R. P. Phill
Modern Thomistic
An Explanation fc
Vol. 2: Metap

editiones scholasticae
Volume 36

R. P. Phillips

Modern Thomistic Philosophy

An Explanation for Students

Volume 2
Metaphysics

editiones scholasticae

Bibliographic information published by Deutsche Nationalbibliothek
The Deutsche Nationalbibliothek lists this publication in the Deutsche Nationalbibliographie; detailed bibliographic data is available in the Internet at http://dnb.ddb.de

This book is a reprint of the third reprinted edition
Westminster, Maryland 1962

Postfach 15 41, D-63133 Heusenstamm
www.editiones-scholasticae.de

ISBN 978-3-86838-540-3

ISBN of the two volume edition
978-3-86838-541-0

2013

Printed on acid-free paper

Printed in Germany
by CPI buchbücher.de

PREFATORY NOTE

THE publication of this second volume affords a welcome opportunity for grateful acknowledgement of the kind reception accorded to the first, and of the many valuable suggestions which have been made for its improvement. In particular my thanks are due to Fr. G. H. Joyce, S.J., for his encouragement and advice; and to Fr. Luke Walker, O.P., for his great kindness in reading the MS. of the present volume, and for his most helpful criticisms. I have also received much assistance in the laborious work of preparing the book for publication from several past and present students of S. John's Seminary.

CONTENTS

MODERN THOMISTIC PHILOSOPHY

METAPHYSICS

PART I.—EPISTEMOLOGY : THE SCIENCE OF KNOWLEDGE

INTRODUCTION

Epistemology the First Part of Metaphysics—Sketch of its History —Its Importance—Division of the Subject.

THE word 'metaphysics' has, no doubt, a somewhat alarming sound, due perhaps to its association with the writings of German philosophers, such as Hegel. It was used originally, however, merely as a label to indicate those works of Aristotle which were put after the Physics, or philosophy of nature, in the arrangement of them by Andronicus of Rhodes.[1] Scholastic usage has given it a meaning which, though less superficial than this, is yet easily grasped ; for whereas the philosophy of nature and of quantity deal with limited classes of being, being which is subject to motion, or to quantity, and so is qualified, metaphysics deals, according to the schoolmen, with being without any such limitation or qualification, with being considered in itself, simply as being.

Such a consideration of naked being must clearly involve the greatest degree of abstraction and the widest universalisation of which the mind is capable, since to attempt to abstract further, i.e. from being itself, would lead us to a contemplation of nothing. As it is therefore the term, the boundary, of thought, it must, unlike the other sciences, be prepared to defend its own possibility and its own principles, for it cannot fall back on any other to do this work for it, since it is the ultimate science. Such a defence is

[1] Cf. Mercier, *Métaphysique Générale*, pp. 5 f.

known as Epistemology, or the science of knowledge ; for it is an essential requirement for the consideration of the science of being that it should be established that the human mind is able to know being.

Theoretically, then, it seems clear that the examination of the value of knowledge, of the capacity of the mind to know being, must be considered to be a part—the first and the introductory part—of metaphysics ; for it does not consider being either as it is subject to motion or to quantity, but purely in the abstract, and—here is the distinction from the rest of metaphysics—as it is related to the human mind. To treat Epistemology as part of metaphysics is, moreover, to follow the normal course and trend of our thinking ; which surely seeks to discover the nature of the intellect (of which we treat in the philosophy of nature), before it reflects on the process of knowing and asks whether, in the light of critical analysis, it can substantiate a claim to put us in touch with being other than ourselves, and give us knowledge of any value with regard to it.

The alternative to this classification is to consider Epistemology as a part of Logic ; and many Scholastic text-books name it Major Logic, Material Logic, or even Real Logic. The impossibility of this view confirms our positive considerations in favour of regarding it as part of Metaphysics ; since Logic, according to the Thomists, deals with being which neither does nor can exist apart from the mind : with logical, not real being. It is therefore impossible for it to study the capacity of the mind for giving us knowledge of real being, so that to count Epistemology as part of logic is to decide in advance of any examination, that the mind can know only its own ideas and processes, and not extra-mental reality. It is, therefore, only by being inconsistent with its own method, and by travelling outside its own field, that logic can take account of the relation of mind to real, as opposed to logical, being.

Since, then, our business here is to see whether we can have knowledge of any being other than our own minds, we ought not to prejudge the issue by identifying our subject with logic. It might turn out, as the result of our investigation, that we cannot maintain that we have such knowledge, and so must identify not only Epistemology but also Metaphysics in general with Logic, since in this case all being would be known being, as Hegel thought. Taking the view advocated above of the character of Epistemology, modern Thomists say that it is that part of metaphysics which is concerned with the ultimate value of human knowledge, examining and judging of its possibility, and its relation to extra-mental being, or as they express it, of its ontological value.

This study has only come into great prominence, in its entirety, in modern times ; for though there have always been men who doubted the possibility of arriving at certainty, and discussed this question, it is far from clear that, as is sometimes maintained, they approached it by the modern road, viz. by critical examination of the validity of our knowledge of the extra-mental world. It certainly seems that attention was first definitely concentrated on this question by the enquiries of Kant. Such a late emergence of fully developed criticism of knowledge might seem surprising if it were forgotten that reflection on action, and so criticism and examination of it, is only possible after the action has taken place ; and we should further observe that if the action leads to satisfactory results, as knowledge appeared to do to the ancient and mediaeval philosophers, there is no disposition to criticise it. When, however, Kant had given the impulse to such criticism there was let loose an avalanche of epistemological discussion and controversy which threatened to sweep away the consideration of all questions but that of the value of knowledge ; so that many seemed to identify philosophy with Epistemology. Whether this view is to be adopted or not will, no doubt, depend on the results we arrive at in Epistemology ; but it may be noticed, in passing, that the prevalent attitude towards it is less extreme than this. While recognising the vital importance of making sure what precisely we can know, since the value of all knowledge whatsoever depends on this, it yet does not refuse to allow that there are subsequent questions which can, and ought to be considered.

It may, perhaps, be thought to be out of place to include a critical examination of knowledge in an account of Thomistic philosophy; and indeed there are some who maintain that this philosophy cannot be critical.[1] Without entering into the details of this controversy, it may be observed, that though, as has been suggested, S. Thomas did not make any separate and systematic epistemological enquiry, yet he did investigate the bases of knowledge critically, and, moreover, that all modern Thomist philosophers do so professedly. It is, therefore, necessary for us to include a survey of their investigations in our summary.

The first form of this kind of enquiry arose, as has been suggested, when notice was taken of the obvious fact that none of us are infallible, and that in fact we are constantly accepting as true, ideas which later we see to be false. What is more, we find contradictories held with equal certainty by different men: one affirming to be certainly true what the other denounces as certainly false. Is it possible, then, it was asked, to determine what is true and what is false? What test or criterion shall we apply, and what are the limits within which certainty is attainable? These and kindred questions form the subject-matter of the earliest critical investigations; and the enquiry once started soon increased in volume and in range. To ask questions as to the possibility of knowledge indicates some doubtfulness with regard to this possibility, so that it is not surprising to find that the answer to this question given by some of the earlier enquirers was a definitely negative one: no knowledge is possible, certainty is unattainable by man. This is the view known as Scepticism and is one which has given rise to lengthy discussions. Others again, who have considered the possibility of knowledge, have come to the conclusion that though some certainty can be arrived at, yet it is confined to our knowledge of the appearances of things, the modifications, that is, which they produce in us, and does not extend to knowledge of the reality (if any) which lies behind

[1] This point has lately gained prominence owing to the discussion which followed from M. Gilson's contention that realism cannot be 'critical.' Cf. *Philosophia Perennis* (Melanges Geyser), *Le Réalisme Méthodique* (Regensburg) Tom. II, pp. 745–755.

such appearances. This view—badly named Idealistic—is characteristic of the modern period ; and is that which has given so much importance to our subject, especially during the last century. The question raised by it is : what, if anything, can be known of realities other than our own mind ?

The two problems just mentioned, besides being distinct in themselves, were also in the forefront of philosophical discussion at distinct periods of its history. The discussion of the Sceptical problem begins at the time of the Sophists, and we have already noticed the Sceptical theses of Gorgias. The New Academy too, founded in the third century B.C. by Arcesilaus, was frankly sceptical. The adherents of this school came to the conclusion that there is no means of discovering what is theoretically true, and consequently that in this sphere one must suspend one's judgement. In practice, however, since it is necessary to act, the more probable opinion should be followed.

The discussion of the Idealistic question, on the other hand, only came into prominence in modern times. The fundamental dogma of Descartes in France, and of Hobbes and Locke in England, is that the mind only knows its own ideas. If this be so, how can we show that these ideas correspond to extra-mental reality ? This is in fact an insoluble problem, but an attempt had to be made to find a solution of it, since then, even more than to-day, everyone was convinced that natural science does give us true knowledge of the world about us. A way out of the impasse was suggested by Kant in his theory that what we know with certainty is not the laws of extra-mental realities as they are in themselves, (i.e. the laws of noumena), but only the laws of the impressions which the mind receives from these realities, or the laws of phenomena. It is these latter which constitute Natural Science ; so that scientific knowledge is secure, though Metaphysics is impossible.

It is hardly necessary to insist on the importance of this whole subject, for it clearly lies at the root of all our knowledge. Unless we are convinced that we can indeed arrive at some certainty with regard to our knowledge of the universe, science and faith alike become impossibilities. Such a reasoned conviction is, of course, peculiarly necessary for Catholics, since a dogmatic religion which did not presuppose this capacity would be a mere fatuity; and it is a fact that in so far as unbelief has an intellectual, as distinguished from a moral basis, this basis is, in most cases, the prevalent belief that certainty, at any rate with regard to ultimate realities, is unattainable.

Division of the Subject.

It will be convenient to set down here the order in which it is proposed to tackle the various questions presented by this enquiry.

In the first place what has been said will have made clear that our subject falls into two main parts, of which the first is a discussion of the Sceptical problem, and the second that of the Idealistic. It has been recently suggested[1] that this division is altogether artificial and unreal, and that in fact there has never been a Sceptic whose scepticism was not based on some sort of Idealism or Phenomenalism, so that it is beating the air to treat the two problems separately. Even if this view be considered to be historically correct, it yet seems that our division is justified on the grounds of method and convenience. There is at least a theoretical difference between the question whether reasoned certainty of any kind can be obtained and the question whether we can have certainties of a particular kind, with regard, namely, to objects other than our own mental states. Moreover, as Scholastic text-books always treat of Scepticism apart from Idealism, it will be more convenient for the student if we follow the same method. Since the Sceptical problem is concerned with the possibility of certain knowledge, it will be necessary to preface it by some remarks as to the various states in which the mind may be with regard to its objects. Again, if after examining the Sceptical attitude we find it to be an impossible one, so that the road to knowledge is not blocked by an impassable barrier, we shall naturally ask what

[1] Cf. e.g. Fr. G. Picard in *Le Problème critique fondamental*, Archives de Philosophie, Vol. I, Cahier II.

means we ought to adopt in order to obtain certain knowledge; in other words, what is the proper attitude of mind in which to begin our enquiry into the value of knowledge. If we can bring these investigations about the value of knowledge in general to a satisfactory conclusion, the way will then be open to an examination of that particular kind of knowledge which professes to be knowledge of the external world. Here we have, or appear to have, two instruments of knowledge, the senses and the intellect, and we shall therefore have to examine under the general head of the Idealistic problem, the extra-mental validity first of sense-experience and then of intellectual knowledge.

In a final section we shall add some considerations with regard to truth in general, and the means of discovering it, i.e. the criteria of truth ; and also as to the distinction and arrangement of the various sciences.

DIVISION I. THE SCEPTICAL PROBLEM

CHAPTER I

THE STATES OF THE MIND WITH REGARD TO ITS OBJECTS

Ignorance—Opinion—Certitude—Various Kinds of Certitude—Doubt.

THE present chapter is an attempt to clear the ground for the discussion which is to be our main concern—that as to the possibility of knowledge—by fixing, at least provisionally, the meaning of some terms which will be constantly occurring in it. These terms are : ignorance, doubt, opinion, and certitude. All these terms denote, of course, states of mind ; and, moreover, cover all the possible states in which the mind may be with regard to the truth of any proposition. For the mind may in no way apprehend it, in which case it is ignorant of it ; or it may in some way apprehend it. If it does this, it may not incline to accept or reject it, and we have the state of doubt ; or it may incline to one side or the other. If it does so, there may go along with this inclination some fear that it may be mistaken, in which case we have opinion ; while if all such fear be absent we have the state of certitude. Evidently this is a complete division, according to the rules of Logic, and so covers the whole ground ; though, of course, further subdivisions of these four states can be made.

We will now examine these states one by one.

Ignorance.

In the first place it is clear that there are many objects which some individual man's mind in no way apprehends, as e.g. the average Englishman has no knowledge of the Pelagian heresy ; or of the office, or perhaps even of the existence, of the Dalai Lama. Such a state of mind is, of course, known as ignorance, being lack of knowledge by someone who is capable of having such knowledge. This last clause is added since we should not consider a stone *ignorant* of scents or colours, or a dog of arithmetic. Since knowledge of these objects, as is generally supposed, cannot be theirs, neither can ignorance. The two examples of ignorance given above are instances of what Scholastics call nescience, since it is not the business of the ordinary Englishman to know about these things; though if a theologian were to be ignorant of the Pelagian heresy, there would be an additional element over and above the mere absence of knowledge in his ignorance, viz. that he is ignorant of something which he ought to know. Such ignorance is named privative ignorance.

If we pass from entire lack of apprehension of any object to any other attitude towards it, this must clearly be some apprehension of it. Such apprehension involves the knowledge of some attribute of the object, for if it is not known as having any at all, it could not be said to be apprehended at all. Now knowledge when formulated is expressed in propositions, as when we say 'snow is white,' and these tell us something with regard to the nature of the object; and therefore something, however little, must be known of the nature of the object before we can be said not to be ignorant of it. With regard to such a proposition the mind may adopt a negative attitude or a positive one; in other words, it may either assent, or not assent to it.

Opinion.

In the first case the assent may be given either to a certainty, or to something not certain; and since it cannot be given to something altogether uncertain, in the latter case it must be assent to a probability. This kind of assent is known as opinion, which is generally defined as assent to one side of a contradiction, given on account of a probable motive, but with fear of the opposite. So Newman describes it as 'an assent to a proposition, not as true, but as probably true, that is, to the probability of that which the proposition enunciates; and, as that probability may vary in strength without limit, so may the cogency and moment of the opinion.'[1]

Thus, though I give an opinionative assent to the proposition, I may, and in the last resort must, give a certain assent at the same time to the probability of the proposition; so that opinion always implies a preceding certainty.

Opinion is sometimes spoken of as 'a weak assent';[2] but this is an expression which is not altogether accurate, since the mind adheres firmly to the probability of the proposition, and does not assent at all to its certainty. If I say: 'Free Trade is probably advantageous,' this is an expression of my opinion. I am, however, certain as to the probability of the advantages of Free Trade, for my remark means: this proposition, 'Free Trade is probably advantageous,' is true. Of this I am certain, though my hold on the certainty may be accidentally more or less strong from various adventitious causes.

This brings us to the consideration of the other member of the division made above: viz. assent given to a certainty, a state or act of the mind known as the state or act of certitude.

Certitude.

We spoke just now of being certain of the probability of any proposition which in our opinion is true, as if we already knew what was meant by this phrase. In fact everyone does know what it is to feel certain of a thing and would probably say he means by the expression that he has no doubt about it, does not question it. Such a state of mind must be due to his having no fear that it will turn out to be untrue. This is the formal element in certitude, which distinguishes it from all other states, that there is no fear of error present in the mind; so that the Scholastics define it as the firm

[1] Newman, *Grammar of Assent*, Chap. IV, § 1–3. Cf. *Apologia pro vita sua* (1865), Chap. I, pp. 20 ff.

[2] Cf. Gredt, *Elementa Philosophiæ Aristotelico-Thomisticæ*, ed. 4ª, sec. 665.

assent of the mind to some knowable proposition without any fear of error. This assent is called firm because it is not easily to be uprooted, for a man who really feels certain must conceive that no sufficient reasons can be brought against the proposition which will oblige him to give it up: if he did not think this he would have fear of error and so not be certain, in our sense of the word.

Division of Certitude.

There are various kinds of certitude. First, the Scholastics distinguish subjective and objective certitude. Now this division is of the kind known as 'analogical,' the word 'certitude' being used in senses which are, if regarded directly, different in the two cases. This is clear, for certitude properly speaking is a state of mind, and so always subjective; though the word is also applied by analogy to the object which is the cause or foundation of this state of mind. Newman calls these two certitude and certainty respectively, but the Scholastic terminology is more expressive. Subjective certitude may be founded on an insufficient basis, and is then *merely* subjective, and illegitimate or false. It is brought about by prejudice, by lack of consideration, and in general by the acceptance, as sufficient to exclude the fear of error, of motives which in fact are not sufficient.

Formal or legitimate certitude, on the other hand, is that which is based on sufficient motives, which require that the thing shall be as it is judged to be. From what has been said it will be seen that the object which supplies such motives is objective certitude. Again, this formal certitude may be based either on evidence of the truth of the proposition accepted as certain, or on evidence of the trustworthiness of some authority which vouches for the truth of a proposition. We thus have two kinds of formal certitude: the certitude of faith and the certitude of evidence.

This last kind of certitude is now commonly divided into metaphysical or absolute certitude and conditional certitude which is either physical or moral. This division presents serious difficulties; but since it is in general use it is necessary to explain here how it is to be understood, without attempting to discuss at length whether it is fully justified.[1] It is said, then, that metaphysical certitude is that which is determined by the very nature or essence of the thing known, so that it is seen that it is absolutely impossible for it to be otherwise; while physical and moral certitudes are those assents which are founded on the constancy of the laws of nature or on the laws which govern man's conduct. An example of physical certitude would be our conviction that the sun will rise to-morrow, while we should be morally certain that the Christian martyrs were sincere in their beliefs.

The phrase 'moral certitude' was unknown to S. Thomas, who uses the expression 'probable certitudes' to designate these states of mind;[2] while our present terminology is derived from the theologians of the sixteenth and seventeenth centuries. This difference of terminology seems to be more than a mere matter of words, for the question really is whether probable arguments can generate true certitudes; for if not it seems that what we call moral and physical certitudes ought to be denied that name. This is a difficult question, with regard to which there is considerable difference of opinion, for, on the one hand, some writers would deny that physical and moral certitudes are formal certitudes at all, since in their view unless all possibility of error is excluded we cannot have formal certitude, as the essence of this is the exclusion of all fear of error.[3] Though perhaps no one, on the other hand, explicitly puts all three certitudes on the same level, yet this would seem to be the logical consequence of the opinion of those authors who hold that they are three species of a single genus; since species share equally in the generic nature. Finally, we have a position which is intermediate between these and asserts that physical and moral certitudes differ essentially from opinion, and exclude fear

[1] A criticism of the division is to be found in the *Dict. de Théologie Catholique*, art. Foi, Vol. VI, col. 211–214.

[2] Cf. *Summa Theol.*, II–II, Q. 70, a. 2 and 3.

[3] This opinion is attributed to Palmieri and Tongiorgi. Jeannière says his opinion is really the same as that of Palmieri. Cf. R. Jeannière, S.J., *Criteriologia* (1912), p. 328.

of error, so that they are properly called formal certitudes; but that they do not exclude it absolutely, or in the same degree. Consequently they are imperfect forms of certitude, the name being applied to them analogically inasmuch as they proportionally share in the essence of formal certitude, the exclusion of fear of error.[1]

This last seems to be the most reasonable view, for the specific difference of certitude from other states of mind is the absence of fear of error, while the certitude is formal or legitimate so long as the mind bases its judgement on motives which in fact show the truth of the proposition. Now both these conditions are verified in the case of physical and moral certitude, for in neither is there any fear of error, there being in fact but a mere possibility of it, due to the fact that we are dealing with contingent things; not any imminent danger of it, nor any positive reason for suspecting it. Just as a man when walking along a level road is not in fear of falling, even though, absolutely speaking, he might fall. Secondly, there is, in both cases, a motive which binds the mind to truth, since the laws of physical and human nature hold in the vast majority of cases; even though, since they admit of exceptions, they do not bind with absolute necessity, and infallibly. Such necessity and infallibility is only found in the case of metaphysical certitude which is, therefore, the only perfect form of certitude, while physical and moral certitude share the common nature of certitude not equally, but proportionally, or in descending degrees; for in the last two the strength of the motive and the consequent firmness of assent decrease progressively. So the legitimate absence of fear of error in the three states of the mind justifies their sharing the common name of certitude; while the progressive decrease in the binding force of the motive does not allow us to apply it to the last two in the same sense as to metaphysical certitude, but analogically or proportionally only.

If this be true, it follows that though certitude implies firmness of adhesion, it does not entail the absolute necessitating of the mind; in other words, probable arguments

[1] So e.g. Geny in his *Critica* (Rome, 1927), No. 151.

can generate certitude. This occurs in the sphere of speculative reason, where the mind finds itself confronted by a probability of so high a degree, or an authority of so great a weight, that it is, as it were, overborne by it, without the will having to intervene. This frequently occurs when the question is decided by external evidence, the witnesses being of supreme competence and probity; and also in scientific research when indications accumulate and all converge towards the justification of a particular view, in such a way as to exclude all plausibility for the contradictory opinion. Probable reasons can also lead to a firm adhesion or certitude under the influence of a good will, though it is impossible to discuss here the very difficult question of how far such influence can justifiably extend.

One last division of certitude, and one of great importance for our subsequent discussion, remains to be mentioned, viz. the distinction of *common and scientific certitude.* The first is the firm assent which we make to a truth, without explicit knowledge of the motives which determine such assent. Such certitude as this is not to be considered to be blind credulity, as it has sometimes been called, for though a man in this state of mind has not reflected on, and analysed his motives for assent, these motives are nevertheless present, and it is they which have determined his assent.

If, and when, he comes so to reflect on his motives, so that he assents to the truth with explicit and reflex knowledge of them, he is said to have scientific certitude.[1]

We have left to the end, because of its connection with what follows, the second of our possible states of mind, viz. that which consists in the withholding of assent to some proposition. This is the state of doubt, which, strictly speaking, is the suspension of assent with regard to both sides of a contradiction, through fear of error. It is called negative if the mind cannot see any reason for assenting to

[1] For the whole subject of certitude the following can be usefully consulted: Newman, *Grammar of Assent*, especially Chapters I to III inclusive and Chapter VII. M. C. D'Arcy, S.J., *The Nature of Belief* (Sheed & Ward, 1931), Chaps. IV and V. A. Gardeil, O.P., *La Certitude Probable*. Geny, *Critica*, Lib. I, cap. II, art. II.

either side: positive if the reasons on both sides appear to be of equal weight.

To what extent such a state of mind is justifiable and necessary are the questions we are to discuss in the following chapters.

CHAPTER II

SCEPTICISM

Preliminary Remarks—Historical Sketch of Scepticism—Sceptical Arguments—The Impossibility of Complete Scepticism—The Ultimate Motive of Certitude: Objective Evidence—Kant's Explanation of the Formation of Judgements—Analysis of the Act of Judgement.

Now that we have seen what meaning is to be given to the word certitude, it is possible for us to consider the question of its attainment. This discussion has two parts, in the first of which we ask whether any certitude can be gained, which is the question of Scepticism; and in the second, if we return an affirmative answer to the first question, what are the proper means of gaining it; or, in other words, what is the right philosophic method.

Preliminary Remarks.

At this stage it is necessary to point out certain general conditions which are imposed on us by the very nature of our enquiry:

(1) We notice that we cannot first doubt the value of the reason and afterwards prove its value by strict demonstration. To do this would be absurd and suicidal, for we have no instrument by which we can judge of the value of the reason except the reason itself.

(2) Epistemology, therefore, discusses, not the value of the faculty itself, but that of its object, about which it asks the following questions: (*a*) Can I form propositions, of which I am justifiably certain, concerning this object; and (*b*) what is the value of this object with regard to its reality? Is it a production of my mind, and to what extent? Is it an external

reality or not ? The question marked (a) is the problem of Scepticism, and those under (b) that of Idealism.

(3) The only means we have in pursuing this investigation, and therefore the means we must use if we are to carry it out at all, is reflection on our mental acts, so that we may discriminate between what may be said to be certain and what doubtful concerning the object of our mental faculty.

(4) Generally speaking, we shall not be able to give strict, and still less direct demonstrations ; usually explanations only will be possible, but these will be entirely sufficient since we are here dealing with fundamental questions, the answers to which, since they presuppose no others, cannot be proved by any premisses. The warrant of their truth can, therefore, not be derived from anything else, but must appear on the face of them when explained and grasped, inasmuch as they are undeniable. Sometimes the fact that they are so may be made plain by indirect demonstration, in which we see the absurdities to which the opposing view leads.

(5) We must be constantly on our guard against a perverted view of knowledge, according to which knowledge of an object is really knowledge of some representation of this object. This representation would, *ex hypothesi*, not be the object ; so that to know the object is, in this view, to know something else, i.e. not to know the object. This is clearly absurd, and a theory of ignorance, not of knowledge ; and, moreover, the process is interminable, for we should have to form a representation of the representation and so on for ever.

Historical Sketch of Scepticism.

The Sceptics (Gr. σκεπτικοί from σκεψίς, a viewing or enquiry), so-called because they were content to look about and enquire without affirming or denying anything, show, by this very attitude, that they are doubtful of the possibility of attaining certitude. We first meet the sceptical spirit in ancient Greece among the Sophists, with Gorgias and Protagoras, but it was Pyrrho (born *c.* 360 B.C.) who founded the school to which the name sceptical became attached. He considered that the impossibility of science was clearly shown by the diversity of opinion which is everywhere found, not only in the market-place, but among men who have devoted themselves to the search for truth. Thus it appears that there are equally good grounds for every opinion, and indeed equally good arguments and authorities can be produced for all. Hence we can arrive at no certainty and nothing can be held to be in itself true or false, good or evil: it merely seems so, owing to the influence of opinion, custom and law. The part, then, of the wise man will be to renounce any preference for particular opinions, or courses of action, and by suspension of judgement, to remain in a state of apathy, such a state being the only one which can be called truly happy. The wise man will try to do nothing at all, but if he is forced to act he will follow probability. That such practical absence of action is the logical conclusion of complete theoretical scepticism can hardly be doubted, but it was not drawn from it by those who held an essentially similar doctrine to that of Pyrrho in the New Academy. Of these the most famous is Carneades, who, though pronouncing knowledge impossible, considered that there were degrees of probability on which action could be based. Finally Sextus Empiricus and others, in the first two centuries of the Christian Era, revived the old arguments of the Pyrrhonians. Aenesidemus, the founder of this movement, put forward ten such arguments or tropes, which a later adherent of the movement, Agrippa, reduced to five; and these five in turn are reducible to three chief points: the contradiction of opinions; the relativity of perceptions 'which vary with the subject; and the impossibility of a demonstration which does not move in a circle, or proceed from presuppositions which are not proved.'[1]

At the time of the Renaissance Scepticism again revived.

[1] Zeller, *Outlines of the History of Greek Philosophy* (Longmans, 1922), p. 302.

To see the causes of this we must go back to the age of S. Thomas. Till then the spheres of reason and of faith had never been defined, and the spirit of the times is summed up in S. Anselm's famous phrase: '*Credo ut intelligam.*' Now S. Thomas drew a clear line between Philosophy and Theology, at the same time asserting that the truths of one could never come into conflict with those of the other. This was very well so long as the lines of the Thomist synthesis were adhered to, but as a result of the attacks made upon it by Scotus, and by the Nominalists, such as William of Ockham, the alliance between dogma and reason was broken. Thus it came to be thought that these two were in disagreement, and that they could not both be true. With some this resulted in the abandonment of the dogmas of faith, with others in doubt or denial of the power of the reason to attain to truth. The theories of Nicolas of Cusa tended in this direction,[1] and Montaigne is usually quoted as typical of this attitude. Hume in the eighteenth century, being a pure phenomenalist, necessarily disallows the possibility of knowledge penetrating behind the changing appearances of things and attaining to certainty. His criticism was equally fatal both to religion and science, though this was not at once realised.[2]

All these, then, more or less despair of the competence of the reason to attain true and certain knowledge, and perhaps Bertrand Russell and Aldous Huxley may be quoted as exemplifying this attitude among living writers; though they are not—as is natural—consistently sceptical.

We are now to ask whether it is possible to adopt an attitude of doubt with regard to the power of the reason to reach any certain truth; and to do this we must first examine what we mean by the sceptical attitude a little more closely. It is essential to notice that it is not to be supposed that the sceptic denies our possession of common certitude. In fact he remarks it, and draws from it an argument for his own position. It is very obvious that men have beliefs and

[1] Cf. *Dict. de Théol. Cath.*, art. Nicolas de Cusa, Vol. XI, col. 607 f.

[2] Cf. Whitehead, *Science and the Modern World* (C.U.P.), p. 65; cf. pp. 4, 5.

opinions, and that they feel certain of some, at least, of these. Even the sceptic, before he began to reflect about it, had no doubt as to his own existence, for example. It is only after reflection that he doubts it ; that is to say, he doubts the possibility of turning his common certitude into scientific. He acknowledges that he has this certitude *de facto*, but can he also have it *de jure*, has he a right to have it ? And this is the question he asks with regard to every certitude whatsoever, and to which he finds no answer. As against this position therefore we are concerned to show, negatively, that such an attitude is indefensible ; and positively, that there is a means by which we can convert our common certitudes, or, at least, some of them, into scientific ones. It is not a waste of time, as has sometimes been asserted, on the ground that absolute scepticism has never appeared in history, to discuss this question. Even if the contention that there has never been a thoroughgoing sceptic be true, as indeed the refutation of scepticism seems to suggest, it is still useful to controvert it ; both because a tendency to such scepticism does exist, and because many people are led to reject the truths of religion, if not the conclusions of science, owing to a feeling that truth and certitude are probably unattainable. The arguments by which this mental atmosphere is engendered are of the following general kinds :

(1) Our cognitive faculties, both sensitive and intellectual, often deceive us : how then can we have any confidence in them ?

(2) There is no question on which men will not hold contradictory views. This sufficiently shows that there is no assertion which compels assent.

(3) No one will maintain that his knowledge extends to all things. Now this ignorance carries with it universal ignorance, for things are so interrelated that ignorance of a part involves ignorance of the whole. To know only part of the truth is to know falsely ; and so, since we cannot know everything, we can know nothing.

(4) The only instrument which we have for gaining

knowledge is the reason. Now it is absurd to trust the reason before we know that it can be trusted, and this we can never do, for we should have to use it in order to test it ; and so trust it before we know that it is trustworthy.

(5) A similar argument to this is the Diallelus ; according to which no ultimate criterion or motive of certitude is possible, since such a criterion would itself need a criterion, and this involves us either in a vicious circle, or in an infinite process.

A sceptical attitude, further, gives a man a feeling of superiority, for he can look down serenely on the contentions and disputes of others, and smile at them, thinking them futile, and being, himself, committed to no opinion.

If the sceptic, then, is in this state of having no opinions, how are we to refute what is non-existent ; or how convince by reason and argument a man who doubts the trustworthiness of the one and the validity of the other ? If the sceptic were, as a matter of fact, in this position we should no doubt be powerless ; but it is sufficiently clear that he is not so, from the very fact that he gives expression to his doubt. In doing this he has already refuted himself, for he who says that all things are to be doubted knows, at least, that all things are to be doubted. Now he knows this either with certainty, or thinks it probable. It is to be supposed that he will not allow that he thinks it certain, since this would be too flagrant a contradiction of his suggestion that nothing is certain. He must then think it probable—it may be true—that no truth is attainable. But here again he is in a desperate position, for to affirm it to be probable implies that he is sure of its probability. It is an opinion to which he assents, though, by his own showing, he should assent to no opinion. He can only avoid contradicting himself, therefore, at the cost of saying he does not think it probable, which is to abandon it altogether. In a word, the sceptic can neither prove his opinion nor even put it forward as an opinion. It is to be observed that, in fact, he puts it forward after reflection and on account of the reasons discovered by such reflection. Though he does not observe it, he does in fact attach some weight to reason, and reflective reason; and is not in fact impartial as to the possibility of attaining scientific certitude. His conclusion as to the impossibility of attaining scientific certitude is thus on the level of scientific, and not of common, certitude, as is sometimes supposed. This is, I say, worth observing, for this manner of arguing against the sceptic has sometimes been ridiculed as showing a complete misunderstanding of his point of view; as if the argument ran (as indeed it sometimes has done): the sceptic who admits any certitude contradicts himself, but all sceptics admit some certitude, therefore they contradict themselves. Such an argument evidently misses the mark; for the sceptic does not impugn all certitude, but only justified, or scientific certitude; and he will properly be said to contradict himself only if he admits any opinion as justified by reflection. Cardinal Mercier, in his *Critériologie Générale,*[1] seems to suggest that the sceptic does not go so far as this, viz. to consider it to be even in the slightest degree more probable that no scientific certitude can be attained than that some can be reached, but merely suspects that it may be so, and so is unwilling to commit himself to any opinion on any subject whatsoever. Actually, the sceptics mentioned above do not seem to have been so cautious. When some truth has been pointed out, it may seem so plain to us, that we find it difficult or even impossible to imagine any intelligent man overlooking or denying it. For example, now it has been shown how easily and simply the Copernican idea of the earth's motion in its orbit explains the planetary motions we may find it difficult to believe in the intelligence of those who formerly denied it. Similarly, before it is pointed out, it may be easy for a man to overlook the fact that he could not suggest the probability of scepticism being true without stultifying himself. So, though it may seem to us difficult to believe that anyone could have failed to observe this, we are not at liberty to conclude that no thoughtful person has ever done so, on the ground of an

[1] *Critériologie Générale* (1918), par. 36, pp. 72 f.

a priori improbability; but ought rather to accept the statements made by the sceptics themselves which seem to show that they have done so. Let us suppose, however, that the sceptic does not suggest that scepticism is true, but merely is in a state of doubt; regarding all knowledge with suspicion. This is a state in which he would be doubtful even of his doubt, i.e. of its validity. So Stuart Mill says: 'Endeavouring to conceive the hazy state of mind of a person who doubts the evidence of his senses, it is quite possible to suppose his doubting even whether he doubts. Most people, I should think, must have found themselves in something like this predicament as to particular facts, of which their assurance is all but perfect; they are not quite certain that they are uncertain.'[1] The question, then, is whether it is possible for a man after reflection to be in this state about all knowledge. We are supposing that the man feels as if he were uncertain about everything, and we ask whether he may not be deluding himself. The test of this will be whether there are any propositions which reflection shows to be in fact indubitable, for, if there are such, it is clear that doubt after reflection cannot be all-embracing, since these propositions must be held to be scientifically certain, and thus exclude what perhaps might be called universal 'scientific' doubt. Now there are in fact two such propositions from doubting which reflection effectively debars us. The first is 'a man doubts when he doubts,' for reflecting on this we see that a doubt of its truth would be a doubt whether the phenomenon of doubtfulness, of which the man is conscious, corresponds to his consciousness of this phenomenon. If it does not, it corresponds to something else; so that consciousness of doubtfulness is in fact consciousness of something other than doubtfulness, i.e. is not consciousness of doubtfulness. But the mind is incapable of entertaining this idea. Similarly, the second proposition which cannot be regarded as doubtful after reflection is the principle of contradiction, for if I say to myself: 'Perhaps to be may be the same as not to be,' reflection shows that this suggestion has no meaning, for if

[1] *An Examination of Sir W. Hamilton's Philosophy*, Stuart Mill (fifth edition), Chap. IX, pp. 164 f.

it were true I could substitute 'to be' for 'not to be,' and the result: 'perhaps to be may be the same as to be' must be equally true. Thus the truth of all contradictory propositions being equal; all thought becomes impossible: for I can neither think: 'perhaps to be is to be' nor yet: 'perhaps to be is not to be.' If a man could think this last, i.e. if he could, after reflection; attach any meaning to it, he would no doubt have committed mental suicide, but in fact he cannot, since in attaching a meaning to it, he acknowledges that this meaning is not its contradictory. It is often said that the final argument against scepticism is that it is suicidal; but in fact it is only attempted suicide, which cannot be fully carried out, since the thought which kills thought still goes on living.

We should also notice that he who doubts knows with certainty, and after reflection, what doubt is, and so what certainty, truth and error are. He knows, too, that it is on account of his fear of error that he doubts; so that his doubt is due to some reason, which, therefore, has some validity. For the very concepts of doubt and probability have no meaning unless there be presupposed some certitude, not merely as to the meaning of such words and notions, but also as to the reason for doubting. For it is to be observed that certitude concerning any object is not abandoned except on account of some other certitude, as e.g. certitude as to the insufficiency of the motives for holding it to be certain; or, at least, certitude that such motives are not evidently sufficient.

Such then is the miserable state of the sceptic, that though he does all in his power to asphyxiate himself with the gas of doubt, it is always cut off before it puts an end to his mental life; and we are justified in saying that complete and universal scepticism is a state of mind impossible and unattainable. If this be so it is plain that there have, in fact, never been any Sceptics of this kind, and therefore it might be urged that the discussion of absolute scepticism is futile. This is not so, however, for men have deluded themselves into supposing that they were complete sceptics; and the bursting of the bubble of this delusion ought to prevent others from having the suspicion that no scientific certitude is possible.

If then we have some such certitude; certitude based on motives which when examined are seen to be sound, it will complete our refutation of scepticism to consider what such motives may be. It is clear enough that when we give certain assent to different propositions the motives which compel us to do so are not the same in each case ; but they do, nevertheless, all possess this character in common, that they compel our assent. Now, if this compelling force were the exclusive property of any one of these particular motives it is obvious that it could not be found in the others, and we must therefore conclude that all particular motives of certitude derive their force from some universal and ultimate motive which underlies them all. It is our business then to discover what this ultimate and universal motive of certitude is.

It is usual, in Scholastic text-books, to discuss at length the ultimate criterion of truth, examining all tests which have any claim to be that by which we can, in the last resort, discriminate between truth and error. For this reason the whole subject of Epistemology has sometimes been named Criteriology, or the study of the criteria of truth. Whatever may be said for or against this method of treating the problem of knowledge, it may be well, for the sake of clarity, to point out that we are not here embarking on a search for the ultimate criterion of truth. For the notions of ultimate motive of certitude and ultimate criterion of truth are not the same. The latter is some instrument by which we test the truth of some opinion, while the former will be some force in the known object which draws us to assent to it as true.

Consequently, if there is any object which draws us to assent to it of itself, in such a way that we cannot refuse assent, we shall not need to look outside this object for some criterion which will enable us to assent to it as true ; though we shall still have a motive for giving our assent, the motive being found in the compelling force of the object which determines our assent. There are in fact some objects which compel our assent in this manner; and in particular 'being'; for, as we have seen, it is impossible to formulate a real doubt as to the truth of the judgement 'being is being.' With regard, therefore, to this judgement, and the other first principles—or *principia per se nota*, as S. Thomas calls them—no *criterion* is required; though we have, of course, a *motive* for assenting to them as true, viz. the compelling force which they exercise on the intellect.

The ultimate motive of certitude, then, for which we are seeking, will be that which receives its force from no other, and is always operative whenever we give a formally certain assent.

The Scholastics are unanimous in asserting that this motive is what they call 'objective evidence,' by which they mean the clarity of the object, by means of which this object manifests itself to the cognitive faculty. The clear vision of the object which results is sometimes called, by analogy, subjective evidence, in the same way as we speak analogically of objective certitude, or the objective concept. Nevertheless, it must be always remembered that evidence is, properly speaking, objective. Hence, if objective evidence be the ultimate and formal motive of certitude, subjective evidence, or apprehension of the clarity of the object, will be required as a condition of certitude; and when the Scholastics assert that objective evidence is the ultimate motive of certitude their meaning is: the ultimate motive of certitude does not, properly speaking, consist in the apprehension of the object, but formally consists in objective evidence; even though the apprehension of the object is required as a condition that the mind may assent with certainty.

In asking what is the ultimate motive of certitude we are in fact asking what it is that, in the last resort, enables us to make a certain judgement; and since judgements are expressed in propositions, we are thus looking for the motive that ultimately justifies us in asserting that the predicate in a proposition about some object agrees with the subject. The Scholastics maintain that the motive and the reason which induces us to assert this agreement is that, when we look at the object, we see *in it* that some predicate is in fact included in it and has it as its subject, so that predicate and subject obviously agree since one is included in the other. In looking, say, at a green leaf, I see greenness in the leaf, and so assert that the subject (leaf) is green.

It might seem, at first sight, that it could not be disputed that we do form our judgements in this way; but Kant pointed out that there is another way in which, theoretically speaking, they might be formed; and which he held to be the way in which they actually are formed. According to his view there are certain modes of thought, which he called categories, which are natural to our minds. When we apprehend any object (which is, of course, some one particular thing), our mind, if it forms a judgement about it, does so by automatically putting it into one of these categories, e.g. that of cause, and we say 'this is cause.' Hence we do not arrive at this judgement by seeing in the object its nature of cause, but apprehending it as a singular thing we assert that it is a cause because it has fallen into that category in our minds. If a man were wearing a pair of spectacles of which one glass was red, the other green, objects seen only through the green glass would appear green, those seen only through the red glass red. If then our minds were internally constituted with different forms or categories in them, an object apprehended through one form might appear to be a cause, through another to be a substance; and so on. If this were the case, it is clear that in the judgement: 'this is a cause,' knowledge of the predicate 'cause' would not be derived from the object, nor would its agreement with the subject be seen in the object, but both would be known in consequence of the application of the category of causality to it by the mind.

This explanation of the way in which we arrive at such judgements seems, at first sight, to be theoretically a possible one; and Kant was led to assert that it is what actually occurs, for two reasons. First, because in his view, it is impossible for us to obtain universal predicates, such as that of cause, from our sensible experience; since this tells us only of particular things. These universal predicates, therefore, must be constituted by the mind. Secondly, because he thought the adoption of this view was the only means of explaining how it is that the conclusions of natural science command universal assent, while those of metaphysics are always in dispute. We shall see later, when we come to consider universals, that neither of these reasons is valid; but, in any case, it does not seem to be a proper method of enquiry to assert that because a certain state of affairs ought, in our opinion, to exist, that it therefore does exist; when it is open to us to discover whether it does exist by examining the facts. Now Kant's explanation of the formation of these judgements is altogether opposed to what we find if we examine the actual process of judging, of which we are conscious. For when we reflect on the act of judgement we see in the first place that it must be a judgement about something. This something must be apprehended; it is an apprehended object, such as, say, this tree, or man; or even something in the knowing subject itself, such as thought. Next we observe in these objects some quality, which we may have observed before, or now abstract for the first time, as green, rational, or incorruptible. Thirdly we notice that the quality is found in the object, which is its subject; and lastly, we affirm that the quality does exist in the subject, and say: 'this tree is green,' 'man is rational,' or 'thought is incorruptible.' In doing so we mean to assert that the agreement expressed by the proposition is in fact found in the object, which is thought of as that which is, as 'being.' This simple analysis of the judgement shows, then, that what we are conscious of doing when we judge is to perceive and affirm the agreement of predicate with subject as appearing to us when we observe the object. This conclusion, however, that a judgement is the affirmation of a relation of agreement as apprehended in the object which is envisaged as 'being,' is altogether opposed to that of Kant for whom the agreement is not apprehended in the object, but formed by the mind; a result arrived at by him, as we said, not on the basis of an analysis of the facts, but of a presupposed theory which we shall consider later.

The nature of the judgement being then such as we have now seen it to be, the question of the ultimate motive of certitude cannot be answered in any other way than by maintaining that it is objective evidence. For it cannot be disputed that when we see clearly the agreement between the subject and predicate in the proposition which expresses a judgement we are certain of it because of our awareness of this manifest agreement. The agreement, however, is manifest in the object, as we have just seen, and manifestation of the object to the mind is objective evidence, so that it follows that we assent with certainty to the proposition because of the evidence of the object.

Thus we see that our initial trust in the possibility of knowledge is justified, as against Scepticism; for we have found the contrary position to be both theoretically indefensible and practically untenable; and have now seen what is the positive basis of certainty.

Having thus cleared away the barrier which would have prevented our seeking knowledge at all, we can now turn our attention to the method by which we ought to seek it.

NOTE.—For a criticism of the arguments used by Sceptics see Mercier, *Critériologie Générale* (1918), pp. 74 ff., and J. G. Vance, *Reality and Truth*, pp. 30-36.

CHAPTER III

PHILOSOPHIC METHOD

Kinds of Doubt—The Method of Descartes—The Dogmatic Method —The Aristoteleian Method—The Method Applied: (1) to the First Principle; (2) to the First Condition.

On the basis that some scientific knowledge is possible we are now to ask what are the means we should use in order to build up the structure of science. Since we are dealing with philosophic science, which is, as we saw, concerned with the primary foundations of things—their ultimate causes—as well as with conclusions, we ask what method we can use to establish the foundations of all scientific knowledge.

Some philosophers have thought that we ought to leave the fundamental principles of knowledge—such as the capacity of the mind for knowing truth—severely alone, without attempting to see whether they are sound, and able to bear the weight of the house of knowledge or not. Now we could not do this even if we wished to, for the Sceptics have already, by their doubts as to the soundness of these foundations, forced us to examine them. We might, however, go to the opposite extreme and say that in order to meet the Sceptics on their own ground, it is necessary to adopt their standpoint, and begin our enquiry by supposing that all propositions are doubtful.

Before beginning to consider the possibility of this second attitude it is necessary to amplify a little what was said earlier as to the state of mind called 'doubt.' We defined it as that state in which the mind assents to neither of two contradictories from fear of error. Now such absence of assent may arise merely from an absence of any reason which inclines the intellect to one side rather than the other. This state of affairs is found, as we saw, when the reasons on both sides are equally balanced, or when no reasons for assenting to either side present themselves to the mind, as in the case of Gallio when asked to judge between S. Paul and the Jews. These two kinds of doubt are known as positive and negative doubt, and are both forms of simple intellectual doubt. There is, however, a more complicated form of doubt than this; and one which arises ultimately from the will, which deliberately prevents the intellect from assenting, or declaring its assent, to a given proposition, in order that the matter may be more fully considered. Such a state of mind is known as methodical doubt, and this also is of two kinds: real and fictitious. The first occurs when the intellect is debarred from giving its assent to that side of a contradiction, to which, for reasons presented to it at the moment, it is prepared to assent. The second is found if, though the intellect has assented in fact to a given proposition, the man forces himself to act as if he had not assented to it, in order to examine it still more thoroughly.

Many Scholastic writers deny the possibility of a state of real methodical doubt, and maintain that it must always be fictitious,[1] but looking at the matter impartially there seems no reason for denying that a man can, and in fact does, prevent himself from assenting; not for any reasons which impugn the truth of a given proposition, but merely in order to pursue the enquiry further. If this is so, though it is true that fictitious doubt is always methodical, methodical doubt is not always fictitious. The division of doubt may therefore be expressed as follows:

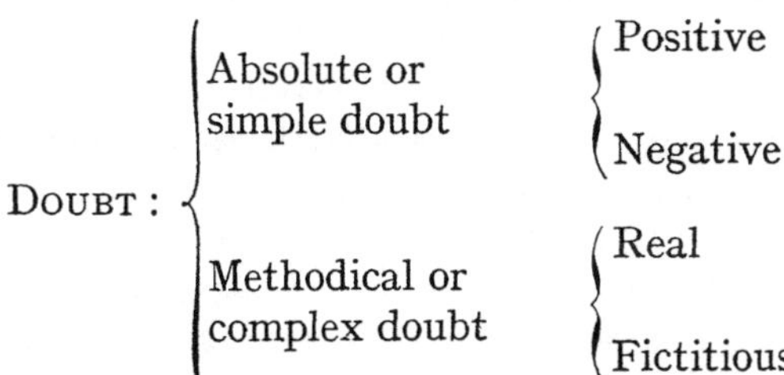

Ought we then, in order to establish knowledge on a firm

[1] So Coffey, *Epistemology*, Vol. I, pp. 95 ff. Gredt, *Elementa Philosophiæ*, Vol. II, No. 676 (ed. 4, 1926).

basis, to employ one or more of the kinds of doubt just enumerated, and, if so, which are the proper ones to employ ?

The most famous answer to this question is probably that given by Descartes, who says :[1] 'As I desired to give my attention solely to the search after truth, I thought . . . that I ought to reject as absolutely false all opinions in regard to which I could suppose the least ground for doubt.' Thus he rejected all the evidence of the senses, all demonstrations, and all the 'presentations that had ever entered into his mind.' In doing this he evidently adopted a state of universal and real doubt, but one which, as he himself points out, was different to that of the Sceptics, inasmuch as it was deliberately adopted in order to arrive at truth, and so was a methodical, not an absolute doubt. The outcome of this doubt in Descartes' own case was unexpected. After describing his initial state of mind he proceeds : 'Immediately upon this I observed that whilst I thus wished to think that all was false, it was absolutely necessary that I who thus thought, should be somewhat, and as I observed that this truth, *I think hence I am,* was so certain and of such evidence that no ground of doubt, however extravagant, could be alleged by the sceptics capable of shaking it, I concluded that I might without scruple accept it as the first principle of the philosophy of which I was in search.'[2] He then enquired why it was that this truth was absolutely indubitable, and found the reason to be that it is perceived clearly and distinctly. Hence he concluded that the clarity and distinctness of an idea is the criterion of its truth. From such ideas as he clearly and distinctly perceived he then proceeded to deduce the existence of God, and from the fact (which he saw clearly) that God is supremely veracious he 'received as certainly true' the existence of the external world ; for if God gave us senses which tell us it exists, and in fact it does not exist, God would in effect be deceiving us, and so not be veracious. He afterwards set out 'the whole chain of truths which I deduced from these primary,'[3] and in fact restored

[1] *Discourse on Method,* Part IV. [2] *Discourse on Method,* ibid.
[3] *Discourse on Method,* Part V.

all and more than all the certainties which had been dissolved by his initial doubt.

What are we to say as to the propriety of the Cartesian method? To answer this question it is essential to notice that it appears to have been a real and absolute universal doubt, extending to all and every truth, even to the first principles such as that of contradiction. That this was indeed its character seems clear, not only from Descartes' own words, but from the very purpose with which it was undertaken, which was to meet the Sceptic on his own ground; while Descartes' good intentions of not remaining in the state of doubt do not alter the fact that he deliberately doubted all truth.

The difficulty which faces us in this question is that of reconciling a real and honest enquiry into the foundations of human knowledge with the fact that the first principles of knowledge are apparently indubitable. Descartes, in his desire for a thorough investigation, applied real methodical doubt to these first principles, and to all immediate judgements. If we do not do this, how can we be sure that we are not, in these matters, assuming something which will vitiate our whole philosophy, and make it one vast '*petitio principii.*' The only safe way seems to be to doubt everything, but, on the other hand, this seems to be an impossibility, and, even if possible, suicidal.

For indeed the fatal objection to the Cartesian method is that it is quite impossible to emerge from the initial state of universal doubt; since it is clear that if we say: 'all that enters my mind is to be considered false,' no notions of any sort can possibly be supposed to be true, not even those of my own act of thinking or of my own existence; inasmuch as these are, if known by me at all, notions in my mind.

Moreover, there is a glaring lack of logic in the acceptance of the principle 'I think therefore I am' and the rejection of the first principles of the reason, and especially that of contradiction. For if we deny that concepts have any meaning and so reject the veracity of the faculty which forms and understands them, viz. the reason, it is obvious we cannot trust it when it tells us that we think and, by implication, are. Also the principle of contradiction being supposed false, thinking may be not-thinking: so that we could say no more than 'I may or may not be thinking, hence I may or may not be,' and indeed we are not justified in going so far as this, since if concepts can be their contradictories, thought of any kind is impossible and words have no meaning.

Moreover, it is clear that Descartes draws illegitimate conclusions from the observation of the fact of thinking, since this fact, taken by itself, does not authorise the assertion that there is a personal subject, an 'I,' who thinks, but is a mere registering of the phenomenon of thought. There is, further, in the statement 'I think hence I am' an unjustified transition from the purely subjective order, the domain of consciousness, to the trans-subjective; for according to Descartes our thought is not the thought of any object; so that we can never arrive, from the observation of the mere fact of thinking, at the certainty: 'I am,' as an entity in the real world; but can only say: 'I am obliged to think I am, because I think.' In fact, as we have just seen, even this is too much to assert, and we ought to put the proposition impersonally: 'There is an obligation to think that there is thought.'

It would appear from what has been said that Descartes went wrong in trying to apply universal and real methodic doubt; and, moreover, as the development of his enquiry shows, he was mistaken in supposing that he actually did so: a mistake which precluded him from using a fictitious doubt.

Whatever may be thought of Descartes' state of mind at the beginning of his philosophising we can see that to employ a real universal and methodical doubt is an unreasonable way of beginning the search for knowledge.

Nevertheless, we cannot altogether abandon the method of doubt with regard to the foundations of knowledge, since this course would enable the Sceptics to say: 'Since you affirm the first principles without examination of their truth, and so gratuitously, we are equally at liberty to deny them.' Some Scholastics, in a reaction from the methodical doubt of Descartes, did attempt to assume the certainty of three fundamental truths, viz. the 'first fact,' that of one's own existence, the 'first principle,' that of contradiction, and the 'first condition,' or the aptitude of the mind for knowledge. Such an assumption, it is plain, begs the question; since the dispute with the Sceptics is concerned precisely with the legitimacy and rationality of our certitude in general, the fact that we *feel* certain of these fundamental propositions being conceded by the Sceptics. It is, therefore, the legitimacy of our certainty with regard to these 'primitive truths' which is here assumed; otherwise the 'Dogmatists' (as those who assume these truths are called) would be in no better position than the Sceptics.

Having seen the impossibility of universal Sceptical doubt, and the irrationality of real universal methodical doubt, and of the dogmatic assertion of the scientific certitude of some one or more fundamental truths, we are led by a process of elimination to conclude that the state of mind which we must adopt is that of *universal doubt*—if we are to avoid Dogmatism—but a doubt which is *not universally real*—if we are to avoid the illogicalities of Cartesianism. Thus, as can be seen from the division of doubt given above, the only state of mind which we have not rejected as illegitimate is that universal methodic doubt which is, in some matters, fictitious, not real. It may be described as a universal attempt to doubt.

Enough has already been said to show that doubt cannot always be real, since such doubt with respect to the first principles would make it impossible ever to attain any certainty; but it may be useful to point out positively why it should be universal, and even though not real, extend to the first principles. This reason is expressed very lucidly by S. Thomas in his commentary on the Metaphysics of Aristotle[1] where he says: 'Other sciences (i.e. other than metaphysics) consider particular branches of truths, and consequently it is their business to doubt about each truth in that particular branch, but to this science' (i.e. metaphysics), 'just as there belongs a universal consideration of truth, so also there belongs to it a universal doubting of

[1] *Comm. in Met.*, Lib. III, Lect. 1.

truth; and so it employs a universal doubt, not about particular branches of truth, but about all together.'

Thus the particular sciences must doubt concerning their particular truths, since their whole purpose is the exclusion of doubt with regard to their own subject-matter; and this purpose cannot be achieved unless they first see what is doubtful. Similarly, a science which deals with truth universally must envisage a universal doubt, since in no other way can it exclude it and arrive at universal truth.

Without abandoning our assurance, then, that the three primary truths named above are indeed true, we can bring before our minds any reasons which have been, or can be, alleged for rejecting them, and so employ fictitious methodic doubt with regard to them. When we come to examine propositions which are not self-evident we shall be able to go a step further; and apply to them real methodic doubt, inasmuch as we shall be aware that their certainty is really doubtful.

To clear the ground we may now apply our method of doubt to the primary truths,[1] before passing on to apply it to those propositions about which real doubt is possible. Thus if we doubt the principle of contradiction we should say: perhaps it is not true that being and not-being are contradictorily opposed. In this case perhaps one is the other; i.e. perhaps being is not-being. Now either we attribute some meaning to this suggestion or none; if none, it is not a suggestion or a thought, but nothing at all. If we do attribute some meaning to it, we must also allow that the meaning is: 'perhaps being is *not* not-being'; while at the same time it is: 'perhaps being is not-being'; since our thought may be its contradictory. These two, however, cancel out; and we are left, as before, without any thought or suggestion at all. Our minds have become, in the strictest sense, a *tabula rasa*. The suggestion, in other words, that the principle of contradiction is false cannot be entertained; it is meaningless. As has been frequently pointed out, we

[1] For a fuller and most lucid exposition of methodic doubt as applied to these truths see Dr. J. G. Vance's *Reality and Truth* (Longmans, 1917), Chap. V, pp. 86–114.

might, in our attempt to doubt this principle, go so far as to deny it ; and so affirm that being is not-being, in which case for not-being in this (or any other) proposition we can substitute the word being, and the proposition becomes : 'being is being' ; which is the principle of identity ; or, alternatively, not-being is not being ; which is the principle of contradiction. The principle might be called a 'boomerang principle,' for even though we cast it away from us, it returns to us again.

We may next try to doubt the first condition : that the mind is capable of attaining truth ; leaving the examination of the first fact—of our own existence—to a later stage.

The first condition has sometimes been misunderstood ; and has been taken to mean that the mind is capable of knowing things as they are in themselves. This, however, is an ambiguous expression ; and seems to imply, in fact, that knowledge is always mediate. It appears to suggest that we first know our own ideas, and then things by their means ; the correspondence between our ideas and things being assured by the principle 'our representations are true, i.e. in agreement with things,' which principle is to be admitted without proof, in the same way as the first condition is. The writers who take the first condition in this sense are thus led to speak of 'the veracity of our faculties' as if we grasped merely what our faculties tell us of things, and not the things themselves. But, in fact, such correspondence, regarded by them as self-evident, needs strict proof, and can be really doubted. Hence the first condition is not to be taken to imply the capacity of the mind for attaining knowledge of external things, but simply the capacity for knowledge of the object : that which lies before, or is presented to the mind.

It is not difficult to see that the proposition taken in this sense is really indubitable, since it is an assertion that we have faculties whose business it is to know their objects, and which, consequently, cannot essentially fail in knowledge of their objects. Now, if we try to doubt this, it is clear that the value of such doubt will depend on the essential rectitude of the very faculties which we are doubting ; since if they be essentially untrustworthy, so will also be our doubt about their trustworthiness. If we are doubtful of the existence of the cognitive faculties which can give us knowledge of truth, we must, *eo ipso*, be doubtful of the reasoning which has led us to doubt their existence. We shall, therefore, be unable to retain our doubt, as even probably true, since we shall be unable to think at all.

We thus see that in the case both of the first principle—the principle of contradiction—and of the first condition, doubt is impossible, since the mind is incapable of entertaining it ; and that therefore as mental facts they are unassailable. We can know objects which are themselves self-consistent ; and so are armed against absolute scepticism.

We have now to turn to the consideration of the nature of these objects, and see whether they have any reality apart from the mind which knows them.

. . . . . .

The discussion of the 'first fact,' the existence of the individual thinking subject, is deferred to a later chapter (Chap. V) as it is not concerned with the conditions of knowledge in general, but with one particular aspect of it.

DIVISION II. THE TRANS-SUBJECTIVE OR ONTOLOGICAL VALUE OF KNOWLEDGE

SECTION I

THE ONTOLOGICAL VALUE OF OUR KNOWLEDGE OF CONCRETE THINGS

CHAPTER IV

IDEALISM AND REALISM

Epistemological and Ontological Objects—Reasons in favour of Idealism—Sense Illusions—Philosophical Considerations—The Principle of Immanence—Varieties of Idealism—Realism—Illationism—Perceptionism—The Questions to be Discussed.

WE have tried to emphasise, throughout the discussion on Scepticism, the distinction, so essential to clarity of thought in Epistemology, between objects considered purely as objects, and objects considered with respect to their own entity. These are the two classes of objects called by Professor Broad[1] 'epistemological' and 'ontological' objects respectively. Thus in what he calls the 'perceptual situations': 'I am hearing a bell' and 'I am seeing pink rats' there is present in both cases an epistemological object, though common sense would not allow that there is an ontological object in the second case, since there are, in fact, no pink rats in the physical world.

It is our business in the present chapter to set down the views on the question whether such perceptual situations ever have 'ontological objects.' If we look at the statement 'I am hearing a bell' it is at once apparent that what I mean is 'I am hearing a sound which comes from a bell.' I suppose the bell to be a definite individual thing outside me

[1] C. D. Broad, *The Mind and Its Place in Nature*, Chap. IV, pp. 141 f.

which has the quality of, or capacity for, producing a certain kind of sound. I am attributing a general character or quality to a concrete subject, the whole: viz. 'the sounding-bell,' being the object of my knowledge. Now it is clear that the two elements in this object: its concrete individuality as the subject of sounding, and this quality of sounding in itself, are of very different kinds; for I attribute the general character of 'sound-producing' to a particular subject. It is therefore convenient to discuss separately the validity of the claims which concrete subjects, and universal attributes and qualities, make to be considered as ontological objects.

That both the universal attributes and the concrete subjects, in the objects of knowledge, do appear to us, in many cases, to be also found as parts of ontological objects, is not disputed. We certainly suppose that there are in the world about us bells, trees, sheep and men which we think possess such universal qualities as sounding, greenness, warmth, and rationality. Can these suppositions be justified? And first are we right in supposing that there are any individual things at all in the world? If there are, they are known by the senses; and hence the first reasons for doubting the existence of such things were drawn from difficulties with regard to sense-knowledge.

Let us shortly consider some of these reasons. The first and most obvious group arise from sense-illusions, which occur in connection with each of our senses. Thus our sight deceives us, especially in cases of refraction and reflection, as e.g. when we see an object in a curved mirror, it appears elongated or contracted in comparison with its appearance when viewed directly. One, at least, therefore of these appearances must be illusory. With regard to refraction we have the classical example of the rod in water which appears bent. Similarly distance, though it may lend enchantment to the view, does so largely by making it appear other than it would appear if close at hand: for distant objects appear smaller in proportion to their distance; and it is often impossible to perceive that they are three-dimensional, as in the case of the moon, which appears as a flat disc. Motion in bodies adds to these illusions: as when a point of light, rapidly rotating, appears to us a circle of light, or 'Newton's disc' in motion appears white;[1] while relative motion makes the telegraph poles appear to be running down the railway line. Again if we put a sea-shell to the ear, we hear in it the roaring of the sea, and we are led astray by echoes. If, as is the case, the same food tastes different at different times, which taste shall we say is the 'true' one? Can I be said to taste the *food* at all? How can I be said to know the *object* by the sense of touch, when a light touch on a polished surface gives the impression of smoothness, a heavier one that of roughness. Crossed fingers, says Aristotle,[2] make an object which appears one to the sight appear two to the touch. As Descartes pointed out, the things we see when dreaming appear real to us, and what reasons have we for supposing that those we perceive when awake are any more real than these? May not our whole life be 'but a sleep'? A second class of reasons for doubting that the objects of the senses have a reality of their own is derived from the conclusions of science. So, for example, physicists assure us that the colours which we perceive as different in quality, as red and green, are not really so, but differ only quantitatively, according as the waves which constitute them are of various lengths. Similar considerations apply to sound and heat. They tell us, too, that the objects which we regard as solid, such as tables and chairs, are in fact not solid at all; they are not continuous and motionless, as they appear to be, but are a mass of whirling electrons. We are further informed that it is the brain, not the senses, which perceives colour, sound, and so on; so that e.g. a colour can be perceived without any colour being present, if a suitable stimulus be given to the brain. The conclusion is that our sensations are mere subjective interpretations of stimuli quite unlike them.

If we turn from these facts, or reputed facts, to philosophical reflection on our knowledge, our doubts as to the existence of ontological objects seem to be confirmed.

[1] Cf. *Encyl. Britannica* (11th ed.), Vol. 28, p. 138, art. 'Vision.'

[2] 4 *Met.*, 1011, a. 33.

For it appears that we can have knowledge only of what affects our own bodies, in other words, of our own subjective states ; so that there is no essential difference in this respect between two such statements as : 'I feel sad,' and : 'I see a table.' What I know in the first case is a certain affection of myself, which is either something mental, or perhaps a sensation in the stomach and head resulting in tears ; while in the second, it is an affection in the eyes. Thus all sensation seems to be entirely subjective, and we can only be said to know our own states. Further, it seems impossible to admit that space and time are realities existing on their own account, since the idea of strict continuity does not appear to be applicable to the physical world ; and it is impossible to suppose that anything of time exists except the present instant : present, that is, to me. Thus both these modes, in which we perceive all objects, seem to be creations of our minds. Moreover, when we assert that objects are substances, causes, and so on, we are endowing them with predicates which can in no way be perceived ; and which reflection even finds to be contradictory ; for how can that which is permanent, and so unchanging, be the subject of change ? If it were it would change ; while change, on the other hand, is impossible without an unchanging subject. It follows from this that causality is also impossible, since it implies change. Such considerations as these—to which many others might be added—seem to lead us to the conclusion that all the fundamental predicates which we apply to things are really only applicable to our own states of mind, and that there are, therefore, no ontological objects at all.

Finally we are faced by the strictly *a priori* argument drawn from the analysis of perception and of thought itself, and known as the Principle of Immanence ; viz. that perception is an immanent action, and therefore cannot get at what is outside us. It is a fact of consciousness which registers only what is internal ; so that to speak of perception of something external is a contradiction in terms. I can only perceive a perception, and only think a thought ; I cannot perceive or think a thing.

Such, in rough outline, are the main arguments on which the opinion of those who deny the ontological value of our knowledge is based. These are called Idealists, since for them all the objects of our knowledge are 'ideas.' Thus Idealism in general is the doctrine which denies that objects of knowledge are trans-subjective, i.e. are things which being in themselves outside the knowing subject yet pass into it in the process of cognition.[1] Such Idealism may be either absolute or partial, according as it does not, or does, allow that any objects of knowledge are trans-subjective; that there is not, or that there is, any reality which is independent of our knowing it. Absolute Idealism is also found in two forms: Pluralistic and Monistic. Pluralistic Positivist Idealism denies any substantial reality and recognizes only the succession of known phenomena; while Monistic Idealism, though it considers that the individual Ego is phenomenal, yet puts forward as the substratum of phenomenal plurality, and as the only real substance, the Universal Ego, or Absolute. This last form of idealistic theory is often called Objective Idealism; and among its representatives are Fichte, Schelling, Hegel, and Bradley.

Turning to Partial Idealism, we have, first, the theory of the founder of modern Idealism, Bishop Berkeley. This theory, which goes by various names—Acosmic Idealism, Immaterialism, Spiritual Realism—holds that the corporeal world is merely a phenomenon of consciousness, while spiritual substances, such as God and the soul, are extra-mental objects of knowledge. Another important form of Partial Idealism is the Transcendental Idealism of Kant and his followers, which maintains that the metaphysical super-sensible world of universal concepts and of abstract universal truths is wholly subjective. While allowing a certain subjective necessity to these truths, the Transcendentalists deny their objective necessity: we are compelled to think of things in this way; but it is not to be supposed that reality

[1] Bertrand Russell defines Idealism as 'the doctrine that whatever exists, or at any rate whatever can be known to exist, must be in some sense mental.' (*Problems of Philosophy*, Chapter IV.) It may be remarked that neither as to the definition of idealism in general, nor as to its various forms, i.e. as to its division, is there entire agreement.

is as we think it. This system allows that it is permissible to postulate the existence of an extra-mental world, but denies that such a world can ever be an object of knowledge. Our knowledge of the world is confined to its appearance; its real nature, the 'thing-in-itself,' must always remain wrapped in mystery. For this reason the theory is sometimes called Phenomenalism. We may notice, too, that some writers call the various forms of Partial Idealism, Subjective Idealism.

Opposed to all these theories stands Realism, which holds that there exist, in their own right, extra-mental objects which constitute a real, external, material universe; the nature of which we can know; at least to some extent. It is clear that Partial Idealism is also Partial Realism, but since the emphasis in such theories as those of Berkeley and Kant is decidedly on the Idealistic side of their doctrine, they are to be reckoned Idealistic rather than Realistic.

It would be to go outside the scope of the present summary to attempt to give an account of the many varieties of Realism which have appeared in recent years; and it is sufficient to mention the two groups of Neo-Realists and Critical Realists in America, as representative of the reaction against Idealism. The views of the last named have some affinities with Thomism. Broadly speaking, realist theories have been of two kinds. Some philosophers assert that though our immediate knowledge is only of subjective objects, yet we can conclude by means of an inference from these that trans-subjective ones, also, exist. This view is known as Illationism or Representationism. Among its adherents some argue from the veracity of God; who could not, being incapable of deceiving us, give us an invincible belief in the existence of the external world, if it did not in fact exist. This was the line taken by Descartes; who, by making the subjective conviction of the existence of the thinking subject the foundation of all certainty, and by his theory of ideas, in fact laid the foundations of all subsequent Idealism; yet did not himself follow out his principles to their logical conclusion, but remained a realist. Other Illationists argue that the subjective world, which is immediately apprehended, requires the trans-subjective as its cause ; and, of these, some think that we can know no more of the trans-subjective than that it is trans-subjective and exists ; while others maintain that since an effect must be proportionate to its cause, we can know at least something of the nature of that trans-subjective world which causes our subjective impressions. This last view has been adopted by some modern Scholastics, as, for example, the Louvain School—following the lead of Cardinal Mercier—though there are some notable exceptions.[1]

The other form of Realism which is defended by Scholastic writers is the traditional theory of Perceptionism. According to this view the trans-subjective is itself perceived—in opposition to the opinion that what is perceived is some subjective representation—though it is conceded that there is a medium through, and by means of which it is so perceived. Such a medium, however, is not known in itself directly ; it is not a representation or copy of the object, which, being first known, leads us on to knowledge of the trans-subjective object itself.

Those who hold this general theory that the external world is immediately perceived, are not however unanimous with regard to the extent of such perception. Some say that it is only the primary sense qualities of things which can be perceived immediately, while others maintain that both primary and secondary qualities are known by immediate perception.

This distinction of primary and secondary sense qualities is one which was familiar to S. Thomas, and has always been in use among his followers ; though the names 'primary' and 'secondary' have only been in general use since the time of Descartes. Since in Descartes' view matter is constituted by extension, he calls quantity, extension, and such like, its primary qualities, the secondary ones being those which he regards as merely subjective impressions, such as colour, sound, and so on.

S. Thomas, approaching the matter, not from the standpoint of a preconceived metaphysical system, but by a direct analysis of sensations as found in our experience, calls

[1] E.g. Dr. Coffey, *Epistemology*, Vol. II, Chaps. XVI to XIX.

colour, sound, odour, savour, resistance and heat, proper sensibles, since these are the qualities of things which are the proper objects of the various senses; giving the name of common sensibles to those qualities which are perceived by more than one sense, such as extension and the like.[1] Six such common sensibles are usually enumerated: extension and number, motion and rest, shape and position.

From what has been said it will be seen that three questions present themselves for discussion: (1) whether the existence of the individual substantial thinking subject is to be admitted; since its reality is denied by the Monistic Idealists; (2) whether we can affirm the real existence of the extra-mental and corporeal world; since this is denied by Idealists generally; and (3) whether our perception of this world (if we return an affirmative answer to the previous question), is mediate or immediate. Finally, we shall have to consider the supplementary question whether immediate perception is universal, extending both to primary and secondary qualities; or partial only, i.e. confined to primary ones; granted that we have come to the conclusion that we have immediate perception at all.

It will be convenient to treat these questions in separate chapters.

[1] Cf. Vol. I, Part 2, Chap. IX.

CHAPTER V

THE EXISTENCE OF THE INDIVIDUAL THINKING SUBJECT

Two Objections Answered—The Meaning of Consciousness—Its Infallibility—Reasons for Asserting our own Individual Exis tence—The Process by which we reach this Affirmation.

We are now to apply the method of methodical doubt, understood in the sense indicated above, as a facing of the difficulties of the question, to the last of the three primary truths: the first fact. The consideration of the truth of the proposition that I, as an individual thinking subject, exist, was deferred from an earlier stage of our discussion,[1] for reasons of convenience; since, unlike the other two truths, that of the capacity of the mind for knowledge, and the principle of non-contradiction, it does not deal with our knowledge in general, but with one part of it, viz. our knowledge of concrete reality.

Before beginning the discussion itself it is necessary to meet two antecedent objections to discussing the matter at all. These are: first, that such a discussion is unnecessary, and second, that it is a wrong way of proceeding. It is thought to be unnecessary because this first fact is so obvious as not to require investigation; for we should not be investigating it unless we existed. To say this, however, is to acknowledge that one has already considered the reasons for its truth; and indeed a reason for holding it to be true is here asserted; so that it is clear that the man who refuses to enter on this discussion has already entered on it, and so is inconsistent. Moreover, the question is not whether there is thinking, or acts of thought, which is all that is immediately required in order that this consideration should be carried out, but whether there is a permanent individual

[1] Cf. Chap. III, p. 38.

subject of these thoughts, an individual Ego ; and this has been called in question by several philosophers ; so that we cannot escape from the obligation of considering the difficulties raised by them.

The second objection is that by starting to enquire as to the reality of the individual Ego we are following the vicious method of Descartes, who made all certainty depend on his assurance of the truth of the Cogito, so closing himself within the circle of his own self, and making it impossible ever to acquire knowledge of the Not-Self, the external world. This is the source of all subsequent Subjectivism and Idealism, and it appears that we also shall doom ourselves to subjectivism if we begin our critical discussion with a consideration of the reality of the individual self.

The reply to this is obvious. Because we ask whether the first fact is a truth, we do not thereby implicitly assert that, if it is, it is the basis of all our knowledge, as Descartes did of the 'Cogito.' Neither do we prejudge the questions whether we have knowledge of realities other than ourselves ; and whether we arrive at such knowledge immediately, or by means of the knowledge which we have of the reality of ourselves. We ask simply whether we have knowledge of the individual Ego, not whether it is the only knowledge we have, or the basis of all other.

If, then, we can legitimately undertake this enquiry, and are, indeed, obliged to do so, there can be little doubt that the answer to it will be found, if it is to be found at all, by introspection, or reflection on our own consciousness. Now this word consciousness has been much misused, for in modern philosophy it is customary to extend its meaning to cover anything which is in any way present to the mind ; a practice which has filtered through into ordinary speech, as when a Foreign Secretary says in Parliament : 'I am deeply conscious of the critical state of affairs in China.' Using the word thus, to say that a thing is within my consciousness is equivalent to saying that it is present to my mind, or an object of knowledge. Thus the data of consciousness embrace all the objects of knowledge, so that what cannot be in my mind, viz. the external object, is not only unknown, but unknowable. This is a palpable misuse of the term, for it is obvious that unless China is in my mind, I cannot be, properly speaking, ' conscious ' of the state of affairs there; and if it were, the task of a statesman would be much simplified, for he would only have to put his mind in order. If we examine what the word itself means, and do not proceed on the basis of a preconceived Conceptualist theory, it is clear that this meaning is: knowledge of what is with us (conscio), i.e., knowledge of those things which belong to the knowing subject. Hence it is precisely defined as the power of perceiving our own internal operations and dispositions, all those things, namely, which are actually present in us. Such consciousness may be either sensitive or intellectual, and the latter either concomitant—sometimes called direct—or reflex. The first is that by which we perceive primarily and principally some internal fact, while secondarily, and in the exercise of the act of perceiving it, we perceive our own perception and ourselves. Reflex consciousness differs from this, since by it we take some act of ours as the object of a new and special consideration, explicitly, and as the formal object of our introspection; or as the Scholastics say: '*in actu signato*.' Thus concomitant consciousness accompanies every act of the cognitive faculties, and knowledge is impossible without it; while reflex consciousness does not accompany every act, and is not necessary to cognition. Strictly speaking, consciousness signifies reflex consciousness, for consciousness means the return of the faculty on its own act and on itself, which return is reflection.

We have said that the exclusive object of our consciousness is our own internal operations and dispositions, as facts which are actually existing in us; and it would therefore seem that the thinking subject cannot be an object of consciousness. This is an objection which was made much of by the Phenomenalists, such as Stuart Mill. It is, nevertheless, not a sound argument, for it is clear that the facts named above are not apprehended in the abstract, but in the concrete, with all their accompanying circumstances, and hence consciousness indirectly tells us of the existence of the subject of these concrete facts.

That consciousness tells us the truth with respect to its proper object is neither in need of, nor susceptible of, proof. It is self-evident, for the witness of consciousness could only be untrue if when I was conscious of some affection, and knew that I had it, I could, at the same time, not have it; which is a plain absurdity. To say 'I feel something' is the same as saying 'I know that I feel something'; they are equivalent statements about my mental state at the moment; I could not say 'I feel' unless I had knowledge that I did feel. So as Mill truly remarks: 'All the world admits that it is impossible to doubt a fact of internal consciousness. To feel, and not to know that we feel, is an impossibility.'[1]

If consciousness sometimes seems to deceive us, this is due, not to any error in its witness, but to a misinterpretation of its data; for there are some judgements which seem to be statements of our immediate conscious perceptions which in fact are arrived at by a process of reasoning, or, at least, by interpretation of our conscious perceptions. So, in locating a pain in a particular part of the body, though it may seem to me that I feel it in that part, yet I really conclude this from the kind of pain which I have, and the habitual association of different pains with the different parts of the nervous system. It is common for persons who have had limbs amputated to assert that they still feel pain in them: the truth is they still feel pain, and since it is in that part of the nervous system which leads to the amputated member, they wrongly locate it in that member. What their consciousness tells them is true, while their interpretation of what it tells them is untrue. The same occurs in the case of neurasthenics, hypnotised persons, and so on; who assert that they have a disease which in fact they have not, though so great is the power of mind on the body, that this conviction may actually engender the disease which they supposed themselves to have.

If then the witness of consciousness is infallible with regard to its direct object—our own internal affections—is it also indubitable with respect to its indirect object, our own

[1] *Examination of Hamilton's Philosophy*, p. 163.

selves? There is no doubt that we do in fact refer all our affections to some permanent substantial subject, and we are asking whether we are certainly justified in so doing.

The Phenomenalists, as Hume, and their successors the Associationists, hold that we are not; and their opinion is shared by those who, like William James, maintain that we can only affirm the existence of a stream of conscious states.

This view is based on the belief that a conscious act can only grasp itself, and cannot go beyond this to affirm a subject of the act; so that James concludes, that 'the thoughts themselves are the thinkers is the final word of psychology.'[1]

This extraordinary theory has gradually fallen into disfavour, and writers like James Ward and McDougall regard the testimony of consciousness as to the existence of the individual self as inescapable.[2]

This last opinion has always been adhered to by the Scholastics, who regard the testimony of consciousness on this point as indubitable. No doubt Scholasticism is 'only common-sense philosophy systematised,' as James remarks; but though he seems to regard it as discreditable to a philosophy to agree with common sense, those who are seeking truth will think it to be a sign that they are following right reason, common sense being the product of man's natural reason.

For indeed there can be no such thought as: 'Perhaps I do not exist': all I can do is to ask myself whether I can attribute any meaning to these words. At once I see that I cannot; for the moment I ask for a meaning I implicitly affirm the existence of a subject to whom the words may mean something. If I did not exist I could not begin to consider whether I did or not.

Moreover, doubt, and still more, denial of our own substantial existence makes it impossible to give any explanation of certain facts in our mental life of which we are immediately conscious. For, if we assert that there exists in us nothing

[1] James, *Principles of Psychology*, Vol. 1, Chap. X.

[2] Cf. Ward, *Psychological Principles*, Cambridge, 1920, Chap. II, par. 2, Chap. XV. McDougall, *Outline of Psychology*, pp. 39 f.

but a series of acts, how are we to account for the assured facts of memory, our capacity for sustained thought, and our sense of moral responsibility? Memory—without which no thought is possible—implies that there is one subject who formerly had a certain experience and now recalls it. Even if, as James grotesquely supposed, one thought could 'keep' another thought 'warm,' how would it be able to find the other? James speaks of the 'warm' one as its 'predecessor,' but in what sense can an unowned thought be supposed to precede any other; and how is the selection made among all the thoughts there are? Unless there is a connecting link in the subject, the thinker, memory of past experiences is wholly inexplicable. Similarly, for following out a process of thought, or developing an argument, time is required; and this involves the presence during it of some subject who can continue thought, and does not disappear. Though memory is involved here again, more than mere memory is needed, in so far as the argument has a unity which it derives, not merely from memory of the premises, but from being worked out by one thinker. The process is entirely different from that of 'Capping verses'; the premises and conclusion are joined not merely by their logical connection, but also because they form the unified consideration of a single mind—my mind. Lastly, it would be absurd to suppose that if all our conscious life were but a 'stream' of acts, one act should feel morally responsible, and worthy of praise or blame, for what another act had done. Such a feeling of responsibility evidently requires and implies a subject who is either meritorious or culpable.

How, then, do we arrive at the formulation of this affirmation 'I am'? It may be an immediate judgement or the conclusion of a syllogism. At first sight, it seems as if it must be the latter, since consciousness only tells us of our present dispositions; and so it appears that we pass from these known facts to argue, by means of the principle of substance,[1] to the existence of the subject. But such an

[1] The principle of substance is formulated as: *omne quod est, est substantia; phenomenon est solum id quo aliquid apparet.* Everything which *is*, is substance; a phenomenon is only that *by means of which* something appears.

analysis of the process is psychologically incorrect, and would, moreover, leave us at the mercy of the Idealists, who would argue as follows: In order to reason from the principle of substance, this principle must first be known; and it cannot be known without the knowledge of substance itself. This notion of substance is, however, unattainable prior to the notion of the thinking subject; for it would have to be formed either from internal or from external perception, or from the notion of accident. Now it cannot be formed from any of these; not from internal perception, since, by hypothesis, this only tells us of internal facts; nor from external perception, which only grasps phenomena, or the corporeal qualities of things; nor from the notion of accident, since we cannot have this notion, viz. of something which inheres in another, until we have first acquired the notion of a support, of substance, its correlative.[1]

The true analysis of the process of reaching the affirmation of our own existence is, then, the following:

There is, in the first place, a confused, habitual and immediate knowledge of the mind by itself, a knowledge which is clearly not actual, and which does not distinguish the substance of the mind from its acts. We now have acts of knowledge directed towards some object; and thirdly, the actual reflection of the intellect on these acts; in which reflection it seizes the act together with its root, i.e. the mind itself. It is clear that what is here grasped is not an act in the abstract, but in the concrete—a twinge of gout is not apprehended in the abstract, but as *this* twinge; so definite that we locate it in a particular limb or part, say, the big toe—it is *this* definite sensation, or the thought of *this* object. So, neither is it the abstract essence of the mind which is grasped, but its concrete reality as the principle of its acts. Consequently, the knowledge gained is not phenomenal, but real: the mind is known as *existing*. We are here dealing, not with the essential, but with the existential order; so that the affirmation of one's own existence is rightly called the first principle of the real order.

It is clear, then, that this affirmation is not reached as the

[1] *Vide* Geny, *Critica.*, Secs. 244, 245.

conclusion of a syllogism. It was doubtfulness on this point, arising from an insufficient analysis of the act of self-knowledge, which prevented Descartes from giving full weight to the first fact as the bridge between the ideal and the real. We have here, in fact, an existential judgement which has the same guarantee of infallibility as the Simple Apprehension, viz. that it is immediately informed by its object, so that we have a judgement of existence—of reality—which is absolutely certain. I, the individual I, exist, and that as a substance.

CHAPTER VI

THE EXISTENCE OF THE EXTRA-MENTAL AND CORPOREAL WORLD

Absolute Idealism—The Primary Intuition of Being—Further Reasons for rejecting Absolute Idealism—Berkeley's Immaterialism—Its Inconsistency—The Principle of Immanence Criticised—The True Nature of Ideas—Summary.

BEING now assured that we can justifiably affirm the existence of the substantial thinking subject, we can proceed to ask whether the existence of anything outside the subject can be asserted. That this can be done is, as we have seen, denied, either completely or in part, by the Idealists. It would, however, be a mistake to suppose that the Absolute Idealist considers that he alone is real, and that there is no reality other than his own individual mind. Such a position is known as Solipsism, and is too absurd to be accepted by anyone. Even if it were, it would be useless to propound it, since, if it were true, there would be no other mind to receive it. Consequently, rejecting the common-sense notion of the individual Ego, the Idealists assert the existence of a universal mind which manifests itself in what are called the 'individual minds' of men.

This absolute mind is regarded in different ways by the various Idealistic philosophers, some holding it to be, to some extent, transcendent; while others consider that it is wholly immanent. For our present purpose these differences are of no consequence, as all agree that the individual Ego is merely phenomenal, and consequently that there can be nothing outside the thinking subject, since this embraces all there is.

In order to discover whether such a view as this is correct or not we have no method at our disposal save that of analysis of, and reflection on, our own acts of knowledge, which are expressed in judgements.

If we were at liberty to identify the notions of 'object and of 'being' in general, our problem would already be solved; since we have seen that we can have true knowledge of objects. Unfortunately we cannot do this, since to be an object is a determinate and specialised mode of being; while the notion of being in general does not imply any relationship to a knowing subject. What it does imply is something which either does or can *exist*, whether it be related to the knowing subject or not. It follows from this that the notion of being is not derived from that of object; but, on the contrary, what we first know is something which either does or can exist, and reflecting on it, we see that by its presentation to the mind it has become an object for us. It first appears as something which does or can exist on its own account, and only as a consequence of its thus appearing does it become an object. An object must *be* before it can be an object, and must be and be presented to me, or appear to me as being, before it can be an object for me. As it so appears the first thing that I immediately perceive in it is that it cannot both be and not be at once; and I see this in the object itself inasmuch as it appears before me as existing (or capable of existing): and this is the first intuition of the mind. Hence the principle of identity (and the same is true of the other first principles) appears before our minds and imposes itself upon us, not because we feel bound to think in accordance with it, but because we see, with the first act of the intellect, the *being* of the object towards which this act is directed. The principles impose themselves on us, we do not impose them on the object; for the being of the object is seen, with objective evidence, to be itself, and not its contradictory; or, in other words we see with objective evidence that the principle of identity is the law of the being of the object, i.e. that this principle is ontologically true, and has a trans-subjective value. An unprejudiced reflection on our own acts of knowledge surely shows us that what we first know—our first intuition—is not ourselves or the internal conditions of knowledge, but something other than ourselves, a non-Ego, a reality external to us.

Further, we are all convinced of the fact of our own

individual existence ; and this is probably the case even with the Absolute Monistic Idealist (though verbally he may deny it). We cannot, however, maintain it to be a fact unless we admit also existences and realities other than ourselves. For how can I know that I am if I did not think and feel ? And how could I think and feel if I did not think and feel this or that ? It is the individual 'this' which, as we saw, determines the act, and the act reveals its subject to me. In proportion as my contact with the 'other' is cut off I lose also knowledge of myself, as in sleep ; and in proportion as I regain this contact with that which is, so do I regain knowledge of myself, the subject which is.[1] Again, no one can dispute that I am conscious of some things as external to myself, of others as internal ; so that among the immediate data of consciousness we find this distinction between the external and internal, and externality.

Such immediate data of consciousness are not to be gainsaid ; but even if they were, the Idealist would be in no better position ; for, at least, he possesses the concept of externality, which cannot be accounted for, on his hypothesis ; since in my consciousness itself there would be nothing which was external, and so nothing which could cause me to have this concept. If a man were living on an estate so vast that he could never reach the boundaries of it he would never know—of his own knowledge—that it had any, and so that there was anything outside it, or that he himself was within it. He could not have the idea of internal and external with respect to it. If, as the Idealists suppose, this state of affairs be extended to all our knowledge, so that we could never know anything external to it, we could know nothing as internal either, and the distinction between the two could not be drawn. What was in fact internal would not be known as something *internal*, but merely as something.

Though, in fact, we are conscious of our own existence by first having knowledge of some being other than ourselves, so that we could not affirm our own existence unless we first affirmed that of other things ; yet, the Idealist who does not

[1] Cf. Sertillanges, art. 'L'Être et la Connaissance' in *Mélanges Thomistes* (Bibliothèque Thomiste—Le Saulchoir, 1923), pp. 177 ff.

admit this to be a fact, and yet is convinced of his own existence, should logically conclude that he alone exists, since he will not admit that we can know any external reality. To extricate himself from this Solipsistic position, which is the logical consequence of his theory, he assures us that his individual Self is only a part of the one great and Absolute Self, which is the only reality, and embraces both the knower and the known. We have, and in the nature of the case can have, no experience of it; nor is there any reason in the nature of things for asserting its existence. It is at best a mere hypothesis; and even so, a contradictory one, since it is supposed to be conscious in that it produces our cognitive acts with their objects, while at the same time it is unconscious of doing so, since we, who are identified with it, are not conscious of being their adequate cause. On the contrary, we are conscious of being finite, morally dependent, and of having duties towards others, our rights being limited by theirs, and so of having moral obligations. This Absolute Ego, therefore, cannot claim to have any justification in experience, and seems to be merely a way of escape from solipsism.[1]

The positive analysis of our cognitive acts therefore results in our being able to assert that there exists some reality or realities outside our own minds. We may, however, still be doubtful whether such realities are of the kind we call material; that is, whether the common-sense view that we are surrounded by a material world is not an illusion. That it is so, is, as we mentioned above,[2] the view of Berkeley, based on his fundamental principle: '*esse est percipi*'—the being of a thing is its being perceived—so that since 'being perceived' is inseparable from a percipient mind, the being of all things must also be inseparable from mind, and so must be of its nature mental, animate, and not purely 'material.' Scholastics, of course, agree with Berkeley in

[1] The arguments for the existence of an extra-mental world are set out more fully than our space allows by Dr. Barron in his *Epistemology* (Burns Oates & Washbourne, 1931), pp. 102 ff. For a searching and detailed analysis of the question cf. Roland-Gosselin, *Essai d'une Étude Critique de la Connaissance* (Paris, Vrin, 1932). Cf. also Maritain, *Les Degrés du Savoir* (Paris, Desclée, 1932), Chap. III, "Le Réalisme Critique."

[2] Cf. Chap. IV, p. 43.

so far as he maintains that for a thing to exist it must be known by the mind of God ; and what force his doctrine has is largely drawn from this truth. But this would apply equally to finite ' spirits ' as to ' matter ' ; and the essential feature of Berkeley's doctrine is that he denies the same kind of real existence to bodies as he allows to finite ' spirits.' This notion is based on his assumption that what we know are not ' things,' but our own sensations and perceptions ; an assumption which Thomists hold to be simply false. For even though we grant that reality must include some formal, ideal, or mental element, inasmuch as it must all be dependent on God who is essentially spiritual, there is no ground for distinction between spiritual and material finite things with respect to reality ; unless we suppose, as Berkeley did, that material things consist of our perceptions and sensations of them. We shall have occasion to return to this notion that what we sense are our own sensations, since it is a fundamental fallacy which has vitiated much modern philosophy ; but it is sufficient to observe here that we cannot sense a sensation unless we are already sensing something, for otherwise we have no sensation to sense. If this something be another sensation we are in the same position once more, so that if we are ever to sense a sensation we must originally sense something other than a sensation ; viz. something which exists in its own right. Sensation, therefore, is primarily directed to something which is not itself, so that colours or sound, etc., are not sensations of colour or sounds. If this be so, the distinction which Berkeley draws between body and spirit with regard to their reality is unfounded and illegitimate ; for the principle ' *esse est percipi* ' would lead us to deny reality to spirit to the same extent as we do to body, and even to a greater extent, since what we directly sense is body, whereas we only know spirit indirectly, and by means of our knowledge of bodies.[1]

If, then, we are to admit that there is a real trans-subjective world at all, as we have seen that we must, and as

[1] Berkeley's theory is discussed at length by Dr. Coffey in his *Epistemology* (Longmans, 1917), Vol. II, pp. 111 ff. where the inconsistency of denying reality to the material, and allowing it to the spiritual world is clearly pointed out.

Berkeley himself does, we cannot maintain that the only realities in it are spirits, but must affirm also the reality, and existence on their own account, of bodies or materially extended things; for the same arguments which would lead us to exclude bodies from reality would also lead us to exclude spirits from it.

The mention of the principle '*esse est percipi*' leads us to examine its truth. It is indeed, as Professor Moore points out,[1] the fundamental principle of Idealism, and if it is found not to be true, in the sense in which it is used by Idealists, we shall have a negative proof of the reality of the trans-subjective world. If the basic principle on which the denial of the existence of an extra-mental world rests is not valid, the denial itself will not be able to be maintained, and with no rival left in the field, the realist view, based as it is on reason and supported by common sense, cannot fail to be adopted.

The principle of immanence, of which '*esse est percipi*' is one formula, has always been, and still is, the chief support of the Idealistic contention that there can be no reality outside the mind. It has naturally received many other formulations. Berkeley applied his—'*esse est percipi*'—only to the world of sensible things; and argued that since what the sense knows is its own sensations, and such sensations can evidently not exist except when we are sensing or perceiving them, nothing which we know by the senses can exist except in so far as it is being perceived; i.e. its existence is constituted by its being perceived. He regarded this as a self-evident truth and writes: 'Some truths there are so near and obvious to the mind, that a man need only open his eyes to see them. Such I take this important one to be, to wit, that all the choir of heaven and furniture of earth, in a word all those bodies which compose the mighty frame of the world, have not any subsistence without a mind, that their being (*esse*) is to be perceived or known.'[2] The reason why he finds it so obvious is given in the preceding para-

[1] G. E. Moore, 'The Refutation of Idealism' in *Philosophical Studies* (Kegan Paul, 1922).

[2] Berkeley, *Principles of Human Knowledge*, Sec. VI.

graph (No. IV). 'What are the forementioned objects' (i.e. all bodies or 'sensible objects'), 'but the things we *perceive* by sense, and what do we perceive *besides our own ideas or sensations*; and is it not plainly repugnant that any one of these or any combination of them should exist unperceived?'[1]

The notion contained in this passage may be put in a generalised form by saying: Perception, since it is a fact of consciousness, cannot have any contact with what is outside the consciousness, and so knowledge of 'the thing in itself' is a contradiction in terms. Or again: Perception is consciousness, and consciousness is knowledge of that which is internal, and it is therefore contradictory to pretend to grasp through perception any external thing.[2]

It is claimed that there is no escape from this objection, and that it is a principle which, if once grasped, will never be abandoned.

Now there is a sense in which these and similar statements are true, and indeed truisms, but this is not the sense in which the Idealists mean them to be taken. For to take them to mean 'we can only think thoughts' is a commonplace which leads us nowhere, unless we interpret it as meaning 'nothing but thoughts can exist.' In this case we should be forced to conclude that our thoughts are indeed 'without content' and so 'empty,' as Kant says. Happily we are not in this state of intellectual aridity, since, in fact, there is ambiguity in all the terms used in arriving at the principle of immanence. Thus those who argue: 'no idea is capable of existing apart from a mind, but every known entity is an idea, therefore no known entity can exist apart from a mind,' are using the term idea in two senses. In the major it is taken to express a mental state; in the minor, an object of thought. If this distinction is introduced into the argument we see at once that though we can agree that no mental state is capable of existing apart from the mind we cannot allow that no object of thought is so, since this is precisely

[1] Italics are Berkeley's.

[2] For a number of formulations of this principle collected from various authors, cf. Geney, *Critica*, p. 204; Jeannière, *Criteriologia*, p. 444.

the proposition which the Idealist is trying to prove; and he does so by introducing it surreptitiously under the cloak of a truism. In fact all the formulæ of the principle of immanence can be taken in two senses, of which one is a truism, the other an absurdity. The truism is: we can only know that objects exist when they are known; the absurdity, we know that objects cannot exist except when they are known. So the principle: 'only what is known to me, or is in my consciousness, can exist,' is a confusion of these two propositions, the absurdity being accepted for the sake of the truism. In general all the terms which refer to knowledge, viz. thought, idea, judgement, and above all consciousness or experience, are ambiguous, being in the first place applicable to mental acts, and then by metonymy, i.e. the transference of the name, applied to the objects of these acts. Such a procedure is clearly sophistical; and moreover we have no right to identify knowledge and consciousness, for though consciousness always accompanies knowledge it in no way follows that all knowledge is consciousness. What we can assert is that when I know, I know that I know, which is a wholly different proposition from: when I know, I know only myself. Thus, to the assertion: 'all cognition is internal' we reply: entitatively, as a kind of being, viz. a state of mind, I concede: intentionally, i.e. in its direction and activity, I deny.

As Father Garrigou-Lagrange points out,[1] the idealist conception of ideas is entirely spatial and materialistic; for the Idealists think of them as if they were portraits or statues, situated in space, and so capable of being considered as objects. S. Thomas, on the contrary, shows us that the idea, or mental presence of the object in the mind, is a living quality, which, being immaterial, is not enclosed and complete in itself, as a photograph is, but is essentially relative to something other than itself. It is, as it were, transparent, so that the mind does not know the idea, but the object through it, and by its means. This relativity constitutes its very nature, for without it, it becomes unintelligible. An idea which is an idea of nothing is not an idea.

[1] *Dieu—Son Existence et Sa Nature* (Paris, Beauchesne, 5e ed., 1928), p. 135.

Though novelty has been claimed for the principle of immanence, so that it was regarded by Idealists as the great discovery and crowning achievement of modern philosophy, in fact it is no new notion, for we find it put forward and refuted by S. Thomas when he asks whether ideas are 'what we know.' In the first objection in this article[1] he says that whatever is actually understood must be in the subject which understands. Now in this subject there is nothing but ideas, and no extra-mental realities, so that we must conclude that we can only know our own ideas. He replies that those things which are actually understood need not necessarily be present in the knowing subject themselves, they may be present in a species or form abstracted from themselves, which is identical with them in nature, though differing from them in its mode of being. Thus, though extra-mental realities cannot be present in the knowing subject in themselves, they can be there by means of their forms or natures which are called the intentional species, and which, being intentional, i.e. relative to the extra-mental reality, essentially lead to knowledge of *it*, and not of themselves; as a telescope is relative to the stars which it makes visible, enabling one to see *them*, and not the telescope itself.[2]

The principle of immanence, then, far from being self-evident and axiomatic is really false in the only sense in which it could be useful as a foundation of Idealism.[3]

We have now seen that we can be absolutely certain of the existence of the individual thinking subject, and that we have solid grounds for asserting the real existence of an

[1] *Summa Theologica*, I, 85, a. 2.

[2] As has been mentioned, the attack on the validity of the principle of immanence among non-scholastic writers was opened by the article 'The Refutation of Idealism,' by Professor Moore (*Mind*, 1903); and since then almost all the neo-realists both in America and in this country have argued against it. A number of these arguments have been collected by Fr. Kremer, C.SS.R., in his two books: *Le Néo-Réalisme Américain* (Paris, Alcan, 1920), pp. 47 ff.; *Le Théorie de la Connaissance chez les Néo-Réalistes Anglais* (Paris, Vrin, 1928), Chap. IX.

[3] Space does not allow of any discussion of the theory of internal relations, which is associated particularly with the name of Bradley, and which was an attempt to show that reality must be an interrelated whole, and that no part taken separately can be real. For a simple and clear criticism of this view, see Barron, *Elements of Epistemology*, pp. 126 ff.

extra-mental world, whose existence is independent of our thought of it. This world cannot, we have shown, be conceived as purely spiritual, but must be extended and material. Finally, even the *a priori* principle of immanence, on which Idealism rests, has been found to be untrue in the sense in which Idealists understand it. Consequently, no basis remains for the Idealists' contention that the external world has no reality independently of our minds, except the arguments derived from the contradictory character of sense knowledge ; and from the fact that perception appears to be mediate, so that what we really perceive are our own bodily states.

If we can show that sense knowledge is intuitive or immediate it is plain that this last objection will fall to the ground. Not only this, but the arguments drawn from the so-called illusions of the senses will also be refuted, inasmuch as it is impossible that what is immediately perceived should be perceived falsely ; since there could be nothing to falsify knowledge if the object is immediately united to the knowing faculty.

It is therefore necessary for a complete vindication of the realist position to consider the question whether the senses perceive their objects immediately, or, whether, on the contrary, they perceive them by means of some medium which is known directly.

CHAPTER VII

THE INTUITIVE CHARACTER OF SENSE KNOWLEDGE

Illationism and Perceptionism—Reasons in favour of Perceptionism—Difficulties of Illationism—An Objection Considered—'Errors of Sense': How Explained by Perceptionism—Extra-mental Reality of Proper or Secondary Sense Objects.

As was pointed out in an earlier chapter (Chap. IV) those who maintain the existence of an extra-mental world and defend the validity of our knowledge of it, i.e. the Realists, are divided into two groups, the members of one group holding that perception is mediate, and those of the other that it is immediate. The former contend that the mind has immediate contact, not with external things, but with ideas or representations of these things formed in the mind. This theory, though historically speaking it is the seed of Idealism, has nevertheless been adopted by many Realists —the Illationists—but it is clear that these will have to justify their assertion that from knowledge of a subjective object we can pass to knowledge of the trans-subjective. To do so they appeal, as we said, either to the veracity of God, or to the principle of causality. Whatever may be thought as to the validity of the argument from our consciousness of passivity in the act of perceiving to an external cause of perceptions—and it seems doubtful whether it is sound—its validity is not here in question; for we are not asking whether we can *prove* the existence of the trans-subjective by means of the principle of causality, but whether, in fact, this is the way in which we acquire our knowledge of the trans-subjective. We are taking it as already proved that an external material world exists, and is known by us, and now merely ask how we come to know it. Do we first know our own perceptions and sensations, and then see that they are likenesses of the world outside, as I might recognise a man from his photograph; or do we know directly, and first of all, the external object? As was mentioned earlier the former view is known as Illationism or Representationism and the latter as Perceptionism. With few exceptions, Scholastics, whether Thomists or not, are advocates of Perceptionism. In this they are plainly in agreement with ordinary experience, for it certainly seems to us that what we sense are the external objects, not our own sensations. In this simple fact we have a very strong foundation for the Perceptionist thesis, for there can be no doubt that this unhesitating adoption of it by the ordinary man is based on the testimony of consciousness. For when we examine our consciousness of our experiences, that which we call external appears to us as being just as real as our internal experiences. The phenomena of colour, sound and so on are just as much 'given' as those of pleasure or pain. At the same time in one respect they are totally unlike; for as soon as we look into the way in which they come to be in us, we cannot fail to see that our emotions are consciously apprehended by us as welling up from within us, and being filled, as it were, by us, so that they have no meaning except as *our* emotions; whereas in external experience we have the exact contrary of this, inasmuch as here the experience appears as coming from outside, as being full, not of us, but of the object experienced. This object has a meaning and existence of its own, and the knowledge that it has these is derived from the object, not produced from ourselves. Thus we have just as much warrant for asserting that our external experience is external as we have for saying that our internal experience is internal and vice versa, since the character of both is guaranteed in precisely the same fashion, namely by our consciousness of this character. If then we are to deny that our external experience comes to us from without, and so assert that it comes from within, from some internal object which mediates between us and the external one, we ought also to be prepared to deny that our internal experience comes from within, our assurance as to the internality of the one having precisely the same ground as that for the externality of the other.

Further, if we examine the processes of imagination and intellectual knowledge we see that in them we produce for ourselves images and concepts, and that we think and imagine by means of such concepts and images, which have been produced by us ; thus making present to ourselves, either in the imagination, or the intellect, things which may not be present in fact ; whereas in external experience, on the contrary, we are conscious that it is not we who conjure up any picture of the object, but it is the object which imposes itself upon us when it presents itself, and not otherwise.

The same idea can be put in a slightly different form by saying that we are conscious of the indetermination of our senses. We know that we can *imagine* any object at will, a landscape, a face, a building ; but we cannot *sense* any object at will—I cannot see my friend just by wishing to, though I can imagine him—and thus my senses remain of themselves passive and undetermined. Evidently then the determination of my senses must come from without ; it cannot come from within from the senses themselves, since they are essentially undetermined. So sensation must be an immediate intuition of something not myself, something not a sensation, but an external present object.

As we noticed earlier[1] the external objects of the senses are of two kinds, the object as it is outside the subject at a distance, such as a bell which is ringing, or a book which is lying on the table ; and an internal object, as the vibration of the air in the ear, or the coloured surface in contact with the eye. It is this latter class of objects which we are here contending must be immediately perceived, since consciousness testifies that I do not sense internal impressions, but something external.

This conclusion is strengthened if we consider the insuperable difficulty by which the theory of mediate perception or illationism, according to which what we sense are modifications of our own senses, is faced. How are we ever to be sure

[1] Vol. I, Part II, Chap. IX, pp. 234 ff.

that such internal modifications correspond truly to the external objects ? If our point of departure is, as in fact it is in this theory, the purely subjective and internal, by what means can we pass from it to the external reality which is supposed to correspond to it, and of which it is imagined to be a copy ? This difficulty is now generally recognised to be destructive of any 'copy theory' of knowledge ; for there is, on this hypothesis, no possible means by which we can assure ourselves that the senses give us true knowledge of the external world ;[1] and once we are doubtful of the validity of sense knowledge we must also be sceptical as to the truth of knowledge in general, since all our knowledge is based on that of the senses. The only way in which we could re-establish our confidence in sense knowledge would be by gaining immediate knowledge of the external object itself, and comparing it with our sensation : a process which is evidently the exact negation of the illationist thesis that we cannot know the external object immediately. The examination of our own sensible experience thus assures us that what we sense are not our own sensations, but external physical objects. On the other hand, it is plain that it is intra-organic objects, not those that are distant from the organ, which are sensed. This is clear from the example of light from a distant star, which may have been extinguished by the time we sense the light which arrives at our eye.

It might perhaps be argued that the difficulty just mentioned with regard to the verification of sense knowledge is as serious for those who hold this latter view as for those who hold that we sense our own sensations, and so sense the external object mediately only.

This objection would take the form of saying that we can never be certain whether the extra-organic object is present, and corresponds to the intra-organic one. It is easy to see, however, that the cases are not parallel ; for we do not here have to pass from an internal subjective state to an assumed external cause of it ; but from one physical fact to another,

[1] For an examination and criticism of the various ways in which Illationists have attempted to escape from this difficulty, cf. J. de Tonquédec, *La Critique de la Connaissance*, pp. 84–90 (Paris, Beauchesne).

both of them belonging to the external world. We can therefore control any particular deliverance of sense knowledge by others, e.g. looking at the distant object from different points of view and using the other senses to determine its character by comparison. In this process the intellect comes into play, judging what sort of cause is necessary to produce a given set of intra-organic objects. Further, the intellect is now not forced to go astray, as it would be in the illationist hypothesis, since in that hypothesis there would be no possibility of the determining whether my subjective sensation corresponded to a trans-subjective object, with regard either to its presence or its nature. To take the example of the light from a distant star, all that the illationist knows is a sensation of light, from which it is impossible to conclude that there is light outside the eye. In our own theory, on the contrary, we immediately perceive a light outside, though in contact with the eye ; a light which is given and presented to me and is not a sensation, i.e. a modification of my sense of sight. We are therefore faced by a physical object which will have a physical cause. Whether it is a lamp or a star, whether it is shining at the time when we see the light in the eye, what its distance and direction are, and so on, being questions which can be determined by further sense experiences.

The conclusion which we have arrived at, by examining our own experience, namely that we sense external, but intra-organic, objects immediately, will be much strengthened by an examination of the objections raised to it. The interpretationist or illationist doctrine, in fact, owes much of its plausibility to the supposed impossibility of accounting for the ' errors of sense ' on the perceptionist hypothesis. That there is no such impossibility is, nevertheless, easily seen if we keep clearly in view the fundamental principles of the perceptionist theory, viz. that what we sense immediately are the essential sense-objects, so that it is only here that the senses are immune from error ; mistakes being possible with regard to all accidental objects of the sense. Thus all subsequent judgements and inferences as to the nature of these essential objects, whether of the sense, e.g. the comparison of two colours, and still more of the intellect, e.g. that a distant object is of a particular shape, size, or nature, are outside the range of immediate sense intuition and so subject to error. There is one class of such judgements which has perhaps a special importance in this connection, namely our judgements as to the exteriority of an object; for the object considered precisely as exterior to us, at a distance from our bodies, is not sensed *per se*, and we may therefore go wrong in attributing exteriority to it; as in the case of a jaundiced eye, which makes the page of a book seem yellow, or the hearing of the sound of a bell which has in fact ceased to ring. It is well to note further that the Thomist theory of immediate intuition in no way implies that we know *the whole* of the sensible object. What we know of it is conditioned by the capacity of the sense—thus the eye can only see a certain range of colours—and by its state, i.e. whether it is functioning absolutely normally, or is in any way defective or diseased.

The confusion between interpretations and intuitions is the main source of the objections to the Thomist doctrine, and it is these objections themselves which are the strength of the opposing view of the Illationists. Thus it is argued that the intuitionist view would oblige us to attribute contradictory predicates to the same realities; for since the colour, size, and shape of objects vary according to their distance from us, the angle from which they are looked at, and the media through which they are viewed, it will follow that we shall have to say that they are simultaneously of different sizes, shapes, and colours: e.g. a penny will be at once half and a quarter of an inch in diameter, both light and dark brown, circular and oval simultaneously. It is, however, plain that according to our theory we do not sense the penny on the table but the projection of light reflected by it to the eye, and this intra-organic object is in fact of different dimensions, shapes and colours according to the point of view from which the penny is looked at. Since, moreover, we cannot regard it simultaneously from more than one point of view it is plain that there can be no discordance between those objects which we actually and immediately see. The same answer will evidently apply to any difficulty which urges that the use of a medium will alter the object—so a microscope will make us see a strange monster when unaided vision will only show us a flea—for the external object, the insect, does not change, but only the object in contact with the eye changes; and this *is*, in the one case, a large and horrible shape, in the other, a tiny speck

Similar considerations show how easily difficulties drawn from the varying dispositions of the subject can be disposed of. So it is objected: I sense water as hot with a hand that is cold, while if the other hand be warm it will sense the water as tepid. The water then must be of different temperatures at the same time. Actually, however, what I sense, and sense truly, is the difference between the temperature of my hand and that of the water, for it is plain that the water cannot give to my hand warmth which the hand already has, and so only communicates to my sense its surplus heat, i.e. the difference of the two temperatures. So, as long as, after putting a cold hand into warm water, I content myself with registering the fact that I sense a considerable degree of heat, I cannot go wrong; but if I exclaim 'this water is boiling,' I have made an unjustified and erroneous judgement with regard to the water itself.

Similar considerations apply to senses in some way disordered or deranged: I am justified in saying 'I see yellow' or 'I see double,' but not that the object outside me *is* yellow or double, relying merely on the testimony of my senses. The object which I see is in fact yellow or double owing to the derangement of the sense, but the judgement as to the nature of the exterior object is evidently not an immediate intuition, but an inference, which may therefore be at fault. The 'errors' of the colour-blind are to be judged in the same way, for, being blind to certain radiations, the whole spectrum is altered for them, and so they see green for red, or even see only the difference between light and shade without being able to distinguish any of the colours of the spectrum. They are right in asserting that they do so see, for in fact the objects are presented to them in this way, while they would be wrong if they inferred that the exterior object is in fact coloured in the same way as the intra-organic one is.

Error, in these and similar cases, if it occurs, is to be attributed chiefly to an error of judgement ; while in the case of hallucinations—such as the ' sensing ' of pain in an amputated leg—the error is due to the intervention of imagination, which has habitually associated a pain in a particular part of the trunk with pain in a definite limb.

We find then that we can without difficulty maintain the infallibility of the senses with regard to their essential objects, while accounting for ' sense errors ' and illusions ; for these are all connected with accidental sensibles, where immunity from error is by no means guaranteed. In this way we see that there is no solid objection to the theory of immediate or intuitive sense perception, and so no solid ground for the illationist or interpretationist view. It is clear that in order to overthrow intuitionism it is necessary to show that the senses go wrong with respect to their essential objects, it being vital to intuitionism to maintain that since no medium is interposed between the sense and its essential object, no distortion of the object, and so no positive error is possible here. The basis of interpretationism is, on the whole, a negative one : for the interpretationist argues that since such errors and illusions as we have been considering are incompatible with intuitionism, the truth must lie with his theory. Thus, in showing that they are not incompatible with it, we have destroyed the foundations of interpretationism, leaving intuitionism in possession of the field ; since the reasons in favour of rejecting it, and substituting interpretationism, are seen not to be cogent.

We noticed earlier the distinction of proper and common sense-objects, which in non-scholastic philosophy are known as secondary and primary sensibles. Since the time of Descartes it has been very generally asserted that even if the common or primary sensibles, such as extension, are to be found in things outside the mind, or, as the Scholastics say, are formally trans-subjective, the same cannot be true of the proper or secondary sensibles, such as colour.[1]

Galileo seems to have been the first to set out this doctrine quite clearly and explicitly. So he says, for example: 'That external bodies, to excite in us these tastes, these odours, and these sounds, demand other than size, figure, number and slow or rapid motion, I do not believe; and I judge that if the ears, the tongue, and the nostrils were taken away, the figures, the numbers, and the motions would indeed remain, but not the odours, nor the tastes, nor the sounds, which, without the living animal, I do not believe are anything else than names.'[2]

Now there is certainly a sense in which this theory is true, for it is plain that no colour would be seen if there were no eyes, and that colour *as seen* differs from colour in an external object, since in the latter it has a physical existence, in the former an intentional or mental one. So if by colour we mean 'colour as seen,' it could not exist without the eye; whereas if by colour we mean the quality which, if it acted on an eye, would result in the perception of colour, there is no reason why such a quality should not exist without any eye to see it. S. Thomas following Aristotle (426 a, 20) explains this (3 de Anima, Lect. 2 *ad fin.*). 'The earlier physicists,' i.e. before Aristotle, 'were wrong in thinking that nothing is white or black except when it is seen; and that there is no savour except when it is tasted; and in like manner concerning the other sensibles and senses. And since they did not believe that any beings other than sensible ones, or any cognitive power other than sense, existed, they thought that the whole being (*esse*) and truth of things consisted in their appearing. . . . In a certain sense they spoke rightly, and in a certain sense, not rightly. For since 'sense' and 'sensible' are of two kinds, viz. with respect to potentiality, and with respect to act: what they said, viz. that there is no sensible without sense, is verified in the case of the sense and sensible with respect to act. But this is not true of the

[1] Vol. I, Part II, Chap. IX, p. 234.

[2] Galileo, Opere IV, 336 ff., quoted by Burtt, *The Metaphysical Foundations of Modern Science*, p. 78.

sense and sensible with respect to potentiality.' Indeed the Aristoteleian and Thomistic saying, 'the sense in act is the sensible in act,' contains all that is true in the doctrine of Berkeley; and it is curious to find these ancient and mediæval philosophers setting out his great 'discovery,' and that in almost his very words—'*esse est apparere*,' and attributing the error in it to the crudity of still more primitive philosophy. Thus Aristotle and S. Thomas meet the difficulty by the distinction: that the sensible in act, what is actually sensed, cannot exist without the sense, I concede; that the sensible in potency, what is able to be sensed, cannot exist without the sense, I deny.

The distinction between primary and secondary qualities with regard to their reality has received a certain amount of support from modern Scholastics, but is, in spite of its superficial plausibility, open to the gravest objections. In the first place, it can hardly be doubted that Berkeley[1] was right in arguing that the same reasons which lead a man to reject the trans-subjective character of secondary qualities, such as colour, must logically lead him to reject also the trans-subjectivity of the primary ones. These are such arguments as those which we have just been examining, drawn from the apparently contradictory character of the proper sensibles if they are supposed to be found in the external object, and from the supposed fact that by 'colour' I really mean my sensation of colour. It is plain, however, that the same arguments apply, e.g. to extension, the same body changing in size as it approaches or recedes from us; and that if colour is merely my perception of colour, we ought also to say that extension is merely my perception of extension.

Further, no one will dispute that we know the primary or common sensibles by means of the secondary or proper ones, and it follows that if the secondary sensibles are merely subjective impressions we can have no possible guarantee that the primary ones are not so also; nor any means of discovering the trans-subjective character of the primary

[1] *Hylas and Philonous.* First Dialogue

sensibles from the secondary sensibles, since all our knowledge of the former si derived from the latter, which are supposed to be entirely subjective, and to have no existence apart from eyes and noses.

Lastly, no satisfactory explanation is forthcoming of the way in which the sense manufactures the proper sensibles, for they would have to make something out of nothing.

Apart from the impossibility of separating the primary and the secondary qualities with respect to their transsubjectivity, the view that the secondary qualities are really due only to ourselves is surely an incredible one. As Dr. Whitehead says: 'Nature gets credit for what should in truth be reserved for ourselves: the rose for its scent: the nightingale for his song: and the sun for his radiance. The poets are entirely mistaken. They should address their lyrics to themselves, and should turn them into odes of self-congratulation on the excellency of the human mind.'[1]

Such a theory, even if it were logically unassailable, is, as Whitehead says, 'quite unbelievable'; and involving, as it does, grave, if not insuperable difficulties must be judged altogether untenable.

NOTE.—In this chapter we have endeavoured to bring out the principles which Thomists make use of in rebutting the objections to their intuitionist theory of sensation, and not to provide an exhaustive criticism of all these objections. For such a full treatment of the question the reader must be referred to works which can treat of the Thomist theory of knowledge more fully than space allows us to do.[2]

[1] Whitehead, *Science and the Modern World*, pp. 68 f.

[2] These objections are discussed at length by J. de Tonquédec, *La Critique de la Connaissance*, Chap. III, pp. 91–132, cf. also Geny, *Critica*, Lib. II, Cap. 1; Gredt, *De Cognitione Sensuum Externorum*.

SECTION II

THE ONTOLOGICAL VALUE OF OUR KNOWLEDGE OF ABSTRACT THINGS

CHAPTER VIII

THE NOTION OF UNIVERSALS

They are General Qualities—Their Importance for Knowledge—Their Kinds—The 'States of Nature'—Analysis of the Universal.

LET us now cast a glance back over the road which we have travelled so far. First we saw that the mind is capable of attaining some certitude, of which the ultimate motive is the evidence of the object. We then began to consider the nature of this object with regard to its extra-mental reality, and we noticed that it appears before us as a complex thing, such as a 'sounding bell,' i.e. it appears as an individual concrete thing having certain sensible qualities or characteristics. So a red rose is first perceived by the senses as a particular patch of a special colour. We therefore went on to ask whether in fact our supposition that there existed such a patch outside us was correct; and next, what was the mode of our perception of it by the senses, whether mediate or immediate. Having decided that we were right in thinking that we immediately sensed an external object, we finally enquired whether such immediate sensation extended to all the qualities of the object: e.g. both to the redness of the rose, and its shape; or only to its 'primary qualities,' such as size. Again, we found it necessary to conclude that sensation is immediate knowledge of the whole concrete thing 'red rose,' and not only of its primary qualities. We have thus reached the conclusion that singular objects which are external to us are known by the senses immediately with regard to all their sensible qualities. Just now we spoke of a *red* rose ; and though it is true that the senses tells us that this object presented to them has a certain definite colour, they do not tell us that this colour is one which is found in other objects, and which we name 'red.' Thus far, then, we have justified the assertion that the senses give us true knowledge of singular concrete things which are actually presented to them ; but we have not discussed whether there exist in the external world such general qualities as redness, which are common to a large number of singular things ; nor whether, if there are such qualities, in what way they can be said to be in the singular things. It is plain, however, that we do seem to have knowledge of such general qualities, and that this knowledge is of an entirely different kind to that which we have, through the senses, of singular things as such. These general qualities, which appear to be found in many different subjects—as redness for example—and which are in fact predicated of many different subjects, as expressing characteristics which are common to many things, are called universals. They are of great importance for knowledge ; since we can only understand things in so far as we can explain them, showing why they are as they are. These explanations, therefore, take the form of general propositions or laws, which apply to a class of objects, indicating a nature which is common to all of them. By means of such laws we are able to understand why a particular thing behaves as it does, knowing that its action must follow a general law which governs all things of its kind ; so that its behaviour will not surprise us, and in fact we shall be able to foresee what it will do. In this way the law of gravitation 'explained' the motion of the heavenly bodies : without such generalisation we could not understand why they move as they do. Thus science deals only with the universal, not with singular things as such ; and all our intellectual judgements about the world are framed in terms of universal notions ; from the simplest judgement, such as 'snow is white'—where snow and white are universal terms—to the widest generalisations, such as the laws of motion. Consequently, just as the discussion of the nature of singular objects was an enquiry into the nature of sense knowledge, so the discussion of universals will be an evaluation of intellectual knowledge. Before beginning to consider the difficult problem which universals present, it is necessary to gain a more accurate notion of what we mean by this word ' universal.' Etymologically it is derived from the two words *unum* and *verto*, and is the adjective formed from universe. So it means that which has a relation to several things which are in some way connected. Thus we speak of a universal church. The universal, then, is opposed to the singular, which, as singular, has no connection with other things, and cannot be shared by other things; or is incommunicable. The relation which the universal may have to the many things with which it communicates, and which are called its ' inferiors,' is of three kinds; for it may be related to them either as a sign of them, or as a cause of them, or as a nature which is common to them. So we have a primary threefold division of the universal into the universal as signifying many things, or as causing them, or as being in them—*universale in significando, in causando,* and *in essendo.* The universal ' *in significando* ' is some sign or symbol which primarily signifies the universal itself, and consequently can be applied to many things, as common names can be. Here it is the very words themselves, as man or donkey (which are audible signs of the universal concept); or material things, such as the barber's pole (which is a visible sign of the universal) which are called universals; for though as sounds or sights they are singular, yet they have a universal character as signs. Very similar to these universal signs are those universals which Scholastics call universals *in repraesentando*—something which represents many things pictorially or typically.[1] So the architect's idea of a building is not exhausted by the construction of one building, but may serve for the production of other similar ones. These universals are *patterns* in accordance with which many things can be made. Though such universals act as ' formal causes ' with regard to the things

[1] In different arts and industries they go by different names, so, e.g. in the manufacture of motor cars they are called ' models.'

which are made after their pattern, yet the name of causative universal or '*universale in causando*' is reserved for those which act as efficient causes of a number of effects.

Though the kinds of universal just mentioned have their importance in various contexts, they are explained here rather for the sake of giving the complete division of universals, than because we are directly concerned with them in Epistemology. It is the last general division of the universal—the universal in being—which we are to investigate here. Aristotle defines it as: ὃ πλείοσιν ὑπάρχειν πέφυκεν (1038 b, 11), that which naturally belongs to more than one thing. Notice that he does not say the universal is that which is actually in many things, but that it is that which is of its nature *fitted* to be in more than one. Since this universal is capable of being in many things it can also be predicated of them, and if the fact that it can so be predicated is taken into account it is called the universal in predication—*universale in prædicando*—which is also called the 'logical' and 'formal' universal; while the universal 'in being'—in so far as it is a certain nature, though without taking into account its capacity for being in *many* things and so predicated of them—is called the metaphysical or direct universal. The reason for the names 'metaphysical' and 'logical' can be seen if we remember what are the objects of these two sciences: for metaphysics considers the natures of things, while logic deals with 'intentions' or the relations which the mind puts into things. Now it is plain that the capacity for being *predicated* of many things is such an 'intention' or mental relation; whereas if a nature be considered without taking into account this capacity for predication, and so whether it is capable of being in many things, we are considering only the *nature* of the thing, and so form the metaphysical universal.

For a fuller understanding of this we must examine the distinction which S. Thomas makes between the various states in which nature can be considered.[1] There are three such states, of which the first is: (1) *the state of nature as it is in itself;* considered, that is to say, absolutely; stripped bare

[1] Cf. *De ente et essentia*, Cap. IV.

of all that does not belong to it as nature. In this state we can only attribute to it essential predicates, for to attribute anything else to it, as *nature*, would be to make a false attribution. For example, man considered simply as a nature is neither whiten or black, tall nor short, these attributes not belonging to the nature of man as such, the only ones which do belong to it being rational and animal; (2) The second state of nature is that in which it is considered *as it exists in singular things*, and here accidental predicates can be attributed to it, as we might say ' man is white,' meaning some particular man, such as Socrates, is white; (3) The third state in which it is considered is *that which it has in the mind*, where, by means of intellectual abstraction, all individuating conditions are omitted.

It will be seen that two of these states are not universal, properly speaking, viz. the state of nature as it is in singular things, which is evidently singular, not universal; and the state of nature considered absolutely as it is in itself. This last is neither universal nor singular. If nature in itself were universal, no singular thing could have it, since what belongs to nature in itself belongs to it always and everywhere: so that if it were universal it would have to carry this universality with it into the singular thing, which would thus be both singular and universal at the same time, which is a contradiction. Neither can nature in itself be singular, for then it would be identical in Socrates and Plato, and could not be made many in different individuals. Thus neither plurality nor unity, universality nor singularity, belong to nature considered absolutely; being accidental to it, as are black and white. In a word, if nature as it is in itself were universal no singular thing could possess it, while if it were singular it could never be communicated to different individuals.

In the third state in which it may be considered, viz. as it exists immaterially through the operation of the intellect, nature, from the very fact that it is abstracted from individuals, and from all conditions that individualise it, ceases to be singular and becomes universal; though, according to the Thomists, not yet formally and actually so. This formal universality is, however, contributed by the mind, considering this nature as capable of being in, and being predicated of, many things. As Fr. Roland-Gosselin says : ' S. Thomas makes his own the strong expression of Averroes : " It is the intelligence which makes the universal." '[1] Nature thus universalised, by abstraction in the intellect, is called by the Scholastics the metaphysical universal *quoad modum concipiendi*, while nature considered absolutely as it is in itself is called by them the metaphysical universal *quoad rem conceptam.*

NATURE
- absolute ; i.e. with respect to essence (neither universal nor singular)
  - Met. Univ., *quoad rem conceptam.*
- as it exists in this or that ; i.e. with respect to existence
  - as it exists in singulars (singular)
  - as it exists in the mind (metaphysical universal, *quoad modum concipiendi*)

It is useful, in order to bring out quite clearly what S. Thomas means by the phrase ' nature as it is in the mind,' i.e. the metaphysical universal *quoad modum concipiendi*, to compare it once more with the logical universal. As we have noted, the latter is the capacity which nature has of being predicated of its inferiors, so that it can be defined as the relation which abstract nature has to its actual inferiors.

Now the logical and metaphysical universal have this in common, that they do not exist actually except in the mind ; in all other respects they are entirely distinct. The metaphysical universal signifies nature as it is abstracted from singular things, its relationship to these things not being taken into account. On the contrary in the logical universal, it is this very relationship of the universal to its inferiors which is its formal constituent.

[1] M-D Roland-Gosselin, O.P., *Le ' De ente et essentia ' de S. Thomas d'Aquin*, Introd., p. xxiii. (Bibliothèque Thomiste VIII, Le Saulchoir, 1926.)

There is one further way in which the universal may be considered, viz. as it is taken abstractly or concretely. If it be taken concretely it signifies both a form and the subject of this form (e.g. man), and the process by which it is arrived at is called total abstraction. If it be taken abstractly it expresses the form only (e.g. humanity), and the process of its formation is called formal abstraction. It will be necessary to add some further remarks about these two kinds of abstraction later.

The universal, then, is a combination of unity and plurality; for being one thing which is naturally capable of being in many—such capacity arising in the first place from its being abstracted from all individuating conditions which would tie it down to the singular—it must include two elements: (1) unity in itself, and (2) capacity for being in many others.

(1) The unity which is required is unity not of name only, but also of that which is expressed by the name. The reason is that we are here dealing with nature which abstracts from individuals; and, consequently, is not differentiated by individual peculiarities, but is all of a kind. Such natures are called 'univocal'; that is to say, the name of the nature is common to all the individuals of that nature, an is,d moreover, applied to them in a sense which is essentially the same in all cases. So the name 'man' is common to Peter, Paul, James and John; and is applied to them in essentially the same way. It is neither applied to them in quite different senses as, for example, the name 'cat' is applied to the animal and the 'cat-o'-nine-tails'; nor even in a sense which is the same only from some particular point of view; as, for example, the word 'healthy' is to the air of a town and the colour of a man's face.

(2) The second element which is required, the capacity for being in many others, implies that the universal should be able to be shared by its inferiors in such a way that the whole nature expressed by the name of the universal should be found in each of them, so that this nature will be multiplied by them, and yet each of them will have the whole of the nature.

It is this simultaneous unity and multiplicity of the universal which constitutes one of the chief difficulties with regard to it, for it seems to be contradictory. On the one hand, it is so unified that it is always the same whatever be the subject in which it is realised ; Peter is a man in precisely the same sense as Paul ; while on the other hand it is so appropriated by, and identified with, the singulars in which it is found that it is unrestrictedly affirmed of each of them, and so made many by them.[1] It would almost seem that it is merely a convenient mental fiction : a label used to designate collectively a number of different things, whose differences are, for certain purposes, of no practical account. It is this problem, and the status of the universal with regard to its trans-subjective reality—its value as an ontological object—which we have now to discuss.

[1] Cf. Geny, *Critica*, No. 312. J. de Tonquédec, op. cit., p. 152.

CHAPTER IX

THE PROBLEM OF UNIVERSALS

The Difficulty Stated—Proposed Solutions—Nominalism: Greek; Mediæval; Modern—Conceptualism: Descartes, Berkeley, Kant—Summary of Kant's View—The Successors of Kant—Extreme Realism: Platonist; Formalistic Realism; Pantheistic Realism.

THE difficulty which we have remarked at the end of the last chapter may also be expressed in the following form: there appears to be a contradiction between the universal character of our concepts and the individual character of things. The things with which we are acquainted are definite, singular, and exclude all multiplicity; while our concepts, on the contrary, imply multiplicity. It would, therefore, seem to be contradictory to assert that our concepts represent the things. There is also a further difficulty. We cannot have any sensible perception of a universal. If I see a rose, or smell its odour, it is this particular redness or sweetness which I perceive: I cannot see colour in general, or smell scent in general. Now my concepts are formed either through or of my percepts; if the latter, so that these two are the same, since I cannot perceive the universal neither can I conceive it; while if they are different, how can my concepts give me knowledge of the thing itself? This is known to me only by percept; and so will not be known by means of anything which differs from percept, i.e. by means of concepts

In the face of such difficulties as these some philosophers excluded the universal character of knowledge altogether. Others claimed that the *only* true knowledge is that of universals, i.e. that reality is in truth universal only, and not individual at all; while some have considered that the difficulties are not insuperable, and have declined to jettison either the universal or the individual.

The theories on this subject are generally grouped by Scholastics under four heads: Nominalism, Conceptualism, Extreme Realism, and Moderate Realism. The first two refuse to recognise that the universal is in any way to be found in the extra-mental world, and so belong to the first tendency just mentioned; the third (Extreme Realism) does not allow that the individual is truly real; while the fourth recognises the reality of both the universal and the individual. We must consider these various points of view in a little more detail.

I. *Nominalism.*

In general, Nominalism is the theory which teaches that universals exist only in their names: or, in other words, that there is no universal entity in nature, nor any universal concept in the mind, which corresponds to these universal terms or names.

All through antiquity and the Middle Ages it is difficult to distinguish between Nominalism and Conceptualism, the latter being the theory which allows that we have universal concepts, but will not admit that there are universal entities in nature. With all the thinkers of these periods the one theory shades off imperceptibly into the other, and the distinction between them is not clearly seen till we come to the modern Empiricists.

Janet[1] names Berkeley as the first avowed nominalist; and, though this might be disputed, it is in any case proved that the philosophers of the earlier periods are classed as nominalist or conceptualist rather on account of the tendencies of their doctrines than because they explicitly held one view as distinguished from the other.

One source of Nominalism in ancient Greece is to be found in the teaching of Heracleitus, who maintained that all things are in a state of perpetual flux. It would follow as a logical consequence from this that universal terms, which

[1] *Histoire de la Philosophie*, par Paul Janet et Gabriel Séailles, 12e edition (Paris, Delagrave, 1921), Vol. 1, p. 536.

remain the same, do not apply to anything in nature, nor even correspond with any concept, since the concept itself will be fluid and changing. This consequence is, however, only implicit with Heracleitus. It was developed and made explicit by his disciples, and notably by Cratylus, who, as Aristotle tells us,[1] denied the possibility of science and even of speech itself.

The diametrically opposite view, put forward by Democritus and the Atomists, that all things are material, also led to the same conclusion. For if concepts are material, and nothing but matter exists in nature ; since that which is material is singular, there can be neither universal concepts nor things.

The teaching of the Sophist Gorgias that knowledge is impossible and incommunicable is also based on Nominalism, for he held that words do not in any way correspond to things, and that therefore things can neither be known nor expressed by means of words.

Later, the Epicureans, as a necessary consequence of their materialism, held the same opinion : for they taught that universal ideas arise from the association and confusion of singular perceptions. Epicurus taught also that we cannot know whether our sensations correspond with their objects ; and so, combining subjectivism with materialism, was led to an absolute denial of universals, that is to Nominalism, on both these grounds. For materialism demands that everything should be singular, while subjectivism refuses to recognise that our concepts can apply to things.

The Greek and mediaeval discussions of this question of the concept are linked by Porphyry (born A.D. 233), the Neo-Platonist, and by Boethius (born about A.D. 480) ; for it was the apparently unanswered question of the former, in his *Isagoge*, which formed the basis of discussion in the Middle Ages. Porphyry's statement was transmitted by Boethius to the mediaeval philosophers in the following form :

' Mox de generibus ac speciebus illud quidem, sive subsistunt, sive in solis nudisque intellectibus posita sunt, sive subsistentia

[1] Aristotle, *Met.*, 1010, a. 12.

corporalia sunt an incorporalia, et utrum separata a sensibilibus an in sensibilibus posita et circa ea constantia, dicere recusabo.' The early Scholastics took up the problem in these terms, and felt themselves bound to the identical expressions here used, being unaware that Porphyry himself had solved the problem of universals in a Platonist sense.[1]

Selecting the best known of the nominalists of the mediaeval period we may mention first Roscelinus (born *c.* 1050), whose writings are lost, with the exception of a single letter, and whose views have therefore to be gathered from his opponents. The chief among these were Abelard and Anselm, who ascribe to him the doctrine that universals are '*flatus vocis,*' which has generally been understood to mean that he thought them to be mere sounds. It is, however, disputed whether his views were precisely Nominalist, as distinguished from anti-realist.[2]

Whatever conclusion may eventually be come to as to the position of Roscelinus in this matter, it is not till two and a half centuries later that we find a clear and fully developed Nominalist or Conceptualist theory. The intervening age had seen the full development of Scholasticism in the teaching of the great masters of the thirteenth century, Albert the Great, Thomas Aquinas and Duns Scotus ; and now in the fourteenth we enter on a period of decadence with the theories of William of Ockham and the Terministic School. Chronologically S. Thomas, Scotus and Ockham form an unbroken chain ; for, according to some, Scotus was born in the very year S. Thomas died (1274), though it now seems to be established that the date of his birth was eight years earlier—while Ockham was eight years old at the death of Scotus (1308). William of Ockham, so called from the Surrey village where he was born, was like Scotus, a Franciscan, but diverged widely from him in his teaching.

In his view, the universal is in no way present in the extra-mental reality, which is wholly individual ; universal terms applying only to the thought-object, and being useful

[1] For a fuller account of this curious affair, cf. M. de Wulf, *Histoire de la Philosophie Mediévale*, Louvain, 1924, 5e ed., Vol. I, pp. 96 ff.

[2] Cf. de Wulf, op. cit., Vol. I, p. 104.

only as mental substitutes (*suppositio*) for a number of individual realities. Thus they are simply labels, which help us to catalogue our apprehensions of individuals. Since these universals are the objects of science, it follows that science is concerned only with terms; hence the name 'Terminist' applied to this school. From this point of view Ockham and his disciples may well be called Nominalists; but since they recognised that universal terms had a meaning and mental value, they are not Nominalists in the sense in which the word is applied to modern Empiricists. One ot the best known of Ockham's followers is John Buridan; while Luther professed himself an 'Occamist.'[1]

The triumph of the Nominalism of Ockham was the destruction of mediaeval scholasticism, for henceforward philosophy is mere juggling with words, which, by hypothesis, can have no relation to reality. At the same time the Humanists of the Renaissance were directing attention to the value of positive studies, such as history, thus giving support to the anti-intellectualist view of the world. So the emphasis was laid rather on the experimental observation of 'facts,' than on their explanation and theoretical co-ordination; and this attitude has lasted to the present day. In this view the only knowledge we have is that of sense experience; and science, at best, is an account of *how* things happen, not of *why* they happen. 'It is a great mistake to conceive this historical revolt'—i.e. the revival of the historical spirit at the Renaissance—'as an appeal to the reason. On the contrary, it was through and through an anti-intellectualist movement. It was a return to the contemplation of brute fact; it was based on a recoil from the inflexible rationality of mediaeval thought.'[2]

It is from England that there comes, in the modern period which was thus inaugurated, a frank and definite expression of philosophical nominalism in the writings of Hobbes, Hume, and Mill.

Thomas Hobbes (1588–1679) says as to this question:

[1] Cf. Denifle, *Luther* (Paris, Picard, 1916), 2nd ed., Tome III, pp. 191 ff., esp. p. 201; where the considerable influence of Ockham's ideas on Luther is shown.

[2] A. N. Whitehead, *Science and the Modern World* (C.U.P., 1927), p.10.

'This word universal is never the name of anything existent in nature, nor of any idea or phantasm formed in the mind, but always the name of some word or name, so that when a living creature, a stone, a spirit, or any other thing is said to be universal, it is not to be understood that any man, stone, etc., ever was or can be universal, but only that these words are universal names, i.e. names common to many things and the concepts corresponding to them are of singular animals or images or phantasms of other things.'[1] His notion of reasoning is equally nominalistic, for, as he says, 'by reasoning I understand computation.[2] It is the collecting together of the reactions to names which we call thoughts, and it is thus a kind of Arithmetic, being carried on by the addition of simple names to one another, or by the subtraction of simpler components from complex names. 'So all reasoning is reduced to the two operations of the mind, addition and subtraction.'[3]

The same notion is also evident in the systems of the two other Nominalists mentioned above: Hume and Mill. According to them there are no such things as universal concepts, properly speaking, and the ideas which we call universal, are, in fact, only a collection of singular percepts accompanied by a common name.

Hume (1711–1776) says that all our general ideas are in reality particular ones, joined to a general term. So he writes: 'A great philosopher (Berkeley) has asserted that all general ideas are nothing but particular ones annexed to a certain term, which gives them a more extensive signification, and makes them recall upon occasion other individuals, which are similar to them. As I look upon this to be one of the greatest and most valuable discoveries which has been made of late in the republic of letters I shall here endeavour to confirm it by some arguments, which I hope will put it beyond all doubt and controversy.'[4]

Again: 'There is no such thing as abstract or general ideas, properly speaking; but all general ideas are, in

[1] Hobbes, *De Corpore*, ii, 9. [2] *Ibid.*, i, 2.
[3] *Ibid.*, i, 2.
[4] Hume, *A Treatise of Human Nature*, Bk. 1, Part 1, Sec. VII.

reality, particular ones, that resemble in certain circumstances the idea present to the mind.'[1]

Essentially the same view of these general ideas is held by Mill, and the explanation he gives of the illusion that general names really represent universal concepts is also substantially the same as that given by Hume; namely that this impression arises owing to the habitual association of images; a theory which is known as Associationism.[2]

It will be seen that these modern Empiricists are Nominalists in the strictest sense of the term, since they do not allow that there is in the mind any universal idea which corresponds to the 'general' term, but regard the 'idea' as singular; this 'idea' being the image or sense impression of a particular object imagined or sensed at the moment.

II.—Conceptualism.

According to this view universal terms correspond, not to singular perceptions as the Nominalists thought, but to universal concepts. Nevertheless, these concepts do not correspond to anything in extra-mental reality; or, at least, if they do, we are incapable of knowing that they do so.

We have already remarked that it is difficult to distinguish, in the Middle Ages, between Conceptualism and Nominalism, so that the theories of Ockham and the Terministic school might well be reckoned as Conceptualist. It is only in the modern period that Conceptualism becomes self-conscious. Its roots are to be found in the philosophy of Descartes, who by basing everything on the subjective fact of thinking, the '*cogito*,' and by making the concept the object and term of thought, enclosed man within the prison of his own mind.[3]

Though Descartes himself was far from realising the implications of his own theories in this as in other matters, the consequences of regarding concepts as the objects of our thought began to be made plain by Locke, Berkeley, and Hume. None of these three can, however, be regarded as the

[1] Hume, *An Enquiry concerning the Human Understanding*, Sect. XII, Note (P).

[2] Cf. Stout, *Manual of Psychology*, Bk. I, Chap. 3, Sec. 3.

[3] Cf. Maritain, *Réflexions sur l'intelligence*, p. 33; and *Trois Réformateurs*, pp. 110 ff.

perfect conceptualist, since Berkeley insisted on the reality of a God and of spiritual beings distinct from the human mind; Locke, though repudiating many features of Cartesianism, went little further than Descartes himself in the direction of explicit conceptualism; while Hume went past it into the extreme of Nominalism.

It is to Kant that we must give the credit, if credit it be, of producing a full-blown conceptualist theory by reversing the rôles of the mind and its object in the process of knowledge. Till his time the supposition that we derive our knowledge, at least to some extent, from objects independent of us had always been accepted, but with Kant the position is reversed; the objects deriving their character from our minds. As he says: 'It has hitherto been assumed that our cognition must conform to the objects. . . . Let us make the experiment whether we may not be more successful in metaphysics, if we assume that the objects must conform to our cognition.'[1] On this hypothesis, the universality of our concepts will not be in any way derived from objects which are in themselves in some sense universal, but from the structure of the mind itself which will impose this character on its thoughts. Thus, though Kant recognises that we have universal concepts, yet since he holds that their universality is derived entirely from the mind itself—from what he calls the '*a priori* categories of the understanding'—he altogether repudiates the notion that universality is to be found in any way in things outside the mind, for the categories cannot apply to the 'thing in itself.'

In order that we may understand Kant's attitude about universals it seems necessary to give a brief synopsis of his system; which in any case can hardly be omitted in an account of the theory of knowledge, for it was owing to Kant's criticism that this subject first came into the centre of philosophic discussion, a position which it has continued to occupy till recent times, if not to the present day.

The year 1769 marks the beginning of Kant's critical

[1] *Kant's Critique of Pure Reason.* Preface to the second edition (Meikle john's translation).

period, with which alone we are here concerned. He received his early philosophic training in the school of Leibniz and Wolff, whose epistemological doctrine was that the laws of knowledge are *a priori*, the chief of them being the principle of sufficient reason. To these views Kant for many years adhered, but the reading of Hume's *Treatise on Human Nature* 'awoke him,' as he says, 'from his dogmatic slumber.' In this work Hume proposed a radical Empiricism which was the direct contradictory of the rationalism of Leibniz. Hume maintained that we have knowledge only of the concrete and particular, but none of the substantial nature of things, of their universal characters or laws; while the Rationalists held that all our knowledge is based on *a priori* principles. How is this contradiction to be resolved? Kant's starting-point was the observation that while the conclusions of physical and mathematical science are universally respected, recognised as true and even indisputable, the same cannot be said of Metaphysics. The explanation of this fact is to be found, according to Kant, in the faulty method adopted by philosophers. He finds defects, or in substance the same defect, in the methods of the two opposing schools with which he was concerned, those of Leibniz and Hume. Neither of them follows the method which has brought about such great triumphs in the field of physical science. For Leibniz, in attempting to construct science by a deductive process from *a priori* principles, neglects a chief element of science, its use of experience; while Hume, on the other hand, with his doctrine that all knowledge consists of sensations, which, since they have no necessary connection among themselves, can give us no necessary or universal laws, excludes the universal or *a priori* element in science, and so is led to a denial of the principle of causation, a concept which is absolutely necessary for science.

Kant is convinced that the object of science must be absolutely necessary and rigorously universal; but he considered, too, that Hume had proved that such universality and necessity cannot be given us by experience. It must therefore come either from the scientific propositions themselves or from our own minds. To say the first would be to relapse into the one-sided rationalism which has already been discarded, and to assert that these propositions are analytic, the subject and predicate being seen to agree inasmuch as the predicate belongs to the subject, as being contained (though implicitly) in it. This Kant refuses to do; and instances such judgements as: $7+5=12$, and the principle of causality; where, he says, the predicate adds something which is not contained in the notion of the subject.[1] These judgements are, therefore, synthetic. It would look as if this added element came from experience; but this cannot be so, for it is indisputable that we attach a universal and necessary sense to such propositions; and since such universality and necessity cannot be derived from experience, the propositions must be *a priori*, in Kant's sense of the phrase.[2] These judgements are therefore at once *synthetic* inasmuch as the predicate adds something to the notion of the subject, and *a priori*, being independent of experience. The problem is therefore: how are such *synthetic-a-priori* judgements possible? They owe their universal character solely to our minds, not to experience (as Hume has shown), nor to a mere analysis of our ideas (as Kant supposes himself to have proved), and as a consequence of this last the predicate adds something to the subject, and they are thus instructive. Where does this something come from?

The solution is to be found in what Kant calls the *a priori* intuitions of space and time.

His reason for so naming them was that they are the conditions which are required in order that external objects may appear to us. Though we cannot conceive of a body, say a chair or table, except as existing in space, we can easily think of space without the chair or table, or even without any

[1] It must be noted that Kant uses the word analytic in a new sense; or at least, a restricted one. What the Scholastics now call analytic judgements include both the first two '*modi dicendi per se*,' or modes of essential predication (as they were named by the mediaeval Scholastics, following Aristotle), i.e., all propositions '*in materia necessaria*,' when the predicate is either contained in, or is *a property of* the subject. Cf. Mercier, *Critériologie*, p. 255 f., and I *Post Anal. S. Thomas*, Lect. X.

[2] 'An *a priori* judgement . . . is simply a judgement which is not *a posteriori*. It is independent of all experience.' H. A. Prichard, *Kant's Theory of Knowledge* (Oxford, 1909), p. 4.

objects at all. So we can have the idea of empty space, but we cannot have the idea of bodies not in space. It follows that the idea of space is prior to that of objects, and knowledge of it prior to knowledge of objects.

Consequently the knowledge of space is prior to experience, for it is its condition. So it does not come to us from experience, but from our own perceptive faculty. It is a form of our own minds : we impose space on things : not vice versa. Kant also argues to the same conclusion on the ground that in order to locate things in space we must already possess the idea of space. Similar arguments apply to time.

Thus, according to Kant, all cognition demands the co-operation of the senses and the understanding. The senses bring passive impressions, the matter of knowledge ; while the perceptive mind, reacting to these impressions, contributes the form of knowledge. As far as the sensibility is concerned, these are space and time ; and it follows that space and time do not in any way belong to the external reality and spatial and temporal objects, in so far as they are spatial and temporal, are not realities at all but appearances. These *a priori* intuitions having rendered the objects intelligible, they can now be dealt with by the understanding, and so form the object of science.

Now, just as Kant had concluded that what is universal and necessary in sensation must be contributed by the mind, since experience cannot give it, so here, in dealing with the understanding, he maintains that the universality and necessity of concepts must be contributed by the mind. It is not necessary for our purpose to follow Kant in his determination of what these universal concepts actually are. He derives them from the purely formal judgements of logic, such as 'Some S is P,' and finds that there are twelve of them, which he calls 'categories.' They include, for example, such concepts as those of substance and cause. These categories are the *a priori* forms of the understanding. Now just as the forms of space and time cannot apply to the thing in itself, since they are forms of the *mind*, i.e. the thing in itself cannot be in space or time, so here the categories cannot apply to the thing in itself: it cannot be substance, cause, etc. It is neither one nor many, it has no quantity, quality, or relation. To say this is to say that it is unknowable. Now it is precisely with these universal categories and the Ideas which unify them—which, according to Kant, are those of the Ego, the World, and God—that metaphysics has always been concerned. If, then, the categories, and consequently the Ideas, do not apply to the thing in itself, metaphysics will deal, not with extra-mental reality, but with forms of thought; not with 'noumena,' but with phenomena. It is because metaphysics has supposed that it can know the truth about these ultimate realities that it has had so little success, and has become involved in contradictions. Natural science, less ambitious, has been content to give an account of *how* things appear to us without asking what they are in themselves, and so, keeping within its proper sphere, has met with success. We can only know phenomena or appearances, the reality which lies behind them cannot be known; and, as a consequence, Metaphysics is impossible.

Kant's system is open to objection at almost every stage, but as Professor Ward remarks, the thing-in-itself is the 'Achilles' heel' of his theory. For it is plain that if it is unknowable we cannot know that it exists; and, moreover, it is contradictory to assert that it does so and is the cause of sense impressions, while denying that existence and causality, as being mental categories, can apply to it. Two courses are therefore open to us: either to re-examine the process which has led to the assertion that the universal categories cannot apply to extra-mental reality; or to abolish the thing-in-itself, and so make the whole object of knowledge, and the entire universe, a product of mind; thus equivalently asserting that nothing is unknowable, or that the mind can know all things. The latter course was the one adopted by the German Transcendentalists, as Fichte, Schelling, and Hegel; while the former will be the course followed by those who consider that a system which ends in a contradiction must itself be faulty or even contradictory. It is impossible for us to embark here on such a re-examination of Kantianism,[1] and we must therefore be content with an attempt to answer the question whether Kant's contention that the categories or universal concepts do not apply to extra-mental reality is tenable; and so deal with it as a Conceptualist theory, which it plainly is.

III.—Extreme Realism.

A few words must be added with regard to those views of the nature of universals which are in extreme opposition to the ones we have just discussed; those, namely, which assert that there correspond to our universal ideas realities which are themselves formally universal.

The first form of this view is that attributed by the Scholastics to the Platonists; and to Plato himself, on the authority of Aristotle. There is much doubt as to Plato's real meaning, and little would be gained by entering into the details of Aristotle's polemic against the opinions which he attributes to Plato. The view attacked is that Universals are entities, subsisting apart from the world of sense, though the objects of sense suggest them to us, since they 'participate' in them. This is not to be taken to mean that they are immanent in individuals, for indeed they are to be conceived of as altogether independent, being neither in things around us, nor yet in any mind, as its thoughts or 'states.' They are the objects of thought only; such as the 'Form,' or Idea, of Man, of the Good, and so on.

S. Augustine had understood the Platonic Forms as being, not self-subsistent entities, but the exemplary ideas which are in the Divine intellect. The Ontologists adopted this view, and asserted that universals are not to be found in created things, nor yet in separation, but only in the mind of God. They held also that we have immediate and intuitive knowledge of God's mind: it is the first thing which we know, and the medium by which we know all other things.

In the Middle Ages there appeared a form of extreme

[1] For criticism of Kant's theories, cf. e.g. Mercier, *Critériologie Générale* (Paris, Alcan, 1918), 7e édition, Livre III, Chap. III. Vance, *Reality and Truth* (Longmans, 1917), Chaps. XI and XII. H. A. Prichard, *Kant's Theory of Knowledge* (Oxford, 1909).

realism known as Empirical or Formalistic Realism. According to this theory, the universal is unique, and identical in all its inferiors; the differences between individuals of the same species being merely accidental. As the waves of the sea are all one and the same water, and differ only in position, shape, and so on, so it was thought by these realists that individual men, for example, were but ripples in the substance or nature of the universal man. The teaching of the school of Chartres in the first half of the twelfth century was of this type.

The Pantheistic systems of John Scotus Erigena, in the ninth century, and of Hegel, in the nineteenth, may, from one point of view, be looked on as advocating an extreme form of realism, inasmuch as they maintained that things are composed of universals, being composed of their attributes.[1] In so far as they identified thought with thing, however, and so denied that universals are in any way to be found outside the mind, they are absolute idealisms. Things are universals; but all things are thoughts, so that thoughts only are universals.

With this reconciling of contradictories we seem to have reached the limit of human ingenuity in constructing theories as to the nature and existence of universals. Our sketch of them shows plainly the complexity of the problem, for every one of the doctrines mentioned—and many others have been omitted—contains at least some truth which must be taken into account in a balanced solution. It is such a solution which S. Thomas sets out to give. In the light of its contrast with the contending theories at which we have glanced, we shall be able to appreciate its merits.

[1] Cf. Stace, *The Philosophy of Hegel*, *passim*, e.g. p. 18. 'Gold is yellow, heavy, soft, etc. The yellowness, heaviness, softness do not exist apart from the gold. But neither can the gold exist apart from its qualities. Strip off in thought the yellowness, the softness, and *all* other predicates, and what is left? Nothing at all. The gold, then, apart from its predicates, is nothing, does not exist.'

CHAPTER X

THE THOMISTIC SOLUTION OF THE PROBLEM OF UNIVERSALS

Criticism of Opposing Views—Nominalism—Conceptualism—Platonic Realism—Ontologism—Empirical Realism—Explanation of the Conceptualist-Realist Theory of S. Thomas—Its Three Elements—Mode of Existence of the Universal.

We can examine this solution in two ways, negatively and positively: negatively, as against Nominalism, Conceptualism, and extreme Realism; and positively, by an explanation of S. Thomas's assertions with regard to the nature and status of universals. This positive exposition of the Thomistic theory will naturally follow from the examination of the other theories; for if universals are in truth concepts, as against Nominalism, and in some way extra-mental, as against Conceptualism, we shall be forced to ask in what way they can be so. If we have decided, as against extreme Realism, that they cannot be said to be in things outside the mind as formally universal we shall already have gone some way towards answering this last question.

A.—Criticism of Opposing Views.

I.—Nominalism.

Let us then first see what is to be said with regard to the Nominalist view that we have no concepts which are, properly speaking, universal. When we reflect we see that we have in our minds *some* idea which corresponds to the common name we utter—such a name, for example, as man. Now reflection also shows us that this idea is not an individual sense impression, nor a collection of parts of similar sense impressions, but something which our mind grasps as being quite distinct from these impressions, though it is really in them and predicable of them. This universality is primarily in the mind, and not in the name. If I say 'man,' the idea in my mind is not that of an individual man, nor yet of a collection of individual men; but is a distinct mental concept, which is known to differ from that of any individual man with whom I am acquainted; but which, at the same time, is known to be applicable to them all, and so predicable of them; and not only of them, but of all similar beings. This is clear from the way in which we use these terms, for when we say 'Peter is a man,' we do not mean 'Peter is a collection of men,' nor do we mean that the name man is to be confined to Peter, so as to exclude Paul, John, etc., as we should if it signified a singular or individual concept. We make a distinction, too, between universal and collective terms, the latter class not being applicable to individuals: so I cannot say, e.g., Peter is an army.

Further, the idea of the universal is itself a universal idea, being that of *one* concept which is capable of being predicated of *many* individuals. If then the Nominalist denies that we have any universal concepts he must also deny that he has the concept of the universal, and so is precluded from discussing this question, since it is useless to talk about what is altogether unknown.

The Nominalists themselves acknowledge that their theory destroys the possibility of science, and so, like Hume, are sceptics; for if we can have no notion of anything which is common to several individuals, we can have none of any connection between them, or of the laws which govern them.

Hume's argument that when we use such a term as 'horse,' 'we figure to ourselves' a particular animal proves nothing more than that an image accompanies our conceiving a universal idea, if indeed this 'figuring' is to be granted to be a fact; which is highly doubtful. Huxley's notion that the universal may be said to be of the same kind as a composite photograph is plainly inadmissible, for such a photograph gives us only an indistinct blur, unless the sitters are just alike, i.e. unless their features are the same. Actually we never get such identity of features, and if we did, a photograph of one of the sitters would serve as well as a photograph of a hundred, for we should be photographing the same thing in each case. So we should have in features what we are asserting we have in the case of universal natures, one thing which is common to many individuals.

II.—Conceptualism.

Let us leave this rather childish view of the Nominalists and pass on to the much more probable one of the Conceptualists.

Apart from the principle of immanence, which we have already discussed, and which would debar us from asserting that anything which we know or conceive can be in any way extra-mental, and so necessarily prevent us from maintaining that universals are, in any way, extra-mental, the Conceptualists seem to have a strong argument in favour of their view, inasmuch as it is clear that nature in itself, nature considered absolutely, is not, and cannot be, outside the mind. There is no such *thing* as ' man as such,' but only individual men. We shall see, however, that this truth is fully recognised in S. Thomas's theory ; and so have only to concern ourselves here with the view that the universal is in no way to be found outside the mind.

Now just as names are the signs of concepts, so concepts are the signs of things. No doubt we can have a misleading sign, as if a waggish employee of the County Council were to erect a direction post which was meant to show the way to London, but which he planted with its arm pointing along the road which led away from that town. But if there were no such place as London the sign would cease to be a sign, and so simultaneously cease to be a misleading sign. A sign, then, which is a sign of nothing is not a sign at all. Similarly an idea which is an idea of nothing is not an idea ; for the whole meaning of the concept or idea is that it should be relative to something other than itself. We cannot empty it of this meaning ; so that to maintain that the universal concept relates to nothing, and is the end and object of our knowledge, is to maintain that it is at once something essentially relative and yet not relative. Kant was, therefore, absolutely right in asserting that ' thoughts without content are empty ' ; conceptions must always be based on sense impressions. And this is the reason why he always clung to the thing-in-itself, even when it was seen to be a contradictory and impossible conception, in view of his own system. And there is no escape for Conceptualism from this difficulty. To be true to itself it must either begin by denying that our concepts are relative to something other than themselves, to do which is to affirm a contradiction, since the concept is essentially relative—or else it must end with the Kantian contradiction of an extra-mental thing which exists, and causes sense impressions, and is known to do so ; even though it can neither be known to exist nor cause, and so is altogether unknowable.

Another consideration to which S. Thomas directs our attention is the difficulty of accounting for error on the Conceptualist hypothesis. For if I know nothing *through* my thoughts, but these thoughts themselves terminate, and are the object of, my thinking, I can never be in error, since to be so would be to be thinking a thought which I was not thinking. If thoughts, as subjective modifications of my mind, are the objects of my knowledge, my knowledge must always be true, since I cannot judge such subjective modification, as known to me, to be other than the known subjective modification. This is clear in an example such as M. Maritain uses :[1] 'If I judge that Rousseau was a madman (meaning : there is in me a mental modification of the particular kind which is expressed by these words) this judgement will be true. And if you judge that Rousseau was a saint (meaning : there is in you a mental modification expressed by these words) this judgement will be true. Thus every opinion will be true, and every assertion, whatever it may be ; which is absurd.'

Lastly, there can be no doubt that if Conceptualism were accepted, all experimental science would go by the board ; for as S. Thomas says : 'All sciences would be concerned, not with things which are outside the mind, but only with the ideas which are in the mind.'[2] Only one science would be left, Psychology, to which all others would be reduced ;

[1] *Réflexions sur l'intelligence,* J. Maritain (Paris, 1924), p. 44.

[2] *Summa Theologica,* I, 85, 2.

and even this would be a sort of logical game, whose object would be to see how our concepts fit in with one another.

We must conclude, then, that our universal concepts have some reference to a universality in things outside the mind, and so we are driven to accept some form of realism.

Do any of the forms of realism mentioned at the end of the last chapter furnish a solution of the problem? This is the next question which requires to be answered.

III.—Extreme Realism.

(*a*) *Platonic Realism.*

As was noticed before, it is extremely difficult to determine Plato's real meaning with regard to the separation of ideas from individuals, and their independent existence. It would be beside the point for us to enter into this historical question; since we only need to see what that theory was which was controverted under the name 'Platonist' by S. Thomas, and on what grounds he objected to it. This we do chiefly to throw light on his own conception of the universal. Let S. Thomas then speak for himself. In the commentary on Aristotle's *Metaphysics*,[1] after relating how Aristotle indicates that Plato acknowledged two classes of beings besides 'sensible things,' namely: 'universal beings which are separate from sensible things,' i.e. the ideas, and 'Mathematica' (the objects of Mathematics, as triangle) which are intermediate between the Ideas and singular things, he continues: 'But it is clear to anyone who looks into Plato's reasons, that he went wrong in taking up this attitude because of his belief that the way in which the thing understood exists is like the way of our understanding of the thing itself. Consequently, since he found that our intellect understands abstract things in two fashions, in one way as we understand universals abstracted from singulars, in another way as "Mathematicals" abstracted from sensibles, he affirmed that to each abstraction of the intellect there corresponds an abstraction in the essences of things; and

[1] *Comm. in Met.*, Lib. I, Lect. X, No. 158.

so he asserted that the Mathematicals and species existed as separated beings. This, however, is not necessary. For though the intellect understands things by being like them with respect to the intelligible species by which it is constituted in act; it is, nevertheless, not fitting that this species should be in the intellect in the way in which it is in the thing understood; for everything which is in any (recipient) is in it according to the mode of that in which it is. Therefore, on account of the nature of the intellect, which differs from the nature of the thing understood, it is necessary that the mode of understanding by which the intellect understands should differ from the mode of being by which the thing exists. For although that which the intellect understands must *be* in the thing, yet it does not exist in the same way in both. Hence although the intellect understands Mathematicals, without understanding sensibles along with them, and universals without particulars, it is, nevertheless, not necessary that mathematicals should exist apart from sensibles, and universals apart from particulars. For we see that the sight also perceives colour without savour, whereas colour and savour are found together in sensible things.'

So in S. Thomas's view this opinion lacks a solid foundation, and it cannot be shown that we must necessarily admit that there are realities which are formally universal. On the contrary, since the mode of being of a thing in itself should differ from its mode of being in the mind, universals as objects of thought should have a different mode of being from that which they have as concepts in the mind.[1]

(*b*) *Ontologism.*

Little need be said with regard to the opinion of the Ontologists, both because it now finds no favour, and because it is, in itself, altogether unsatisfactory. For we are here discussing those universals which in some way constitute the natures of singular things. To identify these with the ideas

[1] For a full discussion of this form of realism, cf. Mercier, *Critériologie Générale*, pp. 336 ff.

in the mind of God would be to identify that which constitutes the natures of singular things with the Divine Nature ; since the Divine ideas are admitted by the Ontologists to be identical with the Divine Nature. Plainly, such a doctrine as this is Pantheistic and the Ontologists reject Pantheism. We can therefore only conclude that they are not dealing with those universals which constitute the natures of singular things. Since it is these very universals which we are here discussing, it is plain that the Ontologists' doctrine is beside the point ; and if it is put forward as a solution of our problem, we can only say that the Ontologists have missed the point of the question.

(c) *Empirical Realism.*

We can dismiss equally shortly the theory of Empirical Realism, according to which universals are formally in individuals. These individuals will either be distinct from one another, or not. If we say that they are not, we fly in the face of experience : both external experience, which distinguishes this from that, and more especially internal experience, by which we clearly perceive the distinction between the Ego and other things. If, however, we say that nature is really multiplied in these individuals, it will be at once both one and many in the same respect, which is contradictory.

It was in such a way as this that Abelard poured ridicule on this theory when it first appeared, pointing out that if the whole of human nature is to be found in Peter at Rome and Socrates at Athens, Socrates will be at Rome too, while remaining at Athens, since he will be present wherever human nature is to be found.

From these considerations of the types of solution of this question which were rejected by S. Thomas we can see that we cannot hold : (1) That universals are merely names for a collection of particulars, or yet simply notions in our minds ; or (2) that though there is something corresponding to them in the extra-mental reality, this something is itself universal, since the universal, as such, is not to be found either in separation from individuals, nor yet in them.

B.—Positive Explanation of the Conceptualist-Realist Theory of S. Thomas.

Turning now to the positive explanation of S. Thomas's solution of the problem of universals, we may summarise it in three statements : (1) The nature which is called universal, which is the object of a direct act of the mind, e.g. ' man ' in Peter or John, exists in things outside the mind.

(2) This same nature in its abstract state, in which the individual characteristics which accompany it in things outside the mind are not included, is to be found only in the mind. This is the metaphysical universal properly so-called, the metaphysical universal *quoad modum concipiendi*.

(3) The formal or logical universal, viz. that which takes account of the multiplication of the one universal nature in many individuals, exists only in the mind.

The truth of the last statement is abundantly clear ; for the logical universal expresses the communicability of nature to many things. Now such communicability cannot be found either in nature as it is in itself ; nor yet in nature as it is in individuals. Nature in the latter state is plainly individual, and so cannot be communicable ; these two being mutually exclusive. Nor can communicability be an attribute of nature as it is in itself ; since this is simply the nature without any addition, and nothing is implied in the concept of nature which would make it able to be shared by many things, for this concept implies essential predicates only ; whereas communicability to many things definitely implies plurality, which is not an essential predicate.

The other two statements, i.e. assertions (1) and (2), follow from the consideration of nature considered absolutely ; for this, as we have seen, is neither universal nor singular, but abstracts from all modes of existence, though without excluding any of them. In this way it is capable of becoming formally universal, in so far as the mind sees on reflection that it is capable of being communicated to many individuals —or of becoming singular, in so far as, in fact, it is the nature of an individual. Similarly it may have an extra-mental existence if it is actually the nature of an individual or of individuals; and a mental existence, if it is in an abstract state in the mind; since, of itself, it requires neither a mental, nor an extra-mental, existence. Being indifferent to these various modes of *existence* it can have any of them; but whatever kind it happens to have, will not affect it in itself, as it is nature; but the same nature which has singular and extra-mental existence in individuals can have a mental existence also, when abstracted from them by the mind. Thus the nature which is called universal exists in things outside the mind, e.g. as the nature of man in Peter and John, and this same nature exists in the mind, but without that mode of existence which it has in the individuals. Nominalism, Conceptualism, and Extreme Realism all overlook this important distinction between the nature which is called universal being the same *nature* in individuals and in the mind, and its *existing in the same way*, or having the same *existence* in both of them. Thus Nominalism, seeing that the nature exists with an individual existence in singulars, concludes it must also have an individual or singular existence in the mind, and so cannot be universal. Similarly Conceptualism, seeing that the nature exists as universal in the mind and cannot have such existence outside it, concludes that it can have no existence in things; not being capable of having in them the same existence as it has in the mind. Extreme realism, lastly, asserts that it must have a universal mode of existence outside the mind since it has such existence in it.

By recognising, then, that nature as such is indifferent to all modes of existence and is unaffected in itself by any of them, since they form no part of it, S. Thomas deprives all these views of their '*raison d'être*,' and at the same time gives a positive explanation of the nature and existence of universals, which satisfies at once the requirements of common sense and those engendered by the philosophical analysis of the question.

From what has been said it will be clear that nature suffers no deformation through being present in an abstract mode in the mind as opposed to the concrete mode which it has in individuals, since these modes of existence are extraneous to it. The mind sees certain characteristics of the thing in separation from all others which may actually be found in it, but does not affirm that they are separated in the thing. The characteristics which are known in separation are really in the thing, though not in separation ; and since external accompaniments of nature do not affect it as it is in itself, there can be no falsification of knowledge owing to the fact that it is conceived without taking account of these accompaniments. For example, the nature of man in itself is not affected by its being accompanied in a particular man by tallness or shortness, blackness or whiteness. It is always 'rational animality,' which is entirely unaffected by the various ways in which it can be realised in individuals. All such modes of existence, including individual existence, are left out of account, and are therefore neither included in, nor excluded from, nature as it is in itself.

The nature, then, which is conceived in the mind, by a direct apprehension, as the metaphysical universal, and, by a further reflective operation as the logical or formal universal, *can* be in things outside the mind, though with an individualised mode of existence ; and *must* be in them, otherwise this concept, though essentially the concept *of something*, and so relative, would, at the same time, be related to nothing, and so not be relative : it would be without content, and empty. We have said that in the concept of nature nothing is taken into account except the essential predicates, even though, in the individual, the nature may be surrounded by many other attributes of the individual. The mental process by which this is done is evidently the process by which the universal is formed. It is called abstraction, and deserves close consideration : since it is impossible to have a proper understanding of the Thomist theory of knowledge unless we see clearly and distinctly what this process is.

CHAPTER XI

THE CAUSE OF UNIVERSALS—ABSTRACTION

A Psychological Difficulty—Nature of Abstraction—Division of Abstraction—Comparison—Two Kinds of Comparison—Distinction of Abstraction and Comparison—The Formation of the Universal—A Misunderstanding—S. Thomas's View of Abstraction compared with Others—Truth of Abstraction.

THE problem of the universal, as we have seen in the objective or ontological consideration of it in the preceding chapters, is twofold : first, whether there are in the mind universal concepts, and secondly, whether such concepts have a foundation in things outside the mind. By answering both these questions affirmatively, and by showing how the individual character of things is to be reconciled with the universal mode of our knowledge of them, we have indicated the solution of the critical problem, properly so-called. In doing so we have seen that our assertions do not carry with them the consequence of maintaining that the universal, formally speaking, exists outside the mind. The solution, therefore, takes account of all the elements in the problem : the conceptualist contention that the universal is something which the mind makes, and the realist one that it must be found in things, unless our knowledge is to be empty and vain.

A fundamental difficulty, however, is now raised, not with regard to the status of the universal as a reality, but as to the possibility of our forming the universal concept. It is a psychological difficulty. It can be put in this way : the mind only knows what is, and that in the way in which it is. Now common nature exists only in individuals, and is even identified with the individual, for the nature of John is not distinct from the individual John. So it seems impossible that it should be *known* apart from the individuating principles.

Even if it be admitted that abstraction is possible, the formation of the universal concept is not thereby explained; for in order to form it we must first compare several things with one another. Now this requires the recognition in them of something which is common to them all; for if they were not alike in some way they could not be compared. To know something as common to several things is, however, to know the universal, or to have a universal concept; so that in order that a universal concept may be formed it must already have been formed; in other words, its formation is evidently impossible. We might illustrate the point of this objection by the case of the Loch Ness monster. We ask: what is it? Some reply: a basking shark; others, a prehistoric animal; others a fishy story, and so on. Now all these answers imply that there can be seen in it points of resemblance to a shark, a prehistoric animal, other tall stories, etc. If it could be compared to nothing we could have no knowledge of its nature.

We have already dealt with the first part of this objection; pointing out first that it is a fundamental mistake to suppose that the way in which anything is conceived and exists in the mind must, or indeed can, be the same as that in which it exists in things; and secondly, that nature is indifferent with respect to the various modes of existence, abstract or concrete, mental or extra-mental.

The second part of the objection remains to be dealt with, and is really a denial of the possibility of abstraction.

In order to understand clearly the answer made by the Thomists we must see what they consider the nature and function of abstraction to be, and in doing so we shall vindicate the teaching of S. Thomas with regard to the nature of universals from a fresh point of view.

Abstraction considered in general is, according to S. Thomas, a mental representation of one or several elements of a thing, the other elements in it not being represented, but at the same time not being excluded, even though they are not included. Such abstraction is sometimes called negative abstraction to distinguish it from positive abstraction or precision, which occurs when the mind definitely *excludes* from its concept those of the other elements which are in fact found along with it in the thing conceived of. Thus, if by abstraction pure and simple, I conceive of the animal nature, say, of a dog, as the principle of sensitive operations and spontaneous movement, I have a concept which can apply to any nature in which these operations are found: but if I join to this a precision, *excluding* from my concept everything that is not the principle of sensibility and spontaneous movement, this concept becomes one which will apply only to certain animal natures and not to all. So the concept formed by pure abstraction will apply to all animals, including man, while the notion gained by precision will not apply to man.[1]

A second division of abstraction is also recognised by S. Thomas, the resulting members of which are called by him, first, 'abstraction of a whole' (*abstractio totius*), or abstraction of the universal from the particular; and secondly the 'abstraction of form from matter.' These are conveniently named by Cajetan[2] 'total' and 'formal' abstraction respectively.

The first kind abstracts universal concepts, as animal; so forming the ideas of our minds; while the second abstracts form from matter, e.g. quantity from sensible matter. These two differ, then, both in their nature and work. The first is produced by the active intellect,[3] and results in the formation of our ideas. These ideas being now in the passive intellect, this is actuated by them, and understands them. It may then perform a further abstractive operation on them, e.g. being given by the active intellect the idea of sensible matter, the passive intellect may abstract from this the form of motion, or quantity. In doing so it forms, not universal concepts or ideas as such, but the objects of the sciences in particular. This latter kind of abstraction, then, is necessary for the formation of the sciences, while the

[1] Cf. S. Thomas, *De Ente et Essentia*, cap. III.

[2] Cajetan, *Comm. in De Ente et Essentia*, Q. I.

[3] For an account of the active and passive intellect (*intellectus agens et possibilis*), cf. Vol. I, Part II, Chaps. XI and XII.

former, that of the active intellect, is necessary for science in general.[1]

Bearing in mind these notions about abstraction, we can now state the Thomist solution of the difficulty with regard to the formation of the universal. This solution takes the form of a distinction, for the Thomists say that different mental processes are required for the formation of the logical and metaphysical (or direct) universal; abstraction *alone* being needed for the second, while an act of comparison must be added to form the first. If, then, no comparison is required in the formation of the metaphysical universal, the objection falls to the ground.

By comparison we mean the act by which the mind knows one thing in its relation to another.

It is plain that there are two kinds of comparison; first, that by which we compare two individuals of a species with one another, as for example, James with John: and in general the inferiors of any universal with one another; and, secondly, that by which we compare the universal, or abstract notion, with its inferiors, and know this universal as having a relation to them; which relation need not be that of really being in them, but may be simply that of a capacity for being in them, in so far as it seems that the abstract notion is not confined to one individual. The first kind of comparison is called composite, the second, simple comparison. It is this second kind which, in the opinion of the Thomists, is used in the formation of the logical universal.

If we now examine our mental processes we can see that this distinction between abstraction and comparison corresponds with the facts. For we are conscious that when we are faced with a particular object, the mind can apprehend, by an act which is proper to it, that of abstraction, the nature alone without including in it anything which makes the object an individual; so, e.g., it apprehends 'man' in Peter, or 'whiteness' in some particular white thing. Now this concept is clearly *one*, since it abstracts from the individuals

[1] For the whole question, cf. S. Thomas, *In Boethium de Trinitate*, Q. V, a. 3.

which might cause it to be differentiated and multiplied, and at the same time it is *capable of being related to many things*, being abstract, and so capable of being differentiated by concrete or individual differences. Here, then, we see that we have acquired a concept of one nature which is, in fact, capable of being related to many individuals; and so a concept which is in fact universal, or, as the Scholastics say, in proximate potentiality to universality, i.e. just on the point of becoming formally universal. Such a concept can be acquired as well from one individual as from half a dozen, so that no comparison of the individuals among themselves is required. But it is plain that this concept is not yet fully universal, i.e. formally and actually so, since the universal is formally made universal by an actual relation of one thing to many. Such a relation is, as we have seen, not taken account of in the metaphysical universal, and so is not actual. It can only be taken account of actually when the mind reflecting on the metaphysical universal sees that there is no impossibility in its being in, and being predicated of, many things, i.e. when it compares it with its inferiors by an act of simple comparison. This is the formation of the logical universal, which, therefore, is brought about by an act of comparison in addition to the abstractive act which is all that is needed for the formation of the metaphysical universal.

We said above that the examination of the way in which the universal is formed would bring out, from a fresh point of view, the truth of the conceptualist-realist theory of S. Thomas. And surely this is so, for it shows us that the logical universal is a mental construction, no such thing as the predicability of one nature of many individuals being found in extra-mental reality. Moreover, since the metaphysical universal is formed by abstraction, and so is abstract, it is evident that this also must be in the mind alone, not in external nature: since there everything is concrete. But though its mode of existence as the metaphysical universal is an abstract mode, it is nevertheless abstracted from some real concrete individual, and so must be present with another mode of existence in that individual; otherwise it could not be drawn out, or abstracted, from it.

Modern writers object to this theory of abstraction that it implies that we have immediate and, as it were, intuitive knowledge of the natures of all things ; whereas the contrary is the fact. The more Science advances, they say, the more evident it becomes that our knowledge of the natures of things is extremely limited. It is, therefore, certain that we have no immediate apprehension of natures ; if we know them at all, it is only after long and laborious research. The objection rests on a misunderstanding of S. Thomas's teaching on this subject. He does not for a moment maintain that the mind at once and intuitively grasps the nature of its object ; at least if we take the word 'nature' in its strict sense, as that which constitutes the inner essence or reality of the thing, by which it is separated, by a clear-cut division, from everything of another kind. All that he and his followers claim is that the mind immediately, and in the first stage of cognition, grasps universal natures, not particular details. My first *intellectual* knowledge of Peter is not of him as an individual, nor yet of his nature as man, which is constituted by the essential components, rational and animal ; but of his general characteristics. So, just as when looking at an object at a little distance I first see it as a vague confused mass, and bit by bit pick out its details, so in intellectual knowledge I first know the thing in the most general way as 'being' or 'thing,' then as 'moving thing,' then perhaps as 'animal,' and at last, by degrees, as 'man.' By degrees : for among all the general characteristics which I apprehend in Peter, e.g. living, white, bearded, musical, humorous, rational and so on, I have to distinguish those that are accidental from those which are essential or proper to him, and also to settle which of these differentiates him generically, and which specifically, from other things. If I ever get to this stage I shall have come to knowledge of that universal which constitutes his nature, and know it as formally universal ; but long before this I shall have had direct knowledge of those general characteristics of his on which this final and definitive knowledge is based. These characteristics are, in fact, universals ; though I may not, and at first do not, know them as such. Thus science, according to S. Thomas, is no easy matter, but requires great assiduity and acuteness; so much so that the natures of things, speaking strictly, are for the most part unknown to us. It is obvious, then, that we have no reason to pride ourselves on the fact that knowledge comes to us by means of abstraction; for, indeed, the necessity for using it arises from the weakness of the intellect. If the mind were capable of knowing all that there is in the thing at one glance, it would not need to abstract.

If we compare S. Thomas's theory of abstraction with those, say, of Mill, Huxley, or even Locke, we see that their views are radically different; for all these later writers confine abstraction to the purely material order, and make it consist of some kind of dissociation of the elements of sensible perception. S. Thomas's view of it is quite different, since for him it consists in the seizing of some characteristic in the object, without considering the fact that it is found in one particular object. There is no question of separating it from others by excluding them; as is done, for example, by a man looking for cornelians among the shingle of the beach, who keeps on throwing away pebbles till he comes on a cornelian; but it is simply a direct apprehension of one thing, no attention being paid to others; a direct apprehension like that of a man who suddenly sees the face of a friend in a crowd. To use a homely example, the nominalist idea of abstraction might be compared to the peeling of an onion, the outer layers being stripped off and discarded; while S. Thomas regards abstraction as being like the action of Jack Horner, who 'put in his thumb and pulled out a plum,' paying no attention to the rest of the pie.

Abstraction, then, in S. Thomas's sense, is spontaneous, producing the direct universal. Dissociation, on the contrary, is always reflective, since it implies that the mind reconsiders its previously acquired perceptions, and submits them: either to a comparison, as Locke[1] thought; or to a process of subtraction, according to Mill[2]; or of addition, according to Huxley.[3]

[1] *Essay on the Human Understanding*, Bk. 2, Chap. VI, Sec. IX.
[2] *Examination of Sir W. Hamilton's Philosophy*, Ch. XVII.
[3] Huxley, *Hume*, p. 95.

We have seen that abstraction does not involve any falsification of the object; since, though it concentrates on one element in it, and omits the rest, yet it does not exclude them, as if to deny that they are also present in the object. It in no way asserts that the element obtained by abstraction has the same sort of existence in the mind and in the thing. Though it is fragmentary and partial knowledge, it is not therefore false; '*abstrahentium non est mendacium.*'[1] It is in fact inevitable, for it enters into all our knowledge, from the first sensible perception, say the sight of the colour of an apple without its scent, right up to the concepts of metaphysics. No doubt it has its dangers, when we begin to mistake the abstract for the concrete. 'The intolerant use of abstractions is the major vice of the intellect,' as Whitehead remarks;[2] though he notes at the same time how abstraction runs through all our knowledge. But if we are on our guard not to take the part for the whole we shall run no risk of falling into positive error; and indeed the more convinced we are of the partial character of our knowledge, the greater will be our efforts to observe reality from many points of view, with the purpose of approximating, more and more closely, to knowledge of the concrete and individual. Our knowledge thus becomes more and more comprehensive and adequate, but in all its stages, though it may be inadequate, it is yet true; so long as we do not make exaggerated claims for it, but recognize its partial character.

[1] Cf. Aristotle, *Physics*, II, c. 2, 193, b. 35.
[2] Whitehead, *Science and the Modern World*, p. 23.

CHAPTER XII

TRUTH AND ERROR

Meaning of Truth—Kinds of Truth—Analysis of the Idea of Truth—Truth Formally Found in the Judgement—Error—Its Nature—Where Error is Found—The Nature of S. Thomas's Theory of Truth.

THE whole of our enquiry so far has been directed to discovering whether we can have legitimate and scientific certitude. We asked this, first of all, with regard to knowledge in general; and having decided that we could acquire some scientifically certain knowledge, we next asked whether we could know with certainty individual sense objects, and the existence of a trans-subjective material world. After giving an affirmative answer to these questions we enquired into the certainty of our knowledge of those universal characters of things which form the predicates in our judgements, and have now concluded that, on reflection on the nature of the universals, and on our mental processes, we are justified in asserting that we can have legitimate certainty with regard to these also.

To say this is to say that we can arrive at truth, or that our knowledge both of individuals and of universals is, or at any rate can be, true.

By this word 'truth' the ordinary man no doubt understands the agreement of his knowledge with reality, or the fidelity of his knowledge to facts. That the battle of Hastings was fought in 1066, or that Paris is the capital of France, he would regard as true statements, since the facts are as represented by them.

Here we have spoken of statements as true, but it is plain that if truth can be attributed to them it can also be attributed to the thought or judgement which lies behind them. So if we think a thing to be what it is independently of our thought of it, such thought would be said to be true, and the expression of our thought would be called a true statement. A statement can also be 'true' in another way. When we say something which expresses the thought in our minds, i.e. when what we say is not at variance with what we think, there is a certain truth in our words even though they may not correspond with the facts. We are 'telling the truth.' Lastly we speak of things themselves as being true, e.g., we say a man is a 'true friend' when he acts in the way in which we think a friend ought to act. Similarly, we speak of 'false pearls,' meaning those which are not in accordance with our idea of what a pearl 'truly' is, being made artificially by man, and not by a natural process by the oyster.

This last kind of truth is called by the Scholastics 'ontological truth'; that which we describe as 'telling the truth' they call 'moral truth,' while the first kind of truth mentioned, the truth of thought, they call 'logical truth.'

If we now compare all these ways in which the word 'truth' is used we shall see that there are some elements common to them all. First, we notice that in all of them truth is ascribed primarily and essentially to the intellect, and only secondarily and derivatively to things and words. Secondly, in all three there is a relation of agreement between two terms, of which one is intellectual while the other is looked upon as being really distinct from the intellect, or at any rate set over against the intellect and compared with it; in other words, as being its object. So, in general, truth will be the agreement between an intellectual and an objective term. If we are speaking of the truth which belongs to thought, i.e. of logical truth, we shall say, in accordance with this general formula, that it is the agreement of the intellect with its object.

Such agreement need not be total, or as it is called, adequate agreement, which ascribes to the object everything that is to be found in it. To insist on such agreement as this would in fact be to make knowledge impossible, as we have not comprehensive knowledge of anything. So comprehensive knowledge of, say, a grain of sand on the sea-shore would entail knowledge of all its constituents—the atoms, etc.—as well as of the rock from which it was formed, the relation of this rock to all others, of the grain of sand to all other objects in the universe, and so of the whole universe. Such knowledge is evidently unattainable. We are thinking truly if we ascribe to the object characters which are really in it, even though it may have many others beside, so long as we do not deny its possession of these others. So to say ' snow is white,' is true, even though snow has many other characteristics besides that of whiteness. The agreement, therefore, spoken of in the definition need only be partial.

Consider next the word ' object.' We have seen from the discussion of Idealism that this object is, in fact, as common sense supposes, an extra-mental reality, our senses not being directed to the perception of our own sensations, but of the thing which causes these sensations, and our minds not being turned in upon themselves to know our own ideas, but using these ideas as means by which, or through which, it knows: we look out through these ideas at the extra-mental thing. In the case of sense knowledge the thing known is a concrete individual, while in intellectual knowledge it is the universal. This universal, though not present with its universal mode in the extra-mental thing, yet is present there as the same nature as is in the mind. The nature or form in the thing is the same as the nature or form in the mind, though it has not the same mode of existence in both.

Consequently, for the word ' agreement ' in our definition we can now substitute the more exact word ' conformity,' and for ' object ' we can write ' thing,' i.e. extra-mental reality. So we have the expression: logical truth is the conformity of the intellect with the thing—the thing and the intellect possess, or are actuated by, one and the same form.

But what precisely do we mean by the word intellect here? It is evidently the intellect in the act of knowing which is in question. Now there are three intellectual acts or operations: simple apprehension, judgement, and reasoning. The first is that by which the intellect seizes some characteristic of the thing by means of its abstractive power, and so knows it, but does not affirm (or deny) anything about it. As was said above, we begin such knowledge with the most general notions, of which the widest of all is being. '*Primum quod cadit in intellectum est ens,*' as S. Thomas says.[1] But at once we attribute this 'being' to the concrete individual in which we have apprehended it; and in doing this we make a judgement, and so affirm (or deny) something of an object, and finally we may connect two or more such judgements in a process of reasoning.

In which of these intellectual operations is truth to be found; or is it present in all three? By logical truth we mean the truth which is proper to the mind, and it is contrasted with ontological truth, the truth of things. If this be so, it will not consist in a conformity between the mind, considered simply *as a thing*, and the object; but requires that the mind *as a mind* shall be so conformed. Now the mind *as a mind* is essentially understanding or knowing, so that logical truth requires that the intellect precisely as it is knowing, shall be conformed with the thing, in other words the conformity required is not the mere fact of conformity but the *known* factof conformity. So for logical truth it is necessary that the intellect should know its own conformity with the thing. This, however, it only does in the judgement, when it asserts explicitly that the character of the thing is as it thinks it to be. In simple apprehension of the object we have indeed the same form in the thing and in the mind, but the fact that it is the same is not yet known by the mind; and therefore we cannot say that we have logical truth, in the proper sense of the word, at this stage. The same considerations *a fortiori* exclude logical truth from sense knowledge.

This conclusion is explicitly maintained by S. Thomas,[2] with whom Suarez is in agreement; as well as most of the leading Thomists. Even those who differ (e.g. Hugon and Zigliara) only do so verbally. They seem to stretch the notion of logical truth, by adhering to the letter of the definition of it, so that any conformity between intellect and

[1] *De Veritate*, I, 1.
[2] *Summa Theologica*, I, 16, 2, cf. I, 17, 2, and *De Veritate*, I, 9.

thing will be logical truth. The definition should, however, be understood formally, in which case by the word intellect we shall mean the intellect formally as intellect, i.e. as knowing.

In saying that for logical truth the intellect must know its conformity with the thing, we do not mean to imply that an act of reflective judgement is required. It is not necessary that the mind should explicitly attend to this conformity; but merely that, in the very exercise of its act of knowing, it perceives that it is conformed to the object. As a man walking along a level road is not attending to the steps he takes, but knows, nevertheless, that he is taking steps. This is an application of the Scholastic distinction between an action *in actu signato* and *in actu exercito*. For logical truth, knowledge of conformity '*in actu exercito*'[1] only is required, not knowledge '*in actu signato*.'

Error.

Since, as we have seen, only partial and not adequate agreement is required for truth, it follows that though there may be incompleteness of conformity with the object, our knowledge will remain true, and therefore that something more than incompleteness of agreement is required for error; which is opposed to truth as its contrary.[2] Such error is called positive error to distinguish it from that inadequacy of knowledge which arises from ignorance It consists in a representation of the object by the mind as other than it, in fact, is; either by ascribing to it something which it does not possess, or by denying to it something which it does possess; for example, if I were to say 'stones are living' or 'man is incapable of thinking.' So there is always positive disagreement between the intellect and the thing in an erroneous judgement. Error is thus a distortion, not something purely negative, and so demands a background of truth just as evil demands a foundation of good. S. Thomas, therefore, asserts that it is a privation, an evil.[3]

[1] Cf. Maritain, *Introduction to Philosophy* (Sheed and Ward), p. 255.

[2] Cf. *Summa Theologica*, I, 17, 4.

[3] *De Veritate*, 18, 6; *De Malo*, 16, 6; *In VI Met.*, Lect. 4; *Summa Theol.*, I, 17, 3; and I, 94, 4.

Being a privation of truth, error will formally be found in the same intellectual act as that in which truth is found, that is to say, in the judgement. Where are we to look for the sources of such error? No doubt in those acts which prepare the way for judgement and are the germ from which it springs. We therefore ask: are there any acts which are exempt from all error? If so, where does error first creep in?

Now error being a privation in a determined nature it cannot affect those acts by which the nature merely finds self-expression, i.e. essential acts. If such an act be posited at all, it will be posited in accordance with the nature, since it springs wholly from it; unless the nature be essentially corrupted, in which case it will have ceased to be. Hence error can never affect the essential acts of the cognitive faculties. Now the essential acts of the senses are those which are directed by each sense to the perception of its proper sense object But we cannot straightway conclude that such acts are immune from error; for this privilege will only belong to such cognitive acts as essentially proceed from a simple nature. If the nature be composite, or subject to external influences, it may happen that some essential part may be in some way defective, or that the external conditions are not present in the requisite degree. Now this is the case with the senses, for the sense organ is essential to it, and there must be some medium between the sense and the external object, which will modify the sensation, or the normal action of the object on the sense. So even essential sense acts will not necessarily be true in all circumstances.

If we pass to the intellect, its only essential acts are those which are directed to its formal object: the natures of things; and these are, of themselves, not liable to error. They may, however, be affected by the intervention of the judgement, and so, *per accidens*, become erroneous. Among judgements, the only ones which are infallible are the first principles, for these simply express the nature of being, which is the object of the essential act of the Simple Apprehension. All existential judgements (e.g. Peter is white) are subject to error, inasmuch as they are not directed towards the formal object of the intellect, viz. nature or essence. Existential judgements must have as their object the individual, and not the universal, since the universal does not exist as universal, in the world about us. Universals, then, such as essence or nature, which are the formal objects of the intellect, cannot be the objects of judgements of existence, and so such judgements are liable to be erroneous.

In the formation of ideas, too, error may creep in. For these are formed progressively, i.e. we begin with the formation of confused ideas which afterwards become distinct. Now this process of clarifying ideas necessarily involves the intervention of the judgement. Hence we can never declare, *a priori*, that any distinct idea, and still less, that any definition, is totally exempt from error. Even the formation of the confused ideas is conditioned by the nature of the intelligence, which is extrinsically dependent on the imagination and the senses, and so can be vitiated by their defects.

Thus we see that there are two root causes of error, defect of the sense organs, and defective conditions of cognition. With regard to the second, from the subjective point of view, erroneous cognition may arise from four causes: the imagination, reasoning, passion and voluntary inattention. It is plain that the imagination is liable to lead to error, since it makes present what is in reality absent. Errors of reasoning arise either from attribution by the mind of the definition of one thing to another, owing to the resemblance or identity of their sensible appearances, or it may be due, and, in the last resort is due, to the failure of the intellect to perceive the differences which underlie the obvious resemblances, so that the intellect goes wrong in the first place by establishing a relation of resemblance. This failure of the intellect, then, depends on the other cause we have mentioned: voluntary inattention; so that the will lies at the root of all false judgements, and all error of judgement will be culpable in some degree.[1] Knowing, then, the causes which lead to error, we can be on our guard against them,

[1] This short sketch of the ways in which error arises is based on the full analysis of this question made by Fr. Roland-Gosselin, O.P., in his essay 'Erreur' in *Mélanges Thomistes* (Bibliothèque Thomiste. Le Saulchoir, 1923), pp. 252–266.

and so avoid error. But if we are to feel any security we shall have to find some means of verifying our judgements, that is, we must have some tests whose application will assure us that our judgements are true, and distinguish them from false ones. This is the question of the criterion of truth which we shall discuss in the next chapter.

Before passing on to this new part of the problem of truth, it will be useful to say something about the nature of the theory of truth which we have been trying to explain.

In the first place it would be misleading to call it, as is sometimes done, a ' correspondence theory ' of truth ; since it is clear that a thing cannot, properly speaking, be said to ' correspond ' with itself. Now according to S. Thomas truth consists in the *same* form being found in the thing and in the mind, though in different ways. He calls it either ' *conformitas* ' or ' *adequatio* ' of the intellect and thing ; and, for this reason, the word ' agreement ' has been avoided, as far as possible, in describing the nature of truth. The Thomist theory is, therefore, not open to the objections which are urged against a ' copy ' theory of truth ; such as that which points out that if our ideas are but copies of things, we can never tell that they are true copies unless we compare them with the original ; which, by hypothesis, we can never do. Now this objection is not valid against the Thomist theory, for this asserts that the mind has the power of abstracting the form of the thing, which form, unchanged in itself, passes into the mind, so that the intellect and the thing known become one. This assertion rests, as we have seen, both on a reflective analysis of our mental processes, and on the necessity of the existence of such an abstractive power if we are to maintain the validity of knowledge at all. Without it we should have to relapse into scepticism.

S. Thomas's theory thus, on the one hand, is clear as to the possibility of attaining truth ; yet, on the other, since it allows that the cognitive faculties are only infallible under certain well-defined conditions, it makes full allowance for the fact of error. This, then, is a second point to notice about this theory ; for no theory of truth can be thought satisfactory which does not make room for the possibility of error. S. Thomas points this out with respect to the theory—which we now call Idealist—that the objects of knowledge are our own ideas. According to such a view all opinions will be true and error will be excluded.[1] The coherence of thought with itself, the description which Idealists are accustomed to give of truth, is thus defective, both because it assumes that we can know nothing but our thoughts, and because it makes no provision for error. This will be the same as partial truth; and all our knowledge will be erroneous, or all true, from different points of view.[2]

In the Thomist definition '*conformitas intellectus et rei*,' the word intellect is not to be interpreted 'objective concept'; this, by common consent among Scholastics (with few exceptions), being the object known by means of the formal or subjective concept,[3] and so identical with the thing.[4] The objective concept is the thing itself as presented to the mind: any other notion of it ought to be sedulously avoided, as leading to Subjectivism.[5]

S. Thomas's theory has, then, no affinities with a coherence theory of truth; but it is decidedly realist, while avoiding the difficulties to which Realism is liable, the difficulties of any form of copy theory. So in this matter, as in others, the Thomist theory preserves the truth of the opposing extremes, rising above them in a higher synthesis.

[1] Cf. *Summa Theologica*, I, 85, 2.

[2] The Coherence Theory of truth has occupied a large place in recent English philosophy; and it is not to be supposed that it can be disposed of in a few words. Indeed it is a subject of such difficulty that it has been thought better to omit the discussion of it altogether from this summary. It may be suggested, however, that what the Coherence theory really gives us is an account of ontological, not logical, truth; and tells us what truth is for God. In fact the identification of thought with existence or reality seems to suggest this; and brings in its train many difficulties.

For the theory see Bradley, *Appearance and Reality*, especially Chapters XV and XVI; for an account and criticism of the theory, see *Knowledge and Truth*, L. A. Reid, Chapter II (Macmillan, 1923).

[3] Cf. Vol. I, Part II, Chap. VIII, p. 224.

[4] Cf. *Joannes a S. Thoma. Cursus Theol.*, Tom. II, Disp. II, a. 2, diff. 1. Suarez, *Disp. Met.*, Disp., II, Sec. I. Geny, *Critica*, pp. 36–37.

[5] Cf. Maritain, *Réflexions sur l'intelligence*, p. 32 f.

CHAPTER XIII

THE ULTIMATE CRITERION OR TEST OF TRUTH

Distinction of Ultimate Criterion and Ultimate Motive—To what Truths does the Ultimate Criterion Apply ?—Its Conditions—Evidence as the Ultimate Criterion—The View of S. Thomas—Justification of this View—Other Opinions as to the Ultimate Criterion.

As was pointed out earlier,[1] we ought not to confuse the notions of an ultimate criterion of truth and an ultimate motive of certitude. Though in every judgement we must have an ultimate motive of certitude, yet we need not test this judgement by any criterion, if it imposes itself upon the mind in such a way as to be undeniable. It would obviously be a foolish waste of time to test the truth of that which we have already accepted as true. It has been, we suppose, recognised on reflection as undeniable ; so that we have full scientific certitude about it. How then can we apply any test to it, or begin to ask whether it is true ?

These remarks, and those made before with regard to this subject, are strictly applicable to those principles which express the notions of being, viz. the principle of identity and non-contradiction, and this only on condition that we understand the word ' criterion ' in its strictest sense, as an instrument by means of which we discriminate between judgements with regard to their truth. The other '*principia per se nota,*' e.g. the principle of causality, can, in a sense, be tested, in so far as we can see that they are necessarily connected with the notion of being, a denial of them leading us inevitably to a denial of the principle of identity ; so that, though indemonstrable, their truth is made plain by a *reductio ad absurdum.*[2] No

[1] Chap. II, p. 25.

[2] Cf. R. Garrigou-Lagrange, *Le sens commun, la philosophie de l'être, et les formules dogmatiques,* Chap. II, Sec. 6. Cf. the same author's *Dieu, son existence et sa nature,* pp. 108–226, and his *De Revelatione,* Vol. I, pp. 252 ff.

doubt, the ultimate motive which makes us assent to these propositions as true is their evidence, inasmuch as we can see that they are necessarily connected with the principle 'being is being' which expresses the notion of being itself. Thus, in a sense, we test these first principles, and acquire scientific certitude with regard to them by applying to them the test of their agreement with, and resolution into, the notion of being. This notion, and its expression in the principles of identity and non-contradiction, is fully evident: if the mind does not grasp this, it knows nothing at all. If this be true, it is not possible to *test* the truth of this notion and these principles by anything else, since, as S. Thomas says: '*primum quod cadit in intellectum est ens.*'[1] If then we use the word 'criterion' in its strict sense, as a test which is to be applied to some judgement to see whether it is true, it ought to be extrinsic to the judgement which is to be tested; otherwise it cannot be applied to it.[2]

As we have seen, in discussing error, the essential acts of the cognitive faculties are necessarily infallible, and will exhibit themselves as necessarily true and indubitable as soon as they are posited; no further sign or guarantee of their truth being required. So with regard to the proper sensation of each sense; the essential act of the intellect directed towards being; and the judgement which immediately expresses this notion of being; no doubt being possible, no criterion or test is required. The motive which impels assent is the object itself. This alone moves the faculty; if the faculty acts at all, this action can only be due to the object. The sense and the intellect see the object as it is, or not at all.

When these primary cognitions are left behind the mind is no longer guaranteed immunity from error, so that its subsequent judgements may be false. No doubt the processes of thought may follow a proper and normal course, but the greater the complication of a train of reasoning becomes, and the longer the distance which separates a judgement from the primary cognitions, the greater also will be the danger of some mistake being made. It is,

[1] *De Veritate*, I, i.

[2] Cf. Geny, *Critica*, Sect. 109.

therefore, all these judgements which we are obliged to verify; i.e. to which we must apply some test to see whether they are true or false.

What is this test? If it is to be an ultimate one, it must not rest on, or derive its force from, some other test; since, if it did, this other test would be ultimate or final. Moreover, it must be universal, applying to every judgement whose truth requires testing. That this is so may be seen by supposing that there were some judgements which could be tested and to the testing of which the ultimate criterion was not applicable. If, then, these are to be verified at all, it will be by some test other than the ultimate criterion. Now this test cannot be something which is prior to the ultimate criterion, from which the latter derives its force; since to suggest this is equivalent to suggesting that the ultimate criterion is not ultimate. Nor can it be a test whose efficaciousness in causing the removal of doubt is independent of the power of the ultimate criterion to do so. If this were so, we should have to say that the one effect—removal of doubt—was due to two entirely unconnected causes. This is plainly impossible, for if one of these causes had the power to remove doubt, the other could not have this power, if they are in no way connected. So it is clear that the hypothesis that the ultimate criterion is not also universal is an impossible one.

If we now try to put a name to this ultimate criterion we find there is a difference—at any rate of expression—among Scholastic writers as to what we should call it. In recent times the opinion that it is objective evidence[1] has been almost universal. It seems that this view rests on a broad use of the word criterion, as meaning that by which we are ultimately assured of the truth of any proposition: in other words, the ultimate motive of assent. In this sense, we have already seen that the opinion is true. If I give a certain assent to a proposition it is because I see it is evident: evidence is the motive which compels me to assent. But I cannot take evidence as some separate thing and apply it to a proposition, to see whether this conforms to it. Take,

[1] Cf. Chap. II, p. 26.

for example, the principle of identity: 'being is being. This is certainly self-evident, but by this we merely mean that it is immediately known as true, and that it is indubitable. To assert that it is evident is merely to assert that it is true, and clearly shows itself as true, so that evidence cannot be a test of its truth. It is the motive of assent, for I say 'being is being' because I clearly perceive the undeniable character of this statement. What we have just said with regard to this primary principle is true also with regard to all other judgements. It is no answer to the question: How do you know that statement is true? to reply: Because I have tested it by evidence, or even, because it is evident. If it is self-evident this only amounts to saying: 'I know it to be true, because it is clearly true'; while if it is not self-evident it is equivalent to saying: 'I know it to be true because I have come to the conclusion that it is clearly true.' The honest enquirer will naturally ask: 'How did you come to that conclusion?' If then, objective evidence be thought of as some mysterious entity which we can apply to judgements to test their truth, as acid is applied to gold to test its quality, then it seems that we are the victims of our own imaginations, and the slaves of words. If, however, we mean that we do not assent with certainty to the truth of any proposition except in so far as we see that it is evident, in other words, that evidence is the ultimate *motive* of certitude, what we say is clearly justified. To say this is the same as saying that I only recognise as clearly true what appears before me as clearly true.

How, then, are we to test the truth of our judgements, if not by evidence?

S. Thomas, who never speaks of objective evidence as the criterion of truth, but only as the motive of certitude,[1] explains very clearly what the ultimate criterion is.

According to him our primary intellectual cognition is of being,[2] and in knowing it we know its identity with itself and the impossibility of its being its contradictory. This we

[1] E.g. III *Sent.*, Dist., XXIII, Q. II, a. 2, sol. 3. '*Certitudo quae est in scientia et intellectu est ex ipsa evidentia eorum quae certa esse dicuntur.*'

[2] *De Veritate*, I, 1.

know immediately, and we cannot have any doubt about the truth of these primary principles, so that the question of testing their truth does not arise.[1] We have here, therefore, a sheet-anchor of truth, so that we shall be able to be certain of the truth of any proposition which is necessarily linked with these first principles,[2] and we shall only know whether a proposition is true or false when we have discovered whether it is so necessarily linked with the first principles which immediately express the notion of being. In other words, our test or criterion of the truth of any judgement, whose truth we are able to question, will be to ask whether such a judgement has a necessary connection with the principles *per se nota,* or not. To find this out we shall have to trace it back, step by step, till we come to these primary principles. Such a procedure is known as an ' analysis ' or analytic resolution, so that the name of the ultimate criterion of truth is, according to S. Thomas, analytic resolution into the primary principles which express the notion of being.

If we can successfully carry out this process with respect to any judgement it is plain that we shall be assured of its truth, for we shall have seen that it cannot be denied without the primary principles being, by implication, denied also; since it is necessarily connected with them. As we know these to be undeniable, and so certainly true, we know also that the judgement we have submitted to this test is certainly true. So S. Thomas says ' there is never falsity in the intellect

[1] Cf. *Post. Anal.*, Lib. I, Lect. VII, Sect. 8. *Ex cognitione principiorum derivatur cognitio conclusionum, quarum proprie est scientia. Ipsa autem principia immediata non per aliquod medium extrinsecum cognoscuntur, sed per cognitionem propriorum terminorum.*

[2] ' *Sciens habet et cogitationem, et assensum; sed cogitationem causantem assensum, et assensum terminantem cogitationem. Ex ipsa enim collatione principiorum ad conclusiones, assentit conclusionibus resolvendo eas in principia, et* ibi *figitur motus cogitantis et quietatur. In scientia enim motus rationis incipit ab intellectu principiorum, et ad eumdem terminatur per viam resolutionis.*' *De Veritate,* XIV, a. 1, cf. Q. X, a. 8. Cf. *Post. Anal.*, Lib. 1, Lect. 1, and I *Sent.* Dist., XIX, Q. V, a. 1. ' *Veritas enuntiationis reducitur in prima principia per se nota sicut in primas causas; et præcipue in hoc principium, quod affirmatio et negatio non sunt simul vera,*' and IV *Sent.*, Dist., IX, a. 4, sol. 1. '*Judicium rectum de conclusione haberi non potest nisi resolvendo ad principia indemonstrabilia.*' Cf. *In Boet. de Trin.*, Q. II, a. 1, ad 5; Q. VI, a. 1, c; a. 4.

if resolution into the first principles be rightly carried out.'[1]

This notion of the ultimate criterion of truth is in entire accord with S. Thomas's general theory of knowledge.[2] In his view, our knowledge of all objects, other than the primary simple data, is due to a prolonged series of cognitions. It is these primary data only which are immune from error, so that to verify other judgements we have no touchstone except their connection with these primary data.

Apart from this theory, experience also shows that this is, in fact, the way in which we verify any judgement. If we are doubtful about any conclusion we trace back the process of reasoning until we find that it either does, or does not, lead us to a first principle which is known in itself and is undeniable. It might be suggested that the test of the truth of these first principles is evidence, so that ultimately the test of the truth of the conclusions is also evidence. This is not so, however, for we cannot *test* the truth of the principle of identity, for example, strictly speaking. We are either aware of it, or not. If we are aware of it we see immediately that it must be accepted: that it is evident. But we do not *test* its truth by evidence. That we might do so it would be necessary that evidence should be regulative of, and so logically prior to, the notion of being expressed in this principle. This is impossible if the notion of being is the first notion we have; and if it were possible it would involve us in an infinite regress. From all points of view, therefore, we are bound to conclude that evidence is not the ultimate criterion of truth, but is the ultimate motive of certitude; the ultimate criterion being analytic resolution into the first principles.

This way of regarding the criterion of truth seems to help us to understand what evidence itself is. To speak of it as a 'light,' and so in parables, seems rather mystifying. It is, in fact, that property of a proposition which makes it undeniable. Now what makes a proposition undeniable is identity of subject and predicate. This may be either com-

[1] *De Veritate,* I, 12.

[2] Cf. *Summa Theologica,* I, 17, 3, ad 1; *Quodlibet,* VIII, Q. II, a. 4.

plete, as in a tautology (e.g. A is A) ; or partial, as in the first principles and indemonstrable propositions. In either case any attempt at denial is doomed to failure, since if we know the subject at all, we must know it as itself, not as something else. To do this would be not to know it. To say a first principle is 'evident' is merely a short and convenient way of expressing this fact.

It may, perhaps, be thought out of place in what professes to be merely an explanation of current Thomistic teaching, to have diverged from what is, on the whole, the more usual way of speaking of the ultimate test of truth. If Thomists were unanimous in their explanation of it, no doubt this criticism would be justified. As they are not, what may be called the minority view,[1] has been chosen for the reasons given. It seems to be a more accurate way of speaking, and the way in which S. Thomas himself always spoke. From the point of view of beginners also it has the advantage of assigning a definite and intelligable test by which to discriminate truth from error; in place of something which can only be described in metaphorical language as a 'light.'

As was said above, however, the view that the ultimate criterion is evidence is not untrue if the word 'criterion' be taken in a wide sense; and so nothing that is here said should be taken as excluding that view, or as in any way derogatory to those authors who think it better to use this form of expression.

For the sake of simplicity the question as to the ultimate criterion has been confined to the verification of purely intellectual judgements which can be, by direct process, resolved into the first principles. Sometimes, however, it will be necessary to trace the link with a primary sense datum, or a simple sensation. The largest class of judgements of all involves both sensations and ideas, and for the verification of these we shall have to work back both to the primary sensation and to the primary idea, that of being.

Many other criteria have been put forward from time to

[1] Though supported by authorities of great weight, e.g. Card. Lorenzelli, Sanseverino, Geny, Roland-Gosselin.

time by non-Scholastic philosophers as the ultimate test of truth. These are dealt with at length by many exponents of the Scholastic view;[1] but in this summary it is neither possible nor necessary to consider them in detail.

They are of two main kinds, for some find the test of truth in some purely subjective feeling, while others look for it in something altogether extrinsic to knowledge itself. Typical of the first attitude are theories that the ultimate criterion consists in a natural instinct, or a free act of the will; and of the second that it is faith in divine revelation, tradition, the general reason, or utility. All these theories labour under a common disadvantage, since the tests they take as being ultimate cannot be accepted unless they are themselves rationally justified; and so cannot, in fact, be ultimate. An instinctive feeling, or an act of the will, both rest on some prior rational conviction, and the same is true of trust in revelation or tradition; while the question of utility must be determined by the reason. Similarly, our natural confidence in common sense as giving us certainty about truths necessary for the conduct of our lives as men, put forward by Reid and the Scotch School as the test of truth, is indeed *a* criterion of truth, but cannot be the ultimate one, inasmuch as we accept this test because the first condition of knowledge—that the essential acts of our cognitive faculties must give us truth—cannot be doubted. Faith in divine revelation, again, presupposes much previous knowledge, which, therefore, obviously cannot be tested by it. The same holds good of tradition taken as the test, for we have to be assured of the claim of the tradition to be true. The founder of Traditionalism, the Vicomte de Bonald, made the interesting suggestion that man cannot think without words, i.e. cannot think without speaking. He truly says: 'man must think his speech before he can speak his thought,' but it does not follow, as he supposed, that he must think his speech before he can *think* his thought, and that therefore he can never learn to speak by his own efforts, but must have gained speech by revelation.

[1] The reader will find a full account and criticism of them, for example, in Dr. Coffey's *Epistemology*, Vol. II, Chaps. XXIV and XXV, pp. 281–366.

Actually, words are but the clothes of thought, and often very ill-fitting ones.

Contrast with all these theories the test proposed by S. Thomas which was outlined above. Here we see that that judgement is to be considered true which cannot be denied without involving a denial of the first principles, and which is therefore, in a sense, contained in them. Since these are immediately seen, as soon as we know them—i.e. understand their terms—to be undeniable, the same is to be said of those judgements which are ' resolved ' into them. Here we have got down to the very foundation of knowledge, and so there can be no question of this criterion presupposing any other.

CHAPTER XIV

SCIENCE AND THE SCIENCES

The Nature of Science—The Classification of the Sciences—Its Importance—Speculative and Practical Science—The Specification of the Sciences—Their Primary Division—Principles of a Complete Division.

THE result of the examination of our knowledge is, first, that some knowledge is possible; next, that this knowledge is not merely knowledge of our own ideas, but is, primarily, knowledge of the trans-subjective world; and, finally, that we can know, with regard to this world, not only facts, or particular events given in sense experience, but also general truths: in other words, that we can have scientific knowledge of the world. To say this is to assume that we already have some notion of what the word science means. No doubt, we have, in fact, a rough idea of what is meant by the expression 'scientific knowledge,' viz. some assured and systematic knowledge. Such a meaning is, nevertheless, a somewhat vague and wide one; and since vagueness in this matter may be, and indeed has been, the cause of much confusion, it is necessary to try and make our notion of science more precise.

SECTION I

The Nature of Science.

The word science, or the phrase scientific knowledge, can be understood in four ways. We sometimes speak of an act of knowledge being 'scientific,' by which we mean that we assent to some proposition because it has been demonstrated. So science as an act may be defined as knowledge of a thing gained through knowledge of its causes. For example, a doctor having knowledge of the causes of malaria could be said to have an act of scientific knowledge about the disease itself.

Secondly, the word is used to signify the habit of science, or habitual science, which a man gains by a series of scientific acts. In this sense, then, it will be a habit acquired by demonstration and helping us in demonstration. That it is acquired by demonstration is plain from what we have just said. It will also help us in demonstration, if it be a habit, since a habit is a ' disposition according to which that which is disposed is either well or ill disposed,' as Aristotle says.[1] Experience shows that an intellectual training does, in fact, help us to pick out the relevant notions, to apply them correctly and readily, and to reach conclusions with ease and assurance. Mathematicians, for example, can omit any explicit reference to many of the steps by which they prove a theorem, which steps would have to be laboriously gone through by a beginner. A practised mathematician sees a whole demonstration almost as one. Action of this kind bears upon itself the marks of habitual action.

Thirdly, science may be understood to mean a scientific system, and so the name may be applied to any body of co-ordinated certainties with regard to any particular matter, these having been arrived at by demonstration.

Fourthly, in modern usage, the word science is frequently restricted to those scientific systems which deal with the objects of the senses, i.e. to Natural Science. This usage has its roots in the Empirical philosophy, and is very inexact and misleading.

Science, then, may be defined as an intellectual habit of certain and evident knowledge of universal and necessary being, which is gained through demonstration.

In saying that scientific knowledge is certain we distinguish it from opinion, which is uncertain, and by saying that it is evident we distinguish it from faith, which is an inevident assent. Its object must be universal, for we can only have *certain* knowledge of what is essential to a thing ; what is accidental is variable and so uncertain. Now

[1] *Met.*, Bk. V, c. XX, 1022 b, 11.

essences are universal, and necessary in the sense that they cannot be changed in themselves, though they may or may not exist.

In connection with what was said in the last chapter about the ultimate criterion of truth, it is interesting to notice the distinction which S. Thomas makes[1] between subalternating and subalternate sciences. Cajetan[2] explains that the essential difference between these two kinds of science is that the conclusions of a subalternating science are seen from, and in, the self-evident principles immediately, while the conclusions of a subalternate science are seen from, and in, these principles mediately; by the medium namely of some other scientific habit, viz. the subalternating science.[3]

SECTION II

The Classification of the Sciences.

That it is proper to consider the classification of the sciences in Epistemology appears from the fact that Epistemology is part of Metaphysics. Now Metaphysics is the highest form of human wisdom, and since it is, as S. Thomas says, the business of the wise man to put order into things, it will be the concern of Metaphysics to determine the order of science itself, that is to classify the sciences. As we shall see, S. Thomas's notion of science, and his method of classifying its branches, is a reaffirmation of his philosophy, and so must be dealt with by Metaphysics in which this philosophy culminates. This is, indeed, true of any classification which is not a random one: it must depend on the philosophic outlook of the classifier.

This problem of the classification of the sciences is one of great importance, for, being fundamental, the view we take of the distinction of the sciences will affect all our treatment

[1] Cf. *Summa Theologica*, I, 1, 2; in *Boet. de Trin.*, Q. V, a 1, ad 5 et ad 6.

[2] *Comm. on the Summa.*, loc. cit.

[3] This subject is fully discussed in treatises on Scholastic Logic, e.g. Gredt, *Elementa Philosophiæ Aristotelico-Thomisticæ*, Vol. I, Sect. 228, 229.

of scientific questions. The sciences deal, in most cases, with the same material object—the same ' thing '—as, for example, biology, zoology, anatomy, etc., all deal with living things. Now if sciences such as these are to be distinct, their ways of considering the object which is common to them must be different. This being so, it is plain that the sphere of one science will not be that of another, since each approaches its objects from different points of view. We might take an illustration from experience. A man looking at a table from above sees some feet of plane surface, and, say, a square shape, while one looking from the side, sees two or more legs and the edge of the table above them. Both see the table, but from different points of view, and neither has the right to insist that what he sees ought to be seen by the other observer, or comes within the other's vision. Similarly, it is essential that the sciences should each keep strictly to its own field, and that a worker in one science should not delude himself by supposing that the conclusions arrived at in it necessarily hold good in the same sense in another. So it would be a mistake to suppose that the results of Chemistry, say, hold good as they stand in Biology.

We are to try and discover, then, how this distinction of the sciences is to be arrived at ; and since false principles of classification would vitiate the work of sciences based on them, since they would lead to a fatal confusion, it is plain that the determination of the true classification is of vital interest for the progress of scientific knowledge.

We may recall what has been said already as to the nature of knowledge.[1] Knowledge is a mode of being. When I know, I share in the being of another ; for there must be union of the knower and the known. That these two may be one there must be some element which is common to the subject as knowing, and the object as known. This element is the form of the thing, which makes it what it is ; and which, being free of the limitations caused by matter, is communicable to the mind which knows. To know, then, is to communicate with the objects as they are incarnate forms

[1] Cf. Vol I, Part II, Chap. VII, pp. 212 ff.

or ideas. We dematerialise these forms, loosing them from the limitations of matter, and making them free to enter our minds. These forms are the very reality of the things themselves: they are the metaphysical universals, which, as we saw, are in a different state, and exist in a different way, in the things and in our minds. So Hegel was right in asserting that the universal is a reality, but wrong in confining the reality of the universal to the metaphysical universal *quoad modum concipiendi*. Now when we communicate with some other thing or person, our purpose in doing so may be either in order that we may receive something from them, or that we may give something to them. This distinction applies to that kind of communication which is knowledge; and so we have a double way of knowledge, and a primary division of science. *Speculative science* receives ideas from the objects, dematerialising the forms and storing them up; while *practical science* embodies them again in some work. This division of science evidently issues naturally, and as it were necessarily, from the fundamental teaching of S. Thomas as to the nature of knowledge.[1]

S. Thomas explains the difference between these two kinds of science as follows:

'The speculative intellect is properly distinguished from the operative or practical by this, that the speculative has as its end the truth which it considers, while the practical directs the truth so considered to operation, as its end; and, consequently, the Philosopher says that they differ by reason of their ends; and in the second book of the *Metaphysics* it is said that the end of speculative science is truth, the end of operative or practical science, action. Since, therefore, matter ought to be proportionate to the end,[2] the matter of the practical sciences must be those things which can be made by our work, in order that the knowledge of them may be directed to operation as if to an end. But the matter of

[1] Cf. A. D. Sertillanges, O.P., art. 'La Science et les Sciences Spéculatives' in *La Revue des Sciences Philosophiques et Théologiques* (1921), pp. 5 ff.

[2] Since matter must be proportionate to form, these being correlatives, and form must be proportionate to the end; the end being, as it were, the expression of form.

the speculative sciences must be those things which are not made by our work; hence the consideration of them cannot be directed to operation as its end; and the speculative sciences must be distinguished in accordance with the distinction of these things.'[1]

The practical sciences, then, will be distinguished in accordance with the different kinds of 'work' which they are designed to produce; while the speculative ones will differ in so far as their objects differ. It is in these latter sciences that the interest of the question of the distinction of the sciences centres; and we must try and see what is the precise meaning of this principle which S. Thomas lays down for their classification, and the reason for it.

This reason is not far to seek, since science is essentially the movement and tendency of the mind towards some subject, some truth. Its whole purpose and *raison d'être* consists in the assimilation of the knowable object. Clearly then, it is incapable of definition except by means of its tendency towards this object; and towards this object precisely as *knowable*. Its species will therefore be determined by the object as knowable. Now the Scholastics name the object considered in this way the 'formal object,' as opposed to the 'material object,' since, as we have seen, it is forms, or universals, which are primarily knowable by the human intellect. Suppose we take any concrete thing, such as the earth, on which we live, it is plain that *as knowable*, it can be considered in many ways. So it may be considered as a body having mass and moving in a certain way, and so considered it forms part of the object of Physics. Or we might investigate its composition, either with respect to its structure and stratification, or its components, e.g. the minerals found in it, when it will be dealt with by the sciences of Geology and Mineralogy respectively; and so on. It is one and the same planet which we investigate in all these cases—the same 'material object'—but different aspects, or natures, or forms, are examined in each case: there are different 'formal objects.'

[1] *In. Boet. de Trinitate*, Q. V, a. 1.

Consequently, the different species of science, or the different sciences, will be determined by the different species or kinds of formal object to which they are directed.

We must, therefore, ask how are these formal objects themselves to be distinguished. They are, as we saw, objects precisely *as knowable,* and must therefore be distinct in so far as they are knowable, i.e. according to their different capacities for being known. Now we have repeatedly seen that a thing is knowable in proportion as it is immaterial, and that the root of cognition is immateriality.[1] The degrees of knowability, then, will correspond to the degrees of immateriality, or abstraction from matter.

If we now look at the objects of human knowledge to see how they differ with respect to immateriality, we find that there are three grades or distinctions among them.

First, we have those objects which are material in themselves and are considered as material by the mind, which studies them precisely as they are embodied in matter or materialised. Such are the natures of bodies studied by chemistry and physics, as well as animal natures investigated by zoology, biology, etc., and even the human body itself as studied by such sciences as physiology.

Secondly, there are objects which are dependent on matter in their being, but whose concept as formed by the mind is immaterial, such as numbers, geometrical figures, points and so on. S. Thomas gives as an illustration of the difference of these two classes snub-nosedness and curvature. Snubness can neither exist nor be thought of except in a nose, whereas curvature, though it cannot exist except in some body, can yet be conceived of without the notion of body being included in this conception.[2]

Thirdly, we have objects which do not depend on matter in any way, being either immaterial realities, such as God; or, at least, being such that their concept in no way implies that of sensible matter: such are being in general, substance, beauty, goodness and so on.

Corresponding to these three groups of objects we shall

[1] Cf. especially Vol. I, Part II, Chap. VII.
[2] S. Thomas, I *Phys.*, Lect. 1.

therefore have three general classes of science: the first group giving those which deal with the material world—what the ancients called *Physica*—and this class includes both the Philosophy of Nature and the Natural Sciences; the second the sciences of quantity, i.e. the Mathematical Sciences;[1] while the third gives that which considers being as such, i.e. Metaphysics.

It is plain that this division is generic only; and to find the specific distinction of the sciences we shall need to apply once more our principle that the sciences are distinguished according to the degree of immateriality of their formal objects. How can this be determined further than has been done already? If we reflect we can see that a general object is more immaterial than a particular one, a simple than a complex one; the whole is less limited, and so less material, than the part; and what is primary or principal is wider, and so less material, than what is secondary or derivative; as S. Thomas explains in the Prooemium to his commentary on Aristotle's *De Coelo*.

We have thus four principles which if applied to the science of nature will enable us to make as detailed a classification of it as we can possibly wish. Thus the philosophy of nature will study the general conditions of motion and change; particular classes of motion, as local motion, being studied by special sciences such as Mechanics. We shall see in the next chapter more precisely how the relation between philosophy and these natural sciences is to be regarded; here it is sufficient to notice that they are distinct in virtue of the more, or less, abstract character of their objects.

If we turn to the second genus of science, which deals with quantity, we are at once faced by a strictly specific division, inasmuch as quantity is of two kinds: continuous

[1] To this group belongs the philosophy of the continuum and of number, and in general the philosophical consideration of quantity; for formally speaking, quantity belongs to the second degree of abstraction; though if we speak materially, i.e. considering those things in which quantity is found, we should say that the philosophy of the continuum and of number belong to the Philosophy of Nature, since, according to Aristotle, they are inseparable from matter. This is, however, a subject of great difficulty, into which it is impossible to enter here, cf. Garrigou-Lagrange, *Le Réalisme du Principe de Finalité* (Desclée, 1932), Chap. IV, Sect. III, p. 251, and Maritain, *Les Degrés du Savoir* (Desclée, 1932), pp. 72, 81.

and discrete. The latter is more abstract, since it takes no account of space. Further divisions can be made in accordance with the four principles mentioned above.

In the third division of speculative science, Metaphysics, we do not find any division which is properly speaking specific, but everything is now considered at the same level of abstraction, that of being as such. Though it is no doubt true that God and wholly immaterial beings are in themselves more immaterial than being which is merely *considered* in a state of abstraction from matter, yet in metaphysics these are not regarded in their own natures, but under the common nature of being. We have, however, an order and classification in this science which accords with our principles, for we first consider being as it is related to our minds, and so, since our knowledge begins with sense knowledge, to material things; then we consider being in itself, which is conceived of as altogether abstracted from matter; and finally being which is not only conceived of as abstracted, but actually *is* abstracted from matter. These considerations give us the three parts of metaphysics which are Epistemology, General Metaphysics or Ontology, and Natural Theology.

From the classification of the speculative sciences here sketched Logic is necessarily excluded, for it is not only a science but also an art. As an art it belongs to the order of practical knowledge. Even as a science, though it makes a negative abstraction from matter, yet since its object is not real, but logical being, which cannot be included among the grades of real being, Logic is not, properly speaking, a philosophical science. Its object is, strictly speaking, neither material nor immaterial, for these are predicates of real being, so that it is an introduction to philosophical science rather than a philosophical science itself. Ethics is excluded from our scheme because it is a practical science, and Sacred Theology because this differs from the Natural Theology which is a part of Metaphysics by reason of its object, its principles, and its method. Its object is God considered in Himself, i.e. the mysteries of the Divine Life, whereas Metaphysics considers Him as He is Being. The principles of Sacred Theology are revealed truths, those of philosophy the principles of the reason. The method of Sacred Theology is the method of authority, that of philosophy the free use of the reason. Hence, as S. Thomas says, these two differ generically. '*Unde Theologia quae ad sacram doctrinam pertinet, differt secundum genus ab illa theologia quae pars philosophiæ ponitur.*'[1]

[1] *Summa Theologica,* I, Q. I, a. 1, ad 2.

CHAPTER XV

EXPERIMENTAL SCIENCE AND PHILOSOPHY

Four Periods in the History of Natural Science—Modern Views as to its Nature—Principles of a Solution—Conclusions.

THE question we have to consider in this chapter is one of great difficulty and importance. It is the question as to the kind of knowledge which is given us by the experimental sciences; and what its value is considered from the point of view of philosophy. The problem is difficult in itself because of its complexity, and is one of which we can find no complete solution in the writings of S. Thomas. Evidently, it is important for us, at the present day, to look for the answer to it, since Natural Science now enjoys a prestige greater than it has had at any previous period of its history. The answers which we give to many questions in Natural Philosophy and even in Metaphysics will be influenced by the view which we take of the nature of experimental science, and may even be determined by it. Similarly in Apologetical Theology many of the most pressing difficulties arise from the apparent conflict between scientific conclusions and revealed truths, e.g. in the question of the possibility of miracles.

S. Thomas, in his own day, was faced by a situation not unlike ours: how the new knowledge derived from the works of Aristotle was to be absorbed into Christian Philosophy. He proceeded, in making his synthesis, on the firm conviction that truth cannot be discordant with itself, and considered that the harmonisation of the new knowledge with the old was to be brought about by a determination of their respective natures or spheres, not by a piecemeal concordance. There can be little doubt that the solution of the modern problem is to be looked for along the same lines.

We have already seen what is the nature of philosophy; how it is universal in its range and how it seeks to penetrate down to the very roots of things: to their last, or as we say nowadays, their first causes. We arrived at this conclusion by a consideration of it as it appears on the stage of history, and it would be desirable to adopt the same method in order to determine the nature of natural science. Unfortunately any attempt to do this would far exceed the limits of space available here; and it is only possible to summarise the results which such an investigation yields.

It seems that we can distinguish four periods in the history of Natural Science. The first extends from the time of Aristotle to that of Galileo, the second from Galileo to Newton, the third from Newton to the end of the nineteenth century, while the last is still in progress.

Observation of nature on a large scale was first practised by Aristotle who was 'the greatest collector and systematiser of knowledge which the ancient world produced.'[1] 'He was one of the founders of the inductive method, and the first to conceive the idea of organised research.'[2] We have already seen that he classed Natural Science among the theoretical sciences, and he held that the collection of observations of nature was valuable rather as the matter with which a deductive science, proceeding from primary rational principles, could be built up, than as constituting the body of scientific knowledge in itself. 'The facts of experience are represented as a confused mass which must be analysed until we see its ultimate implications, the "origins," "causes" or "elements," which are "clear by nature" though to us initially obscure.'[3]

On the whole, then, we can say that neither Aristotle nor his successors in the ancient and mediaeval world made any clear-cut distinction between the philosophy of nature and natural science, though much of what they said of the method of 'saving the appearances' is in accord with modern ideas as to the method of the physical sciences.[4]

[1] W. C. D. Dampier-Whetham, *A History of Science* (C.U.P., 1929), p. 33.
[2] *Ibid.* [3] Ross, *Aristotle*, p. 63.
[4] Cf. P. Duhem, *Le Système du Monde*, t. I, p. 128 f.; S. Thomas, *Summa Theologica*, I, 32, 1, ad 2.

Greek thinkers, then, even those who, like Archimedes and Aristotle, carried observation to a high pitch, did not regard natural science as anything but a branch of philosophy, whose problems were to be solved by the application of the principles of the reason to the observed phenomena. It was essentially a rationalistic method and would give, if successful, information about the ultimate nature of the real world.[1]

This view of natural science may be said to have held the field until the sixteenth century, when Galileo made the great discovery which initiated the modern era. This discovery, attributable in the first place to Galileo, and, as systematised, to Descartes, was 'the possibility of a universal science of nature informed not by philosophy but by mathematics: a physico-mathematical science.'[2] Galileo insists that the book of nature is written in the mathematical language, whose symbols are geometrical figures; and, at the same time, emphasises the necessity of having recourse to experiment. His theory of the mathematical character of nature obliged him to reject, as not really belonging to it, all that cannot be expressed in mathematical terms. Secondary qualities, then, such as colour, had to go, and only primary ones, as extension and shape, remain; and along with them final causes, purpose or design, are discarded, since Mathematics takes no account of these.[3]

Descartes, as we said, systematised this view, and identifying the mathematical universe with the '*res extensa*,' held that nature is a vast machine; so that given the initial data of matter and motion, it would be possible to construct the whole of it by means of mathematical operations. Mind, and everything mental, such as purpose, is to be excluded from the realm with which natural science deals, and the whole material world is declared to be unaffected by any intelligence or design. It is a vast machine which runs unceasingly and blindly. That nature is such a machine, and can be known wholly and only by mathematical methods is, according to Descartes, known to us intuitively, being

[1] Cf. Whitehead, *Science and the Modern World*, p. 9.

[2] Maritain, *Les Degrés du Savoir*, p. 83.

[3] Cf. Burtt, *The Metaphysical Foundations of Modern Science*, Chap. III.

'clearly and distinctly' perceived. When he says the material world is a machine he means that it is so trans-subjectively, and in itself; not that we think of it as a machine, and can deal with it as if it were a machine. In this respect, therefore, his view of natural science is like that of Aristotle in so far as both think that the knowledge obtained by it gives us information as to the real basic nature of the material world, but while Aristotle envisaged this nature in terms of being and becoming, Descartes asserts that it is extension and quantity. This was certainly a great change in the way of regarding nature, for it deposed Metaphysics from its throne, and crowned Mathematics as the Queen of the Sciences. The Mechanistic view introduced in this way by Descartes widened and deepened in the two hundred years which followed, and this was largely due to its astonishing success. One by one all the happenings of nature were found to be reducible to a mechanical and mathematical form. The widest and most far-reaching application of the method was made by Newton, who, in his *Principia, or the Mathematical Principles of Natural Philosophy*, published in 1687, showed that all known motions could be reduced to three laws. But while he takes over the mathematical method from Descartes and is at one with him in asserting that it is mathematics which is the clue to nature, he does not follow him in that part of his theory of science which he shared with Aristotle, namely, that our concept of nature represents nature as it, in fact, is. Whether nature is in fact mathematical, whether the world is a machine, whether light is indeed corpuscular, and so on, he declines to say positively. Thus he is constantly inveighing against hypotheses, and regarded his conclusions, not as deductions from experimental observations, but as statements of those observations in a general form. This method involves an ultimate empiricism,[1] and the exclusion of

[1] This empiricism is explained in the concluding passage of the *Opticks*: 'Hypotheses are not to be regarded in experimental philosophy. And although the arguing from experiments and observations by induction be no demonstration of general conclusions; yet it is the best way of arguing which the nature of things admits of.' See the whole passage quoted by Burtt, op. cit., p. 221.

formal causes from natural science ; as well as of efficient ones, except in so far as we may find it convenient to ascribe these in order to epitomise our observation of the way in which a number of phenomena regularly succeed one another. Natural Science, then, in Newton's view, is a systematic account of phenomena, expressed in mathematical terms, and interpreted according to mathematical law. Its phenomena obey this law, and so move wholly mechanically, but such mechanical movement cannot be asserted of them *a priori*, or beyond the limits of experimental evidence, but only in so far as experiment shows it to be, in fact, justified. It must be admitted that Newton did not adhere consistently to this view, but was led by his interest in metaphysical and theological questions to speculate on the ultimate nature and cause of the universe on the basis of his observations of the 'appearances of things.' Thus he discourses of God whose chief work seems to be the detection and rectification of irregularities in the cosmic system. As more and more of these supposed irregularities were explained according to mechanical laws, the Deity, as Newton had depicted him, seemed to have been put out of business. Thus it appeared that the whole universe could be subjected to the mechanical scheme, so that if we had a complete knowledge of its state at any given moment we should be able to determine from this its whole history, both past and future. 'An intelligence,' writes Laplace,[1] 'who for a given instant should be acquainted with all the forces by which nature is animated, and with the several positions of the beings composing it, if further his intellect were vast enough to submit those data to analysis, would include in one and the same formula the movement of the largest bodies in the universe and those of the lightest atom. Nothing would be uncertain for him ; the future as well as the past would be present to his eyes. The human mind, in the perfection it has been able to give to astronomy, affords a feeble outline of such an intelligence.' This confidence in the ability of science to account for the whole universe by means of a mechanical scheme deepened

[1] Essay on Probability (1812), quoted by E. W. Hobson, *The Domain of Natural Science* (C.U.P.), p. 18.

throughout the eighteenth and nineteenth centuries. Newton's warnings as to the limitations and uncertainties of 'hypotheses' were forgotten, and the Cartesian view of natural science as a mathematico-physical scheme which gives us an explanation of the very nature of the material universe became firmly established. Science, in this view of it, is certainly distinguished from philosophy—which is regarded as defunct—for it bases itself no longer on metaphysical principles, but on observation and mathematical law. It has, however, assumed the function which philosophy was designed to perform, that of giving us knowledge of the real nature of the material world, and even of the universe as a whole.

In the year 1895 a discovery was made which has resulted in a gradual weakening of the confidence of scientists in the universal applicability of a purely mechanical scheme, and the growth of doubts as to the ability of Natural Science to tell us what is the real nature of the physical world.

The first breach in the scheme of Newtonian physics was made by the success of the wave theory of light,[1] due to Young and Fresnel, in the opening years of the nineteenth century, but it was not until the discovery of the X-rays by Rontgen in 1895 that this scheme was seriously questioned by scientists. This year may therefore be said to mark the beginning of the modern scientific period. The discovery of radio-activity led to the formulation by Planck of his quantum theory, according to which radiation is not continuous, but occurs in blocks, or packets. This idea is inconsistent with Newtonian mechanics, according to which movement is strictly continuous. The second break with Newtonian physics occurred when the Michelson-Morley experiment (1905) gave a negative result as to the motion of the earth through the æther. This led Einstein to suggest that the absolute space and time of Newtonian science ought to be abandoned; a suggestion which resulted in a fundamental reconstruction of the notion of mass, which according to the new view increases with velocity, and is equivalent to

[1] Cf. Dampier-Whetham, op. cit., pp. 238 ff.; Bragg, *The Universe of Light*, Chap. IX.

energy. Thus the fundamental conception of classical mechanics—that matter is something permanently extended in space, and persisting in time—vanishes,[1] and with it the beautiful simplicity of the mechanical scheme.

The result of the new knowledge with regard to the concept of science itself has been that some, at any rate, in the ranks both of the scientists and the philosophers have concluded that science is incapable of telling us anything of the nature of things, but must confine itself to descriptions of phenomena.

Before considering this and other views of the nature of natural science which have recently been put forward, it will be useful to glance back and review the transformations which we have noticed in the concept of science.

The earliest view of science took it to be part of philosophy, so revealing the ultimate nature of the material world; and supposed it could arrive at its results by the application of metaphysical principles, so that it would be, to a great extent, an *a priori* construction. The next view, that of Galileo, still maintained that science dealt with the nature of the world, but held that its method must be the application of the principles of mathematics to observed phenomena, excluding metaphysical ideas. Nevertheless, it was so confident that nature was in fact mathematical and mechanical that it was prepared to build up a world from matter and motion, by the aid of mathematical laws, almost *a priori*, as in the Cartesian system. The aprioristic element in this view of science was definitely excluded by Newton, who insisted that its foundation is altogether experimental, and that its conclusions must always be put to the test of experiment. But it was still thought that science did and should fulfil the

[1] It is obviously impossible to give in a summary such as this any account of the history of scientific ideas during the last forty years. The points here set down are only mentioned in order to make it clear that scientists themselves have, during this time, found it necessary to revise their ideas as to the aim and the nature of science, owing to these (and other) discoveries. Numerous books are easily available which deal with this fascinating subject, e.g., Eddington, *The Nature of the Physical World*, and Jeans, *The New Background of Science* (both published by the Cambridge University Press), while the subject is dealt with historically in the *History of Science*, by Dampier-Whetham, already referred to, esp. Chap. IX, 'The New Era in Physics.'

function, which had once been ascribed to philosophy, of telling us what is the nature of trans-subjective reality, at any rate in the material sphere. Thus the decree *nisi* of divorce between science and philosophy granted by Galileo had not yet been made absolute. The attempt to do this has been made in the modern period, in which a new view as to the nature and aim of science has made its appearance.

It is at the opposite extreme to the traditional idea of science—which continues to be widely held—and maintains that the function of science is merely to describe phenomena, and that the relation of these phenomena to the reality (if any) of which they are appearances is unknown and unknowable by it. On its philosophical side the ancestry of this view can be traced through the German Transcendentalists and Kant to the dualism of Descartes, who made a complete separation between mind and matter ; on the scientific, to the writings of Ernst Mach and others, who called natural laws 'abridged descriptions' and 'comprehensive and condensed reports about facts,' and, in general, declare that physical science is concerned with the description of natural motions, and has no concern with their causes. Thus according to Mach, Newton's '*hypotheses non fingo*' means that natural science can tell us nothing as to the nature of forces ; which are, indeed, merely mathematical abstractions. All we know about nature is that we can express certain ranges of phenomena by means of equations. This view is evidently very consonant with a sceptical or agnostic temper of mind, since it allows us to assert that science is the nearest approach which we can get to knowledge, as Bertrand Russell does, and to add with Aldous Huxley: 'Science is no "truer" than common sense or lunacy, than art or religion. It permits us to organize our experience profitably ; but tells us nothing about the real nature of the world to which our experiences are supposed to refer.'[1] So we can say of Nature :

> 'Inscrutable she guards unguessed
> The Riddle of the Sphinx.'

[1] Aldous Huxley, *Do What You Will*. Essay, 'One and Many,' Sect. 2.

In addition to the traditional view of science—which thinks that it intends to give, and succeeds in giving us knowledge of the very reality of the universe, so that light-waves are as real as sea-waves, and tables and chairs are not 'really' solid and permanent, but whirling masses of electrons—and the phenomenalist view just outlined—which thinks that science gives us no knowledge of reality at all, but only of our own thoughts about it—there is a third which holds an intermediate position between these two. According to this opinion there need not be an exact correspondence between a scientific law, or law of nature, and extra-mental facts; still less need there be such correspondence between a scientific *theory* and fact. On the other hand, it holds that there is an essential element of fact which is a primary datum, and to this the law or theory must conform. The truth of it is to be judged by its applicability to a range of phenomena, by its self-consistency and by its simplicity; not by its supposed precise correspondence with a set of relations actually existing in nature, still less by its correspondence with a set of relations between real entities. Evidently these three conditions of applicability, consistency, and simplicity may be fulfilled in scientific theories more or less completely; but that theory will be reckoned true which satisfies them most fully at any given moment. We are not to suppose, then, that scientific entities, such as electrons; or theories, such as the wave-theory of light; or even laws, such as Newton's laws of motion, either represent or are intended to represent entities or relations in nature; except in a very abstract and partial way, and for the particular purposes which science has in view.

This, in rough outline, is the view of the nature and aim of the natural sciences which was expounded, and worked out in its applications to the various sciences by Professor Hobson in his remarkable course of Gifford Lectures delivered in 1921 and 1922.[1]

The general point of view expressed in them has been

[1] E. W. Hobson, *The Domain of Natural Science*, Cambridge University Press, 1923. Cf. also the same author's *The Ideal Aim of Physical Science*, C.U.P., 1925.

endorsed by other scientific writers, such as Prof. J. S. Haldane and Sir A. Eddington. So the former writes: 'Many physicists and other writers are still under the impression that it is the duty of physical science to reveal a complete representation of visible reality or Nature'—but 'physical science does not really set out to interpret reality, but only to discover and make use of such a provisional conception as can be used for certain limited practical purposes.'[1]

After this long preamble we can now ask: Is any of these views of the nature of natural science of the kind which Thomism would find acceptable, and, if so, which is it? We cannot hope to find a cut-and-dried answer to our question in S. Thomas, but he gives us certain principles which may guide us in arriving at our own.

(1) We notice the distinction between '*scientiæ quia*' and '*scientiæ propter quid*,' i.e. between those sciences which tell us *that* things happen so, and those which tell us *why* things happen so. Perhaps we might call them sciences of statement and sciences of explanation.[2] According to S. Thomas the name 'science' is applied in different senses to these two classes.[3]

Thus the philosophy of nature and natural science are sciences of different kinds: the first is explanatory, the second empirical; the first tells us 'why,' the second tells us 'how.'

(2) We are concerned here chiefly with two classes of science: the mathematical and the natural. Now the object of natural science is more complex than that of mathematics, being more material. It follows from this that their principles are not interchangeable, for mathematics, being more abstract, is able to apply its principles to the physical sciences, but the converse cannot be done.[4]

[1] J. S. Haldane, *The Sciences and Philosophy* (Hodder and Stoughton, 1929), p. 243 f. Cf. A. S. Eddington, *The Nature of the Physical World*, especially Chap. XII. Eddington seems to go further in the direction of phenomenalism than either Hobson or Haldane.

[2] Maritain calls them empirical and explanatory. Cf. *Les Degrés du Savoir*, p. 76.

[3] *In Post Anal.*, Lib. I, Lect. 25.

[4] Cf. S. Thomas *In Boet. de Trin.*, Q. V, a. 3, ad 6; *de Coelo*, Lib. 3, Lect. 3.

(3) Modern physics is not under the direction of metaphysics as was that of S. Thomas's day, but under that of mathematics. It is what the ancients called an intermediary science, a science whose subject matter is furnished by the world of nature, but whose formal object and conceptual scheme are mathematical. It is materially physical and formally mathematical.

(4) In so far as modern physics is materially physical, since it begins with experiment and ends with the application of its results to the world of nature, it is not a mere abstract 'description,' but maintains a relation with reality, and so with the philosophy of nature. But in so far as it is formally mathematical it expresses itself by means of a purely abstract conceptual scheme, which includes not merely quantity as such (including geometrical form, which is a kind of quality), but also various fictitious entities (logical beings based on reality) which are useful as helps in developing the mathematical processes. Such entities have been the 'ether,' 'waves,' 'corpuscles,' and so on.

(5) Though it is not true to say that physics deals only with quantity and leaves quality out of account, yet everything it deals with is necessarily expressed in a mathematical form, and so it can give us only a very partial account of the world of nature.

(6) Mathematics eliminates final causes, and this is true also of physico-mathematical science.

We see, therefore, that in constructing a physico-mathematical science we must recognise that we are eliminating from nature (which is the object of the philosophy of nature) a large part of its content. Though the physical world may be amenable to mathematical treatment, yet the resultant expression tells us of one aspect of it only. If we suppose that it corresponds completely and exactly with the entities and relations actually subsisting in this world we are making a false use of abstraction.[1]

Thus the aim of physical science is not to give us an

[1] Cf. Whitehead, *Science and the Modern World*, p. 23.

account of the material world as a whole, but only of that aspect of it which is amenable to mathematical treatment. We must not mistake thoughts for things. This aspect is, however, an aspect of the reality which is the material world; and though science is not directly concerned with the question whether this is so or not, philosophy ought not to forget it.

The truth of scientific theories is of a different kind to philosophical truth.

A physico-mathematical theory will be said to be ' true ' if it is self-consistent, and is the simplest possible scheme of mathematical concepts and explanatory entities which is exactly applicable, from the point of view of measurement, to all the phenomena which have been observed at any given time. It is *not* necessary that a definite nature, or ontological law, should be present in the real world, which is in precise correspondence with each of the mathematical symbols and concepts. Thus physical science and philosophy are wholly distinct; though they are not separated, since both work on the same material, viz. the sensible world.

The view of natural science here suggested is the legitimate child of the theory of ' saving the appearances ' as set out by S. Thomas. So, commenting on the Ptolemaic theory of astronomy—according to which the earth was fixed at the centre of the universe—he says that a reason for accepting a theory may be that the observed effects are consonant with it, as in this case; but such a reason is not demonstrative, since it might be that the appearances could also be ' saved ' by some other theory.[1] With these suggestions as to the way in which Thomism might now regard the physico-mathematical sciences, we must leave this subject. Evidently our sketch of it is very inadequate, and space does not allow of any discussion of the sciences of the biological type. A fuller account of the whole matter

[1] *Summa Theologica,* I, 32, 1, ad 2. Cf. *De Coelo,* Lib. II, Lect. 17, nn. 1, 2, and 8; Lib. I, Lect. 3. *De Trinitate* Q. 4, a. 3, ad 8; XII *Met.*, Lect. 10; *Comm. in Job,* 38, Lect. 2; *Meteorologica I,* Lect II, n. 1; Lect. 1, nn. 7 and 9.

will be found in Maritain's *Les Degrés du Savoir*, already referred to.[1]

Having established the possibility of obtaining true knowledge of real extra-mental being, our next task is to see what this knowledge is, that is to say to consider this real being in general, which is the business of General Metaphysics, or Ontology.

[1] See also H. Poincaré, *La Science et l'Hypothèse*. E. Meyerson, *Identité et Réalité*, Paris, Alcan, 1926, and *De l'Explication dans les Sciences*, Paris, Payot, 1927. The first writer inclines to a phenomenalistic, the second to a realist view of science. Cf. also the communications from Fr. Hoenen, S.J., and Fr. de Munnynck, O.P., in *Acta Primi Congressus Thomistici*, Rome, 1925. Hoenen, *Cosmologia*, nota IV (against Maritain's view). T. Percy Nunn, *Anthropomorphism and Physics* (Milford, 1926).

PART II. GENERAL METAPHYSICS

CHAPTER I

BEING IN GENERAL

Nature of Metaphysics—The Notion of Being—Mistakes as to the Nature of Being.

METAPHYSICS is the science of being, which is considered by it altogether in the abstract, simply as being. We ascend, as it were, into the stratosphere of knowledge, and breathe an air so rarefied that it could not support mental life unless we were first trained in abstract thinking in the more congenial climates of natural philosophy. As the science of being it is the science of the ultimate reality. Is there such a reality, and if so, is it knowable ? The Empiricists doubt whether there is any such reality, and both they and the followers of Kant are convinced that it cannot be known by the speculative reason. We have already met their objections, and so have established the possibility of metaphysics.

What sort of science will this be ? Since being includes everything that is, metaphysics, which has being as its formal object, will also, in a sense, be all-inclusive ; but since it considers being simply as being, and not as any particular kind of being, it will be concerned with the underlying reality of all things, not with the reality of various classes of things. As Whitehead says : 'By metaphysics I mean the science which seeks to discover the general ideas which are indispensably relevant to the analysis of everything that happens.'[1]

Immaterial being is of two kinds : that which is positively immaterial, inasmuch as it never exists in matter ; and that which is negatively immaterial, that is to say something

[1] A. N. Whitehead, *Religion in the Making* (C.U.P., 1926), p. 72 n.

which, though it may sometimes exist in matter, yet does not imply matter in its concept.[1] It is the latter kind of being which is treated of in General Metaphysics. If there exist any absolutely immaterial being, it will naturally form the object of a further division of our subject; and this goes by the name of Natural Theology.

What, then, is this being which implies no matter in its concept?

The term being can be taken in three senses:

A. Grammatically and etymologically it is the participle of the verb 'to be.' Now a participle is a concrete term which implies two things: a form, and the subject of this form. Thus a meeting signifies both the act or form of coming together, and the persons or things which do so. Further, a participle, being a part of a verb, signifies, not a mere quality or action in the abstract, but the exercise of this quality. So, in our example meeting implies the actual coming together of some things, as in the line 'Journeys end in lovers meeting.'[2] Consequently, being signifies something which is composed of existence and of that which has existence, and moreover implies the exercise of existing in actual fact.

B. Secondly, being can be understood *nominally*, i.e. as a noun; and, in this sense, since the meaning of a name is independent of time and has nothing to do with present action, being does not imply the exercise of existing, but something which either has existed, is existing, or can exist. It is in this sense that we speak of the 'writings' of Dr. Johnson.

C. There is a third way in which being can be understood, namely, as S. Thomas says: 'As it is a verbal copula signifying the putting together of some enunciation which the mind makes: whence this "to be" is not anything in the real world, but only in the act of the mind which compounds and divides; and thus "to be" is attributed to everything about which a proposition can be formed, whether it be being, or a privation of being; for we say that blindness is.'[3]

[1] Cf. S. Thomas, *In Boetium de Trinitate*, Q. 5, a. 1.
[2] *Twelfth Night*, Act II, Sc. 3, 44.
[3] *Quodlibet*, IX, a. 3.

This last meaning is mentioned, then, in order to be excluded from metaphysics, since this deals with *real* being.

Which of the other two senses is the one in which being is said to be the object of metaphysics? Though, from a certain point of view, being, in the first sense, as a participle, may be said to be this object, inasmuch as the name 'being' is derived from the act of existing, just as the name animal is derived from its form or '*anima*'; yet, properly speaking, its object is being as a noun,[1] which signifies primarily '*that which* has a relation to existence.' This covers both possible and real being, everything which either is or can be; and so is being in its most general sense.

From this we can arrive at a descriptive definition of being; which because of its simplicity is incapable of strict definition. For it is not in any genus, since the only thing which could differentiate it is 'nothing,' and a definition, strictly speaking, must be by means of genus and difference. The description which S. Thomas gives of it is: 'that whose act is existence.' Thus in the notion of being there are two distinct elements: the subject which has being, and the form or act by which the subject has being. The subject which has being is called 'essence'; the act by which it has it, is called 'existence.'[2]

It is well to recall here the distinction between the objective and the formal concept.[3] The second is the concept properly so-called; the objective concept being called a concept as being the cause of the formal one (i.e. by analogy). The formal concept is a species or form which is expressed in and by the mind, and in which we regard the object. The objective concept, on the other hand, is the thing itself, or the object, which is properly and immediately known, and represented in and through the formal concept. Thus there is immediate knowledge of the object, even though the formal concept is a medium of cognition, since the formal concept is not a medium which, being first known, leads us to know-

[1] Cf. Gredt, *Elementa Philosophiæ,* No. 619, 2.

[2] In Scholastic Latin this last is often called '*esse*': as in the opusculum of S. Thomas, *De Ente et Essentia,* Cap. V, *Essentia* (*Dei*) *est ipsummet esse suum.*

[3] Cf. *supra,* Vol. II, Part I, Chap. XII, p. 124.

ledge of the object—as we know the King or the Pope, say, from their photographs—but a medium *through which* (*medium quo*) the object is known.[1]

It is clear that we are here chiefly concerned, as Suarez says,[2] with the objective concept of being, and since the objective concept is the nature of the thing considered, we can use the two phrases, ' concept of being ' and ' nature of being ' interchangeably.

Now this objective concept of being is a thing of a most general kind, which is predicable of all things which are, or can be. The simple and direct concept of being is a very imperfect and confused one, and is first both in the logical order and in that of time. For that is first in the logical order, or first known, which is included in every other concept, and this is the case with respect to the simple concept of being, since every concept is of some being, or of some determination of being. Similarly it is first in the order of time, for the first idea to be acquired is, as we saw, the most general one, and this is the idea of being. The case is, however, different with regard to the metaphysical concept of being, which can only be acquired as the result of a long process of thought, and so cannot be first.[3]

Being, then, though the first thing known, is also the ultimate term of all knowledge. It is the Alpha and Omega of the speculative reason. It is transcendent (in the Logical sense), belonging to no category.

There are two chief mistakes as to the nature of being, which are in opposition to one another. We mention them here because it will be useful to bear them in mind all through this part of philosophy, if we are to arrive at a balanced view. One extreme view of being, then, is that of the Pantheists, who say that being in general is, as such, a reality outside our minds, and that this being, by its evolution, is the source of all reality. That being in general

[1] Cf. Cajetan, *Comm. in De Ente et Essentia, Prooemium* (ed. de Maria, p. 26). John of S. Thomas, *Cursus Theol.*, Tom. II, Part I, Disp. 2, a. 2, Diff. 1. Suarez, *Disputationes Metaphysicæ*, Disp. 2, Sect. 1. Geny, *Critica*, p. 36, who all explain this distinction in this way.

[2] Suarez, loc. cit.

[3] Cf. Cajetan, *De Ente et Essentia, Prooem* (p. 11, ed. de Maria).

cannot have such reality as this we have seen in our discussion of universals, the mistake of supposing that it has arising from the supposition that general natures have the same mode of existence in our minds and outside them. If being in general were found formally in things, the pantheistic conclusion that all things are one would be unavoidable.

The second mistake, which is at the other extreme to this, is that of the Nominalists, Conceptualists, and Subjectivists, who say that the notion of being is in no way objective, but is a mere fiction of the mind. This also is untrue, for in things, apart from our thought of them, there is something which is related to real existence; there is a capacity for real existence. If this were not so, real and logical being would be on the same footing; but they are not, for the mind cannot confer on logical being a capacity for real existence. Metaphysics, then, which deals with that which has a relation to real existence, is a science of reality, and ought not to be confused with Logic.

CHAPTER II

THE UNITY AND ANALOGY OF BEING

The Unity of Being—Formation of the Concept of Being—The Unity of Being Essential but Imperfect—The Analogy of Being—Analogy—Division of Analogy—The Opinion of Scotus—The Thomist View.

SECTION I

The Unity of Being.

THE question we are to try to answer in this section is whether the objective concept of being, and so its nature, is one concept or a confused accumulation of several. Now it is clear that accidents are not beings in the same sense as substances are, for the notion of accident implies that in order to exist, to be, it must be supported by some thing not itself, while a substance can exist of itself and needs no such support. The same remarks apply *mutatis mutandis* to God and creatures. Now these different ways of existing can evidently only be known, in so far as they differ from one another, by several distinct concepts. On the other hand all these things are known as beings ; all of them, considered in themselves, are or exist. There must, then, be some concept of being distinct from those concepts by which the various ways of being are known. This concept will in some fashion include or cover all the various ways in which a thing may be, and it is this which we name the concept of being in general. We say it includes all these modes, but in what way does it include them ? Is it in the way in which a heap of stones may be said to include the stones, or perhaps in the way that a man, say Peter, includes both soul and body ; or even in the way that the universal concept or nature 'man' includes all individual men ? Is it, that is to say, an essential or an accidental unity ? If it be merely accidental, being will simply be a conglomeration of the various modes of being, so that there will be no concept of being, which is distinct from those of the different modes of being, taken one by one. An essential union will require, at least, that there shall be some one meaning in which all the modes of being agree formally. If we find there is such a meaning, we shall be justified in saying that there is a unified concept which is that of being in general, and of being in general only, and which therefore does not apply to the modes of being in so far as they differ.

No doubt we arrive at the concept of being by some sort of abstraction: this has been plain from the start. Are we to suppose that the abstraction used to form it is of the same kind as that by which the universal is formed? At the first glance it might be natural to think that it is, for being seems to be a kind of universal. If, however, we consider the formation of a universal concept, such as 'man,' we see that in forming it we leave out of account altogether all that differentiates one man from another, so that the universal concept does not, to use the Scholastic phrase, 'actually contain the differences of its inferiors.' If, then, it is this kind of abstraction which we use in forming the concept of being, this concept will not actually contain the differences of its inferiors either. Before asking whether it does so let us consider another possible way in which the concept of being, which is an essential unity, and yet does not possess that unity which we have just found to be an attribute of universals, may be formed. In this case it will actually contain the differences of its inferiors, but if it is still to be an essential unity it must not contain them separated one from another, as, for example, a box of matches actually contains the different matches, but in some unified state, inasmuch as a single relation or proportion is found in them all. Instead of the differences of the inferiors being altogether omitted, as in the case of the universal concept, or simply retained, as in a box of matches or a litter of puppies, they would be retained, though not with regard to something absolute, but to something relative. So half a pound, a hemisphere, half a day, differ in every way except in so far as they all have the relation or proportion of being halves.

If being does not possess unity of either of these kinds it cannot have any essential unity at all, but must be a mere collection of its different modes.

The second kind of essential unity described above, the unity of a relation, or proportional unity, is evidently an imperfect kind of unity as compared with the first sort, the unity of something absolute, such as the inferiors of a universal share with one another. Nevertheless, it is true unity, for every resemblance is a kind of unity, and things which are dissimilar with regard to their absolute reality, may yet be similar with regard to the relation or proportion which each of them has to its corresponding term. This is exemplified in the relation of half to whole above mentioned. Such similarity of things which are, in themselves, absolutely speaking, unlike, is called proportionality; from which it is clear that proportionality implies four terms at least, which form two pairs, and are inter-related in such a way that each term of one pair is, absolutely speaking, dissimilar from each term of the other.

Three views, then, are possible. Either being is perfectly one, like the universal; or a mere collection of different modes, having no internal unity; or imperfectly one, in so far as all its modes are unified in a common relation of proportion. Evidently we are dealing once more with the problem of the one and the many which we considered in a concrete form in Natural Philosophy with respect to individual and specific differences of inanimate and animate bodies. Its solution is the central task of philosophy. Here we see it in its clearest light, freed from the shadows which material things cast upon it. The first view we mentioned is the solution of the Monists; and, verbally at least, the opinion put forward by some Scotists, that being is perfectly one, tends in a monistic direction. The second view is an absolute pluralism which is professed by Nominalists. William James used the word 'pluralist' to describe his idea of the universe, but probably he stands to Nominalism in much the same relation as these Scotists do to Monism.

Thomists maintain that the unity of being is essential,

not merely accidental, so that, as they phrase it, it is formally one. At the same time they will not allow that its unity is complete or perfect, as is the unity of a specific or generic nature, such as man or animal. This doctrine is essentially connected with their theory of knowledge, according to which the proper object of the *human* intellect is the being of sensible things. When we men speak of 'being,' then, it is this being with which we are primarily concerned; and when we ask whether it is one, and so on, we are asking whether it is one as it appears to us when abstracted from sensible things. Does it, like the universal, 'man,' appear as totally abstracted from the difference of its inferiors? If so, it will be perfectly one. Putting the question in this form there can be no doubt as to the answer, for differences which are perfectly abstracted from are in no way retained; so that if being abstracted perfectly from the differences of its inferiors these last would not be being, that is to say, they would be nothing. Unless, therefore, we are to do away with all differentiation in being we must allow that being is not perfectly one. Why the Scotists were able to maintain that it is, was because they did not regard the being of sensible things as the being here in question. We shall see this more plainly when discussing the analogy of being, which is our present question in another form of words.

Even though being (using the word always of abstract being, and being as a noun) is not perfectly one, yet it is not, simply speaking, many; that is to say, the various essences which being in general actually contains within itself, formally agree in some respect one with another. This is surely the case, for each of the essences actually contained within being in general is a definite determined nature. It exists, or can exist, and so must have a definite and determined existence—its own. So it must have a definite relation or proportion to its existence, which will vary as the essence varies, with regard to its terms essence and existence, while remaining the same in so far as it is a proportion of essence to existence. The stone is to its existence as the man to his, or the colour of the violet to this colour's existence. This can only be denied on a purely nominalist view of knowledge.

If we only know singular things it is plain that being must be made up of singulars and so be, simply speaking, many. The advantage of the Thomist doctrine here is that while it is as determined in clinging to the facts, to observation, to singular things, as the most fervent Positivist or Materialist, yet at the same time it recognises the truth of the contention that all that we know is being, and so that all being is one. It asserts: '*nihil in intellectu nisi prius fuerit in sensu*' and at the same time '*primum quod cadit in intellectumest ens.*'

Section II

The Analogy of Being.

The correct meaning of the word analogy (ἀναλογία) is 'proportion' or equality of ratios. The expression is originally a mathematical and quantitative one: ($\frac{a}{b}=\frac{c}{d}$), which has been imported into metaphysics. In Mathematics it signifies the comparison of one quantity with another with respect to some determinate excess of one over the other. Now it is clear that there is no proportion between things which are absolutely unequal or diverse, nor yet between those which are exactly the same; hence in the definition of proportion or analogy we must assert that analogous things are in some respects different and in some the same. They thus fall between the two classes of things which are in their nature the same (which are called univocal things) and those which are in their nature not the same (or equivocal ones). They share, however, to a certain extent in the character of both their neighbours, i.e. in univocacy and equivocacy. The shares analogous things have in each of these cannot, however, be equal shares; for if they were equal, simply speaking, analogous things would be those whose name is common, the notion signified by the name being simply the same and simply different, which is absurd; nor yet can the shares be equal in some particular respect (*secundum quid*), for then the definition becomes: those whose name is common, the notion signified being in some respect the same and in some respect different;

which gives us no more information that we already have in our original notion of analogous things as 'partly the same and partly different.' It follows, then, that the shares of analogous things in univocacy and equivocacy must be unequal. Let us suppose they have a greater share in univocacy and a less in equivocacy. In this case we get in their definition : the notion signified by the common name is, simply speaking, the same and *secundum quid* different. Such a definition cannot be admitted, for it would identify univocacy and analogy ; unless we allow that univocal things do not differ in any respect, so that two men, for example, are absolutely identical in every way. If this be held to be untrue, as it surely is, univocal things must be, simply speaking, the same and *secundum quid* different, so that this notion cannot apply to analogous ones also.

Our conclusion, then, must be that analogous things are those whose name is common and the notion signified by the name is, simply speaking, different and *secundum quid* the same. From this it is clear that, from a logical point of view, analogous things are a subdivision of equivocal ones, and, indeed, they were called by Cajetan '*equivoca a consilio*.'[1]

It may be convenient if we here set down the definitions of these three kinds of things : univocal, equivocal and analogous ones. They are as follows :

Univocal things are those whose name is common and the notion formally signified by the name is, simply speaking, the same.

Equivocal things in general are those whose name is common and the notion formally signified by the name is not, simply speaking, the same.

These are of two kinds : *a casu* and *a consilio*.

Those things are *equivocal a casu* whose name is common and the notion formally signified by the name is altogether different.

These are the things we commonly call 'equivocal' without any qualification. The phrase '*a casu*' indicates that the application of the name to things which it does not formally signify comes about by chance, as when the name vice

[1] In *Prædicamenta Arist.*, fol. 15, col. 1 ; cf. *De Nominum Analogia*, cap. II, and *Comm. in S. T.*, Q. 13, a. 5, No. 12.

is applied to the carpenter's tool and the bad habit. This came about through the chance that the Latin words which signify these things: '*vitis*' and '*vitium*' sound somewhat alike, so that both got the same English form.

Those things are equivocal *a consilio*, or *analogous* whose name is common and the notion formally signified by the name is, simply speaking, different and *secundum quid* the same.

We must now consider shortly the various kinds of analogy, that is, the division of analogy.

In order that this division may be an essential one we must attend to that element of analogy which is essential to it, that is to say, to diversity. The division here must also be a metaphysical one, i.e. drawn from the nature of the thing, not a logical one, one based on modes of predication. Now a thing is what it is on account of its causes, so that our division of analogy will be effected by differentiating the causes or reasons on account of which the diversity of analogous things comes about. These causes are of two kinds: extrinsic and intrinsic; and at once we have a primary division of analogy; for if the diversity comes about by extrinsic causes, then the analogous notion will come to all but one of the analogates from without, i.e. from the one in which it is found intrinsically; while if the diversity comes about by means of intrinsic causes, it will be found intrinsically, though in its own way, in all the analogates.

The first member of this division is named by Thomists 'analogy of attribution,' the second, 'analogy of proportionality.'

Thus: (*a*) Those things are said to be analogous with *analogy of attribution* whose name is common, and the notion signified by the name is in one only intrinsically and formally, in the others extrinsically, by means of some denomination derived from the first or directed towards it, the meaning in each case being, simply speaking, different.

This kind of analogy is subdivided with respect to the four causes which are responsible for the attribution.[1]

[1] Cf. Cajetan, *De Nominum Analogia*, cap. 2; S. Thomas, 4 *Met.*, Lect. 1; 7 *Met.*, Lect. 4; *De Veritate*, Q. 3, a. 2; I *Sent.*, Dist. XIX, 5, 2, ad 1; 1 *Ethic*, Lect. 7.

(*b*) Turning to the second member of our division we see that those things are said to be analogous with *analogy of proportionality* whose name is common, and the notion signified by the name is found in all of them intrinsically, and is simply different, but *secundum quid*, i.e. proportionally, the same in them all. Now this intrinsic meaning can be found in the analogates, either virtually or formally. In the first case we have metaphorical analogy of proportionality, in the second proper analogy of proportionality. These two subdivisions are again divided according to the finitude or infinity of the intrinsic diversity, but enough has now been said for the purposes of our sketch of analogy and its application to metaphysics.

To make these kinds of analogy clear it is worth while to give one or two examples of each of them.

The reader will, no doubt, have grasped that all universal natures are univocal, so Peter, Paul, James, etc., are all man in a sense which is, simply speaking, the same. We have given one example of equivocal things in ' vice.' Another is ' cat ' applied to the animal, the instrument of torture, a part of the tackle of a ship, and so on.

An example of analogy of attribution which is always quoted is that of health: for air, colour, food, exercise, etc., are said to be healthy, inasmuch as they are a sign of, or a cause of, health in man. It is the man who is healthy intrinsically and formally; these others are called healthy owing to their relations to him; but they are not healthy in themselves.

An example of metaphorical analogy of proportionality is: The lion is the king of beasts,' i.e. the lion is to beasts as a king is to his subjects.

An example of proper analogy of proportionality is: the life-principle in man is to his vital operations as the life-principle in plants or animals to theirs.

Now it is clear that those things which are analogous with analogy of attribution and those which are metaphorically analogous cannot have a concept which is a unity, for the unity or ' sameness ' of such things does not consist in anything which is intrinsic in them all, but consists in their extrinsic relation to something else. On the contrary, things which are analogous with proper analogy of proportionality can have a concept which is a unity, even if an imperfect one. The reason for saying they can have one concept is that the analogous notion is found in each of the analogates intrinsically and properly, though in a different way in each. This difference cannot, however, be absolute, otherwise the things would not be analogous, but simply equivocal; and consequently the analogous notion has a certain unity. Such unity is evidently imperfect, for perfect unity implies that the concept which possesses it is purely potential with regard to all the things which share this concept or nature. So animal is not actually either man or horse, etc., but is capable of being either. It becomes actually one or the other by the addition of an actual specific difference. For this reason men, horses, sheep, dogs, etc., all share the nature of animal in exactly the same way. The differences of its inferiors are thus purely potential in the unified nature of animal. This is the unity of the univocal thing, and it is only on condition that the common notion does not contain any differences actually that it will be perfectly one, in which case it will be univocal. Now we have agreed that the unity of an analogous notion cannot be the same as that of an univocal one, for if it were, analogy would be swallowed up in univocacy. It therefore follows that the analogous notion must contain the diversity found in the analogates actually, and so be imperfectly one.

We have now to apply this general doctrine of analogy to the concept of being; and we ask whether this concept is univocal, equivocal, or analogous with regard to the various beings in which it is found.

This is, as we have said, only another way of putting the question already asked: whether being is one or many. Now, in the light of what has been said with regard to analogy, we can treat it with more precision. It is plainly of vital importance, since if we say that being is univocal it appears that there can be no essential plurality of beings, which is Monism. If, on the contrary, we conclude that being is purely equivocal, beings will agree only in name, but there will be no nature common to two or more, so that we shall have knowledge only of the singular ; whereas, as we saw earlier, it is essential for science, or certain knowledge, that we should have knowledge of universals, since these alone are fixed and necessary.[1] Thus we should be committed to a thorough-going Agnosticism.

The Scholastic controversy on this question is a celebrated one as between the school of S. Thomas and that of Scotus. Verbally the views of the two schools are directly contradictory, but whatever may be thought about the opinions of some Scotists as compared with the view of S. Thomas, it is by no means clear that Scotus's own assertion that being is univocal with respect to the ten categories, and to God and creatures, is really in contradiction with the view of S. Thomas that it is not. This may seem rash to suggest after centuries of heated controversy, but the question is whether the being of which Scotus asserts and S. Thomas denies that it is univocal are really the same 'being.' Both agree that being is not a genus, and this admission on Scotus's part would make his assertion that it is univocal unintelligible if he attaches the same meaning to 'being' that S. Thomas does. In fact, it seems that the 'being' which Scotus is speaking of is not that being in general arrived at by abstracting the essence of sensible things, which, according to S. Thomas, is the proper object of the human intellect, but merely the very act of *existing* apart from any further determination. Existence thus considered entirely in itself, is, no doubt, all one and undifferentiated ; and the divergence between Scotus and Aquinas lies not in their doctrine of being, but in their conceptions of the human mind, the first regarding it as a pure intelligence like that of the Angels, the latter holding that it is essentially united with matter.[2]

Now all our examination of the nature of man and of his intellect has confirmed the Thomist view—which is also that of common sense—that the human soul is the immediate

[1] Cf. *Summa Theologica*, I, 13, 5 ; *C.G.*, I, 33 ; *de Potentia*, VII, 7.

[2] *Vide* E. Gilson, *L'Esprit de la Philosophie Médiévale* (Paris, Vrin, 1932) (Gifford Lectures), Deuxième Série, pp. 59 ff.

form of the body, and that it is the whole man who thinks and understands. If this be true we are bound to accept also S. Thomas's doctrine as to its proper formal object, and his view of the nature of being in general as known by us. If we do so, his assertion that being is not univocal presents no difficulty. As John of S. Thomas points out,[1] being is predicated of, and included in, the differences which determine it, if we consider the different kinds of being one by one; or else being includes these differences, if we consider the whole range of being, being as a whole. The truth of the first part of this statement is plain, for if being is predicated of the differences, even with respect to their formal difference, as, in fact, it is—for that by which, e.g. substance, differs from accident is something, is being—it must be included in them. The second part follows from this, for if being is included in the differences, the whole of being will include these differences. Since the differences of being are being, they must be communicated by being, which must, therefore, include these differences, otherwise it could not communicate them.

Again, since it is clear that being is not a genus—for it cannot be differentiated by differences extrinsic to itself, if it were, such differences would be not-being, or nothing—it follows that it cannot be univocal, univocacy being a property of genera and species. Genera and species alone (*a*) agree with their inferiors intrinsically and essentially, the nature expressed by the generic or specific essence being a part of their nature; (*b*) are predicated of all their inferiors in precisely the same way; and (*c*) are perfectly abstracted from, and separated from, their inferiors. These three conditions are also the conditions of univocacy, so that if being were univocal it would be a genus.

Neither is being equivocal, for, as we saw, its concept is truly one and so cannot be equivocal; equivocal concepts not being one but many.

Consequently being must be analogous, this being the only remaining way in which a superior concept can be related to its inferiors. What sort of analogy is it which being

[1] John of S. Thomas, *Logica*, Part II, Q. 14, a. 2; cf. Cajetan, *Enarratio in De Ente et Essentia*, Q. III.

possesses with respect to its inferiors? The Thomists answer that formally it is proper analogy of proportionality, and virtually analogy of attribution. The reason for the first part of this answer is derived from what we saw earlier as to the unity of being. This unity consists in the unity of the relation of the nature of each and every being to its existence. There is always a proportion between the nature of a being and its existence. This evidently obliges us to conclude that if the unity of being consists in a proportion, its analogy must be that of proportionality; for, as we saw, it is the definition of this kind of analogy that the notions signified by the analogical name should be the same according to some proportion.

It cannot, formally speaking, be analogy of attribution, since in this kind of analogy the analogous notion is found intrinsically in one only of the analogates, which is not the case here, since all the inferiors of being are being. Virtually, however, it may be said to be so, inasmuch as this notion of being is found in a higher degree in substance than in accidents, in God than in creatures, so that accidents are dependent on substance for their existence, and creatures on God both for essence and existence.

CHAPTER III

THE PROPERTIES OF BEING

The Transcendental Properties—Their Number—Unity—Truth—Goodness.

HAVING discussed being in itself, we pass, by a natural transition, to a review of its properties. Being in general is, as we remarked, transcendent, i.e. outside of, or transcending the categories ; it is not enclosed in, or confined to, any of them. Its properties, therefore, will also be transcendent in the same sense, and apply to all the categories.

The name *transcendental property* is, however, not applied by the Scholastics to all the properties of being, but is restricted to those which immediately follow on the concept of being as such. S. Thomas enumerates six transcendentals which are predicates of universal application. They are *ens, res, aliquid, unum, verum, bonum.* Of these it is plain that '*ens*' cannot be a transcendental property, since it would then be a property of itself. *Res* is the same as *ens nomen*—' being ' taken as a noun—and so it too is excluded from being a property ; and the transcendental properties will be the last four.

Besides these strictly transcendental properties of being, it has other properties which belong only to certain classes of being. These are called its *general properties* and are such as necessity, contingence, finiteness, etc.

It is worth noticing the reason for saying that *res* or ' thing ' is the same as being taken as a noun. The word ' thing ' is wholly affirmative, and so cannot express distinction from being, or a mode of being, properly so-called, since all addition is by way of difference, i.e. negation or subtraction. Hence it is synonymous with being.[1] The other

[1] Cf. S. Thomas, *De Veritate,* Q. 1, a. 1.

four transcendentals express by means of a negation (so introducing a determination) something which is not explicitly expressed by the word 'being.' For being is negatively opposed, in itself, to not-being, and this negation and division of being and not-being is expressed by the word *aliquid* ('*quasi aliud quid*,' as S. Thomas says), or 'other.' Now if, having thus acquired the idea of division in connection with being, we again proceed to negate division of it, we shall say that being is undivided, i.e. is one. So we have the idea of unity whose two parents are the idea of being and the idea of division. As S. Thomas says: '*primo in intellectu nostro cadit ens, et deinde divisio; et post hoc unum quod divisionem privat.*'[1]

These two, then, otherness and unity, are the explicit expression of properties which being carries in its own bosom, as its own determinations. But there may be other determinations which accrue to each and every being through its relation with something, if, indeed, there is anything to which all being can be relative. That there is such a thing we have already heard, for 'the soul is in a certain fashion all things'; and consequently being, all being, is related to an intellectual nature, which we regard from two sides as intellect and will. Being, then, which is in agreement with intellect is called *True*; being which is in accord with will is called *Good*.

So in being itself we have the determination of its opposition to not-being—which is expressed fully in the principle of non-contradiction—and the determination of its own unity; while the light which comes to it, as it were from without, enables us to see it shining as the true and the good.

Let us glance at these properties one by one. With regard to 'otherness'—*aliquid*—we need only note that as a transcendental property it must be taken in the sense just explained, viz. as the opposition between being and not-being, which we know immediately we know being. It

[1] X *Met.*, Lect. IV, No. 1998 (ed. Cathala). It is interesting to compare this with the Hegelian Dialectic. Which of the two, Hegel or Thomas, more truly represents the genuine working of the intellect?

might be mistakenly understood as expressing the opposition between one being and another ; this is not a transcendental property, for it does not follow immediately on the notion of being.

Unity is not itself one, but of many kinds. It is impossible to enumerate them all here,[1] but two must be mentioned : transcendental, and material or numerical unity.

It is transcendental unity only with which we are concerned in Metaphysics, and this is the negation of division of being as such. Material unity, on the contrary, is that which belongs, and can belong, only to one particular class of beings, viz. material ones, for it is that which belongs to a being which is undivided with regard to its matter ; and so is an individual. Beings such as these are necessarily quantitative, whereas transcendental unity is a property of all being, whether quantitative or not.

It should be clear from the deduction of unity from being that these two are in fact the same, and that being is identified in reality with all its transcendental properties. They merely make explicit what is implicit in the notion of being. If further reason be needed, here is one given by S. Thomas :[2] Every being is either simple or composite. But simple being is undivided, both potentially and actually, while composite being does not exist so long as its parts are divided, but only after they have come together to constitute the

[1] The principle divisions are shown in the following scheme :

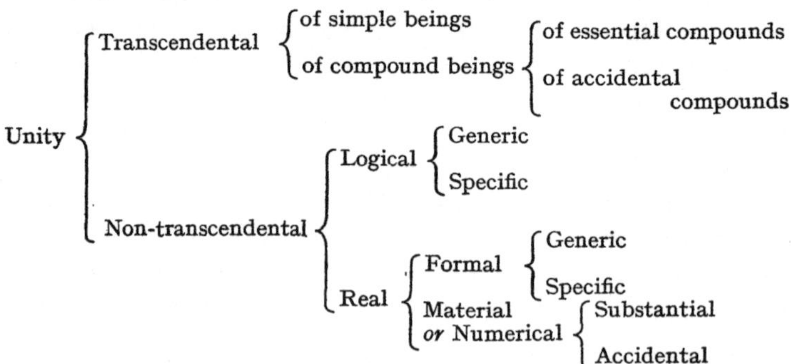

[2] *Summa Theologica*, I, xi, i. In the answer to the first objection he gives another reason

compound. Therefore, every actual being is undivided, or is a unity. This conclusion can also be expressed by saying that it is impossible that two actual beings should form a unity simply speaking. The reason why Scotus dissents from this statement is because, as we saw, he takes a fundamentally different view of the nature of the human intellect to that taken by S. Thomas. To judge which of them is right we must view the Scotist and Thomist systems as wholes—for both are organic and self-consistent syntheses—not wrangle about particular propositions. Fortunately, it is not our business in this summary to decide that the suit cut by S. Thomas fits the universe perfectly while that for which Scotus is responsible does not fit it at all, nor even to show which is the better fit, but merely that the Thomist garment fits well. When the decision between these two masters is taken, however, the final result of their thought must be examined from every angle. It would be ludicrous to suppose that either had botched his work completely; one may have achieved a great measure of success, without the other having completely, or even seriously, failed. We repeat here what was said at the very start,[1] because in the disputed questions with which we shall shortly have to deal, it is essential, in order that the true value of S. Thomas's ideas may be appreciated, that they should be considered in themselves to see whether they are true or not, and that judgement should not be clouded by the supposition that if they are held to be true other views must be worthless or absurd. Those who follow the leadership of S. Thomas do so because they are convinced that he had a clearer vision of the nature of reality, and penetrated into it more deeply than others; from which it by no means follows that the authors of other philosophical systems were blind.

This digression on the value of different systems of philosophy is, of course, concerned with their truth. Some have less negative disagreement with reality than others—approach more nearly to adequacy—while some, no doubt, are in positive disagreement with it, and so are false.[2] Such truth

[1] Cf. Introduction to Vol. I, pp. vii and viii.
[2] Cf. Vol. II, Part I, Chap. XII, pp. 117 f., 120.

as this is, as we saw, known as 'logical truth'; but the truth which is a transcendental property of being is of a different kind. It is called Ontological Truth.

Ontological Truth, then, consists in the possession by the thing of all those characteristics which belong to its essence, so that it is not other than it appears to be to the mind. This being so, nothing can be formally untrue, or false, with respect to the Divine mind; nor even essentially false with respect to the human mind, but only accidentally, in so far as the mind is deceived with regard to the 'true' nature of the thing.

Moreover, it also follows that truth adds nothing to entity except a relation to the mind; in other words, being and the true are *really* the same, and only *logically* distinct. For a thing is true by being what it is, and it is what it is by its entity, so that a thing is true by its entity; its entity is its truth. How a nonentity, a 'nothing,' can be related to the intellect—or to anything—is unknowable; only in so far as a thing is, can it be related to, and be in agreement with, the intellect; only in so far as a thing is, can it be true. On this conception of ontological truth hangs, as Fr. Sertillanges has shown,[1] all the Thomistic doctrine of exemplary ideas in the Divine mind. If the natures of things depend on the Divine mind, so also does their truth, since truth and being are the same, and thus things are true as copies of their patterns in the Divine mind, i.e. of the exemplary ideas.[2] To develop this subject would, however, take us too far afield, and we must pass on to the last of the transcendental properties of being.

Goodness.

In the first sentence of the Ethics, Aristotle approves the description of the good as 'that at which all things aim.'[3] So the good is anything, i.e. being, in so far as it is consonant with desire. Thus a thing is good in so far as it is desirable; and it is desirable in so far as it is perfect; and it is perfect in so far as it is in act; and it is in act in so far as it is being. A thing, then, is good in so far as it is being, or being and the

[1] A. D. Sertillanges, *St. Thomas d'Aquin*, Tome I, Chap. 2 B.
[2] Cf. *Summa Theologica*, I, 16, 1. [3] 1094, a. 2.

good are the same in reality, but differ in so far as being, when related to the will, and drawing it towards itself, is called the good. Notice that if we say, as we must, that truth resides in the intellect, we must also say that goodness resides in things. The directions of the motions of intellect and will are opposite. The goodness of things draws our will towards them, the intellect draws from the things their truth. The action, then, of goodness is the action of an 'end,' of a final cause, and so the divisions of the good are derived from the different ways in which being terminates the motion of the appetite, whether as a desirable means, which is useful for gaining some further end, and hence called '*bonum utile*'; or as that which finally and wholly terminates this motion, which is '*bonum honestum*'; or as the undisturbed possession of that which is ultimately desired, i.e. '*bonum delectabile*.'[1]

Treatises could be written on each of these properties, as well as on the Beautiful, which is a form of the good; but our space allows us only to set down these few hints as to their character; and we must pass on to consider the constituents of being itself.

[1] *Summa Theologica*, I, 5, 6.

CHAPTER IV

POTENCY AND ACT

Meaning of the word Potency—Division of Potency—The Reality of Subjective Potency—Opinions—Its Reality Established—The Nature of Act—The Relation of Potency to Act—The Limitation of Act—S. Thomas's View Explained—Applications of His Principle—An Objection Considered.

THE word potency is derived from the verb '*posse*': to be able, to have power. Indeed, we might use the word 'power' instead of potency, if this had not acquired a certain sense in English which is not quite that of the technical term potentiality.

Among beings we conceive of some that can exist, although in fact they do not do so; while some already exist. Those which can exist, though they do not, are said to be, to exist, in 'potentiality'; those which already exist are, in act. A baby can be a philosopher, though he is not one yet, and is therefore a philosopher in potency; but when he shall have acquired philosophic science he will be a philosopher in act. Neither potency nor act can be defined, in the proper sense of the word; for the understanding of potency is derived from that of act, which is itself simple, and therefore not composed of genus and difference. In general, potency is understood to mean the principle of, or aptitude for, receiving or doing anything; or, more precisely, the principle of action or passion.

Such a principle may be either logical or real—*logical or objective potency* being a logical capacity for receiving existence; so that that which is in logical potency *could* exist, absolutely speaking, since no contradiction would be involved in its doing so. It is called objective, because it does not belong to the thing itself, as it is a reality, but only as it is an object of the mind, and the object of some real potency which could cause the possibility to become actual. It has no real subject, it is mere *possibility*.

Real, or subjective potency, on the contrary, is a real capacity existing in a real subject. It is essential to bear in mind this distinction between objective and subjective potency. They are opposed in every way except that what is subjectively potential is also possible, though the converse is false. Note the exquisite accuracy, from a Realist point of view, of this scholastic terminology. In ordinary speech we should invert the words subjective and objective, calling 'subjective' what is merely in us, and what we observe, 'objective.' This way of speaking comes from a confused subjectivism.

Now this real potency may be either active or passive, according as it is a capacity for action, or for receiving act.

Though these are alike in being real capacities in a real subject, they differ inasmuch as passive potency is imperfect —since a thing cannot receive anything unless it is in some way imperfect; while active potency is a perfection, for act is derived from it, and so must in some way be contained in it. It is therefore a kind of act, which passive potency, *qua* passive, in no sense is.[1]

From this the general meaning of the word 'act' will be plain. It is a completion, a filling-up, a perfection, as contrasted with potency, which is some incompleteness, something unfulfilled, an imperfection.

Aristotle calls potencies 'starting-points'; the primary kind of 'starting-point' being active potency. This last is very clearly a reality, since if there were no power of action, there could never be any action. But this reality of active potency implies the reality of passive, for no action could be effected, if there were nothing capable of being affected by it.[2]

This doctrine seems to have originated with the Academy, for we find a suggestion of it in Plato,[3] but it was Aristotle who recognised its fundamental importance. He made

[1] Cf. *Summa Theologica*, I, 25, 1. c. et ad 1.

[2] Aristotle, *Met.*, 1046, a. 8–15. [3] Theætetus, 197 c.

various applications of it, particularly with regard to matter and form. S. Thomas showed that there is still a wider application than can be made, when he applied it to essence and existence. It has, however, met with constant opposition, especially—among Scholastics—from Scotus and Suarez.[1]

The contention of its opponents is that it is impossible to conceive of a mere and sheer potentiality, which is in no way actual, being a reality; or that a mere capacity is a mere vacuum, that is, a mere nothing. It is essential for us to show that this is a misunderstanding if we are to justify the Thomist philosophy, since this doctrine of the reality of passive potency is its very foundation. We must, therefore, enquire why it is necessary to admit it, and how such potency is distinguished, on the one side from privation and from simple possibility; and on the other, from imperfect act.

The reality of passive potency was denied by the Eleatics, who, with Parmenides, basing their contention on the principle of contradiction, argued that change and multiplicity are impossible. For they said: From being no being can come to be, since it already is; and from nothing, nothing can come, therefore change is impossible. Secondly, being cannot be limited, diversified and multiplied by itself, nor yet by anything else, for what is not being is nothing. Hence being is one, undivided and unique. The same opinion is found in modern times in the philosophy of Spinoza, according to whom there is only one substance.[2] For Aristotle, on the contrary, potency is a reality distinct from act, and these two terms are correlatives. In the first place, then, reality is not all actual, as Parmenides thought, and in the second, it is impossible to deny actuality, or the applicability of the principle of identity to reality, without, at the same time, destroying the correlative notion of potentiality. This denial of actuality is made by Bergson, who, like Heracleitus, identifies being with motion, and says that the only reality is creative evolution.

On the one hand, therefore, Aristotle is concerned to

[1] Cf. L. Rougier, *La Scolastique et le Thomisme* (Paris-Gauthier-Villars), pp. 605, 662.

[2] *Ethica*, Prop. XIV.

explain the reality of motion, and, on the other, to justify the principle of identity as the law of reality.

Only the Absolute Idealist would, to-day, deny the reality of multiplicity; and we have seen, in Epistemology, that this position is untenable. Even he would not dispute the reality of motion and change, for he regards the Absolute as evolving. We can, therefore, take the reality of this last as our starting-point. But if it be indeed a reality, it is inexplicable, unless we admit also the reality of passive potency. For if we do not we shall have to say that only what is actual is real, so that all being will be of the same kind, namely, actual being. If this be so, the principle of identity demands that being—that which is—be already, and so cannot come to be, while not-being is not, so that this, too, cannot come to be. Plainly then becoming and change are, in this hypothesis, altogether impossible.

To escape from the difficulty, without admitting the reality of passive potency, a man might, perhaps, suggest that the principle of identity is only a law of thought and does not apply to trans-subjective reality. Such an attempt to escape would, however, only involve us in greater disasters, for if we deny the applicability of the principle of identity to reality we must affirm that reality is in fact contradictory, and so unintelligible, since it is admitted that we can only think and know in accordance with the principle of identity. What is not in accord with it will therefore be unintelligible.

If, however, we admit the reality of potency we are at once delivered from this impasse, for it allows us to explain change without the sacrifice of the principle of identity. We shall now be able to distinguish between potency and act, and shall say that though it is true that from being in act being cannot come, since it is already being, yet it is not true that from being in potency being in act cannot come, for this potency is neither nothing—it is a reality—nor yet is it complete and perfect being, since, as potency, it is opposed to, and differs from, act, which makes being complete as being. If we take an example of a change brought about artificially by man we can see how this applies. A house cannot come to be from a house, but it can come to be from bricks and mortar, since these are a mutable and determinable subject, and so are a house in potency. This mutable and determinable subject, this potency, is clearly not the same as nothing, for from nothing nothing comes. Nor yet is it merely not-being, i.e. the negation or privation of the form of the thing which is to come to be, e.g. the privation of the form of house. Such a negation is of itself nothing; and moreover the same negation is found in all sorts of other subjects which cannot become a house, such as air, water, or fire. Nor is it merely the nature of the materials from which the house is to be built, since this makes them what they actually are already; nor even their actual shape, size, etc., since this, too, makes them what they are already actually, and in so far as it does so, prevents them from being mutable and determinable. Lastly, this determinable subject is not imperfect act—in our example the partly-built house—since this is not simply determinable, but is the house in process of building, i.e. a movement towards the completed and actual house.

Consequently the determinable subject must be a real capacity for receiving the complete act, a real capacity in the bricks and mortar for receiving the form of a house, such a capacity not being found in other subjects, such as air or water. This is called a real potency for being a house, or a house in potentiality.

Such potentiality is not mere possibility. This would be sufficient for creation where no real subject is required, or indeed possible; but not for change, which presupposes a mutable and determinable *real* subject.

So unless we allow the reality of potency we cannot explain change, and if we do allow it we can see that change involves no contradiction, as Parmenides thought it did, even though there always remains what may be called a 'philosophic mystery.' Our 'explanation' rids change of its absolute unintelligibility, which is contradiction, but it does not make all things plain and clear in this dim twilight world which is the region between being and nothing, the region of becoming.

Turning now to consider act, we recall, what we have already said, that it is that which completes, determines and perfects a thing in any way: it is *perfection* of some kind. It may be that which perfects it as a nature, making it of a determinate kind; this is act in the order of essence. Again, it may be that perfection and completion which makes it an existing thing in the real world; this is act in the order of existence.[1] Lastly, it may be that which perfects the existing thing accidentally, and this is act in the order of accident.

Evidently act is the correlative of potency: it is that which completes and determines its capacity; and so Aristotle describes it as 'the existence of a thing, not in the way which we express by "potentially."'[2]

Though we conceive act in relation to potency, nevertheless it need not in itself, being perfection, involve any imperfection or potentiality; and act which is perfection undiluted by potency—inasmuch as it is neither received in any, nor is itself in potency to any further act—is called by the Scholastics Pure Act. It is absolute perfection, all other act being relative perfection. Such relative perfection may be either formal or entitative act. The first is that perfection by which a thing is determined in its own species, and the second that by which a thing ceases to be a mere possibility, and becomes some existing reality. Having touched on those elements in the notions of potency and act which are most necessary in order that some idea may be gained of the Thomist doctrine on this matter, we must now turn to the consideration of certain aspects of the relation of these two components of mutable being.

The first of these concerns the passage from potency to act, and is stated in some such form as: nothing can be brought from potentiality to actuality except by some being which is in act.

As Dr. Coffey says:[3] 'This assertion, rightly understood,

[1] With the question whether this act is really distinct from that in the order of essence we are not at present concerned. It is plain we can dintinguish them logically, i.e. in our thoughts.

[2] *Met.*, 1048, a. 30.

[3] P. Coffey, *Ontology* (Longmans, 1914), p. 64.

is self-evidently true,' for being in act is one which possesses a perfection, while the correlative potential being is one which lacks this perfection, and so cannot bestow this perfection on itself. This must necessarily be done by something which possesses the perfection in question, that is to say, by being in act.

Another form in which this axiom is often put is: 'Everything which is in motion is moved by another,' where motion is taken in its widest sense to signify the passage from potency to act. That which is moved must be lacking in some act, which it can therefore only receive from some other which has it.

We have seen that the unity of a thing is the same as its entity and it follows that the increase of unity will correspond to the increase of being, and cease when the entity is broken up. Now a being is a being by reason of its existence,[1] and this is its last actuality and perfection. If there were nothing in it but existence, it would be in the highest degree a unity. So, then, if we suppose that we have two beings in act, having each its own entity and perfection, it is plain that the entity and the act of the one cannot be also that of the other, so that they cannot be one single entity. Here we meet again our familiar axiom that from two beings in act cannot be formed a being which is a unity simply speaking. It is an inevitable consequence of the admission of the reality of the purely potential, an admission which is forced upon us if we 'take change seriously.' For the only thing that can complete potency and make a unified entity, is the correlative act—'*potentia est ad actum*'—and so two beings in act being already complete as beings, and actual as beings, cannot also be incomplete and potential. They are incapable of forming one actual being. It was not lack of perspicacity that caused the great Scholastics who were not of the Thomist school to reject this conclusion, but their unwillingness, for various reasons, to accept the reality of pure potentiality. S. Thomas's firm belief in this fundamental conception, and so his whole philosophy, is justified, if it is justified at all, when it is seen how the manifold applications

[1] Cf. Chap. I, p. 159.

which he makes of it enable us to take a coherent and unified view of all reality. No formal proof could be so strong as such a consistent capacity for giving us an intelligible account of all the phases of matter, life and being. It succeeds by success.[1]

It was, it seems, such a spirit of calm confidence in the universal applicability of his fundamental conceptions that caused S. Thomas to set down without comment one of the most hotly contested propositions of his philosophy: act can only be limited on condition of being received in a subjective potency. '*Nullus actus invenitur finiri nisi per potentiam quæ est ejus receptiva.*'[2] This proposition contains as a special case, as we shall shortly see, his famous doctrine of the real distinction between essence and existence; and on account of its fundamental character we must examine it carefully. From a metaphysical point of view it is the initial point of divergence of the Scotist and Suarezian philosophies from that of S. Thomas. The proposition can be precisely stated by saying: while potency contains in itself the reason of its limitation, act can only be limited by being received in a related potency.

S. Thomas never gave a formal demonstration of this principle, but rather, by giving examples of its application, and by using it constantly to elucidate various problems, allowed it to manifest its own truth by its own clarity and applicability.[3] Indeed, formal demonstration, strictly speaking, is impossible: if we mean a direct illation from premisses to conclusion, since the proposition is not a conclusion, but one which is *per se nota* when the terms act and potency have been understood and the reality of subjective potency conceded. The explanation may be put forward under the form of an explanatory argument; and this will be, at the same time, an indirect demonstration.

Act, then, being perfection, is of itself unlimited in its own

[1] Cf. A. D. Sertillanges, *S. Thomas d'Aquin*, Tome I, p. 74.

[2] *Compendium Theologiæ*, c. 18.

[3] So, e.g. in I *C.G.*, 43; *S.T.*, I, 7, 1; I, 44, 1; I, 50, 2 ad 4; II *C.G.*, 15; I *Sent.*, d. 8, 1, 1; I *Sent.*, d. 43, 1, 1; *De Ente et Essentia*, cc. 5 and 6; *Comp. Theol.*, cc. 15, 18; *De Potentia*, I, 2, o; *De Substantiis Separatis*, arts. 1, 8; *De Spiritualibus Creaturis*, a. 1 et ad 1, ad 2; *ibid.*, a. 8; *Quodlibet*, IX, a. 6, ad 3 et ad 4.

order, as is clear in such examples as those of existence or wisdom. For existence in itself is not limited, it is not this or that existence; wisdom is not this or that wisdom—the wisdom of the statesman, the scientist, the philosopher, or even of the Saints—of itself it is none of these. The same applies to all perfection, to all act as such; and so if act is to be limited at all, such limitation must come from something which is not itself, and which is capable of limiting it. What can this be but something which contains a limitation in itself and so is capable of putting an intrinsic limit into act? Such a limit cannot be act, for act is of itself perfection, and therefore not a limit. Neither can it be nothingness, for 'nothing' is not a limit; what is 'limited' by nothing is not limited. So there is no escape from the conclusion that this limit is subjective potency, which, being capacity for perfection, contains within itself a limitation and imperfection.

The suggestion of Suarez[1] that in order that an act may be limited it is sufficient that there should be some extrinsic principle of limitation, and that an intrinsic principle is not required, is unacceptable. For if the extrinsic agent produces a limit which it puts into the act, this limit must, as we have seen, be subjective potency; while if it does not produce such a limit, or put any limit in the act, the act will remain unlimited intrinsically, or in itself. Moreover, the agent can only cause that which is capable of being caused. Consider, then, any actual being. Such a being will have an actual existence, and this, if not intrinsically limited, will be in itself unlimited or infinite. Being, then, infinite existence, it will be necessary, for if it were contingent it would contain a capacity for not-being, which would be an imperfection or limit in it. It is, then, necessary existence, and so cannot not exist, and therefore exists of itself or is uncaused. Consequently, any being whose existence is not intrinsically limited, exists necessarily, and is therefore incapable of being caused. If it exists, such existence must be due to itself, and not to any cause, since it is, of its very nature, existence.

[1] *Met. Disp.*, XXXI, Sect. 13 *versus finem.*

We may, and in fact do, acknowledge that in order that act may be limited, there must be an extrinsic principle of limitation which produces the intrinsic principle which limits the act in itself ; but we are bound to insist that both these principles are required in so far as God Himself cannot produce a limited act without limiting it, that is, without putting an intrinsic limitation to the perfection which constitutes the act.

Some examples of the application of this principle of limitation may help to a clear understanding of it. If we consider the nature of any individual, say of *this* stone, *this* dog, *this* man, we have an act of essence limited to an individual of a species, and so limited within the species. According to our principle this can only be done by the specific principle being received in a potency which is limited in itself, and here the potency is the matter of stone, dog or man. If now we consider not merely the nature of something, but something which actually exists ; the act to be considered in this case will be that of existence, and again, according to our principle, this act must be limited, if at all, by being received in a correlative potency. Plainly this potency, in which existence is received, will be the nature of the individual existing thing, for what exists is an individual which is either a particular example of some specific nature, or an individual which *is* a specific nature. So the nature must itself be potential with regard to the existence. But, it may be said : if this nature is itself an act, how can it be also a potency ? Evidently only by not being completely actual. In the case of an individual thing it is easy to see how this comes about, for that which makes it individual (which the Thomists say is matter) is itself a limitation, a potency, which is joined to the act of essence or nature (the form). If the nature, however, is not a particular one, but the whole of some specific nature, the same principle holds good ; for though, in this case, we shall not have the specific nature received in any potency or matter (for this would make it individual), we shall still have a potency in the nature itself in so far as this is specific, not generic. Though genus and difference are not really distinct, but logically only, yet they presuppose a real distinction in any real being to which they apply.[1] Any specific existent must contain within itself two realities, one corresponding to the generic nature of which it is a species, and the other to the difference which divides it from other species of that genus and so limits it, or puts a potentiality into it. Such an existent is not simply actual, but a limited actuality, a combination of potency and act ; and so when its nature is considered with relation to the act of existence, it is potential with regard to it, and therefore capable of limiting it. If this be understood it will be seen that it meets what is perhaps one of the most serious objections to our principle : namely that in immaterial beings the act of essence, not being received in any matter, will, though limited, not be limited by subjective potency. The answer is that it is itself subjective potency with regard to existence, and so is limited in itself by being a real potentiality with respect to existence. If more limitation than this is required it cannot come from the nature itself, which is entirely actual in so far as it is this specific nature, but must come from some potency outside it (viz. matter), and this will delimit it to be an individual of this nature. The principle of the limitation of act by subjective potency is thus universally valid. It applies to the act of essence of the individual which is limited by the subjective potency of matter, to the act of essence of the immaterial thing which exhausts a specific nature ; for this being limited by the subjective potency which corresponds to the specific difference is itself potential ; and to the act of existence of any finite thing, since this is limited in every case by the subjective potency contained in the nature (whether individual or not) which exists.

The objection referred to above may also be expressed by saying : evidently the abstract notion of act does not contain any idea of limitation, but such an idea *is* found in an act taken in the concrete, which is limited essentially, and of itself ; unless it is, strictly speaking, infinite. True, the

[1] Cf. Capreolus, ed. Paban-Pègues, Vol. I, p. 308a ; *S. Thomas. Quodlibet*, IX, a. 6, ad 3 ; *De Ente et Essentia,* c. 6 (ed. de Maria, pp. 204, 205) and *Comm.*, Cajetani, *ibid.*

concrete is essentially limited, but because it is concrete, that is to say because it is received in a subject. So in this sense God is in no way concrete, nor yet is a subsisting form concrete. This last, consequently, as *a definite kind* of perfection, is unlimited or infinite. Thus the only concrete acts are those which are in a subject, and it is this reception in a subject which makes them both concrete and limited. The dispute is whether an act which is not received in a subject can be limited ; so that it is useless to try and support an affirmative answer to this question by talking of concrete acts, since no unreceived act is concrete.

(*Note.*—For the whole of this question the student should consult the lucid treatment of it by P. Geny, S.J., *Le Problème Métaphysique de la Limitation de l'Acte,* "Rev. de Philosophie," Paris, Rivière, 1919.

The opposing point of view is defended by P. Descoqs, S.J., *Essai Critique sur l'hylémorphisme,* Beauchesne, 1924, Chap. II, and more convincingly by N. Monaco, S.J., *Prælectiones Metaphysicæ Generalis,* Giachetti, 1913, Thesis XXXII ff. See also the further explanations given by Geny, *Gregorianum,* Vol. VI, March, 1925.)

CHAPTER V

ESSENCE AND EXISTENCE

Meaning of Essence—Meaning of Existence—Their Distinction—Opinions—What was S. Thomas's View?—His Proofs of It—A General Argument—A Difficulty Considered—Applications of the Doctrine: With Respect to Cognition, to Being, to Operation, and to God and Creatures.

THE question of the relation of essence to existence is one which has probably caused more controversy in the Schools than any other in the whole range of philosophy. The reason is that Thomists regard their view of this relation as integral with the conception of a transcendent God distinct from creatures, and so as 'the fundamental truth of Christian philosophy,' as Fr. Del Prado puts it; while those who reject the Thomist view are naturally anxious to show that the Christian conception of the universe is in no way dependent on that view.

Before we can form any opinion on the merits of S. Thomas's explanation of this matter we must first gain as precise an idea as possible of the meaning of these terms: essence and existence.

Essence.

Since essence is something which is common to all genera, it cannot be defined, properly speaking; but, according to the point of view from which it is considered, it is described in various ways.

So, considered in itself, it is that by which a thing is constituted in its own genus or species, and, therefore, that by which a thing is made, say, a *substantial* thing, or a *human* being. As it stands in relation to the intellect it is described as that which is first conceived of in a thing; for 'Being,' understood as a noun, is the nature to which existence attaches, and it is this which is known first of all by a mind which has any knowledge of a thing ; for it first knows it as thing, as being. If it be regarded from the point of view of what proceeds from it, it will be said to be the first principle [illegible] of properties and actions ; a description akin to [illegible] Boethius :[1] ‘Nature is either that which can [illegible]ch can be acted upon’ ; which, as he points [illegible] to substances. One of the other senses of [illegible] by him is also worth noting : ‘Nature [illegible]ence which gives form to anything.’[2] [illegible]hough somewhat narrower than, our [illegible]ce ; from which it will be gathered [illegible] it be not taken to cover the whole [illegible] substances alone, is equivalent to [illegible] both substances and accidents have [illegible]cidents possess it only incompletely, [illegible] is extraneous to them in themselves [illegible] their definition ; viz. the subject. [illegible]ition is incomplete, their essence will [illegible] as it were, legless ; and as S. Thomas [illegible] *[m]agis entis, quam ens.*’[3]

[illegible]

T[illegible] common to all genera, can only be descri[illegible] defined. Thus it is said to be the act by whic[illegible]laced outside the state of mere possibility ; o[illegible]h makes a thing to be outside its causes ; or [illegible]ctuality of a thing. We say ‘last actuality,’ for e[illegible] in itself is act, though considered in relation to existe[illegible]t is, as we have seen, potency ; thus humanity expresses a certain act or perfection, but it has not its full actuality until existence is added to it, and we have humanity existing, that is, man.

We are now to ask whether in finite things these two, essence and existence, are in reality the same, and differ only

[1] Boethius, *Contra Eutychen*, I, line 25. ‘*Natura est vel quod facere vel quod pati possit.*’

[2] *Ibid.*, line 57. ‘*Natura est unam quamque rem informans specifica differentia.*’

[3] Cf. e.g. *Summa Theologica*, I, 45, 4.

with regard to the notions which we form of them; or whether they differ in reality. Is the distinction between them a real distinction or only a logical one? By a real distinction is meant some difference which is found in reality; and which is not made, but only recognised by the mind. It is not 'mind-dependent'; whereas a logical distinction is that which obtains in a thing which in reality is one, but which is conceived of by the mind as multiple. So, as we saw, entity and unity are really the same, but we have distinct concepts of them. The waters of a river and the river itself might be *regarded* as differing, and yet in reality they are the same.

The difference which obtains in realities, and which is necessary for a real distinction, must on no account be taken to imply that the realities which so differ are necessarily complete entities. So there is a real distinction between a substance and its accidents, for example, between a man and the colour of his hair, between the soul and its faculties, and yet this colour and these faculties are incomplete entities. So distinction is not separability; nor does it imply it. Hence we see the falsity of such remarks as the following: 'To put forward a real distinction is to put forward a distinction between two things which possess their reality independently one of the other.'[1]

To make the matter in dispute as precise as possible it is well to see how far those who maintain and those who deny the real distinction agree. They all allow:

(1) That in God there is no real distinction of essence and existence.

(2) That in creatures ideal essence, or essence regarded in the abstract, (e.g. the nature of the dinosaur or even that of man in the abstract), is really distinct from existence.

(3) That there is *at least* a logical distinction between real essence and its existence.

The question, therefore, is: is real and actual essence in creatures really distinguished from existence? In other words, is real essence made to be outside its causes by its own power, or by virtue of some other superimposed act

[1] L. Rougier, *La Scholastique et le Thomisme*, Introd., p. xxix.

which is really distinct from it ? Is that act which makes it, not a mere possibility, but an actual existing reality, the same as that which makes it an actual nature ? Is Peter's essence the same reality as his existence ? We are evidently dealing with actually constituted existing realities, not with the realm of mere possibility, and asking whether in a thing, in which essence and existence are both really present, they are the same identical reality or not.

Not only is the answer to this question hotly contested, but there has been considerable dispute with respect to the opinions of great philosophers on this point. So some say[1] that Aristotle held the real distinction, for in the *Posterior Analytics* he says : Τὸ δὲ τί ἐστιν ἄνθρωπος καὶ τὸ εἶναι ἄνθρωπον ἄλλο—' that which a man is and being a man are different ' ;[2] a phrase which Cajetan interprets as being an express affirmation of the real distinction,[3] though in another place he says we have nothing clear on this subject in Aristotle.[4] The germ, at least, of the distinction is to be found among the Neo-Platonists, as for example, in the writings of Proclus.[5] Avicenna (980–1037) certainly makes the distinction, going so far as to say that existence is accidental to essence,[6] and it seems to be due to William of Auvergne (died 1249) that it was introduced into Latin theology. The real distinction was opposed by Averroes (1126–1198) and his school ; and so by the famous Averroist and contemporary of S. Thomas, Siger of Brabant. That S. Thomas held the real distinction, though he did not adopt Avicenna's way of explaining it, can now hardly be doubted. Not only does he express himself in the clearest possible fashion in his earliest writings, and consistently through the whole course of his life, as in favour of the distinction,[7] but, as

[1] E.g. F.-X. Maquart., *Revue Thomiste*, 1926, pp. 62 ff. A résumé of the dispute on the point is given by B. de Solages, ' Le Procès de la Scholastique ' (*Rev. Thom.*, 1927, p. 390) ; cf. also Roland-Gosselin, Le *De Ente et Essentia*, pp. 137 ff.

[2] 92b, 10.

[3] *Comment. in Post. Anal.*, c. 6.

[4] *Comment. in De Ente et Essentia*, c. 5, ed. de Maria, p. 154.

[5] Cf. Roland-Gosselin, op. cit., II, Chap. III.

[6] *Ibid.*, p. 156.

[7] Cf. Del Prado, *De Veritate Fundamentali Philosophiæ Christianæ* Fribourg, 1911), Cap. II.

Mgr. Grabmann has shown,[1] his contemporaries, and notably Siger, were in no doubt as to his opinion.

The aim and extent of our summary of Thomistic philosophy will not allow of any detailed discussion of the question whether the real distinction forms an integral part of S. Thomas's system ; but in affirming that it does we rely upon the consensus of opinion in the Thomist school from the thirteenth century to the present day ; on the testimony of both contemporary opponents and disciples of his doctrine, and on the words of S. Thomas himself. This ought, as Fr. Roland-Gosselin observes, henceforward to be sufficient to convince all that the real distinction is the authentic doctrine of S. Thomas.

If this be granted we are happily delivered from a controversial treatment of this question, since the only business of this summary is to give a simple explanation of Thomist doctrine ; not to criticise other philosophical opinions.

Essence and existence, then, are considered by S. Thomas to be distinct, though not separable, realities ; and essence stands to existence in the same relation as potency stands to act. His opinion differs from that of Avicenna in so far as he will not allow that existence is a predicamental accident of essence ; it is not added to it as accident is to substance,[2] though in a wide sense it may be said to be accidental inasmuch as it does not belong to the definition of substance.

It will be seen from this that S. Thomas's doctrine is an application of the principle that act can only be limited by subjective potency, which was discussed in the last chapter. There is, however, one argument which S. Thomas uses to show the truth of the real distinction which may be independent of that principle.

In the *De Ente et Essentia*[3] it is given in the following form :

[1] Cf. Grabmann, *Doctrina S. Thomæ de distinctione reali inter essentiam et esse ex documentis ineditis sæculi XIII illustrata. Acta Hebdomadæ Thomisticæ*, Rome, 1924, pp. 131 ff.

[2] *De Potentia*, Q. V, a. 4, ad 3um ; *Quodlibet*, XII, a. 5.

[3] *De Ente et Essentia*, cap. 5, ed. De Maria, p. 138. It is given again: I *Sent.*, Dist. VIII, Q. VI, a. 2 ; II *Sent.*, Dist. I, Q. I, a. 1 ; *ibid.*, Dist. III, Q. I, a. 1 ; *Quodlibet*, II, Q. II, a. 3 ; cf. *Totius Logicæ Summa*, tract. 2, q. 2. (This opusculum, though not a genuine work of S. Thomas, gives an authentic account of his doctrine.)

whatever does not belong to the conception or understanding of an essence, is extraneous to this essence, and forms a compound with it, for no essence can be understood without those things which are parts of the essence. If, then, an essence can be understood without this or that characteristic, such characteristic does not belong to the essence as such. If it is attributed to the essence, the attribution is extrinsic. Now every essence can be conceived or understood without anything being understood concerning its existence; for I can understand what a man or phœnix is, and, nevertheless, be ignorant whether it has existence *in rerum natura.* Therefore it is clear that existence is other than essence, unless perhaps there be some thing whose essence is its very existence. Such a thing will be one and first, since, being subsisting existence, and so nothing but existence, it cannot be differentiated by the addition of any form, otherwise it would not be existence only. Hence in anything other than this one first thing its existence must be distinct from its essence.

The point to note especially about this argument is that no part of an essence can be excluded from its concept if we are to avoid a misconception, and have a true concept of the essence. To say, for example, that it does not matter whether man is conceived of as animal or not, is to misconceive man's nature, so that the conception of animality must be included in that of man. Similarly if existence were really a part of essence or identified with it, it would be to misconceive essence to think it apart from existence. Since we do, and must so think it, it is plain that existence is not part of, or identified with, essence. S. Thomas is not suggesting that our notion of any essence explicitly includes all that is part of that essence—this would imply that we have adequate or exhaustive knowledge of such essence—but only that no part must be excluded from our concept.

An attempt has been made to identify this way of reasoning with that used in the 'Ontological Argument,' where the existence of God is proved from the consideration that the definition of God must contain the notion of existence. But it is plain that the conclusion there drawn is of quite a different kind to that of our argument, since there it is said that since the definition of God's essence includes existence, God must exist in reality, whereas here we say that since the definition of essence does not include existence, essence, if and when it exists in reality, cannot include existence. The attempt to involve S. Thomas in a contradiction—since he rejects the Ontological Argument—therefore fails ; and in fact his procedure when *refuting* the ontological argument includes the present reasoning, for he maintains that what that argument proves is that since the definition of God includes existence, it follows that if He exists, He must exist necessarily ; His existence will be, in fact, as it is allowed to be in theory, part of His nature, and so inseparable from it. Our argument does, however, imply a realist theory of knowledge, that is to say, that we can have *true,* though not adequate, knowledge of trans-subjective reality.

There are two other ways in which S. Thomas argues to the same conclusion, that essence and existence in creatures are really distinct. The first is drawn from considering what would be the nature of a being in which essence and existence were really the same, and the second from a consideration of created beings.

In the first way,[1] which has already been touched upon, S. Thomas proceeds on the basis that there is a real multiplicity among the things of which we have knowledge by means of the senses. And this is legitimate, for we are not here trying to refute Monism, but to give an explanation of the fact of multiplicity. Moreover, as we noticed earlier, this multiplicity can only be denied at the cost of denying the validity of our cognition.

Granted, then, that reality, as known to us, is multiple, S. Thomas argues that the existence of these many things cannot be really the same as their essence, since, if it were, they would not be multiple, but one and unique. For a being whose very essence is to exist cannot be differentiated in any other way, and so cannot be multiple. Such a being

[1] I *Sent.*, Dist. VIII, Q. V, a. 2 ; *De Ente et Essentia*, cap. 5 ; *In Boet. De Hebdom.* c. 2 II *C.G.*, 52 ; *Quodlibet*, VII, Q. 3, a. 7 ; IX, Q. 4, a. 6 ; *Summa Theol.*, I, 61, 1 ; *De Spiritualibus Creaturis*, a. 1 ; *Quodlibet*, III, Q. 8, a. 20 ; etc.

would be its own subsisting existence, for its existence is its actual substantial essence, its own substance. That it cannot be multiple is seen first from the fact that existence, being an act, can only be limited and multiplied by subjective potency. Now subsisting existence does not, by hypothesis, inhere in anything, and so cannot be received in any potency; nor can it have any potency in itself, i.e. any capacity for any other act, for this act could only be subsistence or existence, both of which it already possesses. Hence it cannot be multiplied, but must be unique. Secondly, subsisting existence is absolute perfection, since it is perfect both as a being and as a substance. Consequently it can be one only; for if there were two such absolute perfections one of them would have to possess some perfection which the other lacked, otherwise they would not be two, but one. That which lacks some perfection would plainly not be absolutely perfect, so that it is impossible that there should be two absolutely perfect beings.

The last way of arguing to the real distinction of essence and existence in creatures proceeds from the nature of creatures themselves.[1] Inasmuch as they are caused by another, they are given existence by another, and so cannot have it of themselves, of their own nature. For that whose essence is existence, exists of its very nature and so essentially and necessarily. This being so, it is impossible that it should not exist. Existing of itself it cannot receive existence from another, and so cannot be caused. Consequently in things which are in reality caused, existence must in reality be distinct from their actual essence. So, as S. Thomas says,[2] '*Hoc est contra rationem facti, quod essentia rei sit ipsum esse ejus, quia esse subsistens non est esse creatum.*'

A general argument which combines the last two is the following: If the existence of any being were not really distinguished from the essence of this being, such existence would be pure act, for it could neither be received in any potency nor contain any potency in itself; in the Scholastic phrase, it would be unreceived and unreceiving act. This

[1] Cf. I *Sent.*, Dist. VIII, Q. IV, a. 2; I *C.G.*, 22, 43; II *C.G.*, 52.
[2] *Summa Theologica*, I, 7, 2, ad 1.

existence could not be received in any potency, since being really the same as the essence, there would, in fact, be nothing in such a being except existence; and so nothing for existence to be received in. Nor could it receive any further act, and so be itself potential with regard to it; for it is plain that existence is the act which completes the thing as a real being, so that once the thing exists there is no further perfection which can be added to it *as a being*. The existence, then, of such a being, and so the whole being, since it *is* existence, would be pure act. A finite or created thing cannot, however, be pure act, since pure act containing no potency or imperfection, must be altogether perfect and unlimited or infinite, for potency alone limits act. So if we look at the question from the point of view of finite being we see that such a being cannot be pure act, from which it follows that its essence and existence must be really distinguished, since that being in which they are identified will be pure act.

The obvious objection to the Thomist view is that it is by existence and existence alone that a thing passes from being merely possible to being real, all its reality is due to existence, so that all the reality in an existing thing *is* existence. There is no distinct reality which is essence. But this difficulty is due to a confusion of thought, for the reality which existence confers on essence is certainly to make it really existing, so that the reality of really existing, in an existing thing, certainly is existence. It does not follow that all the reality in it is existence; there may, and in fact, must be some real subject of which existence is the act, otherwise what was and remained merely possible would exist and be real. Just as matter is a reality, though one which without form sinks into unreality, so essence is reality, though without existence it sinks to being merely possible. Matter is not real without form; but with it is not the same reality as form: essence is not real in the existential order without existence, and yet with it is not the same reality as existence. These two are indispensable, the one to the other; they are distinct, but not separable. What is not a real capacity for existence cannot receive the act of existence, just as the act of existence cannot actuate anything but a real capacity for receiving it. Essence, as it were, calls out for existence its correlative, so that we see the truth of the dicta '*esse per se consequitur formam*' and '*forma dat esse,*' since substance being defined by the power to be '*in se,*' existence is the fulfilment of this power, the act of this potency; so that as S. Thomas sometimes says: 'existence . . . is, as it were, constituted by the principles of essence,'[1] and so is not added to essence after the fashion of an accident.

It will be useful if we show at this point how this doctrine of the real distinction, or the principle of the limitation of act by subjective potency only, runs through the whole of S. Thomas's system.

I. *Applications with respect to Cognition.*

As potency is in no way act, but is really distinguished from it, so matter is in no way form, and is really distinct from it. So, in itself, it neither exists nor is knowable.[2] (Vol. I, pp. 48–50.) Knowledge, then, comes about by abstraction from matter, and singular material things are not directly intelligible by us (Vol. I, pp. 262 f.). The opinion that they are so is a consequence of the opposing view as to potency and act. Form, on the other hand, not being matter, is of itself capable of being understood directly; it is not of an alien nature to the intellect, so that it can be both in the thing as an objective concept, and in the mind as a formal concept (Vol. I, pp. 225 f., 271). So immateriality is the root of intelligibility and intellectuality, and the degrees of these will be proportionate to the degrees of immateriality (Vol. I, pp. 212 ff.). Hence we see the distinction between intellectual and sensible cognition (Vol. I, p. 259), and the distinction of the sciences (Vol. II, Part I, Chap. XIV). So also we see the falsity of subjective idealism, and the objectivity of knowledge is justified; in so far as the objective concept, being the form, is really in material things. Here, too, we have a refutation of Materialism, since form is irreducible to matter. Metaphysics here finds

[1] In IV *Met.*, Lect. 2 (ed. Cathala, No. 558)
[2] Cf. *Summa Theologica,* I, 15, 3, ad 3.

its justification, for if the real distinction be denied, there will be no real difference between the physical concrete thing and its metaphysical principles, so that metaphysics will be reduced either to physics (as with the Empiricists) or to logic (as with Hegel).

II. Applications with respect to Being.

Granted the Thomist view of act and potency, the principle of individuation will be matter, for act must be limited by potency (Vol. I, Part I, Chap. XII). This is not true for those who oppose S. Thomas's idea of act and potency. Nor is it true for them that in everything composed of matter and form, neither will have existence of itself, and only the compound will exist, so that there will only be one existence of the whole. In the opposing view there will be more than one existence, so that it is difficult to see how there is essential unity in man or any other bodily thing, for both essence and existence will be composite if they are the same, whereas for the Thomists essence is composite, but existence is not (Vol. I, Part I, Chap. X, Q. 1, and pp. 309 f., cf. pp. 48 f.). Material Substance, not being its existence, is not its existence as extended, i.e. its quantity, so that quantity is really distinct from substance (Vol. I, Part I, Chap. IV). Also potency being a reality distinct from act, change and motion are not impossible, as Parmenides and Zeno thought, on the supposition that all reality is actual; but motion is the continuous actuation of potency (Vol. I, Part I, Chaps. V, VIII and IX). So also substantial generation is explained, the new form being neither actually concealed in matter, nor yet wholly extraneous to it and introduced from without, for it is in matter inasmuch as this has a real potentiality for it, a potentiality which is distinct from act (Vol. I, Chap. X, Q. 2). Again, the rational soul will be united to the body in such a way as to be its only substantial form, for otherwise there would be a unity *per accidens*, not *per se*; for from act and act an essential unity does not come about, but only from the union of potency with its correlative act (Vol. I, p. 309). Moreover, the existence of an individual man will be one only, whereas in the opposite view he will have two substantial existences. It follows also from the principle of the limitation of act that a form which is not received in matter cannot be multiplied in its species, which is the reason why S. Thomas held that there could not be two angels of the same species.

III. *Applications with respect to Operation.*

Turning to the order of operation we see that faculties or powers and habits are specified, not by themselves, but by the formal object of the act to which they are essentially directed; and so are distinct both from the essence of the soul (since these acts of the faculties are accidental while the soul is substantial) and from one another (Vol. I, Part II, Chap. III). The real distinction of the active and passive intellects follows similarly, 'because with respect to the same object it is necessary that active potency which makes the object to be in act should be other than passive potency which is moved by the object which exists in act '[1] (Vol. I, pp. 268 ff.). We see, too, that the cognitive faculty and the impressed species are not two partial causes (two acts which would produce an accidental unity) of the act of knowledge, but two total causes, so that the knower and the known are more closely united than matter and form, for the knower becomes the known in a certain way, whereas matter does not become form (Vol. I, Part II, Chap. VII). Hence there is a proportion between the intellect and the species in such a way that the higher the intelligence, the fewer species does it need for understanding.[2] In the same way the intellect and will concur in the production of one free act of choice as two total causes, not as two partial ones ; consequently it is impossible that there should be choice without a last directing judgement (Vol. I, Part II, Chap. XIII). Again, in essentially subordinated causes we cannot have an infinite process ; for it follows from our principle of the limitation of act that whatever is in motion is moved by another. This is not true for the opposing school, so that Suarez is able to admit an infinite series of causes acting together simultaneously (i.e. by *concursus simultaneus*), whereas for S. Thomas no

[1] *Summa Theologica*, I, 79, 7. [2] *Ibid.*, 55, 3.

created cause is its own existence or action, and so none can operate without divine premotion.

IV. *Applications with respect to God and creatures.*

For the sake of completeness we mention here some of the principal applications of the distinction of potency and act with respect to S. Thomas's doctrine concerning God and creatures, though we have not yet considered these.

(1) In God *alone* essence and existence are the same ; a proposition which must evidently be denied by those who identify them in creatures.

(2) God is essentially and really distinct from every creature ; while in creatures, from the same arguments which show that essence and existence are really distinct, we shall conclude that personality and existence are distinct (Vol. II, Part II, Chap. VII).

(3) God alone, since He alone is his own ultimate actuality, can be the subject of no accident, whereas all creatures can receive accidental additions. Hence the operative power of creatures is distinct from their substance, since not being their existence they cannot be their action either.

(4) The truth of creation is proved by means of our distinction, inasmuch as that which is caused must be a real compound of essence and existence, and God alone being subsisting existence, all other beings must receive all their existence from God ; and the continuance of this existence, which is conservation.

(5) The Principle '*Omne quod movetur ab alio movetur*' which immediately follows from the real distinction of potency and act is the foundation of the first way by which S. Thomas proves the existence of God[1] (Vol. II, Part III, Chap. II).

[1] For all these applications cf. R. Garrigou-Lagrange, *De Actu et Potentia, Acta Primi Congressus Thomistici Internationalis*, Rome, 1925, pp. 36 ff. Also Del Prado, *De Veritate Fundamentali Philosophiæ Christianæ*.

CHAPTER VI

SUBSTANCE

The Modern Objection to Substance—The Thomistic Notion—Other Conceptions of It—Further Examination of the Thomist View—The Reality of Substance—Our Knowledge of Substance—Essence and Substance.

'ALL modern philosophy hinges round the difficulty of describing the world in terms of subject and predicate, substance and quality, particular and universal. The result always does violence to that immediate experience which we express in our actions, our hopes, our sympathies, our purposes, and which we enjoy in spite of our lack of phrases for its verbal analysis. We find ourselves in a buzzing world, amid a democracy of fellow creatures ; whereas, under some disguise or other, orthodox philosophy can only introduce us to solitary substances, each enjoying an illusory experience : " O Bottom, thou art changed ! what do I see on thee ? " ' So Dr. Whitehead[1] formulates his chief complaint against the Aristotelean analysis of substance and accident ; a complaint which would probably be justified, if by this division Aristotle meant to give a complete account of reality for all purposes. No doubt he regards substance as the primary object of Metaphysics,[2] yet this science is not confined to the consideration of substance, which is an abstraction made for certain definite purposes, and known to be valid only within certain limits. Moreover, the notion of substance, as developed by Aristotle and S. Thomas, is no simple one, as of something opposed to and underlying

[1] A. N. Whitehead, *Process and Reality* (Cambridge University Press, 1929), p. 68.

[2] *Met.*, 1028, a. 14 : ' While being has all these senses ' (the individual qualitative, quantitative, etc.), ' obviously that which " is " primarily is the " what," which indicates the substance of at hing.' Oxford translation, Vol. VIII, ed. Smith and Ross.

accidents, and still less as of something which is entirely self-sufficient and 'solitary.' No doubt this latter view of it, which is Descartes,' is that 'which led to Locke's empiricism and to Kant's critical philosophy—the two dominant influences from which modern thought is derived '[1]; but is it also true that Descartes' notion is 'a true derivative '[2] from Aristotle's? Rather it seems to be a perversion of it.

Etymologically, the word substance signifies something which 'stands under' (*substat*) others, so that its name is attributed to it in so far as it is a support. But this is only a superficial, and as is plain, 'a nominal' notion or definition of it; the universal experience of mankind attributes the name of 'being' not to such or such being, e.g. walker, corpse, body, but primarily to 'a being,' simply and absolutely, which manifests itself in innumerable ways, as well by all the realities of change, quality and quantity, as in its relations to others. It is this which we call substance. Such qualities and such relations are only intelligible in dependence on a subject which they determine, and this, though it must be their support, must first of all 'be' in itself.[3]

These, then, are the two elements or characters of substance, to subsist, i.e. to be that which immediately receives existence and exists in itself (*in se* or *per se*) and to be the subject of accidents. It will also be apparent that though it belongs to substance to be the subject of accidents, it is not in this that its formal nature consists; for this is something purely relative, whereas its power of subsistence is something absolute. Consequently, all definitions of substance which make of it a permanent and invariable subject are quite foreign to S. Thomas's conception. So the Cartesian definition, alluded to above, which describes it as 'that which needs no other thing in order to exist,'[4] modifies profoundly the Thomistic notion,

[1] A. N. Whitehead, op. cit., p. 69.

[2] *Ibid.*

[3] Cf. Régis Jolivet, *La Notion de Substance* (Paris, Beauchesne, 1929), p. 39. This admirable work gives a full and illuminating account of S. Thomas's doctrine concerning substance. Notice especially how S. Thomas transformed Aristotle's idea owing to his doctrine of creation.

[4] '*Substantia est res, quæ ita existit, ut nulla alia re indigeat ad existendum.*' *Principia Philosophiæ*, I, 51.

for it is no longer thought of as that which exists in itself. If the definition be taken literally it would ascribe absolute independence to substance; it would be not only intrinsically independent, that is independent of any subject, but also extrinsically, and so independent of any cause; so that, as Descartes himself notices, the definition applies, strictly speaking, only to God. It was in this latter sense that Spinoza took up the Cartesian definition, making this meaning still more explicit in his own definition: '*Per substantiam intelligo id, quod in se est, et per se concipitur: hoc est id, cujus conceptus non indiget conceptu alterius rei, a quo formari debeat.*'[1] From this he immediately deduces that it is impossible that one substance should produce another, and consequently that there can be only one substance, which is necessarily infinite. So he concludes: 'There does not exist, and it is impossible to conceive, any substance outside God; and all that exists, exists in God, and nothing can exist or be conceived without God.'[2] So Descartes' conception of thought and extension as the essence of immaterial and material substance respectively, must be abandoned, and these two can be nothing else than attributes or modes of a unique substance; attributes not distinct in themselves, but identified in so far as they are but aspects of a unique substance which is presented in these two ways. We need not pause to consider whether such a conception is Pantheistic; but it is plain, at least, that it can give no account of personality, or, indeed, of any concrete thing. It ought, however, to be recognised that experience of the concrete is at the base of all our knowledge, and any system which is powerless to give some explanation of it is *ipso facto* condemned. Spinoza's notion of substance is only possible by an abuse of abstraction; and is totally divorced from any conception of it which is acceptable to common sense.

Herbert Spencer's idea of substance as permanence, and Leibniz's conception of it as 'the power of action' or

[1] *Ethica*, Pars. I, Def. 3.

[2] '*Præter Deum nulla datur neque concipi potest substantia,*' *Ethica*, Pars. I, Prop. XIV; and '*Quidquid est, in Deo est, et nihil sine Deo esse neque concipi potest,*' ibid., Prop. XV.

'force,'[1] are both imperfect and partial notions, permanence being but an attribute of substance, and the power of action consequent upon its constitution, and so not constitutive, but, at best, characteristic of it. In making such a criticism as this it ought to be recognized that Leibniz's treatment of this subject shows a truly metaphysical spirit. We cannot attempt here any appreciation of his doctrine ; but can only remark some weaknesses in it, of which the chief is its failure to give an adequate account of the unity of compound substances, as was before mentioned ;[2] the device of the '*vinculum substantiale*' being unable to bring into an essential unity the simple substances or monads which are absolute and independent entities. His insistence on the activity of substance emphasises a necessary ingredient of it, and is of the greatest value ; and it was the failure to appreciate this which was one of the chief causes which led the English Empiricists, with Locke and Hume, to discard the notion of substance. The former, though he did not deny that substances exist, maintains that we have no clear idea of them ;[3] for substance, he says, 'is something, we know not what,'[4] and this attitude of his led to the entire rejection of them by later Empiricists. These, identifying knowledge with sense knowledge, are evidently precluded from admitting that we can have any knowledge of substance, since it cannot be sensed ; and therefore hold that it is, at best, a mere hypothesis, and, in fact, a name to cover our ignorance, since even those who believe in substances must admit that they are unknown in themselves. This denial of substance, then, rests on a presupposition as to the nature of knowledge and stands or falls with it.

From what has been said earlier it will be apparent that in S. Thomas's view what primarily defines substance is its capacity for receiving existence immediately and of itself, which is called its '*perseity*,' a property which must denote

[1] Cf. e.g. *New Essays*, Introduction, 'activity is the essence of substance in general.' Also Gerhardt's edition, IV, 508, II, 517.

[2] Cf. Vol. I, Part I, Chap. II.

[3] First Letter to Stillingfleet, Bp. of Worcester.

[4] *Essay on the Human Understanding*, Book I, Chap. IV, Sec. 18, and Book II, Chap. XXIII.

a positive perfection. Thus the received definition of substance among the Thomists is 'essence to whose being is due existence in itself and not in another.' This *perseity* must be its primary formal constituent if it does in fact sustain accidents, for in order to do so it must be capable of existing in itself, otherwise we should have an infinite process. To say this in no way implies that it lies inert and inactive under the accidents which fall on it, like the still waters of a lake over the surface of which pass the shadows of the drifting clouds. Such a misconception of S. Thomas's doctrine has been very prevalent; but he is careful to point out that properties are caused by the essential principles of the substantial subject, going so far as to say that it is their '*causa activa*'; though, inasmuch as it is not their efficient cause, properly speaking, he qualifies the phrase by saying that it is their active cause 'in a certain way.'[1] So proper accidents naturally result, according to him, from the subject, as colour from light.[2] This, however, is not true of contingent accidents, which come and go, such change being caused by some extrinsic agent.[3]

It is by means of these contingent accidents that we are primarily assured of the reality of substance, for we are immediately conscious of changing thoughts, volitions, sensations and so on, and such consciousness implies the equally strong certainty as to our own self-identity. A thought which is not the thought of any mind is, indeed, unintelligible; for it has no power of supporting or sustaining itself, but must be sustained by some subject. If this subject, again, were incapable of sustaining itself, the same problem would recur with regard to it; in other words, it would require a subject which sustains it. This process cannot go on for ever, since if there were no ultimate subject which sustained others while being itself unsustained, nothing would be sustained. We know that there are such realities which are in fact sustained, such as thoughts, and we are therefore obliged to conclude that there is also a reality

[1] *Summa Theologica*, I, 77, 6, ad 2; cf. *De Ente et Essentia*, Cap. VII.
[2] *Summa Theologica*, I, 77, 6, ad 3.
[3] *De Ente et Essentia*, Cap. VII.

which sustains them, as well as sustaining itself. As it does this it has no need to be sustained by any other, and it is this which we call 'substance.'

The same can be seen to be true if we acknowledge the reality of local motion, for this requires that there should be some real subject which passes from one place to another, and it is this subject which we call substance. As Dr. Inge says: 'It is, or should be, a commonplace of philosophy, that only the permanent can change, change being a succession of states within a unity.'[1] Substance, then, for S. Thomas, implies a permanence stretching back into the past and pushing forward into the future; it is not constituted by a negation—a negation of inherence—but by its own enduring self-identity, and that independence in being which belongs to it as that which is primarily being, and to which existence attaches immediately. If this is not real, nothing in nature is real. But this is not to say that it receives nothing and loses nothing: on the contrary, all its 'states' come about through the contributions received from its own activity and that of the environment. But 'the more it changes the more it is the same.' So, as Dr. Whitehead says, 'It is nonsense to conceive of Nature as a static fact, even for an instant devoid of duration. There is no nature apart from transition, and there is no transition apart from temporal duration.'[2] Substance is the basis and ground of temporal reality, and as such is itself pre-eminently real.[3]

If we now turn to consider our knowledge of substance, we see that we come at it, not in, but through sense knowledge. Here, once again, S. Thomas's fundamental conception of man as an essential unity who only understands

[1] W. R. Inge, *The Philosophy of Plotinus*, Vol. I (2nd edn., Longmans, 1923), p. 177.

[2] A. N. Whitehead, *Nature and Life* (Cambridge, 1934), p. 60.

[3] Thus we see that we must acknowledge the reality of substance if we allow that of multiplicity and change. For things that are of themselves diverse cannot of themselves be one, and a sheer multiplicity is unintelligible. So Fr. Garrigou-Lagrange says: 'The many, in fact, are only intelligible as a function of the one, and the transitory as a function of the permanent or identical; because "every being is, of itself, one and the same," which is one of the formulas of the principle of identity. To say that a being is substance is to say that it is one and the same under its multiple and changing appearances.' (*Dieu, son existence et sa nature*, 5e edition, p. 168).

the intelligible in and through the sensible, is exemplified and verified. We are, therefore, more or less at a loss when it comes to dealing with what is not itself sensible ; so that substance, not being able to be sensed, is not directly knowable by natures such as ours. What we know of it is primarily derived from the phenomena ; which oblige us to conclude to it. But if it is unknowable of itself, and only to be known by means of accidents, it is also true that accident can only be understood, and so, properly speaking, known, by means of substance. In its very definition it must include the subject of which it is a manifestation ; colour is the colour of something, change the change of some substance.[1]

Substance, then, is really distinct from accidents, but is manifested to us by their means ; and is, consequently, united with them either necessarily, as in the case of those accidents which follow from its very nature, i.e. its properties ; or contingently, in the case of those which are produced in it by some extrinsic agent. It is only by means of its accidents that we know it ; and this knowledge is, at first, of a very confused and general kind. Two things are to be noticed here : first, that substance belongs to the intelligible order, not the sensible, so that, as Fr. D'Arcy remarks : 'The attempt to replace it by sensible qualities, to make of it nothing but a sum of sensible attributes, is doomed from the outset ';[2] and secondly, that we have no intuitive knowledge of substances ; what we know of them is the consequence of a long continued process of observation of accidents. This process may lead us to knowledge of the essence of the thing.

Are essence and substance then the same ? The answer to this question is that though, speaking quite generally, the word 'essence' has a wider meaning than predicamental substance, since it applies in a certain sense to accidents, which substance evidently does not ; yet, if we are speaking of substantial things, these two, essence and substance, are distinguished only logically and not really. The same reality is the essence of Peter and the substance of Peter ; both of

[1] Cf. Sertillanges, *S. Thomas d'Aquin*, Tome I, pp. 76–78.
[2] M. C. D'Arcy, S.J., *Thomas Aquinas*, p. 121.

them are his primary being, and one thing cannot have two primary beings. On the other hand, when we say 'substance' we are thinking of that primary being by means of which a thing subsists in itself, whereas when we say 'essence' we are thinking of that by whose means it is made a definite, specific kind of thing; so that there is a distinction in thought between the notions of essence and substance. The word 'nature' adds something more to this notion, though not to the reality; for it conveys the idea that the substance is the first principle of operations. Fr. D'Arcy[1] sums this up by saying: 'Generally S. Thomas employs the word essence to express what the thing is, nature to express the essence as the principle of activity, and substance for its mode of existence.' This mode of existence belongs to it in virtue of its subsistence, and we must now try to elucidate this notion.

[1] M. C. D'Arcy, S.J., op. cit., p. 122.

CHAPTER VII

SUBSISTENCE AND PERSONALITY

First and Second Substance—The Notion of Suppositum—Person—The Formal Constituent of Subsistence—The Scotist View—Subsistence and Existence—The Distinction of Suppositum and Individual Nature—The Distinction of Subsistence and Existence—The Nature of Personality—S. Thomas's View—Individuation and Personality.

ARISTOTLE in the *Categories*,[1] and elsewhere, makes the distinction between 'first' and 'second' substance. First substance is that which is neither in a subject nor affirmed of a subject; while second substance, though not in a subject, since it is not inhering, is nevertheless affirmed of a subject as a predicate. First substance is individual, as 'a certain man and a certain horse,' while second substance is universal, and so is only called substance by analogy, since, according to Aristotle, the universal cannot subsist: i.e. be an independent substance. Universals are only affirmed of first substances, so we say: 'Socrates is man,' the universal 'man' expressing the nature of Socrates, but not being in him as in a subject. Substance, then, primarily and properly, is first or individual substance, which the Scholastics call a '*suppositum*.' The Thomists distinguish between the *suppositum* understood denominatively and the *suppositum* understood formally.[2] In the first sense it signifies the individual which subsists, in the second the compound of this individual and its subsistence. Using the word in the first sense, S. Thomas says that in those things which are not composed of matter and form, *suppositum* does not differ from nature. The reason is that there is in their specific

[1] 2a, 11 *sqq.*

[2] Cf. Capreolus in III *Sent.*, Dist. V, Q. 3, art 3, Sec. 2, II, ad 4, edn. Paban-Règues, Tome V, p. 110b; Billot, *De Verbo Incarnato* (1900), p. 61; Hugon, *Cursus Philosophiæ Thomisticæ*, Tome V, p. 247.

natures no composition of potency and act, but the nature of one differs from that of another by being itself more potential with regard to existence; so in this sense that which subsists, or the *suppositum*, and this determined nature are the same.

In its second or formal sense we mean by *suppositum* a substance which is individual, complete, autonomous and incommunicable to another. It is in this sense that the word is used in what follows; and we see that in saying that *suppositum* is complete and autonomous we exclude parts of substance, as well as incomplete substances (such as the soul or the body of man considered separately), from the meaning of the word.

When *suppositum* is said to be incommunicable this term is to be taken in the fullest sense. In this connection three kinds of communicability are possible; that of the universal to the singular (so humanity is communicated to Peter and Paul), that of the part to the whole (so the arm communicates with the whole body), and that of assumption by another *suppositum* (as if a parasite, such as a tapeworm, were supposed to be one individual substance with its host). It is this last kind of incommunicability which is peculiarly the property of *suppositum*, for singular nature, even if incomplete (e.g. the soul of a particular man), excludes the first kind of communicability, while complete singular nature (e.g. Peter's soul and body together) excludes the first two kinds. *Suppositum* alone excludes all three.

There is one class of *supposita* which are of special interest and importance for us, namely, human beings. These are called persons; person being defined by Boethius[1] as '*Naturæ rationabilis individua substantia*,' an individual substance of a rational nature. It is distinguished, therefore, from *suppositum* in general by adding to it the dignity of an intellectual nature; while the word 'individual' in the definition signifies the complete individual who is autonomous and incommunicable.[2] The Greek word '*hypostasis*,' sometimes used in this connection, can be taken to mean

[1] *Contra Entychen*, III, 4.
[2] Cf. *Summa Theologica*, III, 2, 2, ad 3.

either *suppositum* or person, but is more commonly used in the latter sense by the Greek ecclesiastical writers.[1]

If the definition of Boethius be accepted, and we hold to S. Thomas's view of the essential union of soul and body, which being related to one another as potency to act will neither of them be complete substances, it will follow that souls separated from the body are not to be considered to be persons, in the strict sense of the term. They are incomplete and lack an essential part of the nature of man.[2]

That substantial perfection by which an individual substance is made perfectly subsisting and so autonomous and altogether incommunicable is called subsistence.

What is it precisely which formally constitutes this perfection of subsistence and personality ? Various answers have been given to this question. The view taken of individuality and the principle of individuation will necessarily have repercussions on that held by any thinker as to the nature of subsistence and personality, for the *suppositum* and person are *individual* substances. So we find that those who, like Duns Scotus, consider that individuality arises from a formal principle in the nature, whether this be the substantial form (in living things, the soul) or some formality other than this, such as Scotus's '*haecceitas*,' and deny that the principle of individuation can be matter, maintain that there need be no positive addition to nature in order that it may be a *suppositum* or person. For them the individual as such, is made individual by an act, a perfection, so that to say that subsistence is not a positive perfection does not entail for them the consequence that the subsisting thing is constituted as subsisting by a pure negation. Such a position would be surely untenable, since this power of self-sustentation and autonomy must undoubtedly be something positive and a perfection and act. If the Scotist statement that subsistence is something negative be considered as an isolated statement without relation to his views on the individual, or rather, as if he held the Thomist opinion on this point, it becomes inexplicable; but as he had already affirmed that individuation is

[1] Cf. *Summa Theologica*, I, 29, 2, ad 1.

[2] Cf. *De Potentia*, IX, 2, ad 14um; *Summa Theologica*, I, 29, 1, ad 5um; I, 75, 4, ad 2um; 3 *Sent.*, Dist. 5, Q. 3, art. 2; *Tabula Aurea. Anima*, 7.

itself constituted by an act or perfection, it was not necessary for him to maintain that subsistence was a further perfection. In fact he identifies all the three elements which can be considered in person : viz. nature, subsistence, and existence. The difficulty of his position lies in the fact that by making the principle of individuation something formal, he thereby goes far towards sacrificing the unity of the species, and of the individual itself. Of the species, since if each individual has something formal or actual which is peculiarly its own it is difficult to see how all of them can have the same form, and so be constituted of the same nature ; since for him as well as for S. Thomas '*forma dat speciem.*' Of the individual, for we shall now have two acts or forms which constitute it, that which makes it an individual, and that which makes it of a certain nature. So, as M. Gilson says, 'Being sensible of the difficulty of maintaining in his doctrine the unity of the human species, Duns Scotus was obliged to modify profoundly the notion of unity itself in order to reconcile the unity of the species with that of the individual.'[1]

The view, then, that subsistence consists in something negative, namely in not being assumed by some other *suppositum*, is generally rejected ; and the Thomists are unanimous in this, in virtue of their fundamental principle that act can be limited only by potency, from which follows at once that the form or act of any given species or nature can only be multiplied in that nature and made individual by potency or matter and not by form. So for them the principle of individuation must be matter, and subsistence, which gives the individual a positive perfection, making it independent, autonomous, incommunicable and complete, must also be a positive perfection. This view is held by all Scholastics with the exception of the Scotists, but they do not agree on the question whether this positive perfection is that of existence or of something distinct from existence. Some distinguished Thomists, such as Fr. Billot, identify

[1] E. Gilson, *L'Esprit de la Philosophie Médiévale*, Gifford Lectures (1st series), p. 203. There is some slight doubt whether Scotus meant to distinguish as different forms that of corporeality and the human soul. If he did not, the unity of the individual would not be so seriously compromised, though that of the species could with difficulty be maintained.

these two ; but the majority of Thomists[1] hold that there is a real distinction between subsistence and existence. Suarez agrees with this view, but since he does not allow the real distinction between existence and essence, the consequences of the distinction when applied to the theology of the Incarnation are very different for Suarez from those which follow from the Thomist position.

In saying that subsistence is a positive perfection, and not merely something negative, we have already implicitly affirmed that individual nature together with subsistence, i.e. *suppositum*, is really distinct from individual nature alone. Whatever view Thomists take as to the distinction of subsistence and existence, they are all agreed in saying that *suppositum* is really distinct from individual nature. This is, in fact, even clearer for those who deny a real distinction between subsistence and existence than for those who affirm it, for if subsistence *is* existence, since existence is really distinct from individual nature, it is plain that *suppositum*, or individual nature plus subsistence, i.e. plus existence, must be distinct from individual nature alone. *Suppositum*, in this view, is distinct from individual nature because it adds to it a reality, namely existence.

The fact that S. Thomas did not use this argument to prove the distinction between individual nature and *suppositum* tends to show, we may remark in passing, that he did not identify existence and subsistence ; for the argument is a mere corollary from his central thesis of the real distinction between essence and existence. In fact he uses, to prove the present distinction, the argument which is adopted by those Thomists who think that subsistence and existence are not to be identified.

This argument, found in the *Quæstiones Quodlibetales*,[2] is as follows :

In every being to which something may be added which does not belong to it of its very nature, *suppositum* and

[1] E.g. Cajetan, Ferrariensis, Bannez, John of S. Thomas, Salmanticenses, Goudin, Billuart, Zigliara, Del Prado, Mercier, Gredt, Garrigou-Lagrange.

[2] *Quodlibet*, II, a. 4.

nature differ. For in the meaning of nature is included only that which is of the essence of the species, while *suppositum* has not only those things which belong to the essence of the species, but also other things which are accidental to it; so that *suppositum* is a whole, while nature is the formal part. So in material things the individuating principles (*this* matter—matter having a transcendental relation to *this* quantity) are outside the essence of the species, for what makes two material beings numerically different obviously cannot be common to both of them, and so to the nature of the species which both share; and in immaterial beings, since their existence is other than their essence or nature, this existence is accidental to such a being, i.e. belongs to it contingently, not necessarily. So in both classes *suppositum* is that which exists, nature that by which the *suppositum* is specifically constituted, so that existence is attributed to the *suppositum* but not to the nature. In material things the quantitative differentiation of the matter in each of them is outside their specific content and not attributable to it, as are also existence and their accidental characteristics, such as whiteness; and in immaterial beings, though there is nothing which differentiates their species or essence, yet outside their specific content and not attributable to it are existence and their personal acts. *Suppositum*, then, must differ from individual nature in all finite beings, where essence and existence are distinct, for *suppositum* is the subject of existence and other 'accidents'[1] in all of them, while nature cannot conceivably be the *subject* of accidents, being that *by* which an existing thing is constituted specifically, not *that which* exists.

We can be sure, then, that whether we identify subsistence and existence or not, *suppositum* and individual nature are really distinct in finite things; *suppositum* adding to the

[1] The word 'accident' is, of course, not to be supposed to imply that existence is an accident in the ordinary sense of the term, since, as we have seen, S. Thomas repudiates the idea of Avicenna that it is so. (Cf. pp. 195 f. and 201.) It is used to indicate S. Thomas's expression which he repeats continually in this argument: *esse accidit ei*, i.e. to an angel: it is a contingent adjunct, not attributable to its nature, nor belonging to it necessarily. It is contingent also to *suppositum*, but nevertheless attributable to it and 'belongs' to it, inasmuch as it is the *suppositum*, not the nature, which exists or has existence.

nature the positive perfection of being the subject of contingent adjuncts to nature, such as existence.

Coming to the question of the distinction of subsistence and existence, we may notice that there are texts of S. Thomas which are favourable to both views.[1] One favourable to the distinction is found in the *Quodlibet* from which the argument given above is taken, where S. Thomas says explicitly: '*ipsum esse non est de ratione suppositi*' (ad 2um). It is certain, however, that subsistence is '*de ratione suppositi*' since it is this which makes it a *suppositum*. This and other texts are difficult, if not impossible, to explain except on the hypothesis that S. Thomas thought that subsistence is not to be identified with existence, and, as has already been pointed out, it is strange, if he considered them identical, that he did not argue that *suppositum* is nature plus existence, and therefore really distinct from nature, as do the advocates of the identity of existence and subsistence, instead of using the elaborate argument which we find in the *Quodlibet*. Whatever may be thought as to S. Thomas's opinion on this point—and space does not allow us to do more than touch on this historical controversy—it is certain that the majority of Thomists have held that subsistence and existence are really distinct. They say this not without reason; for, according to them, existence is a *contingent attribute* of every finite *suppositum*, and so cannot constitute it as the first *subject* of attribution. To maintain this would be equivalent to saying that the personality, say of Socrates, is his existence; whereas God alone is his existence. Neither the person of Socrates, nor his personality, which formally constitutes the person, can *be* his existence.[2] Again, subsistence belongs to the very nature

[1] Cf. Pègues, *Commentaire de la Somme Théologique* (Paris, Téqui, 1924), Vol. XV, p. 72. The text which he considers opposed to the distinction is: '*Non quodlibet individuum in genere substantiæ, etiam in rationali natura, habet rationem personæ, sed solum illud quod per se existit.*' So that subsistence would be a mode of existence, viz., existence *per se*.

The arguments against the distinction are fully given by Fr. R. R. Welschen, O.P., in the *Revue Thomiste*, 1919, pp. 1–26.

Texts in favour of the distinction are: *S. T.*, III, 17, 2, ad 1um; I, 50, 2, ad 3um; *Quodlibet*, II, a. 4. Against it are quoted: *S. T.*, I, 29, 3; III, 17, 2; III, 19, 1, ad 4um.

[2] Cf. R. Garrigou-Lagrange, O.P., art. 'La Personnalité,' in *Revue Thomiste*, 1933, pp. 262 ff.

and definition of *suppositum*, it is that which formally makes it a *suppositum*, complete as a substance. Existence on the contrary cannot be of the nature and definition of finite *supposita*, otherwise these would exist of their very nature and so necessarily.

Further it is the *suppositum* which exists, it is the subject of existence, and so cannot contain it of itself in the shape of subsistence.[1] How, then, in this view, do individual nature, subsistence, and existence stand to one another? Subsistence, evidently, attaches to nature which it completes as substance, thereby making it the first subject to which are attributed existence and accidental characteristics; so that S. Thomas teaches that it is the compound or *suppositum* which has existence properly speaking, and not the parts or the form; 'existence follows nature, not as that which has existence, but as that by which anything exists, but it follows person or *hypostasis* as that which has existence.'[2] So subsistence completes individual nature and is naturally prior to existence. Moreover, subsistence belongs to nature intrinsically, since it is by subsistence that it is terminated and completed in itself; whereas existence belongs to it extrinsically, being produced by the efficient cause.

So far we have spoken of subsistence in general, without making any distinction between that of non-rational and rational beings. But naturally it is the case of human subsistence, or personality, which is of the greatest interest to us. There have been many views as to its nature, of which one of the most widely adopted is that personality consists in consciousness. So Locke says: 'Since consciousness always accompanies thinking, in this alone consists personal identity.'[3] The reason given is plainly insufficient; but apart from this, how can a man be conscious till he is a being, that is before he has personal identity? Personal identity is presupposed to thinking and consciousness, not consciousness to personal identity. It would seem to

[1] Cf. Cajetan, *Comm. in S. T.*, III, 4, 2; comm. No. 1.

[2] *Esse consequitur naturam, non sicut habentem esse, sed sicut qua aliquid est, personam autem, sive hypostasim, consequitur sicut habentem esse.* *Summa Theologica*, III, 17, 2, ad 1um.

[3] *Essay on the Human Understanding*, Book II, c. 27, Sec. 9.

follow also from this view that personal identity would lapse with consciousness, so that in sleep, or at any rate, under an anæsthetic, we should lose this identity.[1]

What truth there is in this view is, in fact, implied by our definition and analysis of personality. Though this, at first sight, may appear too abstract and restricted, it will be seen on further consideration to be, on the one hand, but a development and unfolding of what common sense has to tell us of personality, and, on the other, to include all those elements which can be discerned in personality by philosophic reflection. Common sense regards a person as the ultimate subject to which are attributed all actions and it is therefore plain that that by which 'person' is constituted must be something substantial, not accidental. Also personality must be the term in which all those things which are attributed to the person meet; and these are individual nature, existence, and operations. The individual nature in question is a rational one, to which personality adds the perfection of being independent and autonomous, so that it is implied that the person has complete self-command, which he could not have without the conscious possession of existence, and freedom of action, so that he is master of his acts. In this sense, then, we may agree with Illingworth that 'the fundamental characteristic of personality is self-consciousness.'[2] Being thus aware of his own self-identity, and that his acts are attributable to himself as his very own, he is obliged to take responsibility for them, so that he has rights and duties, and his actions will be praiseworthy or blameable, for which reason he can be rewarded or punished. He thus is in conscious possession of a rational nature in himself and for himself, a nature which is distinct and separate from every other; or, as S. Thomas says, a person is '*quod per se separatim existit in rationali natura.*'[3] To be oneself, having

[1] Cf. A. N. Whitehead, *Nature and Life*, pp. 82–84. Here in pointing out that our claim to personal identity is one of 'the really fundamental factors of our experience' which must not be excluded from philosophy, he remarks: 'The continuity of the soul—so far as concerns consciousness—has to leap gaps in time. We sleep or we are stunned. And yet it is the same person who recovers consciousness.'

[2] J. R. Illingworth, *Personality, Human and Divine*, Lecture II.

[3] *Summa Theologica*, III, 2, 2, ad 3um.

a being all one's own, with such self-mastery as not to be under the dominion of another, and not to be a part, but an independent whole, this is to be a person in the full sense of the word. Such independence and self-mastery will clearly be proportionate to the nature which is personified, so that the grandeur of personality is not absolute but relative, and depends on the grandeur of the personified nature. As the waters of the incoming tide flow round and take the shape of the objects on the seashore, so the tide of existence is moulded to the personified natures to which it gives being ; and the essence of personality is to be found not in this existence, nor in the individual nature as such, but in the subsistence which makes that nature independent and autonomous. The measure of personality will be the degree of such independence and self-mastery, increasing as this increases ; though, in finite beings, it must always be infinitely removed from complete independence, since their nature never *is* being but *has* it only, and so can never be wholly independent. The greatness of personality is proportionate to the greatness of the personified nature.

Here we see once again[1] what a great gulf separates individuation and personality. Individuation merely divides one thing from another by a purely material and spatial distinction. It is almost negative : this being is not that ; whereas personality and subsistence are positive perfections, increasing in greatness in the same measure as the natures in which they are found, and culminating in absolute and positive independence and complete autonomy. And this is why S. Thomas asserts that '*person* signifies that which is most perfect in the whole of nature.'[2] It is this perfection which allows him to apply the word to God.

[1] Cf. Vol. I, p. 161 f.

[2] *Summa Theologica*, I, 29, 3.

CHAPTER VIII

ACCIDENTAL BEING

Predicamental and Predicable Accidents—The Nature of the Former —Their Reality—The Existence of Accidents—The Objection to the Idea of Accident—Relations—Their Reality.

THE second of the two supreme genera into which Aristotle divided being is that of accident. Perhaps no Aristotelean and Scholastic notion is so out of favour at the present time as this; for though the old empirical objection, which, by abolishing substance, thereby took away the accidental nature of phenomena, is now not generally brought against it, the idea of transitory beings which attached themselves to a permanent substratum and can only exist in such a conjunction, is considered to be a sheer falsification of nature. The reader will already have gathered that to describe accidents in such a way as this would be to give a very erroneous notion of S. Thomas's concept of 'accident'; but before beginning to consider whether his genuine view of it can be justified or not, it will be useful to recall some notions from logic with regard to the nature and division of accident.

The logicians distinguish between predicamental and predicable accident. The latter, which is also called 'logical accident,' expresses the mode in which a thing is predicated of a subject, viz. adjectivally and contingently. It is therefore anything which is not predicated necessarily, and so is opposed to 'property.' A predicamental accident, on the contrary, is a being which is not subsisting but inheres in a subject. So a predicable accident can be anything which is not a property; it can be inhering or subsisting, real or logical. Thus existence is a predicable accident of creatures, though substantial existence is substantial; and this fact shows that it is not a predicamental accident, since this can never be substantial. A being may, of course, be both a predicable and a predicamental accident, which it will be if it is neither a property nor a substance. Here we are only concerned with predicamental accident; and this is described as that whose nature is such that it is fitted to exist in some subject and not in itself. So the natural aptitude for inherence is the distinguishing characteristic of accident.

Can such a notion as this be justified? This really amounts to asking whether there are any such beings, for the notion of a being which exists in another cannot be said to be absurd, or to involve a contradiction. Existence, as such, is merely the act by which a nature is transferred from the order of mere possibilities and made an actual thing in the world: it has nothing to say to the mode of the nature itself, whether it is inhering or subsisting. With regard to the question of fact, both internal and external experience bears witness to this: that beings which retain their essential self-identity do sometimes gain something which they had not before, and do sometimes lose something they previously had. So in ourselves thoughts, desires, volitions pass away and new ones come; while bodies, both our own and those of other things, change in quantity, shape, colour, and so on. The material of which our bodies are composed is continually changing, and after a time is entirely renewed. Now it is clear that these changing characteristics cannot be the very essence or substance of the thing which is subject to change, otherwise it would not remain in any way the same. We should have a succession of different things, not one thing at all; and since the process is continuous we should never have any self-identity, for the instant is not an actual reality, but is the link between past and future. The remark just made about the change of the material of our bodies may serve to dissipate one misunderstanding about the scholastic doctrine on this point; for it is plain that since the Scholastics allow that all the material elements of a body may change, and that the body itself may yet remain the same substantially, they do not identify substance with these elements. In modern English we have come to use the word substantial to mean large and solid; but in scholastic terminology it has nothing to do either with size or solidity. In material things it is the compound of matter and form, made a complete whole and the subject of existence by means of subsistence; and in immaterial beings it is subsisting form. Such a nature remains, or may remain, S. Thomas holds, identical with itself both as *this* nature, and as the subject of existence, notwithstanding great changes in the material elements of which it is composed, or the accession or loss of other characteristics. Nevertheless such loss or gain does not, as has been pointed out several times already, leave it altogether unchanged; for some of its gains are produced by its own activity, while even those which are not, affect it with new relations to the whole universe; though they can, at the same time, leave it the same in its essential nature as a certain kind of thing, and in its substantiality. The word substance, on the lips of S. Thomas, stands for a metaphysical and intellectual concept, not for a material and sensible image; so that these sensible realities which come and go, and which we call accidents, must be really distinct from it. If they are not substance they are not self-sustaining, and since they exist they must be sustained in existence by something other than themselves. Accidents, then, or beings which are incapable of existing in their own right, do yet exist, and are real.

What is the existence of accidents? Is it the same as that by whose means the substance in which they inhere exists?

There has been a certain amount of discussion among Scholastics on this point, and Cardinal Mercier, for example, held that the existence of a substance and its accidents is the same. Those who deny, with Suarez, the real distinction between essence and existence must necessarily maintain that an accident, since it has its own proper essence, will also have its own existence, distinct from that of substance;[1] but it seems that the contrary opinion to this is not inconsistent, if we hold that there is a real distinction of essence and existence. Whether this be so or not, S. Thomas does

[1] Cf. Suarez, *Disputationes Metaphysicæ*, XXXI, Sec. XI.

not adopt the view that the existence of accidents is that of the substance; for though he thinks it impossible to affirm that a thing which is truly one should have several substantial existences, the same does not hold good of accidental ones. In fact, the existence of whiteness in Socrates does not belong to Socrates inasmuch as he is Socrates, but inasmuch as he is white. So 'there is nothing to prevent the multiplication of existence of this kind in one *hypostasis* or person; for the existence whereby Socrates is white is other than that whereby he is a musician.'[1]

Such multiplication of accidents in no way injures the unity of substance itself, and indeed these accidents are the means by which substance, as it were, strikes through the soil of the purely intelligible where it lives and grows, and shows itself in the region of sensible things. Since the proper object of the human intellect is, for S. Thomas, the intelligible in the sensible, it is only by means of accident that we can know substance, and substance in the concrete cannot be understood without accidents. For though, by abstraction, we may be able to consider substance in itself without considering its accidents, we cannot suppose that in concrete reality the one may be found without the other. This would be to mistake our abstractions for realities.

The greater part of the objections of empiricists and others to the Thomist doctrine of substance disappear when once this connection in the concrete between accidents and substance is clearly grasped; for no longer will substance appear as a naked, inert, and undetermined substratum, but as something which though in itself really distinct from accidents yet forms with them one concrete whole.

But, it may be urged, this view of substance carries us too far in the opposite direction. If it forms one whole with accidents these must affect it in its very essence, and it will be changed essentially with each new relation that comes to it by means of its changing accidents. So it will be but a tissue of relations.

It is not surprising that we should again be confronted, in

[1] *Summa Theologica*, III, 17, 2. Cf. also Jolivet, *La Notion de Substance*, pp. 57 ff.

dealing with accidents, with the same difficulty that faced us when considering substance,[1] for these two are mutually complementary. It has already been partially answered, for we saw that substance and accident are not found in separation; for substance cannot be, in the concrete, without accidents, nor accidents without substance; but the whole forms one complete thing, which is the *suppositum*—the self. So the caricature of substance drawn by philosophers of an empirical tendency, as a mere passive indeterminate something hidden away behind accidents—a something which has less connection with the world we know than a *poltergeist* or table-turning spook—has been seen to be a travesty of S. Thomas's conception of it. The fact that natural science—physics, at any rate, and, in the opinion of the empirical philosophers, biology and psychology also—abstracts from everything except sensible appearances, has caused the belief that philosophy, if it is to be adequate to such science, must abstract from everything but phenomena also. The empiricists have, in fact, done just what they charge the metaphysicians with doing; and have mistaken their abstractions for realities. Both 'bodies' and 'persons' are, according to Earl Russell, 'strings of sets of events';[2] though how we can have events without any duration, and which, therefore, must vanish in the same instant that they occur; how these nothingnesses can be made up into 'sets'; and, most marvellous of all, form a continuum or string, is far more mysterious, and difficult to explain, than the concept of substance which it is intended to replace.

If, then, we are bound to assert the existence of something to which events occur, and which is relatively permanent, will not the very occurrence of such events to it radically change it, so that it will not endure any more than the events themselves? Thus we should be brought back once more to the events themselves as the only reality. In other words, the fact that substance, by means of its accidents, is continually acquiring new relations to its environment and to

[1] Cf. Chap. VI.

[2] *An Outline of Philosophy*, p. 171. Cf. Dr. H. S. Box, *The World and God* (S.P.C.K., 1934), Chap. XIII; who shows how this view had its origins in the empiricism of Hume, and criticises it.

the whole world, seems to show that it is, in itself, nothing absolute; but a collection of such relations.

It might suffice to say, in answer to this objection, that to speak of relations where there is nothing which is related is to speak unintelligibly. A more satisfying answer will, however, emerge from an account of the Thomistic analysis of 'relation,' for which this objection provides a suitable occasion.

The general idea of relation is, no doubt, that of the order between two things, which are in some way referred to one another. It is, therefore, necessary, in order that there should be a relation, to have a subject which is referred or related; a term to which it is referred; and some reason for the reference, some aspect under which the subject is so referred. This last is called the foundation of the relation.

Among relations, so generally conceived, we can distinguish two kinds: transcendental and predicamental. A transcendental relation is an order which is included in the very essence of a real thing, by which order its entity is, of its very nature, referred to some other. Such is the relation of matter to form, of a faculty to its actions: the soul has a transcendental relation to the body, the intellect to its acts of knowledge.

A predicamental relation, on the other hand, is, as the name implies, a predicament or category, and so an accident. It is defined by the Thomists as a real accident whose being consists in its reference to some other. Considered as an accident it has the same kind of existence as other accidents, its *esse* is *inesse*; but considered precisely as a relation according to its own nature (*propria ratio*),[1] its relativity is not towards the subject in which it is, but towards something outside it. The other accidents, as quantity and quality, modify the subject itself, but the essence of relation signifies only a respect to something else. So the word 'towards' expresses what is proper and essential to relations as such. Aristotle therefore names relation Τὸ πρός τι, which name S. Thomas adopts under the form *ad aliquid*. It is a 'towardness.'

[1] Cf. *Summa Theologica*, I, 28, art. 1 and 2.

The difficulty with regard to relations centres in the question of their reality. The theory which introduced the discussion of them—that substance is a tissue of relations—evidently does not allow reality to anything else than relations. On the other hand, it has been held that no relation is real in itself, but that only the foundations of relations are real. S. Thomas will not admit the truth of either of these views, for while he recognises that many relations are logical only, he distinguishes between those which are intrinsic to the essence of the related thing, and those which are accidents ; and, finally, with respect to these accidents he maintains that the relation itself is a reality other than its foundation. It is in this last view that he is peculiar ; and, indeed, at first sight, the notion of a reference, a 'towardness' which is itself real, seems almost fantastic. We can see that when a man has a son the act of generation, which is the foundation of the relation of paternity, is something real in him ; but it is difficult to see how this relation to his son can really differ from the fact that he was his father or generator. But if we say this, what in effect do we make of the relation ? Evidently, the act of generation is something in the father, which causes some alteration in him. He, as a man, is somewhat changed. There is nothing relative about this, except in the sense that every accident is relative to its subject, inasmuch as it affects it and inheres in it. This view, therefore, amounts to absorbing relation in the general nature of accident, or in one of its categories, such as quality and action, and so destroys relation altogether. For this is the peculiarity about relation, that while other accidents affect the substance in itself and internally, relation has as its function to add something external to substance, inasmuch as it introduces an order between different substances which leaves them unchanged in themselves. Certainly some accidental change—such as the act of generation—is presupposed in the substance, in order that the relationship may be set up ; but it cannot be this which constitutes the relation itself, for it is something which is *not* relative to anything other than the subject. The existence of a relation is inherence, but its essence is reference. It is a gossamer reality, floating away to something else, though the cause and the reason of its existence, and of its being a reality at all, is to be found in some other accident, which is not relative, but modifies the subject in itself. This accident, which is the foundation of the relation, being its cause, must therefore be really distinct from the relation itself, which is the effect which it produces. The relation is even separable from the foundation; for the foundation may remain as a reality in nature even when the relation ceases. If we have two white objects, they are alike in so far as both are white; but if one object is destroyed the relation of similarity ceases, though the whiteness which is the foundation of this relation, remains in the object which still exists. No sign of real distinction can be more convincing than real separability, for a thing cannot be separated from itself.

To avoid having to admit the reality of so strange an entity as that which is nothing absolute but only a reference, and whose function is merely to introduce one thing to another, some deny the existence of predicamental relations altogether, and retain only transcendental ones. But surely it is true that the greater part of the order and harmony of the world about us, and of our own experiences, is constituted, not by those connections or relations which follow necessarily from the essence of things; but from those which, though inseparable from the substance, are yet contingent to it; and result from the accidental presence together of several things. This seems to be exemplified in the beauty of a landscape; and more strikingly still in the gradations and relations of living things; as, say, in biological adaptation.

If, then, there are in reality relations which are not of the very essence of the related things, as S. Thomas teaches, it is clear, on the one side, that things cannot be held to be a mere tissue of relations; nor, on the other, can it be said that all relations are logical, and merely the way in which our minds envisage the world. To say all things are relations, and so that there are relations but no related things is to contradict reason; to say there are no relations distinct from substance, and so to deny the order of the universe is to contradict experience. An atom is more than its electrons, a family than its members, an army than its soldiers. The fact that the world is ' buzzing ' does not exclude, but rather demands, that it should be composed of ' bees.'

Note.—For a detailed and searching analysis and criticism, from the Thomistic standpoint, of Modern Relativism, the reader should consult : G. Rabeau, *Réalité et Relativité* (Coll. Études Philosophiques), Paris, Rivière, 1927.

CHAPTER IX

THE NATURE OF CAUSALITY

Principle and Cause—Condition—Occasion—Division of Causes—The Principle of Causality—The Principle of the Reason of Being—Experience of Causality—Instrumental Causality.

NATURAL SCIENCE, if it employs the concept of cause at all, must necessarily take it for granted; for it deals, not with what may lie behind the happenings in the world of nature, but with those happenings themselves, and with their co-ordination in the simplest form of conceptual scheme which will cover all the available data. In asserting that events occur in a definite and unvarying sequence it does not seem committed to any metaphysical interpretation of the nature of cause. Even Natural Philosophy, though it receives the notion of cause which it utilises from Metaphysics, does not itself enquire into the validity of this conception, for it is one which applies to all being, and therefore the investigation of it belongs properly to the science which considers being as such, which is Metaphysics. It will be useful, in order tc clarify our ideas as to the meaning of this concept of cause, to compare it with other cognate notions. The first of these is that of 'principle.' This is a wider idea than that of cause, for a thing which is not a cause may yet be a principle. It implies order of some sort, and is that which is first in any order.[1] From this the Aristotelean definition of principle as 'the first point from which a thing either is, or comes to be, or is known,'[2] is derived. S. Thomas, in the Physics, gives a wider definition of principle as 'that from which anything in any way proceeds';[3] so making it clear

[1] S. Thomas, *Comm. in V. Met.*, Lect. I.

[2] 1013a, 18; cf. the whole of this first Chapter of Book V of the Metaphysics.

[3] *Physics*, I, Lect. I.

that principle implies only an order of origin, and does not include any notion of an influence, derived from the principle, on those things which follow it.

Now it is plain from the common sense notion of cause that this differs from the notion of principle: first, as implying a real and positive influence on the things of which it is the cause, whereas principle implies no such influence ; secondly, and as a consequence of this, cause implies that the caused things are dependent on it, but principle implies no such dependence on the part of things which follow it ; thirdly, cause implies some priority to the effect, if not in time, at least in nature. Such priority is not implied by the notion of principle, which signifies merely an order between things, which can be present without any priority.

The second notion with which we may compare that of cause is 'condition.' This is something which is required for the production of some effect : either necessarily, in which case it is called a '*conditio sine qua non,*' or necessary condition ; or else to facilitate the production of the effect. In neither case does it positively pass into the effect itself : there is no influx from the condition into the effect ; and in this it differs from cause.

Again an 'occasion' differs both from condition and from cause, for an occasion is an event of such a kind that, on its occurrence, a free agent is moved to act ; and is thus one which has no influence on the effect, nor even a *necessary* connection with the action of the cause. It is a mere opportunity for action. So cause adds to condition influence on the effect ; condition adds to occasion necessity for the action of the cause. We may illustrate these distinctions by an example. The day begins with the dawn, but the dawn does not make the day, whereas a carpenter makes a table. That he may do so it is necessary that the wood he uses should be soft enough to work in. So the dawn is the beginning or 'principle' of the day, the carpenter the cause of the table, the softness of the wood the condition of its manipulation. If a man sees the sun shining, and decides to go out, the appearance of the sun is the occasion of his going ; but not the cause, nor the necessary condition.

The Scholastics, following Aristotle, recognise four genera of causes, two extrinsic ones, efficient and final; and two intrinsic, material and formal. In ordinary language nowadays we confine the name cause to the first class only, efficient causes, but in fact if cause be that which has a positive influence on the being of something else, as we have seen it is, this meaning will be too narrow. John of S. Thomas, therefore, defines cause as the principle of anything by way of influx or derivation, by means of which something which is dependent in being on the principle naturally follows.

There are then four ways in which the cause may pass into the effect; for it may be that *by* which the effect is produced, and we have an efficient cause; or that *for whose sake* the effect is produced, and we have a final cause; or that *out of which* it is produced, and we have a material cause; or that which makes the effect to be *of a particular kind,* and we have a formal cause.

A man building a house is its efficient cause; it is built to afford protection from the weather, and this is its final cause; it is made of bricks and mortar, its material cause; and it is a building and a building of a particular kind, which is its formal cause. All these four causes must combine in order that the house may be built, and therefore the house, which is the effect, is dependent for its existence on all four of them.

We have now to consider whether this concept of causation is merely a notion in our minds or whether there are real causes in the world, so that one reality is in fact produced by another. That there are such causes seems to be a plain fact; as, for example, that in writing I produce marks on the paper. The chief objections to asserting it to be true come from the Empiricists, such as Hume; who, since they recognise no knowledge except sense knowledge, maintain that it is impossible to know causes, and that the most that we can safely assert is that phenomena succeed one another; for this is, in fact, all that the senses tell us about them. Kant, too, held that cause is an *a priori* category of the mind, and so applies only to the phenomenal order, not to things-in-themselves. So again we should say that every phenomenon presupposes an antecedent phenomenon, not an absolute cause.

The principle of causality, which makes explicit the notion of cause, has as its formula: it is necessary that that which is not of itself should be produced by some other. This applies to efficient causality, and at present we are only concerned with this primary kind of causation.

Modern writers who wish to justify this principle are often inclined to base their defence of it on an appeal to our own internal experience. However valuable in itself, and consonant with current modes of thought, such an appeal may be, it is not the method adopted by S. Thomas, who grounds the certainty of the principle of causality on the metaphysics of being; and it seems that the appeal to consciousness only has its full value if such a metaphysical basis is presupposed.

S. Thomas says: '*Omne enim quod alicui convenit non secundum quod ipsum est, per aliquam causam convenit ei, sicut album homini; nam quod causam non habet, primum et immediatum est.*' So every attribute of a thing which belongs to it otherwise than by reason of its own being belongs to it by the operation of some cause; and it will follow that our principle of causality is a derivative of the principle of reason of being; the simplest formulation of which is: 'everything which is has its reason of being.' Such reason of being is twofold: intrinsic and extrinsic, the intrinsic reason being that by which it is made of a certain determinate nature, say a square rather than a circle. Evidently it is impossible to deny that a thing has in itself that by which it is constituted as that definite kind of thing which it is; since this would be to deny that its nature is its nature, a denial of the principle of identity. But the reason of being of a thing may also be extrinsic. So it may derive its *nature* from something extrinsic to itself, as the nature of properties is derived from that of the thing whose properties they are; or it may derive its *existence* from something else, if it has not existence in its own right. Indeed, if it exists, and does not possess existence in its own right, it must derive its existence from something which does so possess it. For it is plain that if anything is found in a being which does not belong to it in virtue of its own proper constitution, it has no reason of being in this thing itself. So things which are *of themselves* diverse cannot *of themselves* be one ; and if, in fact, they are made one or united, this union must be effected by something other than themselves. In this way the full formula of the principle of reason of being is justified : ' Every being has the reason of being of that which belongs to it either in itself or in some other : in itself, if that which belongs to it is a constituent of it in itself ; in another, if that which belongs to it does so without being a constituent of it in itself.' This principle is not deducible by a direct demonstration from the principle of identity, for it affirms a relation of dependence on another, a relation not affirmed in that principle. Moreover, since it is immediately evident in itself, it cannot be directly demonstrated. It can, nevertheless, be justified by a *reductio ad absurdum* ; which, of course, links it up with the principle of identity, since it is a denial of this principle, i.e. a contradiction, which is, strictly speaking, absurd. For if we deny the principle of the reason of being we affirm that that which does not possess existence of itself, and yet exists, does not derive its existence from any other. Since then it exists, it must have existence as its own proper possession ; and thus both exists of itself, and does not exist of itself.[1]

By cause, as we saw, we mean a principle on which something else depends for *existence* ; and consequently the notion of cause is less general than that of reason of being. Nevertheless it is true to say that the principle of causality

[1] The full analysis of the principle of the reason of being (from which that given here is derived) is to be found in Fr. Garrigou-Lagrange's *Dieu, son existence et sa nature* (5e edn., Paris, Beauchesne, 1928), pp. 171 ff. Rougier (*La Scolastique et le Thomisme*, p. 150) criticises it, saying that it involves a *petitio principii* ; and, what is plainly untrue, that Fr. Garrigou-Lagrange attempts to deduce the principle of the reason of being from that of identity. Both these criticisms miss the mark, for the second is simply false ; while the first is founded on the allegation that to say that a thing is itself *by* what makes it itself is already to introduce surreptitiously the principle of the extrinsic reason of being (i.e. of causality) into that of identity. This is not so, however, since nothing is the efficient cause of itself.

is a derivative of that of the reason of being.[1] For we cannot doubt that, where existence does not belong to a being as a constituent of its own self, if it has existence, it must receive it from something other than itself, or must be caused. Thus change and becoming demand an extrinsic reason of being, or a cause, for change is the successive union of differing things, and an unconditional union of differing things is impossible; otherwise elements which are of themselves differing would be of themselves the same, which is contrary to the principle of identity. Again if we regard change as the transit from potency to act, it is plain that it demands a cause, since what is about to change is potential to that into which it will change, as the bricks and mortar are potential to the house, the child to the philosopher. As we have agreed already that nothing can pass from potency to act except by means of some actual being, the actuation by an actual being (which will therefore be distinct from the thing about to change, which is potential) is required to bring about the change, or the actualisation of the potency in question. Such an actual being is a cause, the changing thing being dependent on it for its actualisation and actual existence. In the same way the multiplicity and diversity of things lead us to the postulation of a cause. For in such a multiplicity we have a number of things which, though differing, agree in some common element; being either parts of one being or else members of one species, or genus; or, at least, having a proportional or analogical unity. This being so, multiplicity implies a union of differing things, and since such a union cannot be unconditional, it demands an extrinsic condition of cause.[2] So S. Thomas says: '*Omne compositum causam habet, quæ enim secundum se diversa sunt, non conveniunt in aliquod unum nisi per aliquam causam adunantem ipsa.*'[3]

Multiplicity, like change, implies a composition of act and

[1] So Fr. D'Arcy, S.J., says: 'Causality is nothing but the application to the real world of the principle of sufficient reason.' (*Thomas Aquinas*, Benn, 1930, p. 143 f.)

[2] *Vide* Garrigou-Lagrange, op. cit., pp. 182 f.

[3] *Summa Theologica*, I, 3, 7.

potency, and cannot be pure act; for the diverse things which compose it are limited, and act can only be limited by potency. In the case of multiplicity, therefore, as well as in that of change the extrinsic reason of being which is demanded by it must be a principle of actualisation, or an efficient cause. The fact is of importance as showing that the notion of efficient cause, and the necessity for its presence, is not limited to the world of motion, to being in a dynamic state, but is equally applicable, and equally requisite in a static world of being to which motion and change do not penetrate, so long as this world is composed of many beings. That the world about us is in fact composed both of changing things and of many things is no more in doubt for S. Thomas than it is for common sense. Denial of this change and multiplicity must rest on a denial of *all* validity to sense perception, which involves denial of all knowledge (if sense knowledge is the basis of all knowledge) and so leads to a denial that we can know that change and multiplicity are not found in nature. So denial of these results in saying we are not entitled to make this denial.

The way in which S. Thomas establishes the legitimacy and necessity of the principle of causality, and the fact of efficient causality in the world shows that this conception is in no way anthropomorphic. It is based, not on our own internal experience of being causes, but on an analysis of what the nature of being necessarily requires. Hume's objection to causality is thus, so to say, side-tracked; for he asserts on the one hand, that we can only know by sense experience the succession of phenomena, never a relation of dependence between them; and, on the other, that our asserting that there is causality in the world about us is due to a transference of our own internal experience into the world at large, so constructing it in our own image. The first part of this objection is seen to be sound in so far as it maintains that sense knowledge gives us no knowledge of causality, but it falsely implies that the mind cannot penetrate beneath the sensible appearances, and by its intellectual power see the necessary laws which govern being itself. The principle and concept of causality is an ontological principle, dealing with what is essentially intelligible, and only accidentally phenomenal or sensible. The second part of the objection to causality cannot touch S. Thomas's defence of it, since he does not argue from our internal experience of causality, but points out what is absolutely demanded if we are to give any intelligible account of reality. To deny causality is, for him, to introduce absurdity, i.e. a contradiction, into the real world.

With this metaphysical foundation, however, we can legitimately have recourse to our own experience of being ourselves causes of thought and action. We produce and direct our thoughts, volitions and bodily movements, and distinguish such activities of ours from states of passivity; as, for example, in the suffering of pain. It should also be noticed that it is not to every regular succession or sequence of events that we attribute the relation of causality and dependence; we do not always say '*post hoc, propter hoc.*' So we name the sun as the cause of the daylight, but not the night as the cause of the day; though as far as regular succession goes, the night has the advantage over the sun.

We may add in conclusion that according to most Thomists the principle of causality is an analytic proposition,[1] and so universal and necessary; and not, as Kant maintained, a synthetic-*a-priori* judgement. The reason of this disagreement is, of course, to be found in their different theories of knowledge; and if it is true that the mind can, as S. Thomas maintains, apprehend the universal in the singular, the reason for supposing that the universality and necessity of this proposition must be derived from an *a priori* form of the mind disappears, and with it Kant's conclusion that the principle and concept of causation apply only to the phenomenal order, and not to the noumenal. S. Thomas asserts that it belongs to the ontological or noumenal order, not to the phenomenal, and so agrees with Hume in saying that it cannot be perceived by the senses, and with Kant in holding that it is universal and necessary.

There are, then, in the world, real causes and real effects; the effects depending on the causes, either for their production,

[1] Cf. Dr. H. S. Box, *The World and God*, Chap. XV.

their coming into existence—as in the case of father and son, the writer and his writing—or for their continuance in existence as well as for their production ; in which way the daylight, and life itself, are dependent on the causality of the sun.

We shall not attempt to discuss the theory of Malebranche and the Occasionalists that creatures are not efficient causes ; all causality being, in their view, Divine, and creatures being merely occasions for the exercise of this Divine causality. This theory which, both logically and historically, is continuous with that of Descartes, has, however, very little actuality to-day. It may, perhaps, suffice to remark that the theory debars us from having any real knowledge of finite things ; since we can only know these through their activities, and if they do not act, as Malebranche supposes, we cannot know them. Moreover, by depriving creatures of causality Malebranche really reduces them all to nonentities ; or, at best, makes them modifications of the Divine Being. As Fontenelle pointed out,[1] all Malebranche's arguments against finite efficacy have equal force against finite entity.

There is one kind of efficient causality which is of particular interest, both from a philosophical and from a theological point of view. This is instrumental causality, as to the nature of which Scholastic opinion has long been divided.

An instrument is, as everyone will acknowledge, something which is used in performing some action ; it is something useful, a tool. It must, therefore, be suitable for the purpose which it is intended to serve ; and so implies some intention, which is determined by the user, or principal agent. Such a purpose and intention is evidently superior to anything which the instrument possesses of itself, for we do not call a thing a tool or instrument which directs its own action, but reserve the name for something which ' no question makes of Ayes and Noes.' So the flamingo which Alice was required to use as a croquet-mallet could hardly be called an instrument because ' it *would* twist itself round and look up into her face,' just as she was going to use it. An instrument, properly so called, performs a function to which it is directed by its

[1] *Doutes sur le système physique des causes occasionelles.*

user, and one which of itself it could not perform; as croquet-mallets cannot of themselves play the game of croquet. So the Scholastics define an instrument as an agent which is raised by the power of the principal cause or agent to produce an effect of a higher order than itself, and one which is proportionate to the power of the principal cause alone.

From this it follows that there are in an instrument two distinct powers: that of the instrument itself, and that which it receives from the principal cause. For though we may attribute an action in which a tool is used chiefly to the user, yet it is clear that the tool also has a power and capacity of its own. So a cutting instrument, such as saw, plane, or chisel, must be used for shaping wood; a brush or hammer would be useless. Such powers as this, however, being native to the instrument, cannot be called 'instrumental power' in the proper sense of the term, for it does not make the thing which has it an instrument, for whether used as an instrument or not, it possesses this capacity. It is the power derived from the principal agent which is instrumental power.

Two conditions must, therefore, be fulfilled if a thing is to be an instrument. First, it must be used to produce an effect which it could not produce in virtue of its own power; for if it did so produce it, the effect would be attributed to it as a *principal* cause, not as an *instrumental* one; and, secondly, it must receive some power which renders it capable of producing such an effect—a power which is an addition to its own—from the principal cause. It is this dependence of the instrument on the principal cause which is the reason for S. Thomas's dictum: '*Est ratio instrumenti in quantum est instrumentum, ut moveat motum.*'[1]

What, then, is the nature of this power which the instrument receives from the principal cause? It is clearly not something native and proper to it, such as a property, nor yet an accident which is found in it even when withdrawn from the actual influence of the principal cause, and so is more or less permanent in it; as is the heat of hot water,

[1] *De Veritate*, Q. 27, a. 4.

for the water heats other things by its own heat, not by that of the fire which originally warmed it. It is a purely transitory power which is only found in the instrument when in actual use ; and so cannot be, as Suarez thought,[1] an active power in it of subserving the ends of the principal cause ; since such a power—which he calls an active obediential power[2]—will be found in it, whether in use or not.

Besides this view of Snarez, there are two others as to the nature of instrumental power ; of which one makes it extrinsic, and the other intrinsic to the instrument. So some theologians say that it is the help which is afforded by the principal cause, and which remains extrinsic to the instrument and assists it in acting. It acts, by a kind of sympathy, in accordance with the motion of the principal cause. It is very difficult to understand with any precision what such an extrinsic assistance may be ; and, in any case, it is not sufficient to explain instrumental causality, if an instrument is something which does in fact produce an effect which it could not produce by its unaided powers. This extrinsic assistance would, in this case, be the sole cause of the superiority of the effect ; and the instrument would contribute nothing to it, for not being in itself affected by this help, its capacity for action would be the same as if it was not being used as an instrument at all.

The Thomists, therefore, unanimously maintain that instrumental power is a transitory entity, which begins and ceases with the action for which it is evoked ; and which is received intrinsically by the instrument, which it perfects. Being thus something which affects the instrument intrinsically, it affects its nature ; and so is said to be a natural or physical entity, as opposed to a moral one, which acts from without ; so drawing a cause on to act, but not altering it in itself. So a donkey might be induced to move by showing it a bunch of carrots, but this would not give more strength to its legs ; whereas a feed of oats will make a horse run better. The first is moral causality, the second physical, affecting the nature in itself. Further, such physical

[1] *Disputationes Metaphysicæ*, Disp. XVII, Sec. 2.
[2] *De Incarn.*, I, Pars., Disp. 31, Sec. 6.

and transitory assistance communicated to the instrument by the principal cause, being essentially a transitory and passing help afforded to the instrument for the purpose of action —and so not something fixed in it, or static, but something passing through it, or dynamic—is called by the Thomists a 'motion'; and, since it is presupposed to the action of the instrument, a premotion. This doctrine of physical premotion has caused some bitter controversies among theologians in connection with the discussions concerning grace and free-will. In the simple form given above it seems harmless and natural enough; if it be granted that an instrument does produce the whole of the effect for which it is used. That it does so seems fairly clear from what has been said already; and this view is strengthened if we consider the difference between an instrument working under the influence of a principal cause, and two causes working side by side. On the canals we sometimes see a horse and man, both towing the same barge, and though some of the elements of instrumental causality are here present, others are absent. It is true that both man and horse combine to make the barge move, that the strength of the horse is far greater than that of the man, and that the man alone could not tow the barge at all, or, at least, not so easily. Yet no one would think of calling the man the instrument of the horse, since all he does he does by his own strength, and receives no intrinsic, but only an extrinsic aid from the horse. In order, then, that of two causes one may be subordinated to the other as an instrument to its user, it is necessary that the inferior activity should *depend* on the superior, and as a consequence, that the power of the superior one should be received intrinsically into the inferior, and so influence its action from within. If it does so, the whole effect will be attributable to the inferior or instrumental cause, and not merely a part of it, as in the case of the man and the horse. So my pen, in writing, will be responsible for making definite signs on the paper, and not merely ink marks; but, of course, only so long as it is being guided by my hand. This, therefore, seems to be the essential character of an instrumental cause, that it is, in contradistinction to a cause which works side by side with another, responsible for the production, of the whole of the effect, and moreover, receives the power to do so in itself ; not merely co-operating with some other cause external to itself, without any change occurring in its own power or causality. Though the instrument is moved in this way by the principal cause, its own native power is not thereby excluded. On the contrary, it is essential that it should retain this power, for otherwise it would cease to be an instrument, and become a mere medium for the passage of the power of the principal cause.

Such, in brief outline, is the Thomistic theory of instrumental causality. We may usefully summarise it in the following propositions :[1]

(1) An instrument is an efficient cause which, under the influence of a principal cause, is rendered capable of producing an effect which surpasses its own natural powers.

(2) It differs from the principal cause in two ways : by achieving an effect which surpasses its own powers, and by working under the influence of an alien and communicated power.

(3) This added power in it is not permanent, but a transitory quality found in it only while the action lasts and in view of the action ; it is also intrinsic to it, and so is a physical motion.

(4) Such motion does not merely accompany the motion of the instrument, being applied along with it to the effect, but modifies the instrument itself when in action, raising it to a higher order and applying it.

(5) Besides its instrumental action the instrument has its own action, which it produces as a principal cause. This action affects that of the principal cause to a certain extent ; since this must use the instruments in a way adapted to their nature.

(6) The action of the instrument, as such, is all one with that of the principal cause, so that a single effect results from their combined efforts. Both instrument and principal cause are thus responsible for the whole of the effect.

[1] Cf. P. Hugon, O.P., *La Causalité Instrumentale en Théologie* (Paris, Téqui, 1907), pp. 31 ff.

CHAPTER X

THE PRINCIPLE OF FINALITY

Existence of Finality—Division of Final Causes—The Attempt to Eliminate Finality—Aristotle and Finality—The Formulation of the Principle of Finality—It is Analogical—Its Truth Established.

IN considering the fact of change and motion we saw that if we are to give any intelligible account of it, and at the same time, uphold the ontological value of the principle of identity, it was necessary to recognise a fundamental division in being, and to distinguish being in potency from being in act. We saw further that the multiplicity and limitation of beings required us to say that all things which were so multiplied and limited must be composed of potency and act, which are really distinct in them. Thus all finite things will have at least two real elements, essence and existence, which stand to one another in the relation of potency to act. If the essence itself is further divisible, so that a species contains several individuals, this again can only come about by a real composition of potency and act in the heart of this essence itself. Since the actual element of these two is what gives the thing its determinate essence or nature, it is called ' form ' ; while the potential element which limits, and so multiplies it, is called matter. Again, in the last chapter, we concluded that change, or the passage from potency to act, demands an extrinsic reason of being, or an efficient cause. Hence this primary division of being into potency and act has already led us to posit, as essentially necessary if we are to recognise the reality of change and motion as well as the validity of thought; three of Aristotle's ' four causes ' of being. In the internal constitution of a being we always find potency which is essentially related to act (matter to form, essence to existence) the act always being that which is the perfection and completion of the potency; so that there is an internal order in all finite beings; their potentiality, as it were, crying out for, and demanding, a correlative actuality to complete and perfect it. There is always, therefore, a certain tendency in the heart of things themselves, one element tending towards the other, the potency tending towards the act which is its perfection and good. The efficient cause also essentially tends to convert the potential into the actual, and so contains in itself a certain tendency, or drive, towards a term which is that for whose sake it acts, and which is the end of its action, the perfection for whose sake it acts. Such a term or end towards which something is directed is that which moves it to act, and is therefore called the final cause. Finality is, then, apparent both in the internal constitution of every being (*potentia est ad actum*), and in the working of the extrinsic efficient cause which makes things change, for this is directed towards the actualisation of potentiality of its very nature. The end is, therefore, that for which the agent operates; and different kinds of end will correspond to differences, either in the object and the way in which it attracts the agent, or to differences in the agent itself, i.e. in its intentions. In Scholastic language we say that the division of ends can be made either from the side of the object, or from that of the subject or agent. If we consider the end objectively in so far as it attracts the agent we have the end for whose sake the action is done, and this is the good which is willed or intended (*finis cujus gratia*), which may be either the good itself which is willed or desired, or else the act by which this good is to be attained. These last are called *finis qui* and *finis quo* respectively. If we now consider the end subjectively, i.e. with respect to the intention of the agent, we have the division of end into *finis operis* and *finis operantis*; the first being the end which the work or action naturally tends to produce (*finis effectus*), or to obtain (*finis obtentus*), as health is produced by exercise, or goods obtained by payment; while the second, the end which the agent has in view when acting, may differ from the *finis operis*, as when the athlete, though gaining health by exercise, takes it, not with this intention, but in order to win a race.

We must now consider whether there is, in fact, such tendency towards an end, such finality, to be found in the world. The principle of finality, which asserts that finality is universally present where there is action, is formulated in various ways: for example: 'Every agent acts for an end,' or 'Nature does nothing in vain.' These, and all similar statements are denied by the materialists, according to whom there are no such things as natural or voluntary tendencies; the most we can say is that things happen in a certain way. We might, perhaps, say with regard to a machine, such as the engine of a motor car, that the explosions do not occur in the cylinders in order to move the pistons, but that if the explosions occur, the pistons will move. Similarly, in the world of nature, the materialists maintain, for example, that certain chemical elements have no tendency to combine, but do combine because they have a certain constitution; bodies have no natural tendency to move in accordance with the law of gravitation, but do so move as a fact; plants have no natural tendency to grow, or to produce flowers or fruit, but if stimulated in certain ways, do produce them; animals do not have eyes and ears in order to see and hear, but see and hear because they have eyes and ears; and finally, man has no purpose in his actions, but acts as he does because he is of a certain kind, and conditioned in a definite way by his environment. That living things can adapt *themselves* to their environment is necessarily denied by this theory; and this is, probably, one of the chief reasons why it has declined in popularity, for the signs of such adaptation have become increasingly clear with the progress of biological investigation. Some instances of variation of action without variation of the environment have already been noticed in connection with the actions of the lower organisms, such as Paramœcium;[1] and they become clearer and more striking as we ascend to the more complicated forms of life. Common sense, of course, has always maintained that a man has eyes in order to see, a

[1] Cf. Vol. I, Part II, Chap. X, esp. p. 248.

bird wings in order to fly. The mechanistic or materialistic doctrine contradicts this and says that a man sees because he has eyes, a bird flies because it has wings. So there would, on this view, be no purpose in the universe as a whole, nor in any part of it, nor even in the life of man, but all things move on to a predestined and inevitable conclusion. Instead of telling the tree by its fruits, and seeking to discover the nature of things by looking at their most perfect and developed forms, materialism rather aims at explaining the perfect by the imperfect, and standing the pyramid on its apex, accounts for intellectual life by means of sensitive, sensitive by means of vegetative; while vegetative life is, in turn, explained as the product of physico-chemical forces.[1]

The origins of this elimination of finality from nature are to be found in the attempt made by Descartes and Spinoza to treat of the physical universe entirely by the methods of mathematics, which take no account of finality. Nevertheless, Descartes admitted internal finality, i.e. that the organs, say, of an animal tend to preserve its life and that of the species; though later even this attenuated form of teleology was dropped, in accordance with the theory that the presence of such and such organs in an animal could be explained, not as tending of themselves to preserve the species, but on the ground that only those animals which had such organs as were in fact of use in doing so, survived. Everything is to be explained by survival value, natural selection blindly eliminating those things which were less fitted to survive. It is plain that this doctrine encounters increasingly formidable difficulties as we pass from the lower to the higher forms of life, and if it is difficult to guess what the survival value of the colours and patterns of a butterfly's wings may be, it is impossible to assign any such value to what we consider man's most desirable character-

[1] Cf. Bertrand Russell's essay on a 'Free Man's Worship' (*Philosophical Essays*, p. 70) which, as Dr. Inge says, leaves no room either for freedom or worship. 'Blind to good and evil, reckless of destruction, omnipotent matter rolls on its relentless way.' This, according to Russell, is the whole truth; but he thinks it is nice for us to pretend that matter is not omnipotent. We are to show our 'freedom' by worshipping something 'which our own hands have built,' and which we know quite well to be a fake and pretence: a foolish 'make-believe.'

istics, his development of mental, æsthetic and moral qualities. In fact, no one has ventured to maintain that intellectual, artistic, or saintly men are more prolific than idiots or criminals ; but rather the reverse, so that the presence of all that we count noblest in human life must be attributed to chance, that is, left without any explanation at all. 'Can we be content,' asks Lord Balfour, 'to regard the highest loyalties, the most devoted love, the most limitless self-abnegation as the useless excesses of a world-system, which, in its efforts to adapt organism to environment, has overshot its mark ? '[1]

Aristotle, as is well known, was a consistent champion of the reality of final causes. In the *Physics*,[2] we find him arguing against this very doctrine, which we generally associate with the name of Darwin, and which we have just outlined; namely, that wherever things 'came about just what they would have been if they had come to be for an end, such things survived, being organised spontaneously in a fitting way ; whereas those which grew otherwise perished and continued to perish.'[3] This theory of natural selection by the survival of the fittest, whereby nature mimics teleology, had been put forward by Empedocles ; and Aristotle argues against it on the ground that it does not explain the permanence of types, and that animals breed true to type, monstrosities being only of rare occurrence. These latter, then, may be ascribed to chance, but not the former ; whereas it is, in fact, the monstrosities which are eliminated, not the permanent type. The fact of the matter is that even if the doctrine of Empedocles and Darwin be accepted, the result is only that it is *easier* to believe in chance and accident as the origin of some variation on types ; but not that the whole process, or the normal development of things, can be accounted for in this way. In fact, according to the theory itself things are fitted to survive ; they are adapted to this end which is survival. So in his biology Aristotle always attempts to explain structure by function, not vice versa ;

[1] Cf. A. J. Balfour, *Theism and Humanism*, pp. 108 ff.
[2] *Phys.*, II, 8.
[3] *Phys.*, 198b, 29–34. (Oxford translation.)

his belief in teleology dominates his whole system. As Professor Ross says : ' One of the most conspicuous features of Aristotle's view of the universe is his thorough-going teleology. Apart from occasional sports and coincidences all that exists or happens exists or happens for an end.'[1] This characteristic of his thought is strikingly exemplified in his notion of God, whose connection with the universe is, in his view, chiefly, if not exclusively, that of a final cause to which it tends. With such whole-hearted advocacy of finality on the part of Aristotle we should be surprised if we did not find a strong conviction of the presence of purpose in the world, and in all its parts, in the philosophy of S. Thomas. Though some say that he modifies Aristotle's doctrine here to a great extent, especially in connection with the idea of God ; whom he makes not only the final, but also the efficient cause, or creator, of the world ; S. Thomas maintains that finality is present in connection with every action. He regards the principle of finality as self-evident, and that it is so independently of the demonstration of the existence of God. If we are to see his point of view about this, it is necessary that the principle should be clearly formulated.

Such expressions of it as ' all that comes to be is directed towards an end ' or ' every being is directed towards an end,' are to be avoided. The first is neither necessary nor evident, since many things come about by chance, such as the configurations of mountain and valley ; for it is not plain that the presence or absence of a hill at a given place subserves any determinate end. The second formula is applicable only partially, to some beings and not to all, for in fact God is independent of all extrinsic cause. The true and precise formula used by S. Thomas and the Scholastics is : ' Every agent acts for (or in view of) an end.' ' *Ubi non est actio non est causa finalis,*' as S. Thomas says,[2] for final cause only causes by moving the efficient cause to act.

It is, however, important to notice that this principle, ' *omne agens agit propter finem,*' must be understood analogically

[1] Ross, *Aristotle*, p. 185. [2] *De Potentia*, Q. V, a. 1.

as it applies to God, to created intellectual agents, and to natural agents not endowed with reason. As regards God and creatures this is clear, for obviously no term can be applied to God in the same sense as that in which it is applied to finite things. Among finite things we can see that 'direction towards an end' has a very different sense as applied to a man and an avalanche. S. Thomas shows that there are three main classes among these analogates of the final cause, classes to which 'action for an end' applies in senses which are, simply speaking, different, though proportionally the same, inasmuch as there is a proportion between each agent and the end of its action.

He distinguishes :[1]

(1) Agents endowed with reason, which act for an end with knowledge of their purpose and of finality itself, and so are said to act *directive formaliter*. Having knowledge of the end as an end to be attained, they are thus able to choose means for its attainment.

(2) Animals which are not rational act for an end with knowledge of the thing for the acquisition of which they act, but not knowing it as an end ; and so are said to act *directive non formaliter sed materialiter tantum*. So an animal, being able to sense the object, e.g. a dog smelling his dinner, is not merely passively moved towards it, but actively moves itself to get this object. It desires the object and acts accordingly, but does not know the object as desirable.

(3) Natural agents which have no knowledge, not even that of the senses, act for an end merely in so far as they act definitely, and so are said to act for an end *executive tantum* ; that is, only by the execution of their action. Such action is determined for them by the laws of their nature. They have, therefore, of themselves, no purpose in their action ; and it is this fact which has led to doubt being thrown on the universal applicability of the principle of finality. So stones have no intention or purpose in falling ; while animals have a purpose or intention in acting, but do not know it as a purpose. Only man, among the beings with which we are familiar, both has and knows his purpose in

[1] *Summa Theologica*, I, 18, 3 ; I, II, 1, 2 ; I, II, 6, 2 ; I, II, 11, 2.

acting. Are we, then, to confine the application of the principle to man, or, at most, extend it also to the animals; and exclude from its scope all things which are destitute of knowledge? Or can we, on the contrary, affirm, quite apart from any demonstration of the existence of God, or of a Divine guidance and ordering of the universe, that every agent acts for an end? S. Thomas is decidedly of the opinion that we can; and supports his contention by arguing both *a posteriori*, from an examination of nature itself, and *a priori*.

If, then, we look over the world of nature we find everywhere facts which are inexplicable if the direction of action towards an end is excluded. So we see in living things the adaptation of organs to their functions, and in both living and inanimate ones the general tendency of all the parts to the perfection of the whole. Moreover, we see in the world order, and constant and invariable law. Now these facts cannot be explained without finality, since, if we rule this out, we should have to attribute them either to the operation of an efficient cause; or seek to explain them by means of the material organisation of the agents; or, finally, say that they come about by chance.

The efficient cause *by itself* cannot afford a sufficient explanation of definite action: for to state that there is such a cause does not provide the answer to the question: why does the agent act rather than remain quiescent, why does it do this rather than that? To assign an efficient cause of an action merely tells us *how* it comes about, not *why*; and is therefore no explanation of it, but merely an assertion of 'brute fact.' Again, the purely material constitution of the agent affords no sufficient explanation of the order of the world; for we want to know not merely what particular configuration of matter will enable an animal to see, for example, but why he possesses that particular organ which enables him to do so. If he does not have it for the purpose of seeing, why does he have it? It is evidently not absolutely necessary; in the same way as it is necessary for the triangle that its angles should together be equal to two right angles. We do not ask why is an animal an animal, but why this portion of matter is an eye rather than an ear. It is very well to say: eyes are not made to see, but man sees because he has eyes; but the question immediately arises: why has he eyes? If we answer: because they have survival value, we come back again in the long run to purpose. If he is to survive he must have eyes, and so only those who have eyes survive. But how did he get these eyes? The only answer could be: by chance. If we are not to say this we must acknowledge that a man has eyes in order to survive, in order that they may be used; that they come to be in order to function in a certain way, not that they function in that way because they chance to have a certain structure. If we are not to explain everything by chance we must admit finality. But perhaps we can do this, and say that chance accounts for everything. A moment's reflection will show that this is impossible, for there can be no chance without law. If there is no rule there can be no exception, so that to say that everything is chance is to deny chance as well. I may chance to find a treasure when digging in my garden, but only if I dig. Moreover, chance is no explanation, and the assigning of it as the cause of all things is not only incredible, but impossible; for then we should have to say that the perfect is produced by the imperfect; order by disorder; what is, by what is not.

The truth of the principle of finality can also be shown *a priori*, that is to say it is evident in itself. There is little or no doubt that this was S. Thomas's opinion: it is sufficient to cite the article of the *Summa*[1] where he deals with the question whether teleological action is proper to rational nature alone. His explanatory argument to show that all agents must act for an end may be summarised as follows. Final cause is the first of all causes. The reason of this is that matter only receives a form if it is made to do so by an agent; for nothing passes from potency to act of itself. Now no agent moves or acts except in so far as it tends towards some end; for if it did not act in order to produce some determined effect, it would not act at all. If some

[1] *Summa Theologica*, I–II, Q. 1, a. 2.

definite thing is produced, its definiteness or determination must be due to the agent which produces it, for if it were not, it would be without any reason of being. Just as the being of the effect must in some way pre-exist in the cause, so also the determination of the effect must be already in some way present in the productive action. Now obviously it is not there actually and formally, as it is in the effect, only virtually; i.e. in the power of the cause whose action is directed to the production of this effect. To deny this direction and tendency is, therefore, equivalent to denying that the actual determination of the effect has any reason of being. This denial is self-contradictory, as we saw when considering the principle of the reason of being; and so it is an absurdity.

Action, then, is essentially intentional. It tends always to the production of some definite effect. Action which had no definite direction or tendency would not be action at all.

To deny finality, even in inanimate things, is thus only possible if we deny them a definite nature and so definite modes of action; a denial consistent neither with experience nor with reason; for things with no definite nature would be altogether unknowable.[1] We may conclude this discussion with the dictum of S. Thomas: '*Omne agens agit propter finem; alioquin ex actione agentis non magis sequeretur hoc quam illud, nisi a casu.*'[2]

[1] For the whole discussion of the principle of finality and its applications *vide* R. P. Garrigou-Lagrange, O.P., *Le Réalisme du Principe de Finalité* (Paris, Desclée, 1932), Chaps. IV and V.

[2] *Summa Theologica*, I, 44, 4; cf. III *Contra Gentiles*, cc. II and III.

CHAPTER XI

THE CO-ORDINATION OF CAUSES

Reciprocal Causation ; where Possible—Its Applications—Possibility of Two Total Causes of One Effect.

To complete our consideration of the Thomistic doctrine of causality something must be said as to the mutual interdependence of the four causes. In assigning these four causes Aristotle makes it plain that he uses the word 'cause' analogically, in so far as the being of a material thing depends in different ways on each of the four ; all four together being necessary for its production. We have already seen that matter is essentially directed to form, and the agent towards the end ; and, in general, the Thomists maintain that causes are causes of one another, though in different genera of causality. Clearly reciprocal causation is impossible in the same genus of causality ; for example, two efficient causes cannot be causes of one another at the same time and with respect to the same effect. For causes of the same genus with respect to the same effect require absolutely the same conditions. If, therefore, they were causes of one another, each would have all the conditions necessary in order that it might cause, and would not have those which are necessary in order that it might be caused ; and the converse would also be true. We are thus led to the contradictory conclusion that each would, and would not, have those conditions necessary for it to cause and be caused. In different genera of causality, on the contrary, this does not hold good ; as can be seen in the example of work and health, where work which does not require over-exertion is an efficient cause of good health, and the good health is the end for which the work is undertaken, or its final cause. This principle of the mutual interdependence of causes is a fundamental one in the Thomist system, and throws light on many obscure problems. So, in sense knowledge, it is applied to the mutual causality of the senses and their objects ;[1] in intellectual knowledge, to the interdependence of sense and intellect ;[2] and in the question of free will to the relations of the will and the intellect.[3] In the purely physical order the principle applies in the question of generation to the relations between the dispositions of the changing subject and its substantial form.[4]

In his commentary on the Metaphysics[5] of Aristotle, S. Thomas explains this mutual subordination of causes. So he points out that the two pairs of causes, extrinsic and intrinsic, correspond one to another. There is a reciprocal correspondence of agents and end, since the agent is the principle of motion, and the end its term. Matter and form correspond similarly, for form gives the specific being and matter receives it. So the agent is the cause of the end, while the end is the cause of the action of the agent. The agent is the cause of the end inasmuch as it effects or produces the end, giving it being and making it a reality ; or by obtaining it, gaining possession of its being for itself ; while the end is the cause of the action, not with respect to the being of the action as such, but as it is a causal action, since the end is the reason why the agent acts. So the agent receives its causality from the end ; being an agent only in so far as it acts, and acting only for the sake of the end.

The same holds good with respect to the two intrinsic causes : matter and form. The form is the cause of the matter inasmuch as it makes it exist actually, while the matter is the cause of the form inasmuch as it sustains the form. So substantial form makes matter a reality ; and accidental form giving some additional being to it, adds to it some accidental existence. Thus we can see that in many cases where, at first sight, there might seem to be a *petitio principii,*

[1] Vol. I, pp. 225 ff.
[2] *Ibid.*, pp. 261 ff.
[3] *Ibid.*, pp. 288 ff.
[4] *Ibid.*, p. 135.
[5] *In Met.*, Lib. V, Lect. II (Ed Cathala, No. 775).

or a vicious circle, there is, in fact, none, owing to the mutual interdependence of causes in different genera of casuality.

So we saw that the dispositions required for the appearance of a new substantial form, i.e. for a substantial generation, precede this form in the order of material causality, while the form precedes the dispositions in the order of formal causality ; and there is no priority of time.

Even in man, the body which is to be informed by a soul will, by its very material constitution, require a soul proportionate to it ; and, on the other hand, it will be a body of a particular material constitution in accordance with the soul which is going to inform it. So the body of an intellectual genius will be adapted to the soul of a genius ; while the reason why the body is so adapted is that it is informed by a soul of great nobility. Again, we saw that in sense knowledge the faculty of sense, such as sight, has an impression made upon it by the object, and so is assimilated to the object ; while, since the object is received in a vital faculty, it is assimilated to this faculty, and so is to a certain extent dematerialised or spiritualised. In this way we can understand how it is possible that in sensation the object should produce a species which is more immaterial, and so more perfect, than itself. This perfection of the species is, indeed, due, not to the perfection of the sense object as a purely material thing, but to its reception in a vital and organic power. So the psychological impression made by the object, being the proximate disposition to the vital action of sensing, precedes this action in the genus of material cause, and follows it in that of formal, efficient, and final cause.

It is not necessary to repeat here what has already been said as to the mutual interaction of intellect and will in a free act : but this is plainly one of the most striking applications of the principle of the mutual interdependence of causes.[1]

It is certain, then, that several causes of different genera can concur to produce one and the same effect. But can two causes of the same genus be causes of one effect ? To answer

[1] Cf. Vol. I, p. 135.

this question we must distinguish between total and partial, adequate and inadequate causes.

A total cause is one which in itself, in its nature, has sufficient power for the production of the whole effect; while that is called an adequate cause which in action, and not merely in nature, is sufficient for the production of the whole effect.[1] A partial cause will, then, be one which in itself has not sufficient power for the production of the whole effect, and an inadequate cause one whose action is not sufficient for the production of the whole effect.

Our question concerns two causes of the same genus, and causes which are not subordinated one to the other; for we have already seen that two subordinated causes, a principal and an instrumental one, can be total causes of one and the same effect; and all Thomists hold that this is also true with regard to created causes acting in subordination to the first cause, or God. So they say that the act of the will is wholly from the will as from its proximate cause, and from God as its first cause.

If, then, we exclude such subordinated causes we find disagreement, as between the Thomists and other Scholastics, as to the possibility of two total and adequate non-subordinated causes producing the same effect; for the Thomists think it to be impossible; others that it is possible supernaturally, though not naturally.

The reason for the Thomists' opinion is that a finite cause is evidently limited, not merely specifically, but also individually; its action being limited to the principle from which it proceeds, and to the term to which it is directed. Consequently, an action which has once been produced by one agent cannot be produced by another and remain the same action, and an action which has once reached an individual term cannot reach another individual term and remain the same action. So the supposition that we could have two total, adequate, and non-subordinated causes of the same effect is contradictory, for each would be an actual total cause, by hypothesis, and at the same time each would not be a total cause, since each leaves room for the causality of the other.

[1] *Joannes a S. Thoma. Phil. Nat.*, I.P., Q. X., A. V.

We have had occasion earlier to consider one case of this principle when discussing the possibility of the plurality of substantial forms, where we saw that substantial form bestows being, simply speaking, and thus the being having been once constituted a specific substantial being by one substantial form cannot be so constituted anew by another, so that any further form will be an accidental one; and it is, therefore, impossible to have two substantial forms which actuate the same individual matter.

The brief review of the nature of causality which has now been given, leads naturally to the next and last division of Metaphysics, which deals with being which is in itself altogether immaterial; for such being is God, who is primarily considered by S. Thomas, from a philosophical point of view, as the First Cause of all things. The immediate foundation of the classical proofs of God's existence is, as Fr. Garrigou-Lagrange points out, the principle of efficient causality; both it and the principle of finality being derivatives of that of the reason of being.

PART III. NATURAL THEOLOGY

CHAPTER I

THE DEMONSTRABILITY OF THE EXISTENCE OF GOD

Natural Theology a Part of Metaphysics—Two Objections: God is the Object of Faith; God is Unknowable—The Answer to the First Objection—Is the Existence of God Self-evident?—The Ontological Argument—Rejected by S. Thomas—The Second Objection—Hume and Kant—Conditions of a Rigorous Demonstration—The Transcendent Value of the First Notions and Principles.

IT is unnecessary to repeat here what has already been said as to the nature, scope and division of metaphysics; but it may be useful to recall that we saw that being which is positively immaterial, i.e. which never exists in matter, will, if it exists at all, have to form the subject of a special part of metaphysics, inasmuch as its nature must be different to that of all other being. Since God is conceived of as immaterial in this way, the name Natural Theology or Theodicy is applied to the section of this second part of metaphysics which treats of God. There may seem to be a surprising discontinuity between a discussion of the Divine existence, nature, and attributes and the investigation into the natures of things which we have, so far, been carrying out; for the word 'God' has for us primarily a religious signification; and we have become accustomed to the notion that God can be known, if at all, only by faith and not by reason. S. Thomas would never consent to such a mutilation of human knowledge, which, if allowed, would exclude us from knowing anything of the source and ground of things. On the contrary he maintains that metaphysics, the science of being, must deal with the ultimate principles of being.

Consequently, there must be a part of metaphysics which will treat of the ultimate principle or source of being, which we call God, if metaphysics is to be properly speaking the science of being, i.e. the knowledge of being through its causes. On the other hand, there can be no natural knowledge of God outside metaphysics, since it is proper to this science to treat of being and its causes, and it is only as the ultimate cause of being that we consider God in Natural Theology.

It will be necessary, therefore, in the first place, for us to ask whether there really exists in fact such an ultimate cause of being ; for it would plainly be a waste of time to consider the nature of this cause unless we were first assured that it existed. Can we know, then, by the use of reason, that God exists ?

To this question a negative answer is often given : either on the ground that God is the object of faith, not of knowledge, or because it is supposed that human reason is incompetent to decide whether God exists or not. It is to be observed that the two reasons just mentioned as precluding us from having such knowledge are of very different kinds. For those who maintain that God can only be known by faith and not by reason, do not deny or even doubt that He exists, their objection is concerned only with the manner in which we are assured of His existence. The position of those who affirm the incompetence of the reason in this matter is quite other ; for these are doubtful not merely as to the true method of assuring ourselves of the Divine existence, but as to the fact of that existence itself. This theoretical Agnosticism, or profession of ignorance as to whether God exists or not, evidently amounts in practice to a denial of His existence : since He is to be ignored. The objection, moreover, is one which denies that the human mind by its natural powers, i.e. by reasoning, can conclude to the existence of God, and is therefore a direct objection against the demonstrability of this existence. The first reason renders all discussion of the demonstrability of God's existence vain, since if we are already assured of it by faith, there is no need to enquire further ; and so it is indirectly aimed against this demonstrability. It will therefore be logical to discuss the two objections in the order named, and we shall thus clear the ground progressively. It is, in fact, the order adopted by S. Thomas, who puts in the first place the objection which would render the discussion of the possibility of demonstration futile,[1] and then those which attack this possibility in itself.[2]

Just as in S. Thomas's day there were those who maintained that the existence of God is to be accepted by faith alone, and so is not to be demonstrated, so there are also in our own. It is, in fact, felt by those who take this view to be, in some sort, impious to attempt to prove what they firmly believe; and possibly there is mixed with this attitude a kind of false mysticism, as if they had already a kind of direct intuition of God. All that has been said earlier as to the nature of the human intellect and its proper object runs counter to such an idea as this, for we are convinced that we know the immaterial and supersensible by means of the material and sensible; the proper object of man's intellect being the natures of material things. Moreover, it is clear that to say that we know God's existence by faith is to make an assertion which refutes itself, since no one can accept anything on the authority of God, i.e. by faith, who is not first convinced that there is a God. Hence S. Thomas says here in answer to this objection, that the existence of God is not an article of faith, but one of the '*præambula*' to the articles of faith, natural knowledge being presupposed by faith, as nature is by grace, and in general that which is perfectible by perfection.

To this the Thomists[3] add that the existence of God which is proved by reason relates to God as He is the author of the natural order, while faith in His existence can coexist with this natural certainty in so far as He is believed to exist as the author of the supernatural order. This belief in God's existence as the first cause of the supernatural order is an

[1] *Summa Theologica*, I, 2, 2, 1.
[2] *Ibid.*, I, 2, 2 et 3.
[3] Cf. Gonet, *Clypeus Thomisticus*, Tom. IV, De fide, Disp. I, a. VI, Sec. II; Garrigou-Lagrange, *De Revelatione*, Vol. I, p. 438.

article of faith, whereas knowledge of His existence as the first cause of the natural order is a preamble to faith.[1]

If, then, the question of the existence of God is one which is not confined to the sphere of faith, but falls also within that of reason, it may be that it is still in no need of demonstration because it is self-evident. S. Thomas therefore prefaces his consideration of the objections raised to the possibility of demonstrating it by one concerning the necessity of doing so.[2]

He states and confutes, in various places,[3] at least thirteen arguments which are intended to show that the proposition 'God is' is self-evident. We cannot discuss them in detail, but they all revolve round the notion that existence and essence are identical in God, so that to conceive of His essence is to conceive of His existence. Thus the denial of the proposition 'God is' is impossible, involving the manifest contradiction of saying: 'that which *is* existence does not exist.' If the predicate of a proposition is included in (or is identical with) the subject the proposition is self-evident; in which way the principles of identity and non-contradiction or the proposition that the whole is greater than its part are self-evident.

Now there are two things to be noticed about this suggestion. First, that any attempt to prove a self-evident proposition proves that the man who makes it does not consider it self-evident; and secondly, that though a proposition may be self-evident, it only shows itself as such to me if I understand its terms. No abstract proposition is self-evident to a dog or a cat, and the proposition 'the whole is greater than its part' is not evident to a man unless he understands all its terms.[4] Now in the proposition which asserts God's existence, though I may understand what I mean by existence, I do not understand the nature of God in itself. My knowledge of the Divine nature is analogical,

[1] Cf. *De Veritate*, Q. 14, a. 9, ad 8.

[2] *Summa Theologica*, I, 2, 1.

[3] *Summa Theologica*, I, 2, 1; I *Sent.*, Dist. III, Q. 1, a. 2; I *Contra Gentiles*, c. 10; *De Veritate*, Q. 10, a. 12.

[4] And if we are talking of metaphysical self-evidence, and not merely logical, we shall not be able to confine ourselves to an analysis of the terms, but shall have to understand the 'things.'

and does not apply to the nature in itself but to this nature regarded as in some way similar to creatures, which alone I know directly. What God is in His own proper nature, with regard to the mode of the Divine perfections, we know only negatively and relatively. In this way we form an idea of God's essence; deriving from our knowledge of creatures concepts of the Divine perfections, their mode in God remaining unknown.[1] So though we may, and indeed must, conclude, on examining the notion of the Divine essence so formed, that it must be identical with existence, we do not see this in the essence itself which we know; but conclude by a process of reasoning that the existence of such a being as that whose essence we have thus conceived must be identical with that essence. So the proposition 'God is,' though self-evident in itself, since in fact essence and existence in God are identical, is not self-evident as far as we are concerned, for we never intuit God's essence and see therein His existence. We may, as the result of a process of reasoning, know that the proposition 'God is' is self-evident, we never know its self-evidence.

The most famous attempt to show that the proposition 'God is' is a self-evident one is that made by S. Anselm in his *Proslogium*. It is what is known as the Ontological Argument, and its rejection by almost all Catholic theologians is no doubt due, in great measure, to the clarity with which S. Thomas pointed out its inconclusiveness. S. Anselm argued as follows: Our idea of God is that of a Being than whom no greater can be conceived. But that than whom no greater can be conceived cannot be in the understanding alone, i.e. a mere idea which has no reality apart from the

[1] As S. Thomas says (in *Boet. de Trin.*, Q. 1, a. 2) a thing may be known either *per formam propriam*, if we know its very nature in itself; or else we may know it *per formam alterius sibi similis*. This last is the way we know God, not knowing His quiddity 'for we have neither his genus, nor difference, nor definition,' as Capreolus notes in I *Sent.*, Dist. II, Q. 1, a. 1 conclusio V.

So we can say that we know the essence though we do not know it essentially (*cognoscimus quidditatem sed non quidditative*) inasmuch as we have positive though analogical knowledge of some essential predicates. This is the distinction made by Cajetan (*Comm. in De Ente et Essentia*, Cap. VI, Q. XV). '*Cognoscit leonis quidditatem quicumque novit aliquod ejus prædicatum essentiale. Cognoscit autem quidditative non nisi ille, qui omnia prædicata quidditativa usque ad ultimam differentiam novit.*'

mind, for if it were, and did not exist, something greater than this could be conceived, namely a being which had all that the first had and existence in addition, which would thus be a Being greater than the greatest conceivable one. This Being, then, which we call God must exist in reality as well as in idea.

The answer to this argument is to be seen by distinguishing the minor : if the most perfect being did not exist and were not conceived of as existing of itself, one could conceive of a more perfect one, I concede : if the most perfect being, though not existing, were conceived as existing of itself, one could conceive of a more perfect one, I deny. So we cannot conclude that God exists, but only that if He exists He must exist of Himself. So if He exists, He exists not contingently but necessarily, but it is not necessary that He should exist. The fact that we conceive, and must conceive, of God in a certain way, namely as existing of Himself, in no way shows that in fact there is a Being which exists of itself, but merely that if there is a Being to whose concept existence attaches necessarily, He will, if He exists at all, exist necessarily.

This argument was put forward again both by Descartes and Leibniz, and is not without its champions at the present day. Kant, on the other hand, criticised it ; and indeed his rejection of those other arguments for the existence of God which he examined, is based on the rejection of the ontological ; at least in so far as it is a criticism of the arguments themselves and not a corollary derived from his theory of knowledge. For he holds the other arguments to be invalid inasmuch as, in his opinion, they make a surreptitious and illicit appeal to the ontological argument, which is itself invalid. Curiously enough, though so much seems to depend on his showing the fallacy of the ontological argument, his criticism of it is, in fact, faulty ; and indeed, as Professor Sorley has pointed out, irrelevant.[1] It may be noticed that while Descartes' restatement of the argument leaves it essentially unchanged and so open to S. Thomas's criticism, the form given to it by Leibniz (that God is possible, and if He

[1] W. R. Sorley, *Moral Values and the Idea of God* (C.U.P., 1924), p. 310.

is possible, He must exist)[1] somewhat modifies it ; and the answer to this way of arguing is that we cannot, since we have no intuition of God's nature, know *a priori* that He is possible.[2] As far as Descartes' form of the argument is concerned Leibniz associates himself with the criticism of Aquinas ;[3] and throughout his discussion of it shows a much keener insight into the strength and weakness of the proof than does Kant.

Some modern writers, as Lotze, Caird, and Bosanquet, have tried to restore the credit of the ontological argument which they wrongly supposed to have been destroyed by Kant's criticisms. As Fr. Joyce clearly shows,[4] these restatements have little or no connection with the argument of S. Anselm and Descartes. Space does not allow us to consider them, nor yet the other arguments used to show that the existence of God is self-evident which are refuted by S. Thomas,[5] and which have some affinity with them ; but we must pass on to the objections raised against the demonstrability of the Divine existence by those who take up a position at the other extreme to that which we have been considering.

In place of saying that the existence of God is indemonstrable because it is self-evident, these declare that it lies outside the range of what can be attained by the working of man's mind.

The grounds on which this allegation are based differ widely in themselves but are one in their effect, which is to exclude metaphysical concepts and principles from claiming to be valid of objective reality. The ground taken by the Empiricists is that all our knowledge is in essence sense knowledge, while that of Idealistic Agnostics is that we clothe everything in the forms of our own minds, and so can

[1] *Monadology*, Secs. 44 and 45.

[2] Cf. Leibniz, *The Monadology*, etc., ed. Latta (O.U.P., 1925), Appendix G., p. 274 ; Garrigou-Lagrange, *Dieu*, p. 69.

[3] *Meditationes de Cognitione, Veritate et Ideis.*

[4] G. H. Joyce, S.J., *Principles of Natural Theology* (Longmans, 1924), pp. 211-215.

[5] *Summa Theologica*, I, 2, 1, ad 1 et 3 ; *De Veritate*, Q. X, a. 12 ; cf. Sertillanges, *S. Thomas d'Aquin*, Vol. I, pp. 135 ff. ; *Foundations of Thomistic Philosophy* (Sands), pp. 58 ff.

never have knowledge of objective realities but only of phenomena. The protagonists of these two views are Hume and Kant; of whom the latter was, as is well known, profoundly influenced by the former.

Hume's attack, as far as our present subject is concerned, was chiefly directed against the ontological value of the principle of causality; though, of course, his whole notion that we can only know particulars, and never universals, since the senses only supply us with knowledge of concrete singular things, is involved. As we saw, it follows from this that causality is merely the regular sequence of phenomena, so that the 'cause' of any phenomenon would be but the sum of the phenomena which immediately precede and accompany it; these phenomena being merely antecedent or simultaneous, and having no power or influence over the phenomenon which we call their effect. We have no right to say, according to this view, that one thing gives being to another and really influences it, we can only assert the succession of phenomena. As Fr. Joyce points out,[1] essentially the same result is reached in the Bergsonian philosophy which repudiates the intellectual division of reality by such concepts as cause and effect, agent and patient, substance and accident, which freeze what is essentially motion into immobility, and so falsify reality altogether. Now we have shown, at length, that the very foundations of this Empiricist view are unsound; since the intellect must be admitted to be a faculty distinct from sense, having as its proper object being, an object which is plainly of a different kind to those of the senses, or even of the imagination, which represents things to us, not as things or beings, but as definite sensible determinations: shapes, colours, and so on. We have seen, moreover, that it is necessary to attribute causality to real beings if we are to give an intelligible account of either change or multiplicity; and if the Empiricist urges that we cannot give such an intelligible account, having no intellects but only senses, he is clearly condemned out of his own mouth, for this supposition, and all the arguments which he uses, appeal, not to the senses—for they have no shape or

[1] G. H. Joyce, op. cit., p. 24.

colour or sound or scent—but only to the intellect. Such an *argumentum ad hominem* will carry us, however, but a very little way, since the end of all Empiricism is Scepticism, and it is impossible to pursue the Empiricists into this abyss of intellectual annihilation. The condemnation of Empiricism is to be found in the discussion of Nominalism in Epistemology, where we saw that this theory satisfies the requirements neither of experience nor of reason.

We turn, then, to the Agnosticism which was introduced by Kant's theory of knowledge. This theory is no less fatal than that of Hume and Mill to the concepts on which a demonstration of the existence of God must be based, of which the chief is that of causality.

Kant, as we noticed earlier, regards all metaphysical concepts including those of substance and cause as *a priori* forms of our understanding; and the principle of causality as a synthetic *a priori* principle, not one which imposes itself by its own evidence. We have already seen reason to reject both these positions (of which the second is, logically speaking, a corollary of the first), as being inconsistent with experience and contradictory in themselves. Inconsistent with experience, since no reason can be assigned for the application of the different categories to different classes of phenomena, as Fichte points out; though experience shows that we do apply them regularly and furnishes the reason, viz. that we see that they are applicable in the things themselves; and contradictory, as in Kant's view the idea of cause and causality itself cannot attach to things-in-themselves, and yet he allows that the things-in-themselves are causes of sensation.

We have only to note here that what Kant considers the speculative reason incapable of doing, viz. proving any metaphysical proposition, including the proposition that God exists, he allows to be within the powers of the practical reason, which, seeing that God's existence is inseparably connected with the moral law, is bound to assert it.

Kant's objection to the demonstrability of the existence of God is thus, like that of the Empiricists, directed against the principle of causality; though, unlike theirs, it does not deny the necessity of this principle, but maintains that it is a necessary law of thought which is not applicable to extra-mental reality. It thus denies the ontological value of the principle, and consequently its transcendent value also; that is, it denies that it is applicable to infinite being. It may be useful to recall here that by the ontological value of a principle is meant the capacity of that principle to give us knowledge, not merely of phenomena perceived by the senses or the consciousness, but also of being, of which phenomena are only the sensible manifestation; while by transcendent value we mean the capacity of the notion or principle for giving us true knowledge of God conceived as the first cause which transcends, and is distinct from, finite being; and not merely that such notions and principles are valid for being and its properties, which transcend the categories.

It is quite clear that we cannot hope to demonstrate the existence of God *a priori*.[1] The nearest approach to such a demonstration is the ontological argument; and this, considered as a purely rational argument is, as we have seen, fallacious. Moreover, it is not an *a priori* proof, properly speaking, since such a proof proceeds from a known cause to demonstrate its proper effect, and it is clear that neither the idea of God, not yet His nature, is properly speaking the *cause* of His existence. Nor can any cause of God be conceived of, since nothing can be prior to Him either in nature

[1] In order to avoid any misunderstanding it is necessary to notice that the phrase '*a priori* proof' is used in quite different senses by the Scholastics and by many modern writers who have adopted Kant's phraseology.

For the Scholastic it means one which from a cause argues to its effect, while an *a posteriori* proof is one which argues from effect to cause. In modern non-Scholastic works an *a priori* argument is often identified with a deductive one, an *a posteriori* argument with an inductive. (Cf. Joseph, *An Introduction to Logic*, p. 437.) In such a use of the phrases no argument will be called *a posteriori* which does not rest wholly on experience, and exclude all appeal, in reaching its conclusions, to self-evident principles. So a recent writer (Dr. R. Leet Patterson, *The Conception of God in the Philosophy of Aquinas*, pp. 24, 25, 55 ff.) maintains that all the proofs given by S. Thomas of God's existence (with the possible exception of the fifth) are '*a priori*,' as involving an appeal to the principle of causality. This way of speaking no doubt originates in Kant's theory of knowledge; and is, to say the least, liable to lead to confusion. It really implies that all necessity and universality in propositions are contributed to them by the mind.

or being. Hence, if any demonstration of God's existence is possible it will be a demonstration *a posteriori*, i.e. from effect to cause.

That such a demonstration may be possible, it is necessary hat certain conditions should be fulfilled.

First, it must, if it is to be rigorous, proceed from a *proper* effect to its proper cause, the cause on which the effect depends necessarily and immediately. This is the cause without which, not only could the effect not have come into being, but that without which it could not now exist. So we cannot argue from the existence of a man to his father's present existence, but we can argue from it to a cause which preserves his existence, since his existence is not something which, of himself, he is bound to have; but something which might cease at any moment. Such causes are called by the Scholastics equivocal causes, since the effect produced by them is not of the same nature as the cause. Thus it is necessary for the preservation of life on this planet that the sun's rays should continually come to it, though the nature of the sun differs from that of life. Similarly, that water may be boiling and not merely come to the boil, heat must be continually applied; it will cease to vaporise if the heat be removed. If then it is steadily vaporising we can conclude that the cause of the vaporisation is present.

Such an argument from effect to cause will clearly not show what is the nature of the cause, but merely that the cause of this effect *exists*. The demonstration is, therefore, not one which shows *why* the predicate in the conclusion agrees with the subject but simply *that* it does so; in the case in point *that* the cause exists. It is what the Scholastics call a *demonstratio quia* not *propter quid*. It ends in a judgement of fact, and though the cause to whose existence we conclude is of a different nature to the effect, so that we cannot tell what it is in itself, we are not therefore deprived of all knowledge of it, since it is the cause on which the effect essentially depends; and so must have *some* similarity to it.

Secondly, that an argument which appeals to the principle of causality may be conclusive, it is necessary that the series of effects and causes which are considered should be a series of essentially subordinated causes which are causing in the present, not an accidentally subordinated series of causes which have caused in the past. We have implicitly stated this condition already, for such essentially subordinated causes are those which cause only in so far as each of them is, here and now, under the dominion of a superior cause, namely the one next above it in the series. In such a series the causality of each cause ceases if the causality of the one next above it ceases. So a vital action causing some effect, say motion from place to place, can only cause so long as the life-principle causes, and this can only cause so long as the temperature and other conditions of life remain normal. It would be useless to try and argue through a series of accidentally subordinated causes, causes which are only causes of the becoming of the effect, as father and son, to a cause which is necessarily required. So we cannot arrive at a first cause in the series father and son, for fathers might have generated sons for ever. There is no necessary end to this series, and consequently the arguments which prove that there is a first cause of the universe have no connection with the question whether the universe has had a beginning in time. As is well known, S. Thomas thought that reason was incapable of proving that the world was not eternal, and yet is very clear that it has a first cause. Moreover, inasmuch as we are not concerned here with a series of accidentally subordinated causes stretching back into the past, the question is freed from being involved in any complication with the controverted one as to the possibility of an actually infinite multitude, which was discussed earlier.[1]

Thirdly, the proper cause of an effect, which when the effect is known we are obliged to posit, and behind which we cannot go, is not only the necessary cause of this effect, but also its immediate cause ; so it is the man as a singer, not merely as a man who is the immediate cause of song. Thus motion will lead us to a first mover, contingent being to necessary being, and so on, and the proofs of God's existence will lead up to Divine attributes, which have afterwards to be proved to be attributes which can only belong to a Being

[1] Cf. Vol. I, pp. 105–108.

who is Being itself; i.e. One in which essence and existence are identified; and which in consequence of this identification will be shown to be absolutely perfect, good, immutable, eternal, omniscient, distinct from the world, etc.; in a word, to be God. So as Fr. Sertillanges remarks: 'The proof of God is the work of the whole Theodicy,' and is not completed, as is sometimes supposed, in the five arguments which are given by S. Thomas to show that God exists.

These conditions for the application of the principle of causality being borne in mind, we can see that S. Thomas's statement that from any effect the existence of its proper cause can be demonstrated[1] is justified; provided, as we have already seen is the case, the principle of causality applies to real being. For this principle, as well as those of identity and finality, and the primary ideas of being, unity, etc., as well as that of substance, are not essentially sensible, and so cannot be ideas of phenomena, but must have an ontological, and not a merely phenomenal value. The essential distinction, which we have so often remarked, between the senses and the intellect must entail an essential difference in their objects, so that being and the principles and properties which derive from it must be essentially different to phenomena, which are all that the senses can know.[2]

But we are not dealing here with being which is divided into the ten categories, but are proposing to prove that there exists some cause which transcends all finite being. Perhaps, then, the principle of causality and the other first principles will not be applicable to such a cause, even if they are allowed to be valid for the categories of being. We seem, indeed, almost to have allowed that this is the case, for in rejecting the idea that the existence of God is self-evident, our objection was based on the ground that we do not know 'what God is'; we do not know the modes of the Divine perfections positively. Now it is necessary to observe that this objection of S. Thomas to S. Anselm's argument, and to all assertions that we can arrive at God's existence *a priori*,

[1] *Summa Theologica*, I, 2, 2. '*Ex quolibet effectu potest demonstrari propria causa ejus esse.*'
[2] Cf. R. Garrigou-Lagrange, *Dieu, son existence et sa nature*, pp. 123 ff.

are based on his profound conviction that the nature of man is such that he must always derive his knowledge of the supersensible from the sensible, of the immaterial from the material. Thus whatever knowledge he may *naturally* acquire of God will be based on his knowledge of material things, of the world about him; and so, of necessity, will not be of God as He is in Himself, since this must be altogether immaterial. Nevertheless, it does not follow that man can have *no* knowledge about God by natural reason, even if he cannot have positive knowledge of the infinite modes of the Divine perfections (*quid est*). For he may be able to conclude negatively that He is *not* material, *not* finite and so on, having as a basis to work on that which he knows directly, namely, the material and the finite. Further, this '*via remotionis*' or way of negation is not the only road by which man may attain to some knowledge about God; if it be true that some, at least, of the ideas which he has derived from his knowledge of material things are of such a kind that they do not, of themselves, imply any limitation or imperfection, and are moreover seen to be applicable, though in different ways, to beings which differ essentially; i.e. if they are notions of absolute and analogical perfections. For we have seen that analogous notions are those whose name is common while the idea signified by the name is different, simply speaking, though the same in some respect, i.e. according to a certain proportion. Hence they are applicable to things which differ essentially, and yet are proportionally true of them all. Thus such notions as these, if they exist, would be able to give us knowledge of a God who is essentially distinct from finite beings; though it is true that such knowledge will never be knowledge of His nature, as it is in itself, but as it were extrinsically; in so far as we know that we can affirm of God certain perfections which we see in creatures, His nature remaining unknown with regard to the mode of the Divine perfections. So as one result of our investigation we may be able to say that in God essence and existence are identical, and that therefore the proposition 'God exists' is self-evident in itself, since God is His existence; but it will nevertheless not become self-evident to us since we cannot know His nature in itself, and so, by inspecting it, see how it is the same as His existence. We shall know the fact but not the reason of the fact, as we should do in the case of a proposition which is self-evident to us.

Have we then any such ideas: ideas which express absolute and analogical perfections? It seems plain that we have, for the ideas of being and its properties, of cause, of knowledge and love, of intellect and will, do not in themselves involve any imperfection; and are known to be analogical among finite things.

Thus the formal nature of being involves no imperfection, for it abstracts from all matter, all limitation, and is not confined to any genus or species. 'Being is not a genus,' S. Thomas often insists, and we have seen why this must be so. It is therefore an analogous, not a univocal notion; and what is true of being must be true of its properties, unity, truth, and goodness, since these are really the same as being.

Moreover, the ideas of final and efficient cause imply, in themselves, no imperfection; since, as such, they involve a relation to being as such, and are not limited to the production of any particular mode of being—as heat is to the production of warmth—but are the 'reasons of being' without any limitation or imperfection. Also, in finite things, the notion of cause is seen to be an analogical one, for it is applied analogically to the four causes, while principal and instrumental causes have the name 'cause' applied to them in different senses, i.e. analogically. Similarly the name final cause is applied analogically in finite things to the last end in any genus, and to the intermediate subordinate ends.

The same is true of the intellect and will, for the intellect is directly related to being, the will to good, and their objects being, of themselves, unlimited and involving no imperfection, the ideas of intellect and will also imply, of themselves, no imperfection. Further being essentially related to being and good, they must be, as being and good are, analogical; and we see in finite things that both knowledge and desire are predicated analogically of sense and intellect, and of the sensitive appetite and the intellectual appetite or will.[1]

Thus all these notions are fitted to express analogically but properly something concerning the absolutely perfect being, concerning God. This examination of the foundations on which S. Thomas's arguments for the existence of God rest was absolutely necessary, if we are to feel secure as to the results of the arguments themselves, and not be haunted by doubts that perhaps they make some unjustifiable assumption. Even so, it is but a summary of the points upon which doubt might be cast ; and though it is to be hoped that nothing essential has been omitted, it is evidently by no means exhaustive.

[1] Cf. Garrigou-Lagrange, *De Revelatione*, Vol. I, pp. 301 ff.

CHAPTER II

THE DEMONSTRATION OF THE EXISTENCE OF GOD

It is a Demonstration *a posteriori*—The Impossibility of an Infinite Regress in Essentially Subordinated Causes—The Argument from Motion—The Cartesian Conception of Motion—The Principle of Inertia—The Argument from Efficient Causality—The Argument from Contingence—Its Relation to Other Arguments—The Henological Argument—Its Distinction from the Ontological Argument—The Argument from Finality—The Five Classical Arguments all Lead to One and the Same Being: Subsisting Existence.

WE will consider in this chapter the *Quinque Viae* by which S. Thomas leads our reason to knowledge that God exists.

The principles on which these five ways rest are, first, the principle of causality, and secondly, the impossibility, under certain conditions, of an infinite series.

All the proofs start with some observation concerning the things which constitute the world as known directly by the senses; and so all contain an empirical element, and are founded on experience. They are, therefore, not *a priori* but *a posteriori* proofs; unless by *a priori* proofs we mean such as appeal to any self-evident principle, such as the principle of causality or identity; in which case all proofs, and indeed all reasoning, even such inductive reasoning as leads to a probable conclusion, must be reckoned to be *a priori.*

Before setting down the proofs themselves it will be convenient to explain why it is impossible to have an infinite series of essentially subordinated causes; a truth which is often referred to shortly, by means of the Aristotelean phrase, as the principle *ἀνάγκη στῆναι*, i.e. it is necessary to stop at a first cause in such a series. If it is clearly understood that we are dealing with a series of causes which are actually and essentially subordinated, this principle is evident. For in a series of this kind, since each member of it is here and now dependent for its causality, and so for being a member of the series, on the actual causality of the member next before it in the series—the priority of one over the other being a priority, not of time, but of the superior over the inferior—it follows that any member of the series which we like to choose can only cause so long as it is dependent on the member next above it. If then, we were to suppose that this series went on without end, i.e. was an infinite series, we should have to say that there was no first member of it, and consequently no second or any other member. If each member of the series is a cause only as being in dependence on a superior member, no member of the series can cause if causality is never imparted to the series; in other words, if there is not a first in the series of causes. In a goods train each truck is moved and moves by the action of the one immediately in front of it. If then we suppose the train to be infinite, i.e. that there is no end to it, and so no engine which starts the motion, it is plain that no truck will move. To lengthen it out to infinity will not give it what no member of it possesses of itself, viz. the power of drawing the truck behind it. If then we see any truck in motion we know there must be an end to the series of trucks which gives causality to the whole. If no water enters the system of water pipes in a house from the main, there can be no water at the taps. To suppose that we could get causality in some cause which essentially depends for its causality on another by having an infinite series of such causes is like hoping to get water at the tap by prolonging the pipes for ever, but never connecting them up with the main.

This is evidently not true in a series of accidentally subordinated causes which form a series stretching back into the past; as in the case of a dentist who uses one instrument after another. If he was eternal this succession of instruments might go on to infinity, but we should be obliged to look outside the series to find a cause which moved all the instruments, i.e. the dentist, inasmuch as none of the instruments moves itself.

Thus we see that in a series of essentially subordinated

causes it is useless to prolong the series to infinity in the hope that by so doing we shall account for the presence of causality in the members of the series in which we observe it. An infinity of causes which can only cause in dependence on some other is as powerless to impart causality as one such cause would be; so that if causality is known to be exerted by *any* member of the series, we are bound to say that the series of dependent causes is not infinite, but begins with some first cause which is not dependent for its causality on another, but gives it to all the rest. The dependent thus demands the independent, the relative the absolute.

With these preliminaries we can now proceed to set down the 'Five Ways'; and since the object of this summary is primarily to explain the usual Thomistic teaching, it is unnecessary to apologise for giving them in a Scholastic form, in which the articulation of the arguments is most apparent; nor for retaining S. Thomas's own order, which has certain striking advantages over any other.

The First Way.

There is motion in the world, as is plain from experience; but everything which is in motion is moved by another, and it is impossible to proceed to infinity in a series of movers which are actually and essentially subordinated; therefore there exists a first mover which is moved of none, and this we call God.

In the last phrase, which recurs equivalently at the end of each way, S. Thomas indicates that we have arrived at an attribute which is generally allowed to be a Divine attribute; that is, as the Scholastics say, that this attribute is a nominal definition of God.

What does S. Thomas mean by motion here? The Thomists unanimously reply that he means any transit from potency to act. It is certain that 'motion' is not to be confined to local motion; rather the word is taken in its most general sense, no particular kind of mutation, whether substantial or accidental, spiritual or sensible, local or qualitative being intended in distinction from any other. That change of some kind is to be found in the universe is an empirical fact which we are forced to admit, both from internal and external experience. Even if, as Zeno contended, it were unintelligible, it would still be a fact.

In the minor there are two propositions. The first is that everything which is in motion is moved by another. This is proved as follows: movement is the passage from potency to act, therefore to be moved is to be in potency, and to move is precisely the contrary, it is to be in act. Now the same thing in the same respect cannot be both in potency and in act, and therefore everything which is moved is incapable of moving itself, and must therefore be moved by another. Hence this first proposition rests on the very notion of movement or becoming, that is, on the real distinction between potency and act and on the principle of non-contradiction.

The second proposition is that it is impossible to proceed to infinity in such a series of movers which are actually and essentially subordinated. We have seen the reason for it above; and it rests on the notion of causality itself, and not on the impossibility of an actually infinite multitude; still less, on a shrinking of the mind from the contemplation of an infinite series as such, for we have seen that an infinite series of accidentally subordinated causes is not impossible.

As has been said, the word motion here is not to be confined to local motion; if it is so confined, a difficulty arises from the conflict between the Cartesian view of motion, which is dominant in physics, and the metaphysical one. Descartes treated motion as something added to a fully actualised entity; whereas, from the point of view of metaphysics, it is, on the contrary, the passage to actualisation. Secondly, he treated it as a state; but metaphysically it cannot be considered as a state, which is a permanent condition, whereas motion is essentially transitive. So also he imagined that the motion of one body passes into another; but such an idea is not philosophically sound, for a motion, not being a complete entity in itself, cannot be handed on; all that is possible is that the force which generates and maintains motion in one body should generate a second motion in another, as occurs when two billiard balls strike.

It is untrue to say that the motion of the first ball is communicated to the second : what occurs is that a new motion is generated in the second ball.

If such Cartesian conceptions of motion as these are assumed to be philosophically sound, the proposition '*omne quod movetur ab alio movetur*' would have to be abandoned in the case of local motion ; and it is therefore important to notice that however helpful they may have been in physical science, and as giving us a picture of movement which is easily imagined, they are metaphysically incoherent.

A difficulty similar to these arises in connection with Newton's first law of motion, which states that every body perseveres in its state of rest or of uniform motion in a straight line, except in so far as it is compelled to change that state by impressed forces. The principle embodied in this law is called the principle of inertia ; and from it would follow the conclusion that a body, under the imagined conditions, would, if started moving, go on moving for ever ; so that a finite impulse would produce an infinite effect, and a body would move without being moved by another. We may notice in connection with this law that it is incapable of verification either experimentally, since we can never produce the necessary conditions ; or theoretically and *a priori*. It is a wide induction made from certain observed facts. In so far as it asserts that an inanimate body is incapable of setting itself in motion it is indubitably true both physically and metaphysically ; but the assertion that once such a body is moving it will continue to do so for ever unless stopped by impressed forces is, philosophically speaking, very doubtful. The reason why it has been accepted without question is because the Cartesian idea of motion, according to which local motion adds nothing real to a body, was already accepted. In the view of Descartes all that is acquired by local motion is a mere change of position, and there is no passage from potency to act ; local motion being regarded not as a 'becoming' but as a 'state.' Such a 'state,' being contingent, would need a conserving cause, but not a continuously operating mover. We have already seen some of the difficulties of this view ; and if it is not accepted we shall have to allow that there must be some force, over and above the native forces of the body itself, which keeps it moving, i.e. passing from potency to act. John of S. Thomas[1] regards this force as an impulse or impetus imparted to the projected body, at the moment when motion is started, by the efficient cause which initiates the motion; and which remains in it as a transient and instrumental power so long as the motion lasts. Thus as Fr. Garrigou-Lagrange says: 'The projectile is in act with respect to its dynamic quality, and in potency with respect to its local positions.'[2]

This explanation of the motion of projectiles has had a long history, going back to Hipparchus and Themistius, a commentator on Aristotle. It evidently involves a refusal to recognise the philosophical validity of the principle of inertia in so far as this asserts that a moving body will continue in motion indefinitely unless stopped; the grounds of this refusal being that the impulse, being finite, will be exhausted in a finite time, and that local motion involves a real and continuous actuation.

To avoid this partial rejection of the principle of inertia, and because of other difficulties which he finds in the theory of an 'impulse,' Fr. Joyce has adopted another explanation, according to which there must be two orders of movers, the external or impressed forces of Newtonian physics, and a higher mover which is continuously at work as a principal cause, using the impressed mechanical forces as its instruments.[3]

Either of these two explanations safeguards the truth of the principle '*quidquid movetur,* etc.'; but it should be noticed that even if both of them are rejected, and local motion be considered to be not a true 'becoming' at all, S. Thomas's argument from motion is still valid; for the principle: '*quidquid movetur ab alio movetur*' will in any case apply strictly to motions of increase, or qualitative movements.

[1] *John of S. Thomas. Phil. Nat.*, P. I., Q. 25, a. 2.

[2] R. Garrigou-Lagrange, O.P., *Dieu*, p. 253.

[3] G. H. Joyce, S.J., op. cit., pp. 100 ff. As this book is readily accessible to English readers it seems better to refer them to the original than to attempt to give a summary of the theory here: a summary which would necessarily be inadequate

Motion and change, then, are not self-explanatory. Every movement implies a mover, and if this is also moved as well as moving, it again implies a further mover. At last, therefore, there must be a mover which is moved of none, otherwise the motions we observe could not occur.

The argument is thus quite independent of any particular physical theory of movement, whether Aristotelean or modern.[1] It is based on the metaphysical analysis of change, of becoming, which is quite unaffected by differences of scientific outlook, so long as the principles of identity and reason of being are held to be valid.

In concluding our account of this first way, we may observe, with Cajetan, that we know no more of the source of motion by means of it than that it is an unmoved mover. S. Thomas is not here concerned to show that this mover is to be identified with the *ens perfectissimum* which we call God, but only that in reality there really exists an unmoved mover; and he does not concern himself with the question whether this be the 'soul of the heaven or of the world,' or anything else.[2]

Similar remarks apply to the predicates—which are in fact Divine attributes—which are concluded to in the remaining four ways: it will therefore be unnecessary to repeat this observation in each case.[3]

The Second Way.

This way has as its starting-point, not becoming or change,

[1] So Dr. Wicksteed seems to be mistaken in thinking that the proof was dependent on the superseded Aristotelean science; and also in giving it a new dependence on the second law of thermodynamics. Cf. P. H. Wicksteed, *The Reactions between Dogma and Philosophy* (Constable, 1926), pp. 232 f.

[2] Cajetan, *Comm in I.*, 2, 3, Sec. III.

'These reasons . . . can be adduced to prove that certain predicates are found in *rerum natura*, which are in truth predicates of God: without troubling about how they exist. It is for this purpose that they are here adduced . . . so for the first way it is sufficient that it can be inferred "therefore there exists a first immobile mover" without caring whether this be the soul of the heaven or of the world: for this will be inquired into in the following question.'

[3] It is obviously impossible to treat here of all the objections which have been brought against these arguments. The reader is referred to the full discussion of them by Fr. Garrigou-Lagrange in the work already cited, which has recently been published in an English translation. (Herder, 2 vols., 1935, trans. by Fr. Bede Rose, O.S.B.)

but being and permanence. It argues from what is enduring in the world, and so from what may be called the static aspect of it, not the dynamic.

It observes as a fact of experience that there are in the world causes which are causes not merely of the production, but also of the conservation, of their effects. They are causes not merely *in fieri*, but also *in esse*; and, as such, must act continuously. If they cease to act the effect will cease to be. Such are all the conditions of atmospheric constitution and pressure, warmth, etc., which are necessary not only that a living thing may come into existence, but that life, and so the living thing, may be preserved. Now if such causes as these do not exist of themselves, they must, in their turn, be essentially dependent on other causes, since nothing can cause itself. We cannot, however, go on for ever in this series or 'order' of causes which are essentially subordinated one to the other, for in this case, there being no first cause in the series, it could impart no causality to the series as a whole, so that there would be no causality at all, which is contrary to what we have observed. Hence there must be a first cause on which the whole series of essentially and actually subordinated causes depends, and this cause will exist of itself, and not be caused. It will be an uncaused cause; and such an uncaused cause we call God. God, then, exists.

It is evident that in this argument we are speaking of efficient causes only; and causes *in esse*. So each member of the series of causes possesses being solely by virtue of the actual present operation of a superior cause. In the example already given life is dependent, *inter alia*, on a certain atmospheric pressure, this again on the continual operation of physical forces, whose being and operation depends on the position of the earth in the solar system, which itself must endure relatively unchanged, a state of being which can only be continuously produced by a definite—if unknown—constitution of the material universe. *This* constitution, however, cannot be its own cause. That a thing should cause itself is impossible: for in order that it may cause it is necessary for it to exist, which it cannot do, on the hypothesis, until it has been caused. So it must *be* in order to cause itself, and it cannot *be* until it has caused itself. Thus, not being uncaused nor yet its own cause, it must be caused by another, which produces and preserves it. It is plain, then, that as no member of this series possesses being except in virtue of the actual present operation of a superior cause, if there be no first cause actually operating none of the dependent causes could operate either. We are thus irresistibly led to posit a first efficient cause which, while itself uncaused, shall impart causality to a whole series.

It is even clearer in this way than in the last that the series of causes which we are considering is not one which stretches back into the past; so that we are not demanding a beginning of the world at some definite moment reckoning back from the present, but an actual cause now operating, to account for the present being of things.

The Third Way.

This way starts with the observation of the contingency of the things in the world around us; that is from the fact that these beings are such that they need not exist. Thus the first way considers these beings as changing, or subject to change, the second as they are actually existing, and the third as they are capable of ceasing to exist.

It is, then, a fact of common experience that contingent beings exist; for we see all around us beings which do not always exist. Plants and animals come into existence and pass away. Chemical compounds, too, arise through the coming together of their elements, and are resolved again into their elementary constituents. Even if it be thought that there is no true novelty here, the generation and corruption of living things is sufficient for our present purpose.

If so much be granted we can establish the existence of a necessary being which exists of itself and cannot not exist.

In fact, it is clear that any existing being which can cease to exist does not contain in itself the reason of its own existence, and must therefore derive its reason of being from something else; and, in the long run, from a being which exists of itself; for we cannot proceed to infinity in a series of beings which derive their reason of being from some other. To suppose that some contingent being, or the series of such beings, is eternal, does not in any way account for their existence, or relieve us of the necessity of demanding a necessary being as the cause of such eternal existence. Even if the series is eternal, it is eternally insufficient. Moreover, as S. Thomas here points out, if the universe is constituted only of contingent beings, at some moment nothing at all existed, for such beings do not of themselves require to exist. We are forced, therefore, to ask how it comes about that anything does exist now; for it is clear that if at any moment nothing had existed nothing would exist now. Why then do contingent beings exist? Not owing to the necessity of their own natures which of themselves demand existence, for then they would not be contingent; but—for this is the only alternative—in virtue of their production by a being which is not contingent but necessary: one which must exist of its very nature.

We are not asking as yet what is the nature of this necessary being, for, as was said before, each way leads up to some real predicate—which in fact is a Divine predicate—and to nothing more. It may, however, be as well to point out that whatever be the character of necessary being it cannot be the sum of all contingent ones, their natures being opposed in such a way that necessary being *has* in itself the reason of its existence, which contingent beings have not. To add together a great or even, if it were possible, an infinite number of 'have nots' will not produce one 'have.' No addition of noughts or nothings can make something.

This way, which S. Thomas places in the centre of his five ways, is indeed central among them. In it is expressed in the clearest fashion the main theme of them all; and moreover, since its starting-point is 'being considered in itself,' and not as changing, or as an effect, or as partial, or as an end, but purely with respect to that which makes it being, its existence related to its essence, it is concerned with the very heart of metaphysics. So, while the first way starts from being in process of coming to be, the second from being which is permanent, already constituted in essence, this third way starts from the very nature of finite being considered in itself, from that whose essence is not its existence, nor implies its existence, but is really distinct from it. Thus though it is, in a sense, true that all the 'ways' constitute one argument, for all proceed by application of the same method and medium of demonstration to the same reality, finite being; yet, in another sense, they are not the same, for the aspect of this being envisaged in each is different, and they proceed by a progressively penetrating insight into its nature. Thus they differ formally, though materially they are the same.[1]

The Fourth Way.

This way has received the name of the 'henological argument,' since it argues from the multiple to the one. The starting-point in the world which is known to us through our experience is that there exist in it beings which have varying degrees of truth, goodness, and nobility, and the argument proceeds to show that there must be a being who is absolutely Good, True, and Perfect.

With regard to the characteristics which S. Thomas thus selects, we notice first, that they are transcendentals and as such are susceptible of degrees; for being is not a genus and so is not diversified by extrinsic differences as a genus is; but by being found in varying degrees. While generic and specific attributes are found in the same way in all members of a genus or species, being and the transcendentals are found in the different classes of beings in different ways. So, for example, the goodness of iron differs from that of a horse, as this does from human goodness; and clearly we have here an ascending scale of goodness. They are, in the second place, attributes which involve in themselves no limitation or imperfection,[2] and are analogous not univocal.[3]

The argument based on the observation of the degrees of being and the transcendentals is of Platonic origin, and may

[1] Cf. R. Leet Patterson, op. cit., Chap. IV, where this question of the distinction of the five ways is considered at length. The author, considering the first three ways materially rather than formally, comes to the conclusion that they are identical. The word 'ways' which S. Thomas uses is significant. Together they form a cord with five strands, which is not easily broken.

[2] Cf. Part III, Chap. I. [3] Cf. Part II, Chap. II, Sec. II.

be thought to have a kind of charm not to be found in the others.

It runs as follows:

There exist in the world things which have more or less truth, more or less goodness, more or less being; the transcendental aspects of being are found in reality in a hierarchically graded order. Now, when a concept which implies no imperfection is found realised in different degrees in different beings, none of those which have it in a more limited degree can account for its own possession of this perfection, but must derive it from some being which possesses it in an unlimited degree, and which *is* this very perfection. Consequently, since we do in fact find these perfections in a limited degree, there must exist also a Being who is Being, Goodness and Truth itself; and this we call God.

There are implicit in this 'dialectic of love,' as Fr. Garrigou-Lagrange calls it,[1] two principles of whose truth it is necessary that we should be fully convinced.

The first is: If one and the same characteristic is found in several beings, it is impossible that each of them should possess it of itself, and they therefore receive it from some other, which is unity. Multiplicity is inexplicable without a unity as its cause. S. Thomas shows the truth of this. He says: 'If any one thing is found as a common characteristic in many things, it must be caused in them by some one cause; for it is impossible that it should belong to each of them of itself, since each as it is in itself is distinct from any other, and the diversity of causes produces diversity of effects.'[2] By hypothesis, the things in which the common characteristic is found are *of themselves* different, and therefore they cannot *of themselves* be the same. That which constitutes them, constitutes them as distinct, and cannot therefore also constitute them as not distinct, that is as one. As we saw earlier,[3] to assert that things which are of themselves diverse can, of themselves, also be one, is to be led to a denial of the principle of identity. '*Quæ secundum se diversa sunt non conveniunt in aliquod unum, nisi per aliquam causam*

[1] G. Garrigou-Lagrange, *Dieu*, pp. 282 f.
[2] *De Potentia*, III, 5.
[3] Cf. Part II, Chap. 9.

adunantem ipsa.'[1] So multiplicity demands unity as its cause.

The second principle implicit in the proof asserts that gradation of perfection, like multiplication of it, demands as its cause some being which possesses it of itself. This is complementary of the first; and is expressed exactly by saying: if a characteristic, whose concept does not imply imperfection, is found in some being in an imperfect state, this being does not possess it of itself, but receives it from some other which possesses it of itself.

It is seen to be true if we consider that in any kind of perfection which does not imply imperfection and which admits degrees, anything which has not the highest degree of perfection, but something less, has not that perfection by virtue of its nature, for what belongs to a thing of its nature cannot be lessened or deficient.[2] A thing either has a certain nature or not, it cannot have the *nature* in a greater or less degree, though it may have a less or greater power of exercising its natural functions. Consequently any being which possesses such a perfection as these of which we are speaking in a limited degree, cannot possess it of its own nature, and therefore must receive it from some other, and, in the last resort, from some other which possesses this perfection of its own nature.

This argument, then, following the lead of Plato, passes from the fact of imperfection, of potentiality, in the world about us, to the existence of a Being who is absolutely perfect, and in which there is no potentiality; which is Pure Act.

It is not to be confused with the Ontological argument, for it does not, from the analysis of the *idea* of imperfection conclude that the absolutely perfect being must exist; but starting with *fact* of multiplication and gradation of imperfections shows that they must have a unified and absolutely perfect cause. S. Anselm rightly thought that if an infinite being is possible it must exist, but did not observe that we cannot know its possibility either by intuition or *a priori*, and therefore must base our argument on what we do know by experience; which is the procedure here adopted by

[1] *Summa Theologica*, I, 3, 7. [2] II *C.G.*, c. 15.

S. Thomas to arrive at the existence of the absolutely perfect being.

Thus, like the three preceding arguments, it rests on a fact of experience, for the interpretation of which we call in the principle of causality. It no doubt enriches the content of our idea of God considerably, by adding to the attributes of unmoved mover, first efficient cause and necessary being—attributes which sound absolutely impersonal and even inanimate—those of Goodness, Truth, Unity, and fullness of Being or perfection.

The Fifth Way.

The argument we have just considered prepares the way for this last proof given by S. Thomas ; which, in its turn, supplements and completes the preceding ones. As the fourth way passes from multiplicity to unity, this proceeds from the ordered multiplicity of the world to an ordering intelligence. Whether we are to call it the argument from design depends on what is meant by that name, for it certainly is not the same as that which is often associated with the name of Paley.

It is stated very succinctly by S. Thomas. He says : We see that some things which lack cognition act on account of an end, which appears from the fact that they always, or at least in the majority of cases, act in the same way in order to attain what is best for them. From this it is clear that it is not by chance, but as a result of intention that they thus attain their end. Now those things which have no knowledge, do not tend towards an end unless they are directed by some being who has knowledge and intelligence, as the arrow is directed by the archer. Therefore there exists some intelligent being, by which all natural things, things which lack cognition, are directed to their end, and this being we call God.

Fr. Garrigou-Lagrange expresses the argument in a short syllogism.[1] 'A means cannot be directed towards an end except by an intelligent cause. But there exist in nature, among beings which are destitute of intelligence, means

[1] R. Garrigou-Lagrange, *Dieu*, p. 315.

which are directed to ends. Therefore nature is the effect of an intelligent cause.'

S. Thomas is here appealing to the fact of internal finality, not external; to the finality which is observable in things destitute of intelligence taken separately; as that the eye is directed to seeing, the ear to hearing, wings to flight. External finality, the purpose of some noxious animal, such as a viper, or of a disease germ, is often difficult to discover; whereas internal finality, such as the purpose of the organs of the body, is plain.

But even this internal finality has often been denied, especially by those who uphold the theory of mechanistic evolution in its entirety. We have seen earlier, however, that this explanation is incapable of accounting for the origin of variations except by chance, and has no explanation to offer either of evolution itself, or of the perfection of the evolutionary process.[1] To appeal to chance is, however, not to explain, but to abandon explanation, and to say that everything comes about by chance is really to assert something unintelligible or absurd. For if everything is by chance and nothing by rule, there is nothing to which chance can occur. I may chance to meet my friend in the street, but only if I am walking along in it in a definite way. If nothing occurs in any definite way, nothing can occur by chance or in an accidental way. It is in this sense that the 'exception proves the rule.' If there is no rule there can be no exception: if there is nothing essential there can be nothing accidental or by chance.

But even if such finality be admitted, is it certain that it must be attributed to an intelligence? The answer is that the finality which we observe in nature is direction of operations to ends, precisely as ends, i.e. in view of the end to be attained. The means are related to the ends precisely in so far it is in the ends that they have their reason of being; their whole constitution is directed towards the attainment of these ends. Such a relation as this can evidently only be known and established by a being who knows the reasons of being of things; that is to say, by an intelligent being.

[1] Cf. Vol. I, pp. 336 ff.

We are now in a position to draw together the results of the five classical arguments for the existence of God. They lead us to five attributes which, in fact, are proper to God; namely: *primum movens, primum efficiens, primum necessarium, primum et maxime ens, primum gubernans intelligendo.*[1] These attributes can, in fact, only belong to a being whose essence and existence are identical; and the proof of the existence of God is essentially incomplete until this has been shown to be true; and we have seen that these attributes belong, and are peculiar to, a being who stands at the meeting-point of the five ways.

(1) The first mover, since it is unmoved, does not pass from potency to act with regard to its action; its action is always in act, and contains no element of potentiality. Now the mode of action of a thing is a consequence of its mode of being; hence, if the first mover is pure act in the order of operation, it will be so also in the order of being. That this may be true it must contain no potentiality in its being, and therefore will not have a nature which is merely *capable* of existing, so standing to existence in the relation of potency to act. It will, therefore, be of the nature of the first mover to exist, it will exist essentially, its essence will be identified with its existence. This conclusion is confirmed by the fourth way where it is shown that whatever is in a thing without belonging to it as a proper constituent of it, is caused in it. For wherever there is diversity and composition we are in the presence of the conditioned and not the unconditional: this is only arrived at where there is pure identity. Hence that alone can exist of itself whose existence constitutes it, which is existence itself.

(2) The first cause, being uncaused, must contain in itself the reason of its own existence. Now it cannot cause itself, since to do so it must *be*, and it cannot *be*, on this hypothesis, except as the effect of being already. Thus to suppose that it receives existence from itself is contradictory, and being uncaused, it cannot receive it from any other; and so does not *receive* it at all, but is existence. Its existence is its essence.

[1] Cf. Cajetan, *Comm. in S. T.*, I, 2, 3.

(3) Necessary being, which is absolutely incapable of not existing, must have existence as an essential predicate. It does not receive existence, but is existence. Its existence is its essence.

(4) The Supreme Being, as we have pointed out above (cf. (1)), cannot be composite, and so cannot have a share of existence; but its existence must be constitutive of it, so that its essence will be existence.

(5) With regard to the first intelligence, who ordains all things, it may, perhaps, be maintained that if the teleological argument be considered quite apart from the other arguments, it does not establish anything more than the existence of a most powerful intelligence, which is capable of constructing the order of things, not an intelligence of infinite power. But, first, there is not the slightest reason for dissociating this argument from the others, and as we have already proved that there exists an absolutely perfect being on which all nature depends, the proof that there exists a supreme intelligence is confirmatory of this; secondly, if we see what is required of such a supreme intelligence we shall be obliged to say that it must be Pure Act, for if it were essentially related to an object of intelligence, distinct from itself, such a relation would, in virtue of the teleological argument itself, have to be produced by a higher intelligence, and finally by one which was not so extrinsically related to being, but was Being itself and Pure Act.

We see, therefore, that the five ways all lead up to a Being in which essence and existence are identical, and which exists of its very nature. This is made particularly clear in the third way which shows the existence of Necessary Being, and we find here the essential distinction between God and the world, inasmuch as in God alone are essence and existence identical. It is therefore not true to say that the arguments do not lead us to a transcendent God, distinct from the world. As this God is also seen to be absolutely unchangeable, wholly perfect, subsisting Being, Truth and Goodness, and the Supreme Intelligence which is the source of all order in the world, we have evidently arrived at the existence of God as He is conceived of by Theists.

CHAPTER III

FURTHER CONSIDERATIONS CONCERNING THE EXISTENCE OF GOD

I. The Question of the Distinction of the First Three Ways. II. Kant's Criticism of the Traditional Arguments. The Nature of His Criticism—The Reply to It. III. Other Arguments for the Existence of God. The Argument from the Eternal Truths—The Argument from Natural Desire—The Argument from Moral Obligation—A General Argument.

I. *The question of the distinction of the first three ways.*

It is not possible in the space at our disposal to treat fully of the distinction of the five ways by which S. Thomas arrives at the existence of God ; but we may note that their starting-points are different, so that though they all use the same means of arriving at the conclusion, they are not, therefore, to be pronounced identical. They are like different ascents of a mountain-side which all meet at the summit. So though both the first and second ways argue from causation, the first applies it to the transition from potency to act in the becoming of things, while the second applies it to the being of things which demands a cause for its preservation and continuance. Nor is the second way identical with the third, for although both deal with the essential dependence in being of finite things on a first cause, the second way starts from the observation of causes which continuously bestow on things a certain kind of being, and the third with the observation of things which do not possess being of any kind of themselves, and so must receive being simply speaking, and not only a particular kind of being. Thus the second way observes causes such as the sun, which continuously preserves things in life as well as causing them to be generated, while the third argument begins with the fact that since in finite things existence is distinct from nature, these must receive being simply speaking, since they do not possess it essentially. It thus has a wider basis than the second, for it starts with all finite being, not only with those that are causes *per se*. Similarly, the basis of this second way is wider than that of the first, which deals only with causes *secundum fieri*, while the second deals also with causes *secundum esse*.

From the point of view of what is most easily known by us, also, there is a progression from the first to the third way, motion being most easily discernible, then the preservation of things, and finally the fact that their very being, considered in itself, is dependent. The last two ways supplement the conclusions arrived at in the first three, and make their content much richer, the third way being the culminating point of the five, and so placed by S. Thomas in the central position. It is this way also which places in the clearest light what S. Thomas conceives to be the distinguishing character of the Deity, that in God alone essence and existence are identical. From this point of view the other four ways may perhaps be regarded as buttresses of the third.

II. *Kant's criticism of the traditional arguments.*

Owing to the controversial importance of the subject, some short account must be given of Kant's objections to the traditional proofs of the existence of God.

That he considered them to be invalid is well known, and since his time they have been commonly dismissed without examination on the ground that they have been finally and irrietrievably demolished by his criticisms. We ought, however, to notice in the first place that he did not examine them all, but only the cosmological[1] and teleological arguments. Even if the first three ways be held to be substantially the same, the fourth way escaped his criticism altogether. What is perhaps even more unfortunate is that he did not examine them in the shape in which they are formulated by S. Thomas, but in one in which they are much more open to criticism.

[1] Kant's 'Cosmological' argument is his version of the 'Third Way.'

He criticises them in two ways: on the basis of his theory of knowledge, and in themselves; though, of course, the second criticism is, as presented by Kant, coloured by his presupposition that substance and causality are *a priori* forms of the mind. If these presuppositions are accepted, it is useless to go further, since it is plain that the *Quinque Viæ*, resting as they do on the principle of reason of being, cannot, on Kant's hypothesis, hope to give us knowledge of reality. Many, however, consider that quite apart from his epistemological theory his particular criticisms of the cosmological, and what he calls the physico-theological, arguments, which correspond to the third and fifth ways of S. Thomas, have completely demolished them. Kant, as we have noticed already, agrees with S. Thomas in regarding the ontological argument as invalid; and his criticism of the cosmological proof is dependent on his rejection of it. He maintains that the latter argument only concludes by surreptitiously having recourse to the former. The cosmological argument, starting with observations of contingent being, arrives, by the use of the principle of the reason of being, at the assertion of the existence of necessary being. It is thus founded on an observation of fact to the explanation of which rational principles are applied, so that it can hardly be maintained that the fallacy of the ontological argument—an illicit transition from the logical to the real order—makes its appearance here, since the argument from start to finish is concerned with the real order. But having arrived at the existence of necessary being it is impossible, according to Kant, to pass to the affirmation of God—which he calls the *ens realissimum*—without calling to our aid the ontological argument. The only way, he considers, by which the identification of necessary being and the *ens realissimum* can be assured is by use of the ontological argument. Is this criticism justified?

Now it has already been pointed out that the third way, like the others, does not profess to conclude to anything more than a single attribute of God, viz. to necessary being, and has nothing to say of the *ens realissimum*, which on Kant's lips, means the being whose existence is logically included in the concept of its essence. What S. Thomas does is to show later (I, Q. 3, a. 4) that necessary being is such that its essence is identical with its existence, since, if it exists, it must exist of its very nature, for it cannot not exist. He does not, however, seek to show, on account of this logical implication, that it must exist, as S. Anselm did; but having arrived at its existence independently, he merely shows by a logical deduction that this being must be such that essence and existence are identical in it, and that it will be altogether perfect. His assertion of the *fact* of its existence in no way rests on this development of its character. Thus it seems abundantly clear that no appeal is made in the argument from contingence to the ontological argument, and that, therefore, Kant's criticism of it falls to the ground. It may be long before the truth of this statement is universally recognised, owing to the strong prejudice that exists against allowing that God's existence can be proved by reason.[1]

Kant's further criticisms of the cosmological argument are either variations of this one, and contain the same misunderstanding, or are based on his general theory of knowledge. The latter class will only be thought valid by those who agree with that theory, and in any case can have no greater certainty than the theory itself.[2]

With regard to the teleological argument the criticism made of it by Kant is substantially the same, for he says that this argument cannot carry us further than the existence of an architect of the universe: it does not show us that he is its creator, or indeed give us any determinate idea of him, unless we fall back on the cosmological proof, which he supposes himself to have shown to be fallacious.

But it is not claimed by S. Thomas that this argument does prove the existence of a Creator. To prove that the Cause who governs the world also created it is something which is

[1] Recently the justice of the Scholastic contention as to the inconclusiveness of Kant's criticisms in this respect has been acknowledged by some non-Scholastic writers. E.g. R. Leet Patterson, op. cit., pp. 96 ff; cf. C. C. J. Webb, *Philosophy*, 1934, p. 106.

[2] For an examination of these criticisms cf. Joyce, *Principles of Natural Theology*, pp. 224 ff.

to be done independently and subsequently, if at all. Moreover, with regard to the second criticism—even if it be true, which is by no means clear, that this argument does not lead us necessarily to assert the existence of a perfect intelligence always in act—since we have seen that Kant's criticism of the cosmological argument does not invalidate it, we can have recourse to it to supplement the conclusion of the teleological without involving ourselves in any fallacy.

With these few remarks we must conclude our consideration of the objections raised by Kant against the *Quinque Viæ*, and turn to that of other arguments which have been advanced with the object of showing that God exists.

III. *Other arguments for the existence of God.*

We give here a short account of a few of these arguments. For the most part they have nothing distinctly Thomist about them, and to that extent lie outside the scope of this summary.

(1) *The argument from the eternal truths.*

Possible natures and abstract necessary truths presuppose the existence of God. For possible things are modes of being, which presuppose the existence of subsisting being as a foundation on which they depend. The nature of the dinosaur is quite independent of the existence of any individual animal of this kind, but is a real possibility, which is, and can only be and be permanently a real possibility, if so conceived by an immutable being. This is more evident with respect to necessary truths ; for the ratio, for example, of the circumference of a circle to its diameter is always constant, quite apart from any existing circle, and this proportion necessarily holds good always. It therefore has eternal truth, a truth not given it by the human mind, which receives truth and does not make it, and consequently a truth which is dependent on an eternal mind. So S. Thomas says that these truths, which are understood by us, are eternal not with respect to that 'by which they are understood,' that is, by virtue of some mental power—this would involve the eternity of our minds, were it true—

but with respect to that which is understood, 'from which we can conclude that these truths are based on something eternal, for they are based on the first truth, as on a universal cause containing all truth.'[1]

This argument is a favourite one with S. Augustine, and was endorsed by Leibniz. It is not explained separately by S. Thomas, because it is reducible to the fourth way, where from the degrees of truth the essence of the First Truth is shown.

It is evidently in the Platonic tradition.

(2) *The argument from natural desire for perfect good.*

Since our will has for its object universal good it cannot find satisfaction in any finite good nor even in an infinity of finite goods, for they would not constitute an actual infinity of perfection. This is borne out by experience, since we are never satisfied with any good, but always continue to seek a higher. Hence we conclude that we have a natural desire for perfect good and perfect happiness. Now such a desire cannot be for ever incapable of realisation ; for nature, and so natural desire, cannot be the product of chance, and it would be contrary to the principle of finality to affirm that a natural desire can be essentially vain, for then it would not be directed to an end, being a desire for an unattainable one, and so would be without reason of being. We must, therefore, conclude that there exists an absolute good which can satisfy all our desires, and such an infinite good can be nothing other than God.

The proposition that 'a natural desire cannot be empty' has been the subject of much controversy ;[2] and some contend that its proof is dependent on our proving antecedently that God exists and is the author of our nature. This does not, however, seem to be necessary, for the reasons

[1] II *C.G.*, c. 84. '*Potest concludi . . . quod veritates intellectæ fundentur in aliquo æterno ; fundantur enim in prima veritate, sicut in causa universali contentiva omnis veritatis.*' Cf. the commentary of Ferrariensis on this chapter, section 2, where he shows that these truths to be eternal must be based on the exemplary ideas in the Divine Mind. Since they are eternal such a Mind must exist.

[2] Cf. J. E. O'Mahoney, *The Desire of God in the Philosophy of S. Thomas Aquinas* (Longmans, 1929). M. D. Roland-Gosselin, *Rev. des Sciences Philosophiques et Théologiques*, 1924, pp. 162 ff.

suggested above. This argument, also, is reducible to the fourth way.

(3) *The argument from moral obligation.*

The moral law imposes itself upon us as an imperative obligation, so that we feel ourselves required unconditionally to avoid evil and do good. The good *ought* to be willed, independently of any considerations of expediency or self-satisfaction. Thus the moral law dominates all our actions, and we feel assured that it is immutably binding on all moral life whatsoever. It cannot, therefore, be other than necessary and eternal, and must be founded in an eternal and necessary Good, which therefore exists.

So Dr. Rashdall says : 'The belief in God . . . is the logical presupposition of an "objective" or absolute morality. A moral ideal can exist nowhere and nohow but in a mind ; an absolute moral ideal can exist only in a mind from which all Reality is derived.[1] Our moral ideal can only claim objective validity in so far as it can rationally be regarded as the revelation of a moral ideal eternally existing in the mind of God.'[2]

This argument is evidently allied to that given by Kant from the necessity of a sufficient sanction of moral law. According to him the obligation of morality being unconditional, the moral law obliging us by a Categorical Imperative, the consciousness of this obligation carries with it a demand that Reality shall be in agreement with the requirements of morality. Such agreement can only be brought about by a being who will eventually unite and harmonise virtue with happiness. If such a harmony is not realised virtue would be in the end frustrated, and good would not be good. The only being, however, who can realise such a harmony is God, who, therefore, must exist.

It is not possible here to discuss the implications of this

[1] 'Or at least a mind by which all Reality is controlled.' Dr. Rashdall's footnote.

[2] H. Rashdall, *The Theory of Good and Evil* (1907), Vol. II, p. 212, quoted by Prof. Sorley, *Moral Values and the Idea of God* (C.U.P., 1924), pp. 347 f. For a full discussion of the moral argument cf. the whole of this Lecture XIII of Prof. Sorley's work ; also Joyce, op. cit., Chap. V, Sec. 1 ; Garrigou-Lagrange, *Dieu*, pp. 308 ff.

argument, but it will be seen to be connected on the one side with the argument from the degrees of being, and on the other with that from the order of the world (the fourth and fifth ways).

As confirming the arguments which have already been given. that from the universal agreement of mankind as to the existence of a Supreme Being is usually adduced. Such a belief can only be explained if we grant the force of these arguments, which are in essence the arguments of common sense. We cannot enter into the question of fact :[1] whether such a belief is universal—but granted that it is, the Agnostic finds himself in opposition to the natural reason of man.

It may be useful to conclude our consideration of the proofs of the existence of God with a summary of the general argument given by Fr. Garrigou-Lagrange, which, as he says, includes the 'five ways,' and rests on the principle : 'the greater cannot come from the less.'

We observe in the world beings which belong to different orders, and form an ascending scale of perfection. First, there is the order of inanimate matter, then that of plant-life, then that of animal life, and finally the intellectual and moral life of man. None of the beings in these various orders exist of themselves, but come into existence and disappear. How, then, do they come to be at all ?

If there are beings now, there must always have existed something, for, from nothing, nothing comes.[2] This something cannot have been one belonging to the series of beings which come into existence, for, unable to account for its own existence, it plainly cannot explain that of all the rest. Hence, there must be a First Being, who, possessing existence of itself, is able to impart it to all the rest.

Living beings exist now, and life is essentially superior to inanimate matter.[3] Hence it cannot have arisen simply from matter, unless we allow that the greater can be produced by the less. It must therefore be derived from a First Being who is living. Again, since intelligence is found in man, and since intellect is essentially superior, not only to

[1] For some part of the evidence of fact cf. Joyce, op. cit., pp. 179 ff.

[2] Vol. II, Part II, Chap. IX.

[3] Vol. I, Part II, Chap. V.

brute matter but to vegetative and sensitive life,[1] it follows that it cannot originate from any of these inferior degrees of being, but there must have existed from all eternity a Being who is intelligent ; a conclusion which the observation of the order of the world also enforces, for how can there be order without an ordering intelligence ?

The principles which govern both our thinking and reality itself are necessary, and so superior to the contingent intellects and realities which they control. Hence they must be founded on a necessary and supreme Intelligence who must possess Truth immutably and primarily.

Lastly, we find in the world goodness and even heroic sanctity, which are plainly superior to what is neither good nor holy, and so we are obliged to admit that there must ever have been a Being who is morally Good and Holy. The moral law too is seen to impose itself on us objectively and necessarily, and must therefore be founded on a necessary and eternal law of morality, on a Being who is sovereignly Good.

Thus, unless we are willing to admit that the less can produce the greater, we must allow that there has existed eternally a Being who is Life, Intelligence, Supreme Truth, Altogether Holy, and the Sovereign Good.

So the truth of the existence of God is seen as the culmination of all our previous investigations into the nature of the material world, of knowledge, and of being itself. It is that on which the ladder of being, which we have ascended step by step, finally rests.

We see in this general proof the impossibility of allowing the theory of materialistic evolution as an adequate explanation of the world as we know it : and it excludes also the theory of Idealistic Pantheism, for the First Being is seen to be absolutely independent in being of the contingent world ; and since, in addition, it is Intelligence and Will, it must be Personal. Excluding, as it does, all change and becoming, since eternally it possesses the plenitude of the perfections of being, intelligence, truth and goodness, we cannot be modes of it ; so that it is not the Absolute, but a transcendent, personal God.

[1] Vol. I, Part II, Chaps. XI and XIV.

CHAPTER IV

THE NATURE OF GOD

Agnosticism and Anthropomorphism—The Way of Analogy—The Via Remotionis and the Via Eminentiæ—The Formal Constituent of the Divine Nature—Various Views—The Thomist Opinion—In What Way are the Divine Attributes Found in God ?—The Entitative Attributes—The Unity of God—The Truth of God—The Goodness of God—A Note on Pantheism.

St. Thomas's denial that we can know 'what God is' might lead us to suppose that we can know nothing whatever of His nature. The expression is, however, a technical one, and is intended to deny to us an essential or quidditative knowledge of God. Such a denial is both legitimate and necessary. Legitimate, in so far as we may know with certainty *that* some attribute does in fact belong to some subject without knowing *how* it does so; and necessary, if we are to avoid both agnosticism and anthropomorphism. If we were simply to deny any positive knowledge of God's nature we should fall into agnosticism; while if we were to affirm, without qualification, that we can know positively what this nature is, we should be bound to allow that God is of the same nature as the world, of which alone we have positive knowledge, and so conceive God anthropomorphically, that is, in our own image.

S. Thomas, by the distinction he makes between the knowledge that God is and what He is (*quia est* and *quid est*), manages to avoid both these extremes, for though he will not allow that we naturally have knowledge of God's essence as it is in itself, he affirms that we can positively know that certain perfections are attributable to God, though we remain ignorant as to the way in which these perfections exist in Him. To suppose that we are altogether ignorant as to the nature of God would evidently render the proofs of His existence valueless, and indeed they could not be constructed at all on this supposition, for it is impossible to prove the existence of some thing of whose nature—and even that it is being—you remain entirely ignorant.

Now if we knew directly and positively what God is in the way in which we know positively the nature of man our knowledge of His nature would be univocal, that is to say, the predicates which we affirm of Him, such as 'Good,' would be used in the same sense with regard both to God and to creatures. On the other hand, if we were to deny that we have *any* positive knowledge of the Divine Nature, such a denial could only result from a conviction that all attributes are ascribed to God equivocally; that is to say, in a sense wholly different from that in which they are used by us in describing the things which we know directly. Consequently, to say that we know God's nature analogically only is another way of expressing the distinction between knowing *quia est* and *quid est*. We can, S. Thomas maintains, have positive knowledge that certain perfections belong to the Divine Nature, but since they must be in it in a way which is not simply speaking, but only proportionally the same as that in which they are found in creatures, we cannot know the mode of these perfections in God, and so how they are all identified in the perfect unity of His Nature.

Our ignorance, however, as to the mode of the Divine perfections is to a certain extent lessened if we consider that we are not at liberty to attribute to God, as He is in Himself, any imperfection; and further, that those perfections which we can positively assert to belong to Him must do so in an infinite degree. These ways of approach to some knowledge of God's nature are known as the Via Remotionis or Via Negativa and the Via Eminentiæ respectively. Though these considerations put some limit to our ignorance of God's nature it is clear that it still remains vast, and though S. Thomas's doctrine is far removed from Agnosticism it is equally distant from Anthropomorphism.

We are bound then to think and speak of God according to a mode of knowledge which is essentially imperfect, inasmuch as it is derived from our knowledge of finite things;

but it is, nevertheless, legitimate to think of Him in this way. Thus we attribute to God different perfections, because to us one perfection is different from another. Our concepts are necessarily limited and finite, but when applied to God are not intended to indicate any limitations or differentiation in Him. It is legitimate and necessary for us to use them if we are to learn anything, however imperfectly, of the Divine Nature.

Proceeding, then, on this basis, it is natural to ask if, among the various attributes which we can ascribe analogically to God, there is one which, according to our imperfect mode of knowledge, characterises Him as Divine and distinct from creatures, and which we ought to regard as the source of all those other perfections which we attribute to Him. Among the attributes which we know to be Divine, and which we ascribe to God properly and formally though analogically, is there one which, from our point of view, can be considered to be the formal constituent of the Divine Nature ?

To the question thus propounded a variety of answers have been given.

The Nominalists replied that the Divine Essence is constituted by the sum of all the perfections. This answer is equivalent to denying the legitimacy of the question, and to asserting that we ought not to think of God in terms of differentiated concepts. If this be so, we cannot think of Him at all, and the view, since it leads to Agnosticism, clearly excludes the possibility of theological science.

Among those who allow the legitimacy of the question, Scotus regards infinity as the primary Divine attribute, while some Thomists assert that it is subsisting Intelligence which is always in act. A few writers give the priority to Goodness, and some modern thinkers to Liberty. But how can liberty be conceived of as prior to intelligence ? Intelligence can be conceived without liberty, though liberty is inconceivable without intelligence. So intelligence is logically prior to liberty, not vice versa. Similarly, being is logically prior to the Good, for goodness adds a further notion to Being ; so that if we consider God in Himself, and not relatively to ourselves, He must be said to be primarily Being, and secondarily the Good.

This last remark suggests the answer which the majority of Thomists give to the question. When asked : What it is which formally constitutes the Divine Essence, distinguishing God from creatures, and which, according to our imperfect way of knowledge, is the fundamental principle of the Divine attributes ? they reply : It is Subsisting Existence. This is the Divine Essence : '*Ipsum esse subsistens.*' We have shown in Ontology that all creatures, all finite beings, must be composed of essence and existence which are really distinct. The proof of this assertion rested on the basic principle of Thomistic metaphysics, the distinction between potency and act. The same principle, applied here, immediately shows that what is characteristic of God, as distinguished from creatures, is, from our point of view, the fact that His essence is not distinct from His Existence, but *is* His Existence. It is to this conception of God as Subsisting Existence that the Five Ways lead us. For (*a*) the first mover must be its own activity, and so being pure act in the order of action must be pure act in that of being ; so that its essence is not merely capable of receiving existence, or merely potential to it, but *is* Existence.

Similarly, (*b*) the first cause cannot receive existence but *is* existence ;[1] and (*c*) necessary being exists necessarily, and so existence being an essential predicate of it, its essence *is* existence. (*d*) An absolutely perfect being cannot be limited, and so cannot share existence, but must *be* Existence ; if not, both its Essence and Existence would be limited and imperfect. Lastly, (*e*) the first intelligence, which orders all things, cannot be itself related to being distinct from itself, it must be the plenitude of Being, or Subsisting Existence.

We see therefore that even the attribute of Subsisting Intelligence is, from our point of view, derivative from that of Subsisting Existence, for the former is based on the immateriality of God, on His lack of imperfection, on the fact that His essence *is* His Existence. So also God's radical

[1] *Summa Theologica,* I, Q. 3, a. 4, 1ª ratio.

infinity and requirement of all perfections is only conceivable if His Essence contains this requirement ; and the reason why it does so is that it is not susceptible of existence, but *is* Existence.

Subsisting Existence, then, the formal constituent of the Divine Nature, is the fundamental conception of God from which it is possible to proceed to a deduction of the Divine Attributes. There is here no recourse to the Ontological Argument ; but merely an intellectual scrutiny of the nature of a Being which we have independently proved to be an existing reality.

These Divine Attributes are those absolutely simple perfections, unmixed with imperfection, which exist necessarily and formally, though in a higher mode, in God. So perfections which are essentially combined with imperfection, such as rationality, cannot be called Divine attributes. They are present in God, not formally, but virtually only, inasmuch as God has the power of producing them ; whereas the absolute perfections are in God in themselves and formally ; a distinction which again safeguards us from the twofold danger of Agnosticism and Anthropomorphism.

There are two classes of these Divine Attributes : the Entitative and the Operative ones. The first class consists of those which relate to the very being of God, the second of those relating to His operations, whether immanent, or productive of an effect '*ad extra*.'

These attributes are all deducible from the conception of God as Subsisting Being, at which we have already arrived ; so that we do not make God ' in our own image,' but simply discover what subsisting Existence logically implies.

In the first place every being is, as we saw, one ; so that God must be supremely a Unity and absolutely indivisible or Simple. Secondly, all being is true and good, and God is therefore Truth Itself, and the Sovereign Good. Being Good he must be without any imperfection, and so entirely Perfect, and unlimited or Infinite. Being Infinite His power must extend to all things, and so can be in all things and places ; an attribute known as Immensity ; and His Infinity also implies Immutability, for having no limit he can receive nothing and so cannot change. Eternity, too, is implied in infinity, for to be temporal is to be limited. Being unlimited, He is immaterial, for matter is a limitation ; and this carries with it the consequence that He is supremely intelligent, for immateriality is the root of intellectuality and intelligibility. He is thus Intelligence Itself always in act, and in Him the identification of thought with reality, which Hegel asserted of thought in general, is verified. This intelligence is in the highest degree Life, and an intelligent living being must be endowed with Will, the inclination which follows the intelligence, and this Will is Free with regard to all finite good, for He is absolutely independent of them all.

His Being and Will are infinite and so is His power : He is omnipotent with regard to all being. This does not imply ability to do what is contradictory, for what is contradictory is not being.

We will now consider these attributes singly.

I.—The Unity of God.

(*a*) *God is unique.* For if there were more than one God, there would be in each of them an essence, which would be common to all, being divine, and something which differentiated and individuated them. Hence there would be two or more divine existences, and essence and existence would not be identified in the deity. God would not be Subsisting Existence. Further, if there were more than one God, in order that these gods might be distinct one would have to possess some perfection not found in the others. Hence those who did not possess this perfection could not be God, being to that extent imperfect ; and moreover one would be limited by the other, and dependent on it.

(*b*) *God is absolutely simple.* In God there is no composition, for He is Being Itself, and unity is a transcendental property of being, so that perfect Being must be perfectly One. Moreover, every compound presupposes a cause, for, in order that the parts may be united there must be some unifying cause. God is Subsisting Existence and so is uncaused. Hence He cannot be a compound. There is only one reality in God, Subsisting Existence, and this is undivided and is His Essence. Consequently the Divine Attributes are not really distinct from the Divine Nature, but in the undivided and indivisible reality which is God we can know some things which afford a ground for our making a logical distinction both between them and the Divine Essence. This is what the Thomists call a 'virtual distinction.' It is not itself a distinction, but the foundation, from our point of view, of a distinction.

II.—The Truth of God.

God is the supreme and first truth; for all being is true with ontological truth, in so far as it conforms to its eternal type, while a judgement is true in so far as it conforms to the thing judged of, which is logical or formal truth. Now God, or Subsisting Existence, is not merely in agreement with an eternal type known by the Divine Intelligence, but by reason of His Absolute Simplicity, is the Divine Intelligence itself; so that God is the first truth, and in Him are identified ontological and logical truth, the real and the ideal.

III.—The Goodness of God.

A thing is good in so far as it is perfect, so we have to consider the perfection of God; and His goodness precisely as goodness, that is, as desirable.

Perfections are either simple or mixed with some imperfection. The first class do not imply any imperfection in their concept, so that it is better, absolutely speaking, to have them than not to have them. Such are being, wisdom, etc. All other perfections imply some imperfection, such as sensation, growth, etc. These latter therefore cannot be attributed to God formally but virtually only, whereas simple perfections are to be attributed to Him formally. In both cases, of course, the mode of these perfections in God is not the same as their mode in created things; so He is said to possess them in an 'eminent' degree.

These perfections, or rather perfection itself, is in fact infinite in God: not with that infinity which is ascribed to first matter inasmuch as it is not any actuality, but with the positive infinity of Pure Act. The idea which has recently been much in vogue of God as an evolving entity seems to imply that His infinity is of the former kind, but the root of it is a reaction against the notion that God is a static, inactive, unmoving being. This is not implied in S. Thomas's view of Him as absolutely Perfect and so incapable of acquiring any perfection ; for the plenitude of perfection is the plenitude of life.

That God is good follows immediately from the fact that He is Being itself, since the good and being are the same. God, therefore, is the highest good, and so, since the goodness of a being is that which renders it desirable, God is also supremely desirable. So S. Thomas says : 'every creature is by nature inclined to love God, in its own way, more than itself'.[1]

God, then, is infinitely perfect ; and so we must refuse to recognise in Him any limitation, whether of space ; so that there belong to Him the attributes of immensity and ubiquity ; or of time : and so He is eternal.

Though it would be far beyond the scope of this summary to give an account of Pantheistic theories, it seems not to be out of place to notice that if God's essence be, as S. Thomas maintains, subsisting existence, He is distinct from the world, as possessing as His nature what is not found in the nature of any other thing, namely existence. The difficulty is not to see that Pantheism or Monism which identify the world and God are untrue, but rather how, since there is this infinite gulf between the being of God and that of the world, there can be any connection between them. Pantheism in making God one with the contingent and imperfect world destroys God, but does not Theism in making Him the plenitude of Being and Perfection, destroy the world ? This would certainly be the case if being were univocal, for then there could be only one Being ; but we have seen already that it is analogical, even in the realm of finite and contingent things, so that the relation of essence to existence is simply speaking different in substance and accident, and only proportionally

[1] *Summa Theologica*, I, 60, 5.

the same. Consequently, God's existence, which is identified with His Essence, does not exhaust all the possibilities of existence; since there may exist natures which possess existence, not in their own right as natures, but by a participation of existence from God who exists of Himself. Their existence will thus be utterly dependent on God, though in so far as they receive it in a limited mode, proportional to their natures, it will be their own existence, not God's.

This double truth of the distinction of God and the world, and of the entire dependence in existence of the world on God, and so of the connection between them, will be confirmed by a consideration of God's operations with regard to the world, of His operative attributes, to which we must now turn our attention.

CHAPTER V

GOD'S KNOWLEDGE

The Existence of Knowledge in God—Its Object—His Knowledge of Creatures—His Knowledge of Possible Things—The Science of Simple Intelligence and the Science of Vision—His Knowledge of Individuals—The 'Aristotelean God'—Another Difficulty—The Unity of God and the Multiplicity of Creatures—God's Knowledge of Future Contingent Things—The Medium of this Knowledge—Scientia Media—The Thomist View—Some Difficulties in Either View.

It may, at first sight, seem strange that the discussion of God's operative attributes should open with that of the Divine Knowledge; for, in human knowledge, man is dependent on the things which he knows and does not make them, so that it is, from this point of view, passive; and we should not begin a consideration of man's practical operations with a discussion of it. Divine Knowledge, on the contrary, is altogether independent, and is, as we shall see, causative with respect to the world which it knows. It resembles human knowledge, however, in being activity and immanent activity.

That there is knowledge and intelligence in God, and that in the highest degree, is abundantly clear. Since God is absolutely immaterial without limitation of any kind, He must be supremely intelligent, for immateriality is the root of cognition. We have seen the truth of this, both by analysing the nature of knowledge in itself, when it appeared that it consists in a union with the *forms* of the objects known; and by means of our observation of the knowledge of the senses and the intellect. In intellectual knowledge we saw how the human intellect is relative to the being of things, and this relation and dependence is an imperfection in it. In God there is no such relativity, for He is Being Itself, so that the Divine Intelligence is Being which is always actually known. It is a single act identified with the Divine Essence, an eternal intellection of infinite truth. The Divine Essence is not potential with respect to this act, nor the act with respect to its object. For what is this object? Being infinite, it can be nothing else than the Divine Being itself, which is at the summit of intelligibility, as it is at that of intellectuality, being wholly immaterial. Hence as S. Thomas says: 'It is plain that in God intellect, and that which is understood, and the intelligible species, and intellection itself, are altogether one and the same. Whence it is clear that in saying that God is intelligent, no multiplicity is posited in His substance.'[1] Thus God, knowing His own infinite Being, knows all things, so that His knowledge of creatures implies no potentiality or multiplicity in Him. This infinite Being of God Himself is therefore called the primary object of the Divine Intelligence, for it is that which is first and essentially known by the Divine Intellect, and by its means God knows all other things. We speak here, as we are bound to do, in accordance with an analogy drawn from created knowledge, and it is not to be supposed that it is implied that there is any progress in the Divine Intellect from its primary to its secondary objects, or any priority of one over the other, but all are known simultaneously, perfectly, and eternally. Nevertheless, in accordance with our imperfect way of regarding it, we shall say that the Divine Intellect, being absolutely perfect, knows all things in that order in which they are intelligible. Now there can be no doubt that the Divine Essence is first in the order of intelligibility, and so is 'first' known by God. Further, God in knowing His infinite Being, or Essence, must know all things in and through it, for there can be no being independent of the infinite Being of God. So He will know all things in the way in which they are presented by His Essence, that is to say, first He knows His Essence, and secondarily all other things which are participations of His Essence.

[1] *Summa Theologica*, I, 14, 4. '*Patet . . . quod in Deo intellectus, et id quod intelligitur, et species intelligibilis, et ipsum intelligere, sunt omnino unum et idem. Unde patet quod per hoc quod Deus dicitur intelligens, nulla multiplicitas ponitur in ejus substantia.*'

Consequently, it is true to say that God knows only Himself, and yet knows things other than Himself, for these are wholly dependent on Him for their being, and ' are ' only in so far as they participate the Divine existence. Thus God knows all things other than Himself perfectly, and these things constitute the secondary object of Divine Science. Knowing His own Essence perfectly and comprehensively, He must also perfectly comprehend His Power, and all things to which it can extend. Now this power, being infinite, extends to all things other than God, and can extend to all possible things, and so God's knowledge, too, extends to all actual and possible things. The knowledge by which God knows possible things is called ' the science of simple intelligence,' because to it there is not joined any act of the will, nor does it presuppose the existence of its object. The divine knowledge of all that has been, is, or will be, is called ' the science of vision,' since, like sight, it is directed not to what is merely possible, but to actual existents.

To deny God knowledge of all possible things, down to their least detail, would evidently be to limit His knowledge, for the Divine Essence being infinite is infinitely capable of diverse imitations ; and so His knowledge comprehends all the details of individual possible things. Among all these possibilities God, by a free choice, has decided to bring into existence that world which actually is, has been, or will be. This, too, He knows in His Essence, but now not with a sheer knowledge of the *natures* of the things which constitute it, as possible things, but, inasmuch as to the act of intelligence is also joined an act of will, as actual existents. For the science of God, unlike our own, is not measured by the things which it knows, but is the cause of things. To suggest the opposite would be to make God dependent on the things which He knows, learning from them; which is altogether impossible. This union of the Divine knowledge and the Divine Will, by means of which God knows all actual things, is the Divine Decree. We see from this how erroneous is the view that God knows things immediately in themselves, or even that He knows them both in themselves and in Himself, for either view would make God's knowledge partially dependent on creatures, and so limited and imperfect. The Divine Intelligence would, in accordance with these views, be immediately specified by a created object, and would contain a finite representation of finite things, received from the things themselves, and so dependent on them.

God, thus knowing Himself, must know all things perfectly : nothing can be substracted from His knowledge, not even the individuality or details of things or their materiality, or even evil. Does He then know His Essence as individualised and limited ? No, knowing it perfectly as the cause of all things, He knows them all in a higher unity. Knowing the whole, He knows the parts. His intellect is not to be thought of as containing creatures one after another, or one beside another, as a mirror reflects the objects in a room, but all together in His infinite causality, which, in the effects produced, will be limited and finite. As the light of the sun contains in itself all the prismatic colours, so the knowledge of God contains all the differentiations of creatures.

To say this is not equivalent to saying that God knows particular things confusedly. This was, in S. Thomas's day, the doctrine of the Averroists ; and later something like it reappears in Deism. According to many modern critics of Thomism it is here more than at any other point that the philosophy of S. Thomas breaks down. S. Thomas, they say, took over in its entirety the Aristotelean conception of God who is Pure Act, and who is, consequently, devoid of all limitation and potentiality whatsoever. He must also be absolutely simple, and there can be no multiplicity either in the objects of His knowledge, nor yet any duality of subject and object in His knowing. Yet, in spite of this, S. Thomas informs us that He knows all things, and their very individuality and limitation. Such a view might be consistent, they think, with Platonism, but is absolutely at variance with the Aristotelean God, who 'Thought of thought,' is absorbed entirely in contemplation of Himself and knows nothing of any finite thing, except in the sense in which He may be said to know them under the general concept of Being, since He himself is Being. So some say that the Aristotelean theory has been 'mutilated and mangled' by

S. Thomas in order to make it fit into the theological scheme ; and others that the ideas of Plato and Aristotle have been, as it were, glued together and it is impossible 'not to see the cracks.' These criticisms are severe. It is not our business, however, to decide whether S. Thomas is a faithful follower of Aristotle, but whether his system is coherent in itself. Now the root of all these objections to S. Thomas's presentation of the science of God is the conviction that Aristotle's God is not, and could not be, the efficient cause of the world. Whether or no Aristotle so conceived Him—and this historical question is not, as is often assumed, to be settled out of hand by a simple denial that he did so—it is abundantly clear that S. Thomas does regard Him as the First Efficient Cause. Is this inconsistent with the fundamental principles of Thomist metaphysics ? It can hardly be so, since the conclusion is arrived at as a result of the application of these very principles, as is to be seen in the first three arguments for God's existence. In fact Aristotelianism was not thoroughly thought out by Aristotle, for no one will deny that efficient causality plays a prominent part in the drama of the material world, as he conceived it ; and yet he did not link up the universe in one by carrying to their logical conclusion the implications contained in his basic principles.

If then we grant that the reasoning contained in the first three proofs of the existence of God, given by Aquinas, is sound ; and at the same time allow, as we surely must, that God knows in His Essence, which is subsisting Being, all that has the nature of Being ; it will follow as a necessary consequence that all that in any way is, exists and is known in the Divine Essence as in its first source. Now finite substance possesses being, accidental forms are certain modes of Being, even matter and potentiality are being, for they are potential being, a reality and not mere privation or nonentity. They must, therefore, and can be known by Him who knows all being and from whom all being proceeds. If the real being of potentiality is denied it would be impossible for God either to cause or know it and He would be consequently cut off from all knowledge of the material and individual, and could know only Himself, the infinite. But it is one of the most strongly marked characteristics of genuine and undisputed Aristoteleanism that potential being is real being, and therefore, as S. Thomas saw, it is certainly knowable by the Intelligence which knows all being. The chief controversy of S. Thomas's life was, as is well known, that with the Averroists, such as Siger of Brabant, who denied to God all efficient causality, as a consequence of which they further denied that He has knowledge of finite and individual things. This doctrine found in S. Thomas its most determined opponent, and his interest in the problem was not an historical one, to determine in fact what Aristotle had thought, but a vital one, the desire to discover and elucidate the truth. He follows his principles to their inevitable conclusion, and so establishes, first, that God is Subsisting Being and the efficient cause of all being other than Himself; secondly, that as its cause He must know it: and thirdly, that since finite forms, and matter, and potency itself, are beings, all these must be known by Him. The mode of this perfection of knowledge is unknown to us, for we do not know 'what God is'; but we do know that such knowledge can positively be ascribed to Him, even if we are ignorant of the way in which His Infinite Essence contains the finitude and particularity of created things.

A lesser difficulty in this connection sometimes arises from overlooking the distinction between those perfections which we attribute to God formally and those which we ascribe to Him virtually only. Knowledge is in God formally, but animality or humanity can be in Him only virtually, in so far as He is their cause. *A fortiori* the same holds good of material substance, accidental being, and potential being. Thus God is not a stone nor an apple, but being the cause of all the reality that is in one or the other, He contains them in His Essence.[1]

God, who is Subsisting Being, is the plenitude of Being;

[1] Dr. Leet Patterson seems to confuse these two modes of attribution when he says: 'An apple enjoys a certain degree of being, and in so far as it does so, imitates God. But the apple is round and coloured, while God is neither round nor coloured.' God is not formally round or coloured, but is so virtually in so far as He is the cause of these accidental forms.

and His inexhaustible nature is able to be shared by other beings, which are distinct from Him in so far as they only have, but are not, existence, whereas God *is* His Existence; and which are within the sphere of the Infinite Being of God in so far as all their existence is but a scintilla of being derived from, and continually supported by, the Divine Being. It is thus, in one sense, a different kind or grade of being to that which is Divine, and so is truly other than God, and yet its very being is wholly dependent on the Divine, so that it is not an addition to the infinite being of God. As the light flashes in many rays from the facets of a diamond, but is only one light, so the Being of God and all His Perfection, which is an absolute unity, is reflected in diverse ways by finite things. The plurality is in the facets, not in the light; the multiplicity is in the things, not in God. So God, knowing His own causal Power, as able to produce this multiplicity, knows also the multitudinous natures of things down to their last detail, and their individual distinction and characteristics.

This conclusion, then, far from being inconsistent with the fundamental principles of Thomism, follows rigorously from those principles, for it is implicit in the five ways, which are themselves a magnificent synthesis of Platonism and Aristoteleanism.

From this fascinating subject of God's knowledge of singular things we must now turn to that of His knowledge of future contingent ones. As Deism and Theism separate from one another on the question of God's knowledge of singular things, so there is a cleavage here among Theists themselves as to the way in which God knows future contingent events, and especially free future actions.

Before going any further it is well to notice the difference between a future event and a merely possible one. Evidently there is more reality about the former; and this arises from the fact that an event which is in fact going to happen in the future will then happen as the effect of some cause or causes. Consequently, just before it happens it will be prepared for in its cause, and thus its relation to existence is that of a thing whose cause is already in existence, whereas a merely possible thing has no such relation to existence, but is merely something which can, without contradiction, be conceived of as existing. So S. Thomas says: 'That which now is, was future for the reason that it was in its cause that it should come to be; hence, if the cause were removed, that thing's coming to be would not be future.'[1] Consequently, the whole nature of the future is to be sought in its cause, and it is only determinately future if it is already determinately in its cause.

Now future things are of two kinds, necessary and contingent ones; necessary ones proceeding from necessary causes which act invariably, and contingent ones proceeding from causes which can be frustrated either from without or from within. A special class of this latter kind are free future things which proceed from causes which are indifferent with respect to alternatives.

That God knows all future things cannot be denied if we allow that the knowledge of God is the cause of things, and includes all that is. For, as S. Thomas points out,[2] since God knows things which actually are, and His knowledge is 'measured by eternity,' and so is not successive, He knows future things as present, and so infallibly. For though, from our point of view, we can only conjecture whether future events will come about by examining their causes, God's knowledge is not of this kind, but He sees them as present, even though they are still future with respect to the causes which will produce them. To maintain the contrary would be to assert that the being of future contingent things is independent of God, and that He is not their cause; and that the knowledge of God is passive with regard to such things, and is determined by them instead of determining them. This would destroy the perfection of His knowledge, and be a denial that God is Pure Act, by positing potentiality in Him with respect to such things.

That God must certainly know all future things, including contingent ones and free future actions, is clear from the

[1] *Summa Theologica*, I, 16, 7, ad 3.
[2] *Ibid.*, I, 14, 13, cf. a. 9.

fact that He is the cause of all being and that His knowledge is eternal, not successive. So the fact of His knowledge of them is certain, but we should wish to know not only that He has such knowledge, but, as far as our understanding will allow, how He has it ; that is, what is the medium in which He knows contingent, and especially free, future events.

The question then is : How out of the infinite number of possible things, some are known as future ? It cannot be merely because God knows them, otherwise all possible things would be future. Now all Scholastics agree that God knows necessary future things in His Essence as it is taken in conjunction with the free decree of the Divine Will ; but differ as to the medium of His knowledge of contingent and free future things.

Thus Molina and those who follow him maintain that free future things are known by God in their secondary causes, inasmuch as these are supercomprehended by God, who thus knows what a creature would do if it were placed in a particular set of circumstances. Since He wills to place it in a determinate set of circumstances, He therefore knows what it will do in fact. This knowledge is called by Molina '*scientia media*' because it is intermediary between the science of vision by which God knows actual things and the 'science of simple intelligence' by which He knows possible ones. These conditional future things—'what a creature would do in a certain set of circumstances'—are regarded by Him as neither actual nor yet merely possible. They are not merely possible, since they would come about if a certain condition or conditions were fulfilled ; and not actual, since they will not come about unless certain conditions are fulfilled. Thus in this view we have a distinction between '*scientia simplicis intelligentiæ*' which concerns possible things only, '*scientia media*' which knows what is conditionally future and includes the free acts of human wills, and '*scientia visionis*' by which God sees what will actually happen after His decree. So by *scientia media*, say those who hold this view, God knew, eternally, and apart from any predetermining decree on His part, what every free creature would do in any particular case, if, while enjoying the use of free-will, it were placed in any particular set of circumstances; while by the science of vision God sees what will follow after His decree, and so ordains that those things shall be future which by *scientia media* He foresees would flow from the liberty of their proximate causes.

This doctrine of '*scientia media*' is the one which is most distinctive of Molinism, though, of course, corresponding doctrines of free-will—and, in Theology, of grace—go along with it. Though, in its general outline, it is, and has been, accepted by a large number of Scholastic philosophers and theologians, yet there is considerable difference among them as to the way it should be explained.

So Molina himself thought that God so perfectly understands all the circumstances and motives which can influence the will, as well as the nature of the will itself, that He knows with certainty, not merely what the will in certain circumstances could do, but also in fact what it would do.

Suarez thought this explanation of the way in which God gains *scientia media* to be destructive of creative liberty. As Fr. Joyce truly says: 'If a knowledge of the agent's nature, combined with that of the circumstances in which it is placed, granted only that it be sufficiently comprehensive, reveals to its possessor what course that agent will adopt, this can only be because the action is determined—because given these conditions it must of necessity follow. But if this be so, the agent is not free. . . .'[1] Suarez, therefore, rejected Molina's explanation of *scientia media*, and maintained that God has it by knowing both His decree, in accordance with which He concurs with the realisation of free acts, and by knowing also the part which the free-will is to play in realising them. But since our wills, being free, are essentially undetermined, so that the outcome of their action is uncertain, how does God know certainly what part they will play? Suarez suggests[2] that He knows it from the formal truth of the propositions concerning the event. Of two contradictory propositions one is true, the other false; for example, at a certain moment, and under determined

[1] G. H. Joyce, S.J., *Principles of Natural Theology*, p. 361.
[2] Cf. Mahieu, *Suarez*, p. 232.

conditions, of the two propositions 'John will sit,' and 'John will not sit,' one is true and the other false, since both cannot be true or false. This is sufficient, thinks Suarez, for infinite intelligence to know determinately what John will do, all things being present to it in eternity.

This may be another way of saying that it is useless for us to try and discover the way in which God knows free future events, or how He comes to have '*scientia media*.' In any case, this last is the point of view of some writers, as Fr. Kleutgen, who confesses that the way in which God knows by means of '*scientia media*' is an inscrutable mystery, but maintains that its existence must be admitted as the only means of safeguarding human liberty. So also Fr. Joyce says: 'It may frankly be admitted that it is beyond our power to give any explanation how God can know the choice which a free agent would make were he placed in given circumstances.'[1] So he thinks that to try and explain how God knows free future things is beyond the reach of the human mind, and all we can do is to assert that He does so by means of '*scientia media*.' Others who do not think it necessary to introduce the idea of '*scientia media*' at all take a similar view, and say that we are certain that God knows all things since all are eternally present to Him, and with this we ought to rest content.

The majority of Thomists, however, like the greater part of their opponents, are not satisfied to let the matter rest here. While acknowledging that we cannot know the mode of the Divine perfections as they exist in God, they think that reason can exclude from them certain characteristics, and particularly that there is any passivity or dependence in God and in His knowledge. Thus they think it impossible that He should know any object—as indeed that there should be any object—whose whole entity did not depend on the Divine Will. According to them two kinds of science only can be conceived of in God: the science of simple intelligence, and the science of vision. By the science of vision God knows all things which acquire existence through His decree, and so to it belongs the knowledge of free future

[1] *Principles of Natural Theology*, p. 357.

events, and even of those conditional free future events—known as futuribles—which would certainly come about if some condition were fulfilled which never will in fact be fulfilled. In their view the certainty of these events is, and must be, due solely to the decree of God ; it is His decree which produces them, even though only conditionally. Both Thomists and those who disagree with them regard the science of simple intelligence as concerned with merely possible things and events.

Thus according to the Thomists God knows future things of all kinds in His Essence as it is determined by His own free decree. This decree they call predetermining, not only because from all eternity it preordains free acts, but also because the movement which it gives to a free cause, in time, is previous to the determination of created will.

It is impossible to enter here on the discussion whether this doctrine is that of S. Thomas himself. This historical question has been the subject of much controversy, and the reader must be referred to works which deal professedly with this subject.[1]

What are the reasons which the Thomists advance in defence of their doctrine ? They are of two kinds : positive and negative. Positively, they deduce it from fundamental metaphysical principles ; and negatively, they endeavour to show that the opposing doctrine is involved in insuperable difficulties. It will be convenient to set down first the positive reasons given by them for alleging that God knows future things in general, and free future events in particular, in His Essence as it is determined by His own free decree. It is plain, they say, that there can be no potentiality or passivity in God, who is Pure Act, and therefore that every being, every reality must be dependent for its being on Him. If not, it would be independent, and God would be dependent on it. This being manifestly impossible, it is clear that God

[1] Cf. e.g. art. 'Molinisme' in *Dict. de Théologie Catholique*, especially col. 2183, 2184 ; N. Monaco, S.J., *Theologia Naturalis*, Nos. 179, 180, 187, 289, 290 ; Garrigou-Lagrange, *Dieu*, pp. 408 ff. ; Del Prado, O.P., *De Gratia et Libero Arbitrio*, Tom. II ; Dummermuth, *Sanctus Thomas et doctrina præmotionis physicæ*, Paris, 1886 ; Massoulié, *Divus Thomas sui interpres*, Rome, 1692.

must, by His Science, be the cause not only of necessary beings, but also of contingent ones ; and not only of present realities, but also of all future ones, including free future events. If in this way God is the cause of contingent and free future events it follows that He knows them in Himself as their cause. '*Scientia Dei est causa rerum, secundum quod habet voluntatem conjunctam,*' says S. Thomas.[1] Consequently, God knows future things of all kinds in His essence as determined by His decree, including the free acts of our will. 'Therefore God knows all things to which His causality extends, by knowing His own Essence. It extends, however, to the operations of the intellect and will.'[2] Later in the same chapter of the *Contra Gentiles* S. Thomas points out that though free-will excludes the determination of the will, as well as violence, which proceed from some cause which acts on it externally, it does not exclude the influence of a higher cause from which proceeds both its being and operation. Thus the Divine causality, which is most efficacious, causes the will to will in accordance with its nature, i.e. freely, and when the will wills the good its power and that of the First Cause are all one ; while even when it falls away and wills evil, God eternally knows this, for by a permissive decree He eternally allows the will's defection. Thus both the act of willing and the mode of that act which is freedom proceed from God, and so are known by Him in His essence as determined by His decree.

The Thomists argue further that apart from God's decree free acts are not contained certainly and determinately, but only conjecturally, in created wills ; and could therefore only be known by God conjecturally, and not certainly. If, then, we say, as we must, that God knows all our free acts certainly, it follows that He must know them by virtue of His decree. The same result is, in the opinion of the Thomists, capable of being established negatively and indirectly by a consideration of the weaknesses of the other suggested explanations. Thus it seems plain, and there is now a general agreement on the point, that free future events

[1] I, 14, 8.
[2] I *C. G.*, c. 68, and see the whole chapter.

cannot be known by God in the formal truth of the propositions concerning them. For though it is true, that of two contradictory propositions one excludes the other, so that they cannot *both* be true or false; yet it is not true, that in virtue of the contradiction, one rather than the other is definitely true or false. Hence of two contradictory propositions about future contingent things neither is definitely true or false, except it be divinely decreed as future; so that all that can be alleged is that the disjunctive proposition: 'it will be or will not be,' is true so long as one side or the other is not determined and fixed by the secondary cause, since this is by supposition undetermined, and must therefore be certainly determined by the first cause if it is to be certainly known. If we suppose that free acts come about determinately and certainly independently of God's decree, this can only be because they are determinately and certainly in their causes and *must* follow from them, in which case it is absurd to pretend that they are produced freely by these causes.

This is one of the difficulties attaching to the theory of *scientia media*, especially as put forward by its originator; and was the reason which led Suarez to reject Molina's explanation. For if God by means of His intimate knowledge of the nature of a man's will, and all the circumstances in which he is placed can tell certainly from all eternity what the man will do, this can only be because he cannot, in those circumstances, act otherwise than in a determinate way; and so we are involved in the determinism of circumstances, and man is no longer free. In order to be free he must make his own motives, not receive them either from his surroundings nor yet from the nature of the will itself. As he goes on more and more making his motives for himself, and not being led captive by anything other than himself, he becomes more and more his own master and so free; and it will become more and more probable that he will act in a certain characteristic fashion in any given situation. It will, however, remain probable only, and not certain, if we consider the man as an independent free cause; so that what he will do cannot, by examining him and his circumstances, with whatever penetration, even if it be infinite, be certainly known.

There must, therefore, be some self-originated motion in the man which seizes a particular motive and makes it a determining one for him, and since this motion cannot be absolutely self-originated—otherwise the man would be the first cause, not a secondary cause—it must also be originated by the first cause, who, in causing it, knows it, and the consequent action of the man. In the Thomist view, therefore, God's premotion and predetermination, far from destroying man's liberty, causes it.

So the Thomists maintain that, though their view does not remove all obscurities, yet it is founded on first principles, and arises as a natural result from the necessary and legitimate application of them; while they think that the explanation by means of *scientia media* is an *ad hoc* theory devised merely to safeguard human liberty—and a particular view of it—without due regard being paid to the absolute dependence of the being of all things on God, and the principle of causality.

Their opponents make somewhat similar charges against them, and particularly with regard to free-will, which they hold to be entirely abolished by the Thomist theory. For, they say, it is of the essence of freedom that, in willing, we might have chosen to act otherwise than in that way in which we actually did choose to act. If, however, God predetermines us to choose in one way we cannot choose the contradictory, so that our freedom is gone. There is no doubt that this is a powerful objection, and no explanation will clear it away altogether, for to do this we should have to know the mode of the Divine action, and how He harmonises this with the action of the human will. We shall have occasion to deal with this question again in relation to the Divine Motion; and here will only point out that the objection assumes a particular view of freedom, according to which the will can act *or* not act even after the last practico-practical judgement has been made, and is not bound to follow it, so that it could have chosen a course of action to which this judgement did not lead. Secondly, the objection suggests that the Divine motion is thought of as something external to the will, whereas in fact it is in the will itself, the object which is chosen being found by the will to be good, and so accepted, because the will itself is under the influence of the Divine motion, and therefore wills of itself, and thus freely, what God wills in it. For indeed freedom does not imply random action in any direction, but rather self-mastery, in accordance with which the man is able to choose what appears to him good ; the reason of its so appearing being the whole state of the will at the moment, which state, according to the Thomists, includes the divine premotion. So, though the determinate choice is a necessary consequence of this state, the choice itself is not necessary. It would have been different in fact if the state of the will had been different. The will thus preserves its dominion over its choice, for this is its very own. It would be unreasonable to maintain that a choice is not free because when made it is necessarily made and cannot not be made as, for, example, when a man chooses to sit he cannot also choose not to sit. He is then determined, but he has determined himself, which is to be free ; and so also under the Divine motion he determines himself. The fact that he cannot determine himself in opposition to the Divine motion no more interferes with his self-determination than the fact that he cannot determine himself in a sense opposite to that of his actual determination ; for the Divine motion is within him, and is thus, in a sense, himself.

In the case of a sinful act no motion is required from God to constitute the act as sinful, since the sin is a defect or privation in the act, morally considered. So the sin comes about by God's permission, as both schools acknowledge, and arises because the will does not co-operate with the motion towards good afforded to it. Thus sin arises entirely from the defectibility of the human will and is in no way imputable to God, for it does not require a positive motion from Him, but only that He should not prevent it. Evidently He does not always do so, so that if this be taken to constitute Him the author of sin there seems little to choose between the two theories in this respect, for both allow that He permits it. Here, however, we are touching on the theological discussion concerning grace, and this question can only be fully elucidated in a theological context, where, however, *why* God permits sin, and, in general, the mode of God's action on human wills remain mysterious. Thus both solutions are professedly incomplete, and it seems that they appeal to different types of mind, the Thomist opinion seeming better to those who are strongly convinced of the power of the reason to lead us on the way to truth, while the contrary view seems preferable to those who consider that we should take our stand on the fact of human freedom, and so are more influenced by practical than theoretical considerations. Thus the choice of one or other solution is a free choice : *qualis unusquisque est talis finis videtur ei.*

CHAPTER VI

THE DIVINE WILL AND ITS EFFECTS

Its Object—Its Independence—Its Diffusion of Goodness—The Notion of Creation—It is not a Change—It is a Relation—It is not Contradictory, and so is Possible—It is a Fact—Conservation is continued Creation—Creation and Time—Two Objections to Creation—Multiplicity and Unity.

THE certainty that there is in God intellect and perfect knowledge makes it equally certain that He also has Will. The relationship between cognition and volition is indeed a necessary one, since the will is an inclination to the good as apprehended by the intellect. Now God by His intellect apprehends Himself as the highest good, and good so apprehended as good is necessarily loved, an operation which belongs to the will.[1] Thus the essence of God is the primary object of His Will, and this He wills and loves necessarily, since it is Infinite Good ; so that He *is* Love : Love is His very Nature. Just as we said earlier that the primary object of God's science is His own self as the first truth, so now we see that the primary object of His Will is His essence as the highest Good. Since this Good is Infinite and Perfect, will it not follow that God wills nothing but Himself, for what can be Good or Desirable which is not the Infinite Good ? This conclusion is true in the same sense as the twin statement 'God knows nothing but Himself' is true ; that is to say God neither knows nor wills anything except in His essence and for Himself. God knows all things other than Himself in knowing His own essence, and wills all other things in willing Himself. God is thus in no way dependent on these things either in knowledge or love. This absolute independence of God is the truth which is

[1] Cf. I *C.G.*, 72 ; *Compendium Theologiæ*, Cap. 31 ; *Summa Theologica*, I, 19, 1.

intended to be preserved in the Deist notion of Him as a Being who neither knows nor cares for the world; though in fact it is thereby destroyed, for such a world would be independent of God, who would, therefore, not be the only independent Being, but would be limited by the world. Only in the Theist doctrine, in which the world is seen as the overflowing of the Infinite perfection and Goodness of God, can His independence be fully maintained. '*Bonum est diffusivum sui,*' say the Scholastics; for just as every being wills its good, so it also wills the diffusion of this good, for such diffusion is itself a good. It is only in so far as a good is limited and partial that its diffusion is checked; as a shipwrecked man may try to seize all the water in the ship's boat, though if the supply were ample he would wish it distributed, for what would be good for others would indirectly benefit himself. If, then, we consider infinite good, it is plain that it will be in the highest degree desirable for it to be communicated; and we should expect to find such communication of His perfections to be characteristic of the Summum Bonum. Therefore we shall find no difficulty in the doctrine that the Will of God is active, and throws out, as it were, showers of goodness, giving out a participated being, goodness, truth, beauty and all perfections, in so far as His Essence is capable of imitation, thereby constituting the finite universe. We might indeed be so carried away by the idea that goodness must act thus as to conceive that God could not refrain from so diffusing His perfections, but is necessitated in creating beings to whom they must be in some measure communicated. If so, we should be losing sight of another fundamental truth, namely the infinite goodness of God in Himself, so that all His willing must be satisfied in so far as He wills Himself. If, therefore, God had not willed to communicate His goodness by creation He would still have willed the Perfect Good, and if He wills so to diffuse it, He wills no more and nothing better, but always the perfect good which is Himself. If He does not create, it is good; if He does create, it is no better; for always He wills perfect Good, whether in its own infinite immanent perfection, or as reflected in creatures, whose whole goodness is derived from it, and which are willed only as tending to that infinite goodness. God thus wills things other than Himself with absolute freedom, for they are in no way necessary means for attaining the good which He wills necessarily, namely Himself. If we wish to cross the sea, we must necessarily wish for a ship, but if we wish to make a journey on land we need not wish for a train, for we might go by car or on foot ; and thus God does not necessarily will creatures, for He possesses His perfection perfectly without them. Just as the being of creatures adds nothing to the being of God, so also the goodness which God pours out adds nothing to His Goodness, but is included in it. He is thus absolutely transcendent, independent and free. As Fr. Sertillanges says : 'There is no other good for God than God ; all the rest is only good through Him, not for Him.'[1]

In the preceding paragraphs, the words creation and creature have been used to indicate God's action in the production of the finite universe, and the nature of this universe. Are these expressions justified ; and is God in fact the creator of the world ?

However brief may be a sketch of S. Thomas's view of the nature and attributes of God, this question of creation must occupy an important place. His view of it, indeed, is all one with his proofs of God's existence, all of which include the idea of the entire dependence of the world on God. Whatever may be the true interpretation of Aristotle's fragmentary discussion of the relation of the world to God, there can be no doubt that in S. Thomas's view He is required as its first efficient cause and the ground of its being ; and creation signifies the particular way in which, according to S. Thomas, God acted in this efficient causation of the world. What, then, is meant by this word 'creation' ? It is the making of the world from nothing ; or in the exact phrase used by Scholastic writers : the total production of a thing from nothingness, it being produced neither from itself nor from any presupposed subject. In modern language the word creation is often used very loosely, as when we speak of a

[1] Sertillanges, *S. Thomas d'Aquin.*, Vol. I, p. 246.

'creative genius' or a 'Paris creation'; though these phrases are not amiss if they are recognised to be metaphorical analogies.

Creation, then, is to be distinguished from the two other forms of production: generation and alteration. In the first we have the production of a new substantial form, but the matter remains throughout the change; as appears in the generation of animals, where the germinal cells receive a new substantial form, the matter of the germinal cells being found in them both prior to, and after, its coming. Similarly, by alteration an accidental form comes into being, but the substance remains through the change. An artist painting a picture alters the arrangement of the paint and canvas, but does not call these into being. So creation is not, properly speaking, a change at all; for a change involves something which is changed, something with which the change begins and something with which it ends. Creation does not begin with anything, and so is not a change either of the thing which comes to be by its means, nor yet of any other thing.

This shows plainly that when we speak of production 'from nothing' we are not conceiving 'nothing' as something of which the created thing is made. This would no doubt imply—if it were not too foolish even to be entertained for a moment—that the creature also, being 'made of nothing,' is nothing.

It is essential, then, to grasp very clearly, at the outset, that the idea of creation in no way implies a change, a movement, 'a becoming,' as this term is used of substantial or accidental mutations; for here there is no point of departure, nothing to 'become' this or that. So the idea of creation does not imply any passing from one state to another, a passage from the state of nothingness to the state of being, but only the entire dependence, for the whole of its being, of the creature on the creator;[1] and thus creation, considered in the creature, belongs not to the genus of action and passion, but to that of relation; and creation itself is not an action

[1] So the source and beginning of the creature is the creator to whom it is related, '*cum quadam novitate seu inceptione*' (I, 45, 3, ad 3).

which is an intermediary between the creature and the creator, but, like all relations, is logically posterior to the thing related. So the phrase 'a created being' signifies primarily 'being,' and then a relation of absolute dependence of this being on its first principle and source.

The fact that by creation we mean absolute dependence, with respect to being, of the created thing on its source implies another important truth: that to create is proper to the First Cause. For being is the most universal of all effects, so that its total production can only be attributed to a cause which is also universal and extends to the whole of being. Moreover, the capacity of nothing for becoming something is nil, and so all the power for the production of being must come from the producer, and must correspond to the effect to be produced, namely, to bridge the infinite gulf between not-being and being, and so must be itself infinite. The effect is infinite, for the gulf between being and nothing has only one side. To build a bridge with only one end, which stretches out for ever from one bank, an infinite power is required, and an infinite power can only be found in an infinite cause. God alone, then, who is Infinite, has power to create.

In saying this we must be on our guard against falling into the misapprehension of supposing that creation is, formally speaking, a transitive action in God emanating from Him after the fashion of that of a potter moulding a vase. On the contrary, it is formally immanent in Him, and is the infinite activity of the Divine intellect and will. Inasmuch as this produces an effect which is other than God, though it produces no addition to His Being or Goodness, it is said to be virtually transitive, and establishes in the creature a real relation of absolute dependence on God. On the other hand, no real relation can be set up in God towards the creature, for the relation being one of absolute dependence, it is that of the conditioned to Being which is absolutely unconditioned, and so unrelated and independent of anything but Itself.

The notion of creation, then, though a difficult one—since it affords no foot-hold for the imagination—is nevertheless not a contradictory or absurd one. There is nothing in the nature of contingent being to prevent its being totally produced with respect to its being, since it is of such a kind that it has of itself no necessary claim to being. Again, if we ask if it is contradictory to say that the world of contingent beings should be totally produced by God, we see that it is not ; for God, who is infinite and necessary being, is the universal cause of all being and so capable of producing being in its totality.

From these considerations of the idea and of the possibility of creation, we pass to the question whether, in fact, the world owes its production to a creative act. We are not here asking whether it had a beginning, in the sense of not having existed always, but merely whether the whole of its reality is derived from a Divine act of causation, apart from which it would not be at all.

If we are already convinced that God is necessary being and the world contingent, this question does not present any particular difficulty. Contingent being, if it exists, (and we know that it does so), since it does not possess existence of itself and of its own nature—for then it would be necessary, not contingent—must receive existence from something else, and, in the last resort, from necessary being, or from God. This is simply the third argument for the existence of God looked at from another point of view. Now all beings other than God are contingent, as it is impossible that there should be more than one necessary being ; and consequently the world as a whole owes its existence entirely to God. But could not God have produced being from some pre-existing subject ? The answer is plain, for if this subject were contingent, the question of the production of its being would again recur, and we have already excluded the possibility of an infinite series of contingent beings which owe their being to another. If, on the contrary, this subject were necessary being itself, that is, the Divine Essence, we are faced with a contradiction, inasmuch as that which is essentially unlimited would be limited, and the unchangeable would change. We must, therefore, conclude that the whole being of contingent things is produced by God, and there is no subject from which these things are produced. They are created. In this creative act, there being nothing on which the act takes effect, and to which, therefore, its power is communicated, it is clear that no tool is used; in other words, that no creature can be an instrumental cause in the act of creation.

We speak of the *act* of creation, a phrase which, on account of the association of the word 'act' with the actions of creatures, may, perhaps, seem to suggest an act which is not continuous, but is one out of a succession of actions. That creative act is not of this kind is apparent from the fact that it is nothing else than the eternal will of God diffusing its own goodness. It is, therefore, in itself, not successive, but eternal.

But if God is eternal and 'outside' the time-sequence, creatures are nevertheless subject to it and exist successively. Their whole being is, as we saw, entirely dependent on God; and so at every moment of their existence they depend on Him for that being. Such continuous dependence on God is called by S. Thomas the 'conservation of beings,' and is evidently not something distinct from creation, but, as far as the creatures are concerned, a continuation of it. It is as imperatively demanded by the nature of contingent things that they should be preserved in being, if they are to continue to exist, as that their being should be totally produced by God in order that they may exist. So S. Thomas says: 'The conservation of things by God is not effected by means of any new action, but by a continuation of the action which gives existence; which action is apart from motion and time; as also the conservation of light in the air is effected by means of a continued influence from the sun.'[1]

The dependence of contingent being on God bears no relationship to time, but is an absolute dependence; so that the idea that a creature can continue in being independently of God's act in imparting being to it, or conserving it in being, is as absurd as the idea that it possesses being of itself,

[1] *Summa Theologica*, I, 104, 1, ad 4.

and is not created. The fact that we do not observe such Divine action in conserving creatures, since it is accompanied by no change in them, makes it, perhaps, even more difficult to grasp the truth of conservation than that of creation, for the imagination fails us altogether. Reason, however, gives us certainty of its necessity ; and it is indubitable that, apart from God's conservation, the whole created world would cease to be.

The time-sequence, therefore, considered as a duration, is dependent on God ; for it is nothing else than contingent being as subject to change and becoming, and this being is wholly dependent on God.

We see, then, that what creation essentially implies is the relation of absolute dependence of the being of the world on God. Since creatures exist successively, or in time, we are naturally led to ask whether this successive existence had a beginning, or is it, perhaps, 'eternal,' like the creative action of God Himself ?

If the notion of creation which has just been explained be regarded as true, it will be obvious that no analysis of it will be able to furnish the answer to this question ; for the idea of creation contains no reference to time, and so none to a beginning of creatures in, or with, time, regarded as a measure. If, then, created being implies nothing with regard to duration for a finite time, there is no impossibility involved in the notion of a created world to which the conception of a temporal beginning does not apply. Essence, as such, has nothing to say to determinate duration, and like the universal concept which we form of it, abstracts altogether from time. Nor can the relation of dependence which is the essence of passive creation,[1] involve any necessity, for a temporal beginning of the created world—a first movement—for it implies, doubtless, a priority of being in God as the cause of the creature, but not that He is prior to the world in time, or existed before the world was. It is natural to us to imagine the creation of the world in this latter way,

[1] By 'active creation' the Scholastics mean the Divine action by whose means creatures are brought into being ; while passive creation is the predicamental relation thereby established in creatures, the relation of dependence of being on God.

not only because we are familiar with the notion of a finite duration of the created universe from the teaching of the Faith, but also because we are inclined to picture God's action on the pattern of our own ; and so, as the artist exists before the statue, the architect before the building, we represent to ourselves God as bringing the world into existence at a certain point in His Life, and thereby existing before it with a temporal priority. All this, it is unnecessary to point out, is hopelessly at variance with the conception of an eternal unchanging God ; for to Him none of these concepts of temporal succession apply. Consequently, just as we cannot show that the notion of creation and the creature involves the idea of a temporal beginning, so, also, no proof of the impossibility of a created universe which had no temporal beginning can be derived from the consideration of God's creative action, for this is eternal. Thus, neither from the side of the creature, nor yet from that of the creator, is a beginning of the world in time demanded. If this be so, it almost seems as if we were driven to the contrary conclusion, and should be forced to admit that the world must have been created *ab æterno*. This could only be proved, however, if God were necessitated to create, if the act of creation belongs to His very nature in the same way as the love of His own goodness does. Now we have already seen that the love which God bestows on creatures, which is the source of their being and goodness, cannot be necessitated, but must be free. God is no greater or happier in that He has created the world than He would have been had He not done so, for He wills creatures to be, not for themselves, but for Himself ; and creatures make no addition to His Being or Goodness, but are known and loved in His own Essence. They are in no sense necessary for the fullness of His perfection, as they would be were He obliged to create them ; nor even do they, in themselves, contribute to it. So He is in no way determined or necessitated by them, but they by Him. Hence what being He wills to give them, and so what mode of being or duration He wills them to have, is entirely dependent on His own free choice. Whether their duration is determinate or not, and so whether, from the point of view of the created world, there was a beginning of its succession, duration or time, or no such temporal beginning, God, as actively creating, will remain unchanged; for in either case His action is eternal; and these temporal concepts do not apply to it. So it cannot be urged that the notion of creation 'in time,' as we say, is an impossible one, as involving a change in God, for His will to create, whether 'in time' or '*ab æterno*,' is itself eternal. The words 'in time' are placed in inverted commas because the expression itself, though a convenient one, is clearly inexact, since time begins with the world; so that, as S. Augustine says, we ought to speak of creation 'with time' rather than 'in time.' We mean by it, that reckoning back from the present moment we should come to the end of creatures and so of time, whereas the notion of creation '*ab æterno*' implies that we should never arrive at such a first moment.

In arguing above that such an idea involves no impossibility, it was not implied that some particular creature, or group of creatures, are not incapable of existing '*ab æterno*'; but that the created universe as a whole might do so.

From all this it will appear that, in the opinion of S. Thomas, reason is powerless to decide the question whether creation is or is not '*ab æterno*'; for an answer to it we need to know what, in fact, God freely willed with regard to it, and this can only be known by revelation. In spite of the violent attacks which were made on this doctrine, S. Thomas always steadfastly adhered to his opinion; and, indeed, with increasing energy. The reason of his attaching so much importance to it was, in the first place, no doubt, that its truth was perspicuously clear to him; while a second, and even stronger motive was that he perceived the danger to the Christian faith if its dogmas were supposed to be necessarily linked up with doubtful philosophical opinions. They might then be involved in the collapse of such opinions. This is what actually happened in the decadence of Scholasticism, for the views of theologians, and even in the minds of many, the Christian faith itself, shared the downfall of the natural philosophy of Aristotle, to which the later Scholastics were inordinately attached.

It has already been pointed out that creation, whether 'in time' or 'from eternity,' involves no change in God. It will, however, be well to conclude this chapter with a few remarks on this point, as perhaps it is this which constitutes for many the greatest difficulty in accepting the doctrine of creation.

It is urged, in the first place, that the production of something which did not exist before implies a new action on the part of its cause; and that this is more evidently the case if the created world is not eternal, for then God would have existed before the world was, and later would have produced it. Now we have already seen that such conceptions as those of 'before' and 'after,' new and old, cannot in any sense apply to a Being who is altogether apart from the succession of time, for all the action of such a Being will be simultaneous, not successive. So to talk of God existing *before* the world was is meaningless; and since God is free, He can freely determine the mode of the duration of the world, as He can freely determine that it shall exist. Thus the production of the world is a novelty as far as the creature is concerned, but in God the eternal decree that it be produced is one and unchangeable. Even so, it is further objected that though, perhaps, there be no new action on the part of God, it is clear that after creation there would be new beings and more being than formerly, which is impossible, since so the greater would be produced by the less, and moreover something would be added to God. In this objection two misapprehensions are contained. For creation does not imply that a greater perfection comes to be in the universe through its means, but only that the perfection of God, eternally the same, is made known to, and expressed in the creature by its coming into being. Thus there is no more being, after creation considered passively, than 'before' but there is an increase of beings. And this implies no addition to the infinite being of God, for the being of creatures is not their own, but is bestowed on them by God, His infinite perfection being infinitely imitable in finite perfections, and by such imitation suffering neither loss nor addition. So when many candles are kindled with one taper, there is no more fire than formerly, but more fires, and the flame of the taper is not diminished as one candle after another lights from it.[1] Nor, as we have seen, does the coming into being of creatures imply any added perfection in God; for even though He had not freely willed that His creative activity should take the form which is the production of creatures, it would still be fully present and perfectly exercised in His own immanent action.

Lastly, it has seemed to many that the multiplicity and diversity of creatures cannot be derived from the absolute unity and simplicity of God. Doubtless, no account of the problem of the one and the many is complete, and in the end we are faced with a mystery, though not a contradiction. For the unity and simplicity of God is not a negative unity or a mere negation of parts, but a positive harmony of intense activity, His infinite action being also His infinite Substance; and so this unity and simplicity is at the opposite extreme to such a unity as that of matter, which must be diversified by form, or to the simplicity of a point, which has no parts. Moreover, when we speak of the Being of God we are using an analogous term, and such analogous being does not need to be diversified by anything extrinsic to itself, as a univocal being does, whether by specific difference or a principle of individuation; but contains actually and implicitly within itself the differences of its inferiors; in the case in point, the diversity of creatures.

Thus God's activity, though one and simple, is able to produce a multiplicity of effects; as the sunlight penetrating the foliage throws a dappled light on the grass beneath, though in itself it is one.

Inadequate as these brief remarks on so mysterious a subject admittedly are, they may perhaps suggest the direction in which we should turn in our consideration of it, and help to show that we are not here faced with a contradiction, but with a truth which we are unable to penetrate.

[1] The example, being an example of Divine action, is bound to limp. Oscar Wilde had a curious fancy that by telling your thought to another you diminished or destroyed it in your own mind. We know this is not so; and, indeed, could only be if thought were material. The idea that there is an addition or loss to God through creation seems to be a fancy of a similar kind.

In the alternative theory of Pantheism, in which the finite is placed within the infinite, we are truly in the presence of a contradiction, with a thing at once infinite and finite; a situation which must result either in the absorption of God in the world, which contradicts the first principles of reason, or of the world in God, which runs counter to evident experience. Thus it will be seen that the doctrine of creation is an integral part of Theism and by its means S. Thomas altogether separates himself from every form of Monism, while preserving both the Immanence and Transcendence of God in a harmonious synthesis. From God, distinct from the world, as being Subsisting Existence while creatures only have existence, all the existence of creatures is derived; and He pours out on them all that they are and have of goodness and beauty, being, as S. Thomas delights to repeat, the Fountain of Goodness—*Fons bonitatis.*

CHAPTER VII

THE DIVINE MOTION

The Fact of Divine Motion in Created Action—Views as to its Nature: Occasionalism, Molinism, Thomism—Six Characteristics of Physical Premotion—The Crucial Point of the Dispute between Molinists and Thomists—Arguments in favour of Premotion—An Objection—Determination and Necessitation—A Distinction Explained—A Further Objection.

It will be convenient to devote a separate chapter to those effects of the Will of God which affect the actions rather than the being of creatures, namely, the Divine motion, whereby God concurs with creatures in their actions.

Since God is the omnipotent first cause, it is certain that not only the being of creatures, but also their action depends immediately on Him. The affirmative answer to the question put by S. Thomas, '*Utrum Deus operetur in omni operante*'—whether God acts in every acting agent—is given by all Scholastic philosophers. The matter is perfectly clear in reason, for we know that Subsisting Being must be the cause of all that is, so that no reality can be withdrawn from His power. The actions of creatures are realities, no less than their being, and are therefore subject to the power and influence of God. The only question which remains to be determined is, therefore, the mode of the Divine influence or motion.

There are three opinions as to its nature. First, the Occasionalists maintain that all the reality of the action of creatures comes from God, the creatures themselves being but the occasions of His action; so that fire does not itself heat anything, but it is God who does so, taking the presence of the fire as the occasion of doing it.

We have already seen that this view is erroneous, and we may add, that since it destroys all real causality and action of creatures, it tends also towards the destruction of the reality of their being. For what reality can a substance have which neither does, nor can, act? '*Agere sequitur esse*' is our guide in discovering the natures of things; and if there is no possibility of action there will be no being either. This view, therefore, tends to deprive the created world of all reality, and to end in Pantheism.

The extreme contrary to this opinion would be one which denied that God has any influence in the action of creatures; but since we have already seen the impossibility of this hypothesis, we can confine ourselves to a consideration of that view which, while acknowledging the reality of the Divine motion in connection with the created action, yet does not allow that such motion affects the action of creatures intrinsically, but maintains that the motion falls on the action and the effect produced by the created agent, not on the agent itself, which is the cause of the action. This is the view of Molina, according to whom the immediate influence of God's motion takes effect, not on the second cause, so premoving it to act and to produce its effect, but on the action and the effect, where it acts side by side with the second cause; so that God and the second cause are both partially responsible for the production of the effect, since they both act on it immediately and simultaneously, 'not otherwise than when two drag a ship.'[1] It is clear that in this view the passing into *action* of created causes is quite independent of God's motion, only the effect produced by created causes, i.e. their action and its term, being in any way dependent on the influence of the Divine concurrence with the action of creatures. The opinion is, therefore, in thorough-going opposition to Occasionalism, which deprives the action of creatures of any reality at all. Neither of these views in their original form finds much support at the present day, but while that of the Occasionalists has been entirely abandoned by Scholastics, modifications of Molina's opinion are still defended by many theologians.

The Thomists have always maintained that in order to safeguard the independence and entire actuality of God, as

[2] Molina, *Concordia*, Q. XVI, a. 13, Disp. XXVI.

well as the freedom of human action, it is necessary to assert that God's motion bears, not merely on the action and its effect, but also on the agent as the cause of the action itself, inasmuch as it applies the agent to act, and causes in it and with it both the action and its mode, whether this mode be necessary or free. According to them, therefore, the motion of God is a previous motion ; previous, that is, to the motion of the creature ; and a physical motion, which is concerned with the exercise of the act and not merely with its specification, as a moral motion would be. This priority which they postulate in the motion of God is a priority, not of time, but of nature, since '*motio moventis præcedit motum mobilis ratione et causa*,' as S. Thomas says,[1] and thus, though temporarily simultaneous with the motion of the creature, it is logically and causally prior to it.

This Divine motion and action can be considered in two ways. First, actively, as it is in God, and here, like all Divine activity, it is formally immanent and only virtually transitive. Secondly, it may be considered passively, as received in creatures, who by its means are moved by God to become actually active, whereas before the reception of the Divine motion they had only the power of acting. This distinction is the same as that which was noticed above with respect to active and passive creation.

Since premotion, as understood by the Thomists, applies the secondary cause to act, it is plain that it does not rule out the action of this cause or render it superfluous. Hence it is opposed to Occasionalism. Secondly, since premotion is a Divine influence it is universal in its effectiveness, and produces not only the actions of creatures, but also the mode of these actions, whether necessary, contingent, or free.

Thirdly, it is not to be thought to be merely a simultaneous concurrence of the Divine motion with the created action, but it applies the created cause to act, and so bears not merely on the action and its effect, but also on the initiation of the action, its passing from the power of acting to actual action. It is thus previous motion, its priority to the action of the creature being one, not of time, but of nature and causality.

[1] III *C.G.*, c. 149 (ed. Leonina).

Fourthly, the Thomists, in accordance with their fundamental principle that it is impossible that there should be any potentiality or passivity in God, who is Pure Act, maintain that this premotion cannot be an indeterminate motion, which is in itself indifferent, and which can be made definite and determinate by the will which determines itself, and so the Divine motion also, towards the production of a particular determinate action. Such a determination, since by hypothesis it comes not from God, but from the created will, would involve a passivity in Pure Act, inasmuch as God would not be the author but the observer of this determination, and so would be passive with regard to it. Thus the motion of God must be, according to the Thomists, predetermining.

Fifthly, it is a motion which is passively received in the created cause which it applies to act, and to act freely, if it be a free cause. It is thus something distinct both from the Divine action itself which is called active motion, and from the action of the creature which issues from it. To illustrate this the example of the action of heat on water is often used, for there is an active heat in the fire corresponding to the active motion of God ; a heat received in the water, and so passively received, which corresponds to physical premotion ; and the subsequent action of the hot water on bodies which are in contact with it, corresponding to the action of creatures following on the Divine premotion.

Sixthly, this premotion is called physical, not in opposition to metaphysical or spiritual motion, but as opposed to moral motion, a motion caused by some attraction of a desirable end, as when we say to a child : 'If you are good you shall have some sweets.' Such a motion as this causes the person to act in a certain way, i.e. as S. Thomas says, with regard to the specification of the action ; while a physical motion causes a person to act rather than remain quiescent, and so is concerned with the exercise of the action.[1]

The crucial point in the discussion between the Thomists and their opponents is whether the initial transition of the will from the capacity for willing, when it is in a state of

[1] Cf. *Summa Theologica*, I, 105, a. 4 ; I–IIæ, 10, 2.

potential indifference, to the act of willing, when it is in a state of actual indifference—though the act is already determined—proceeds from God or from the created will. The opponents of the Thomist view all maintain that the assertion that this transition proceeds determinately from God destroys human freedom, while the Thomists not only deny this, but say such a predetermining Divine motion causes human freedom, and that without it the absolute supremacy of God over all being would be impaired. Consequently, their arguments to prove the necessity of this Divine premotion are drawn from the universal causality of God and from the weakness of created causes, and especially of the free-will of man.

If we speak principally of free causes, rather than of necessary or contingent ones, it is because the difficulty of the question centres chiefly in the relation of the Divine motion to these; and if it is shown that free causes are physically premoved, in the sense explained, it will follow, *a fortiori*, that necessary and contingent ones are so moved also.

In the first place the Thomists argue, therefore, that since the transition of a free cause from potency to act is an entity and a perfection, and, in fact, the highest perfection to be found in the natural order, it must proceed from the universal cause of all being and perfection, that is to say, from God. Now this motion of the first cause must precede the motion of the second in nature and causality, inasmuch as the first cause is the mover, while the second cause is that which is moved. It is therefore premotion, and since it is directed towards the exercise of a determinate act it is physical and predetermining premotion.

Neither a purely simultaneous motion from God, nor yet an indeterminate motion which did not apply the will to act in a determinate way, would produce the result required, for in either case something, some entity and perfection, would be produced by the created will independently of the Divine motion. In the first case the *transition* from potency to act would be from the will alone, for to accept or not to accept the divine concurrence, and so to act or not to act would depend solely on the creature; while in the second case the *determination* of its act would be effected by the created will alone, independently of God; and this also, being determination, is an act and a perfection.

Secondly, the Thomists argue, from the weakness of created causes, that every cause which is not of itself in act with respect to action, but only in potency, so that it is capable or acting, needs to be physically premoved by God in order that it may actually act. Such potentiality, however, with tegard to action is found in all created causes, even free ones; so that all must be physically premoved if they are to act.

The major of this argument is plain, for actually to act is a perfection over and above the mere capacity for action, and therefore must be ascribed to God, otherwise what is more perfect would be produced by what is less perfect. It is also clear, as the minor asserts, that all created causes are of this kind, for otherwise they would always be actually in act, and so their action would be their being, and they would not be in potency at all, but be Pure Act.

It is urged against this opinion of the Thomists that it destroys liberty, inasmuch as under the Divine motion the will cannot act except in the way in which it is moved by God, so that it behaves like an inert tool in the hands of a workman. The answer to this objection is to be seen by a closer examination of the nature of liberty, while bearing in mind the infinite efficaciousness of the Divine motion which extends, not merely to the production of the free act as an act, but also to the production of it as free.

Now we saw earlier that the root of freedom is to be found in the universal capacity of the will for desiring good in general, or universal good; so that no particular good, which falls short of being desirable from every point of view, can necessitate the will. Thus, when faced by any particular good the will always remains free. Its state of freedom when simply confronted by such a good, and before it has definitely accepted or rejected it, is called passive or potential indifference; while when it has done so, and has determined itself to act in a certain way, its state is said to be one of active or actual indifference. Now it is plain that the second state, when the will is definitely striking out in a particular direction, is more perfect, from the point of view of actuality, than the former, where the will keeps standing on and off, like a ship in a light breeze. Nevertheless, the will in the second state is determined; but since it has determined itself it is not necessitated. So it remains free, even though it be fixed in its determination. The first point to be noticed, then, is that determination and liberty are not opposed, so that an act of the will may be determined and yet free; and even that every free act must be determined. What is essential is that it should be self-determined, that is determined by what is intrinsic to the will and the man himself, and not determined by some force outside himself, whether of object, circumstances, or inherent character. Thus for complete freedom of action it is necessary that the potential indifference of the will should be overcome, giving place to that actual indifference which is a determinate and dominating self-mastery. Now such self-mastery must come from the inner recesses of the will itself, and when we look into the heart of the will, we see there the power of the will itself and also the power of God, who gives it being, establishes its nature as free, and who, in it and with it, is able to make it pass from the capacity for willing to the act of willing, and to move it in a way which is in conformity with its own nature, i.e. freely. For having power over all being and all its modes, God is able to produce not only the act of the will, but also its mode, which is freedom. Thus the will under the motion of God determines itself to act in a definite way, and so, though determined, and predetermined (since the decrees of God are eternal), it yet remains free. In fact it cannot come by the exercise of freedom except in virtue of such determination by God, since it is unable to effect for itself the passage from the capacity of willing to the act of willing, from potential indifference to active.

It would be universally acknowledged that though a man had freely come to a determinate decision he still retains the power to act in another way or not to act, though, while his decision stands, he will infallibly act in the sense in which he has decided; so also under the influence of physical premotion the will still retains the power of resistance, or of acting or not acting, though it infallibly posits the act to which it is predetermined. In fact premotion will never be found along with abstention from the act towards which it is directed, though the will still retains its power of abstention, since it is not extrinsically necessitated. This is the meaning of the famous distinction: *in sensu composito* and *in sensu diviso*. The will which is premoved to action retains under premotion the power not to act, or to act in another way, but it cannot make this power effective, and so combine the execution of its power with the power itself. So under physical premotion the man is said to be able to act or not to act, and to act in another way *in sensu diviso*, but not *in sensu composito*. For example, under the influence of predetermination and premotion to sitting, the man has a real *power* of standing, although in fact the *act* of standing can never be combined with the premotion to sitting; just as the act of standing can never be simultaneous with the act of sitting, though the power of standing is simultaneous both with the power of sitting and with the act of sitting. So that *sensus compositus* is the power of simultaneity, when an act is simultaneous with the power from which it derives; while *sensus divisus* is the simultaneity of power, when two real powers are present at once, only one of which, however, can be made effective. Thus a man, when sitting, has the power of sitting and also that of standing, but the latter power cannot be combined with the act of standing. he therefore has the power of standing *in sensu diviso* only, whereas he has the power of sitting *in sensu composito*.

S. Thomas[1] illustrates this distinction by saying that the proposition: 'that which is white can be black' is true *in sensu diviso*, although that which is white cannot at the same time be black, i.e. the white cannot be black *in sensu composito*.

So with regard to the case in point he says:[2] 'If God moves the will to anything, it is not possible along with this

[1] *Summa Theologica*, I, 14, 13, ad 3.
[2] *Ibid.*, I–IIæ, 10, 4, ad 3.

position that the will should not be moved to it ; but it is not impossible simply speaking, whence it does not follow that the will is moved of necessity.' There is necessity of the consequence, but not necessity of the consequent.

Or again, he explains that an effect which is willed by God *can* not be, though its not being in fact is not possible along with the Divine willing, so that though it may fail to be *in sensu diviso,* i.e. if we regard only the *power* of acting or failing to act, yet it cannot fail to be *in sensu composito,* when we take into account not only the power but the act which follows from this power. This act must necessarily come about, but it does not come about necessarily, since it proceeds from a cause which *can* fail.

He adds : ' It is not impossible for these two to be found together : God wills this man to be saved and he *can* be damned ; but it is impossible that these two should be found together : God wills this man to be saved and he *is* damned.'[1]

In view of the fact that this distinction has been adopted by S. Thomas and all the leading Thomists, it seems strange that it should be called ' frivolous ' ; as if it were a trick to escape from a difficulty. On the contrary, it embodies profound truths. It will only be thought absurd if we regard the action of God moving the will intrinsically, as of precisely the same kind as that of a man who should bind another hand and foot, and then tell him he is quite free to go where he wishes. Actually the determination of the will by God no more limits liberty than does that of the will by itself, indeed the latter is only possible, and actually effected, as a result of the former. God moves the will from within, making it able to determine itself in a certain way, and the fact that, being so determined, it must necessarily act according to this determination, does not cause it to act necessarily, but rather causes it to act freely.

The other principal objection which is urged against the Thomists' doctrine of physical premotion is that it would make God the cause of evil, and even of sin. It will be more convenient to postpone the consideration of this until we can examine the problem of evil as a whole, and at present

[1] *De Veritate,* Q. 23, a. 5, ad 3.

to continue the consideration of God's will, in connection with created action, in a special case, viz.: that of miraculous events. It may, however, be permissible to remark, in anticipation of what will be said later, that evil comes about only by God's permission, no positive motion being required to produce an effect which is in itself a privation and a defect, and therefore well able to be produced by the secondary causes, which are liable to fail, being finite. If they do fail, evil is the result.

CHAPTER VIII

THE DIVINE OMNIPOTENCE AND MIRACLES

The Nature of Miracle: The Scholastic View—The Determinist Conception—The View of the Agnostics—Three Classes of Miracle. The Possibility of Miracle: The Foundation of the Proof of its Possibility—The Laws of Nature—How far Necessary—Miracle involves no Contradiction. The Actuality of Miracles: An Objection Stated—The Reply—How an Event can be Known to be Miraculous—Summary of Conclusions.

THAT our survey of the operation of God's will and power may be at least moderately complete it is necessary to give a brief sketch of the Thomist doctrine with regard to miracles.

The allegation of miraculous occurrences by the Christian Church has, for some time past, been a great difficulty for many who are affected, though perhaps vaguely, by the naturalistic philosophy which has its roots in the ideas of the Empiricists and Materialists.

The objections to miracles are, at least on the surface, directed against either their possibility, or against their actual occurrence; so that the treatment of this question falls naturally into three parts: first, the nature of miracle; that is, what is meant by this word; secondly, the possibility of miracles; and thirdly, their actuality.

I.—The Nature of Miracle.

The name itself indicates that a miracle is something which provokes wonder or admiration. Now wonder is excited when the cause of some phenomenon which we see is hidden from us, as a savage is filled with wonder at hearing a voice proceed from a gramophone; or when the effect itself is exceptional, and outside our ordinary experience, as in the case of many feats of conjuring. So S. Thomas defines miracles as those things which come to pass by Divine intervention, outside the order which is commonly held to in things.[1]

Their cause being God, it is '*simpliciter occulta,*' as he here notes, though when it is said that the cause is concealed, it is not implied that it is absolutely undiscoverable, but only that we cannot know what is its nature. This statement thus connects with what was said above as to our incapacity to know '*quid sit Deus.*'

The general Scholastic notion of miracle is that it is a fact which is beyond the powers of all created nature to produce, and even beyond those of any nature which could be created. It should be noticed that in saying that miracle is beyond the powers of created nature we confine its surpassing of nature to the sphere of action, and do not imply that it is an effect which surpasses these created natures as regards their being. The effect is a natural one, such as the restoration of natural life to a corpse. But inasmuch as it exceeds created power, it is distinguished from extraordinary natural events.

Other conceptions of miracle fall into two groups; the first of which has its roots in Determinism, i.e. the denial of freedom to God; while the second is based on Agnosticism. According to the Determinists a miracle is an extraordinary natural fact, which has not yet been scientifically explained; and according to the Agnostics, a miracle is an exception, not to the laws of nature, but only to our way of conceiving of these laws.

A. To the first school belongs Spinoza, who denied absolutely the possibility of miracle, since he held that God acts always from the necessity of His nature, so that His action is invariable. The Deists, consistently with their theory that God takes no account of particular things and events, held that God could not intervene in natural events. Malebranche and Leibniz, on account of their absolute optimism, which requires that God shall always do the best possible, hold that He is morally necessitated. If this were true, miracles would be morally necessary. The most widespread view of all is that which has been popularised by

[1] *Summa Theologica*, I, 105, 7

many Liberal Protestants,[1] who think that miracles are only unexplained phenomena.

B. In recent times, many philosophers and physicists have put forward the view that the laws of nature are statistical generalisations, and so are not in any way necessary; their apparent fixity being due to our way of conceiving them. This idea derives, on its philosophical side, from the phenomenalism of Kant, who thought, as we have seen, that we cannot gain knowledge by the use of the speculative reason of the natures of things, but only of their appearances. Now physical science may well use such an hypothesis as this for its own purposes, but it is illegitimate to transfer it into metaphysics, and assert that since science can deal with its data most conveniently on this assumption, the natures of things themselves are, therefore, not determinate, but purely contingent.

If they were so, we could not talk about the course of nature; and so, by implication, could not recognise miracle, i.e. a deviation from this course of nature, either. In this view, then, miracles are but apparent exceptions to an apparent rule.

Both these conceptions of miracle are, of course, quite alien to the mind of S. Thomas, who, when explaining the nature of miracle says: '*ex hoc aliquid dicitur miraculum, quod sit præter ordinem totius naturæ creatæ; hoc autem non potest facere nisi Deus.*'[2] It is outside the order of the whole of created nature, and its only author is God. In accordance with this conception miracle will be defined as a fact produced by God in the world, which is outside the order of action of the whole of created nature.

A miracle, in addition to being a 'wonder,' a *mirum*, is often also a 'sign,' a word frequently applied to miracles in the Gospels. If it is to be so, it must be a sensible phenomenon, for to authenticate the message of a prophet it must be observable by those who do not consent to that message without it. But, in itself, a miracle need not be something

[1] E.g. Professor Tennant, *Miracle and its Philosophical Presuppositions* (C.U.P.).

[2] *Summa Theologica*, I, 110, 4; cf. I, 105, 7; *De Potentia*, VI, 2; III *C.G.*, 101.

which is knowable by the senses, and S. Thomas neither defines it as sensible, nor holds that all miracles are sensible. (Cf. *S. T.*, III, 29, 1, ad 2; 4 *Sent.*, d. 11, Q. 1, a. 3, sol. 3; *De Potentia*, VI, 2, ad 2; et ad 3; etc.) It is not sufficient, in order that an event may be reckoned a miracle, that it should be beyond the powers of some particular nature to produce. When I raise up a weight with my hand, I do something which brute matter of itself cannot do, and, though in a sense I may be said to suspend the action of the law of gravity, what I do is not comparable with a miracle.

Since what is distinctive of miracle is that it exceeds the powers of the whole of created nature, there will be different classes of miracles which correspond to the different ways in which natural forces are surpassed. S. Thomas enumerates three such classes.[1] The first class consists of those which exceed natural power with regard to the nature of the thing done (*quoad substantiam facti*), e.g. if two bodies are made to be in one place. The second class are those which exceed the powers of nature with respect to the subject in which the miracle is done. So though it is not beyond the powers of nature to transmit life, and give it to new bodies, it is beyond its power to give it to inanimate bodies, or to restore a corpse to life. The raising of the dead, then, falls within this second class of miracles. Thirdly, there is a class of miracles which exceed the powers of nature with respect to the way in which the thing is done, such as *instantaneous* cure of a disease.

II.—The Possibility of Miracle.

It would evidently be absurd to argue with an atheist or a thoroughgoing Agnostic as to the possibility of miracle. As he does not acknowledge the existence of God, to discuss whether God can work miracles would be a waste of time. We may notice, in connection with this remark, that miracles

[1] *Summa Theologica*, I, 105, 8.
Another classification is given in *De Potentia*, VI, 2, ad 3, into miracles *supra*, *contra* and *præter naturam*. These two classifications do not coincide, and S. Thomas seems, in his later years, to have preferred the one given in the text. For this question cf. Van Hove, *La Doctrine du Miracle chez Saint Thomas* (Paris, Gabalda, 1927), pp. 59 ff.

cannot be used to prove the existence of God to a man who doubts or denies it. Miracles, indeed, cannot be shown to be possible unless we admit: (*a*) that God is the cause of all being; (*b*) that He knows particulars; and (*c*) that He acts freely *ad extra*; and unless miracles are acknowledged to be possible they cannot be adduced as evidential facts, so that the fundamental theses of Natural Theology and of Theism are presupposed by the discussion of miracle, and cannot be proved by it.

Though, in a sense, both Determinists and Agnostics reject the possibility of miracle, it is most directly attacked by the former, who deny the fundamental theses as to God's nature and action mentioned above. In addition they hold that the laws of nature are absolutely, and not only conditionally, necessary.

If the possibility of miracle is to be maintained against the Determinists it is, therefore, necessary to base our argument on the Divine Omnipotence as it is subject to the Divine Liberty, for an argument founded on the absolute power of God would be insufficient, inasmuch as miracles depend on the ordinated power of God,[1] and on His power of exceptional intervention in the course of nature. So Spinoza's rejection of miracle is based on his denial of God's liberty, not directly on a denial of His omnipotence. The Deists reject miracles on the ground that God has no intentions as to particular events; while Leibniz, holding that God is morally necessitated, destroys their evidential value as signs freely given by God to authenticate a revelation.

It would be necessary for an adequate treatment of this question to discuss the varieties of Determinism, and particularly to consider at length the arguments in favour of scientific determinism advanced by Mill. Such a course would, however, require a volume, not a chapter, and we must be content to set down the fundamental reason on which S. Thomas's defence of the possibility of miracle is based, from which the answers to the objections of Hume

[1] i.e. the power of God as subject to and regulated by the free decrees of His will.

and Mill can be derived. This defence rests on a consideration of the Divine Nature and action, on the one hand, and the character of natural law, on the other.

To take this latter first, if we ask what we are to understand by a law of nature, we might reply that it is 'a uniform mode of activity which natural agents of the same type observe when placed in similar circumstances.'[1] This is, in fact, the way in which we now generally regard a law of nature, as an empirically observed uniformity; and in itself such an idea does not imply necessity in these laws. S. Thomas, however, considers natural laws as necessary. The world is, for him, made up of a variety of beings, each and all of which have their specific and generic natures, and which, except in the case of free agents, act necessarily in accordance with these natures. Thus the laws of nature are not merely observed uniformities of action on the part of creatures, but govern them necessarily. If this be so, how is any exception to such action possible? The answer is that since the laws we are speaking of attach to the *action* of creatures, and not to their *being*, they affect them as efficient and final causes, not as formal and material ones. Now efficient and final causes are extrinsic ones, acting externally, and so can be prevented from taking effect without their nature or action being altered in itself; as the intrinsic ones (formal and material) could not be. A form always and invariably makes its matter of a certain kind if it acts at all, whereas an agent does not always produce the external effect which it is fitted to produce, since it may be prevented from doing so. Thus the laws of nature, though necessary, are not absolutely and unconditionally necessary, but only hypothetically; that is, creatures will necessarily act in a certain way if their action is not impeded. Since their action is not identified with their nature, it is not necessary in the same way as their nature is; so that their nature is not destroyed even if they are hindered in some way from acting in accordance with it. The laws of nature are not, therefore, absolutely necessary in the sense that it is absolutely necessary that the circumference of a circle should have a constant proportion to its

[1] Joyce, op. cit., p. 428.

radius; for this depends on, or is included in, the nature of this geometrical figure. If natural law were, as Spinoza supposed, of the same type as this sort of mathematical law, no exception to it would be possible; but, as a fact, it is not so, for it rests on the extrinsic, not the intrinsic causes of things. If some natural agent acts, and if the conditions under which is does so are of such and such a kind, a certain effect will necessarily be produced.

Granted, then, the hypothetically necessary character of the laws of nature, which few perhaps would deny, we can turn to consider the nature of God, and of the relation of natural law to Him.

First, then, we assert that God is omnipotent. This does not mean that He can do anything, however contradictory. If so, without more ado we could conclude: therefore He can work miracles, even if they are in themselves impossible. It does mean that His power is infinite, and so not limited by anything except the contradictory. God cannot make a triangle not having three sides, since to do so would be to make nothing. His power extends to all being, and is limited by nothing. That which is contradictory is essentially not-being. God, then, so far as His power goes, could work miracles, provided that to do so does not involve a contradiction either in created things or in Himself.

Now it does not involve a contradiction in Himself, since He is free, as we have seen earlier, and so can do anything which has the nature of being or good. Variations of natural law must come within the scope of this liberty, for God, in establishing the natures of creatures, and their action or natural law, did so freely: inasmuch as there is an infinite distance between the Divine Goodness and any created good, so that God could have created an infinity of worlds which differ from the present one both in their nature and their laws. He therefore acted freely in the creation of this one. Moreover, God is free with respect to the application and working of these laws, in the universe as at present constituted, for this application and exercise depends immediately on the action of the natural agent, whose action in turn depends on the first agent, or God. Thus the application of all hypothetically necessary laws depends on the free-will of God which is not tied down by such laws, nor bound to apply them; so that to prevent or modify the action of these laws does not involve any contradiction in the nature of God. From the point of view of God's action there is, therefore, nothing which would make it impossible for Him to work miracles.

Nor is there any impossibility or contradiction involved on the side of created things themselves; for, as we have seen, the natural laws are only hypothetically, and not absolutely, necessary; so that if the conditions necessary for their action in any given case are not fulfilled, the action will not necessarily follow. As, then, it depends on God's free-will to apply or not to apply these laws as He pleases, He can, without any contradiction, act outside them, or work miracles; if not, He would not be free with regard to them, nor have control of them.

Doubtless, such intervention on the part of God acting beyond and outside the domain of natural law will not be arbitrary, but have a sufficient motive, the motive of some greater good; and in asking whether any particular event is miraculous we shall rightly look to see whether any such motive is discernible. This consideration belongs rather to the question of the actuality of miracle than to that of its possibility. We may, however, notice in passing that this motive cannot be, as has often been supposed, an attempt by God to remedy the defects of the nature which He has created, or as Newton said to 'reform its irregularities.' Such an idea is clearly derogatory to the wisdom of God.

It will be observed that an integral part of the defence of the possibility of miracle is the assertion that natural law is necessary, though only conditionally necessary. If not, that is to say if nature follows no law or rule at all, there could be no exception to such law, and so no miracle; but that natural laws are necessary in this way is clearly seen if we consider that the natures of things being fixed and determined, their mode of action must normally be fixed and determined also.

If this be so, the Agnostic objection, that miracles are

impossible because the laws of nature are purely contingent, breaks down. But the objection is often put in the form that since these laws are contingent we cannot discriminate between a miracle and an extraordinary natural event.

This brings us to the third section of our enquiry, that which deals with the discernibility of miracles.

III.—The Actuality or Discernibility of Miracles.

With the diminution among scientists of the popularity of scientific determinism, objection to miracles has, to a great extent, ceased to be directed against their possibility, and is now generally aimed against their actuality. Instead of saying, 'miracles can't happen,' the modern Agnostic says, 'miracles don't happen.' This assertion of a universal negative is made by Agnostics with the greatest assurance, on the ground that miracles can never be distinguished from extraordinary natural facts, so that we can never be sure that any event which purports to be miraculous really is so.

This time-worn objection is stated clearly and concisely by Dr. Tennant in his lectures on miracles, and he considers it to be unanswerable. He says: 'We have seen that a miracle, in order to possess the evidential value which theology used to ascribe to it, must be caused by the immediate activity of God. Such activity is compatible with science and its reign of law, and is not antecedently unreasonable from the presuppositions of theism; but that a given event, however marvellous, unquestionably is so caused, can never be asserted so long as our scientific knowledge of nature is inexhaustive.'[1]

Thus, since we certainly do not know, and presumably never can know, *all* the powers and laws of nature, it is impossible to know with absolute certainty that any fact exceeds these powers.

This objection rests on a principle which is plainly fallacious: that to know what an agent cannot do, we must first know what he can do. In the case of alleged miraculous events we are not concerned to discover what nature can do,

[1] F. R. Tennant, *Miracle and its Philosophical Presuppositions* (C.U.P., 1925), Lect. III.

and so show that these events do not come within their powers ; we shall be equally certain that they do not result from natural forces if we show that they are of such a character as to demand a cause of infinite power, so that they cannot be produced by a finite cause, whatever its capabilities may be.

No doubt the motives which assure us of the impossibility of natural forces producing the effects which are asserted to be miraculous will vary with different cases, for in some it may involve a contradiction that a particular effect should result from a finite cause ; while in others the impossibility of their being so produced will be of a less absolute kind, namely, a physical or moral impossibility. The objection, however, that miracles can *never* be distinguished from natural facts is disposed of if we can show that even one alleged miracle can be so distinguished. The statement ' miracles don't happen ' can admit of no single exception if it is to be maintained at all.

Now the whole of our discussion of Natural Theology up to this point has shown that there are certain effects which are *proper* to God, that is, which demand an infinite cause. The five arguments for God's existence, as well as those for creation, conservation, and Divine motion are all variations on this theme.

Thus it is metaphysically certain that God alone can produce being as being, and as a consequence cause a change in it without using any intermediary. Similarly God alone can produce, and so immediately change, first matter, material substances without the mediation of accidents, the human soul, intellect, and will. To say that He alone can produce being as such is equivalently to say He alone can create, and we have already seen the truth of this. Creative power is also required for the production of first matter, and of the human soul, intellect and will, since these last, being spiritual, can be produced only by creation, and not by generation ; while first matter has no subject. Now the same universality is required in the cause which produces immediate change in these realities as in that which immediately produces them as beings ; for it must affect them in themselves and from within, and so must have entire dominion over them.

There are, in fact, some alleged miraculous events in which such immediate change is stated to occur; and if it does occur, we can be certain that it is not due to the forces of nature but to God alone, even though we do not know all that nature can achieve. Examples of such events are the presence of two bodies in the same place, since to be so they must remain distinct only with respect to their being, inasmuch as the natural cause of their distinction, viz. distinction in place, is removed. Again, the reunion of a soul with a dead body, without the accidental dispositions required for generation, requires immediate control both of matter and the spiritual soul, and this reunion is asserted to occur in the resurrection of the dead. Other examples are the instantaneous change of one substance into another without the mediation of any preliminary accidental alterations, as in the case of the instantaneous conversion of water into wine.

If such events as these are shown to occur, then we can be sure that they are not caused by any natural forces but only by God; and, in the abstract, we may even have metaphysical or absolute certitude as to the Divine origin of such an event. In the concrete, however, we cannot be certain in this way that a particular event is a miracle in the strict sense, since we cannot have more than physical, and usually can only have moral certitude that the event was such as it is alleged to have been. Such a certitude is to be arrived at by a diligent examination of all the circumstances, physical, moral, and religious, which surround the alleged miraculous event.

To enter into an examination of these criteria for distinguishing a true miracle would take us far beyond what can be attempted in a short summary; it is sufficient to have indicated that miracles are possible, and that we can assure ourselves that some events can be attributed to no other cause than immediate Divine intervention.

We may summarise the results arrived at in this chapter as follows:

A miracle is a fact produced by God in the world which is outside the action of the whole of created nature.

Such action on the part of God is not impossible, since He is wholly free, both as regards specification and exercise, in His dealing with creatures; while natural law is not absolutely, but only hypothetically, determined. Further, we can distinguish a true miracle, whose only cause can be God, from an extraordinary natural event; since the laws of nature are not purely contingent; and even though we do not know all the powers of nature positively, we do know negatively what they cannot do; namely, produce an effect which demands a cause of infinite power.

Note.—A complete discussion of the question of miracle with all necessary developments as to its accord with scientific knowledge and the means by which we may assure ourselves of the miraculous character of certain events, is to be found in the work quoted above: *La Doctrine du Miracle chez Saint Thomas,* by A. Van Hove, Paris, 1927.

CHAPTER IX

PROVIDENCE AND THE PROBLEM OF EVIL

Section I

The General Problem—The Opinion of Deists—Optimism—The Nature of Evil—Essentially a Privation—The Origin of Physical Evil—Evil in Human Life—Moral Evil—Not attributable to Freedom—The Physical Act of Sin and God's Causality—The Thomist Explanation—Conclusion.

The General Problem.

Since we have considered at some length the knowledge and foreknowledge of God we need add but little as to His Providence. Just as we foresee the future, to a certain extent, and make plans for it, so we conceive of God as planning the order of the world, though of course His planning is to be thought of without any of the temporal conditions which attach to our own. That God must plan and foresee in this way is evident from the fact that He is the universal cause of all being, and since every agent acts for an end, He too must act for an end in the causation, that is, the production, conservation and motion of every being, intentionally ordering all things in the universe to that end which is Himself, the manifestation of His goodness and perfection.

The idea of the Deists, then, that God's plan affects only the general laws of the universe, and not its details, cannot be sustained, if, as is the case, these details are realities.

If this be so, it might seem that we were committed to a theory of unmitigated Optimism: to affirming that the world as it exists is the best of all possible worlds. For how could a God who is Infinite both in Power and Goodness make anything defective? On the surface, at least, this theory seems to get rid of the most serious objection to

Theism at one stroke ; the objection namely that God cannot be an Omnipotent and Good Creator if the world which He has produced contains evil. If it is the best possible, its defects will not be attributable to God, but to its own inherent defectiveness. But in fact it cannot be maintained that a world with less evil and defect is inconceivable, so that it is not intrinsically the best possible. Nor can we say that it is the best that God could do, for this would be to deny Him omnipotence.

The foremost defenders of Optimism are Malebranche[1] and Leibniz,[2] who maintain that since God must act in accordance with what He is, and He is perfectly good, He could not make the world better than it is. S. Thomas replies to this, that it is true that He could not make a world in a better way than He has done, for His way of acting must be perfectly adapted to what He has in view ; but He might have made an infinity of worlds which are better in themselves than this one, since there is an infinite distance between His own goodness and the goodness of any created being, however perfect. If the word perfect is used as an adverb, God could not have done better ; if it is used as an adjective, He could have made a better world.

Not only does Optimism contain a logical fallacy, but it is, in itself, almost a revolting doctrine, for it attempts to treat both suffering and sin as matters of small account ; whereas pain, sorrow, and, above all, moral evil are terrible realities.

To say this is not to say that there is not a certain truth in Optimism, in so far as it recognises that it is essential to maintain that the world which God has created is that in which His purpose in creating and the end which He had in view are most perfectly realised. Since we can have but a most defective understanding of that end, it follows that we can see but glimpses of the wisdom of His plan.

If, then, we are not to ascribe the evil which is present in the world solely to the inherent limitation of this, the best of all possible worlds, to what can it be due ?

[1] Malebranche, *Dialogues on Metaphysics and on Religion,* Dialogue IX, Sections ix *et seq.*, trans. by Morris Ginsberg (Library of Philosophy, Allen and Unwin, 1923).

[2] *Theodicy,* 119, etc.

The Nature of Evil.

Before attempting to answer this question, it is necessary to clarify our ideas as to the meaning of this word 'evil.'

Evidently it implies some lack of perfection, for what is absolutely perfect cannot be evil. Moreover, it is a lack of a due perfection, if it is to be called evil in any strict sense. So it is not an evil for a peasant not to know Greek, though it would be an evil for the student of the Bible.[1] Thus evil is the lack of a perfection in a subject to which this perfection is due. Being the lack of a perfection it is not anything positive, but something negative, a privation ; and it therefore implies a positive subject in which this privation is found. This positive subject has a definite being, and in so far as it has it, is good. Evil, therefore, presupposes good.

This is not, be it noted, a denial of evil, nor an attempt to evade the fact that it, and its consequences, are among the most obvious and pressing realities of life ; but to take it for what it is, a privation. It is not something in itself and for itself. Certainly the philosophy which insists so strongly on the reality of potency, of matter, of limitation, is not likely to deny all reality to that privation which we call evil, though at the same time it preserves the balance by declaring that its reality is not positive, but negative ; a defect, a disharmony in the good.

The Origin of Physical Evil.

If this be true, we have not to look for a proper cause of evil, that is, one which of itself and by reason of its nature shall produce it. Thus, though there must be some reason why evil comes about, we are not obliged, as we are in the case of being or good, to trace its descent to the first principle of all things, and assert either that there is a Supreme Principle of Evil side by side with the Supreme Good, or

[1] 'If a man has not wings, it is not an evil for him, because it is not natural for him to have them ; if also a man has not golden hair, it is not an evil, for although it would be natural for him to have it, yet it is not due to his nature : but it is an evil if he has no hands, which are both natural and due to him if he is to be perfect ; but this same is no evil to a bird.' (III *C.G.*, c. 6.)

else that God has deliberately caused evil as such in the world. Rather evil arises indirectly, accidentally, apart from the essential intention, in the course of an action in itself good ; as if, when walking, I fall. So even the most determined opponent of Theism would allow that we need not, and indeed cannot, attribute the evil in the will to the deliberate willing of it as such by God. Apart from any other consideration the fact that evil, not being in itself good, cannot be in itself desirable, shows that God cannot will it in and for itself.

Nevertheless, the fact remains, that even if we put the best possible face on it, God does will those things on which evil is attendant, at least in the physical order. So He wills those laws of nature which sometimes result in earthquakes or volcanic eruptions, which cause thousands of deaths and immense sufferings, the existence and multiplication of disease germs, which kill and torture millions ; and the unceasing war of one species with another in the animal world, the world of nature, 'red in tooth and claw.' Even if He does not will the suffering as such, God wills that which inevitably brings it about. Unless what is good for the individual is also good for the species, and what is good for the species is also good for all other species, this state of conflict is bound to arise ; if there are individuals or species at all. The remedy for evil would therefore seem to be not to create, and so the only way of abolishing it would be to abolish the good to which it attaches. This has not been done, and are we then to conclude that God is either feeble or malicious ? Recently, the tendency has been to pick the first of these alternatives, and say that since the world contains so much physical suffering—for it is this which seems most revolting to our contemporaries—God evidently was limited in His capacity for making a good world, and made a very defective one. He is, then, finite ; which is a rather obscure way of saying that there is no First Cause of all things, who is independent in being and action ; that is, there is no God. Reason will not allow us to accept this conclusion, and when we look at the premise on which it is based we see that the evil which is found in the world is due to the fact that this world is one of limited beings, so that if it exists at all, it will contain privations and defects. Not to have made a perfect world argues not limitation in the omnipotence of God, but an essential limitation in the perfection of the creature. God did not make a perfect world because a perfect world cannot be made, since a perfect being is not a creature. A creation in which there is no limitation and imperfection is a contradiction.

But would it not have been better not to have made a world at all, rather than to make one which contains evil? If so, it would seem that God's action is not truly good, and the evil of the world would be imputable to him. This objection would be unanswerable if the last word that can be said about the universe is that it contains evil, but indeed the very defects and privations of the parts contribute to the good of the whole. So, to take a striking example, without death the earth would have become a seething mass of living things; so that though with respect to the individual it is an evil, with respect to the whole body of living creatures it is beneficial. In this way the evils of the parts are transcended in the good of the whole, the evils of individuals in the good of the species.

Evil in Human Life.

So far we have spoken almost exclusively of physical evil, and of this as affecting creatures other than man; though what has been said will apply also to the physical evils to which men are subject, in so far as we consider them as units in the world order. Nevertheless, it is plain that man occupies a peculiar position, both because, in his case, physical evil is much more acutely felt and occasions much more distress than does such evil among the lower animals, and because here, for the first time, we encounter that evil which is directly opposed to the nature of God, namely, moral evil.

Man suffers much more than do the other animals both because of the extreme delicacy of his nervous system, and because, being able to think and understand, the physical evil is always naturally joined with mental suffering. When a calf is taken away from its mother, she will spend perhaps a day or a little more lowing for it, and to all appearances suffering; but after such a short time as this she will forget it and again be quite content. The sorrow of a human mother is not so easily assuaged and may last a lifetime. Thus in the case of man the problem of *pain* is aggravated; but it does not follow that the problem of evil is also made more difficult, since pain is not in itself evil, but is its effect. Pleasure, Aristotle tells us, is the flower of good; if so, pain and suffering are flowers of evil. If man's sufferings are more intense and prolonged than those of the beasts, so are his joys; and his very sufferings lead sometimes to his greater physical good, and more often still can be used by him to promote his moral and religious good. Anyone who has watched a painful illness patiently borne knows well that out of the most acute suffering heroic goodness may come; a goodness and a peace which for the sufferer outweighs the pain, however much those who witness the suffering may rebel. So out of evil comes good.

Moral Evil.

But what shall we say of moral evil? This is directly opposed to the nature of God, and therefore cannot be willed by Him in any way; not even, as in the case of physical evil, that a greater good may be produced by its means. Nevertheless, we must allow that it is permitted by Him, since nothing comes about save either by the will or permission of God. Yet though He cannot will it in order that good may come of it, we can be sure that God would not have permitted moral evil, if it were not that He foresaw that even this could be turned to a good end, and brought within His divine purposes of mercy and of justice.

Can we say, as has often been suggested, that God could not have created beings with free-will without at the same time opening the door to moral evil, inasmuch as a free nature must necessarily be capable of sinning? This suggestion, plausible as it is, is eminently unsatisfactory. We have seen already[1] that capacity to sin is no necessary

[1] Vol. I, pp. 291 ff.

part of freedom; for the will and free-will are essentially directed towards good, and the will is not more, but less, free in so far as it is diverted from it. So, as S. Augustine tells us, it is a greater liberty not to be able to sin than to be able not to sin, the former being the liberty of God and the saints in glory, the latter that of the first man.[1]

It is true that if there is no liberty there is no possibility of sin, just as there is no possibility of virtue; but it is not true that if there is liberty the possibility of sin necessarily follows, and indeed this possibility has nothing whatever to do with the possession of full liberty, but is possible because of the imperfection of our freedom. The answer, then, to the question why did God permit moral evil cannot be: because He would have to have refrained from giving man free-will if it was to be impossible. Indeed, if God had endowed man with full and perfect freedom it would have been impossible. Why did He not do so? To a great extent we may have to confess our inability to answer this question, as one beyond the scope of the powers of our finite minds. Being certain that God is good, we ought to be sure that even His permission of evil is good, however dark and unintelligible to us the fashion of its goodness may be. It is to argue from the unknown to say that since we cannot see why evil should be permitted if there is a good God, therefore there is no God; as so many do. Rather we should say that evil itself shows there is a God, for it can only arise as a disorder, and this in turn as a deviation from order, which order can find no explanation if there is no fount and source of goodness, order being itself a good. In doing so we should base ourselves on what we know and what is sure, not on what we do not know.

Though, then, it is right to face this obscure question with a due sense of our own ignorance and limitations, yet there are here certain gleams of light which make the darkness less opaque.

And, first, we ought to consider that a genuine struggle to overcome evil is of the highest value in promoting moral growth, and the actual defections of those who offend

[1] Cf. *De Civitate Dei*, XXII, 30.

against the moral law intensify this struggle, and so, by increasing its difficulty, increase also the virtue of those who resist these evil influences.

Again, though it is true that freedom as such does not carry with it as a necessary consequence the capacity to sin, yet the freedom which would make man incapable of sinning is the fullness and perfection of freedom. Now it is not clear that it would not have been contradictory for God to have created a being which possessed such freedom as this of its nature, and of itself. For such an incapacity for sinning seems to come from a complete and perfect knowledge of the good, so that the bad loses all attractiveness. This, to be possessed by any being of its own nature, would demand in it infinity, so that it could not be a created or finite being. It would be a finite infinite, a contradiction, something to which God's omnipotence does not extend.

This, if it be true, will only explain why God did not create beings which of their nature are incapable of sinning, and not why He created those who are capable of it, and which He saw would sin. As to this we have to confess our ignorance, only saying that the defections from good are outweighed by the adhesions and that 'there is more goodness and happiness in the universe by far than there is unhappiness and evil.'[1]

As to the contribution of Christianity to the solution of this mysterious problem this is not the place to speak; but it may be pointed out that the way in which it diminishes its urgency, and takes the sting out of it, is not by any theoretical explanations, but by a practical transcendence of it for those who are willing to learn at the foot of the Cross.

Section II

The Physical Act of Sin and God's Causality.

We have left to the last a special difficulty which concerns the reconciliation of the goodness and omnipotence of God with the fact of evil actions—of sin. Since all the actions

[1] Von Hugel, *The Reality of God*, p. 125.

of creatures require the Divine concurrence, the acts of the will which are in fact sinful will require it also. This is true whatever view we take as to the nature of this concurrence of God with free acts; whether, that is, we regard God's motion as being alongside of and simultaneous with the human action, or whether we acknowledge that the very passage from potency to act, from the capacity for willing to the act of willing, must come from God. In either view the motion of God bears on the action itself and on its term or effect, and in the latter it is also responsible with the will for its self-determination, for its passing into action.

Hence, anyone who allows that God acts in every active agent, be he Molinist or Thomist, must allow also that God operates in the physical act which is in fact sinful, or morally evil. It is urged that the difficulty of reconciling such co-operation of God with the sinful act is especially acute in the Thomist theory, for here the self-determination of the human will is attributable to God; and moreover, the man will only sin if God has not predetermined him to good. The latter part of this statement touches closely on the theological question of grace; but before discussing even the purely philosophical aspect of the difficulty it is important to remark that no sin could come about unless God gives, not only His permission, but also a Divine motion, whether simultaneous or previous, for the physical act of sin. Whatever view, then, we take of God's co-operation with creatures we have to meet this difficulty: how can God co-operate in causing a sinful act, and yet not be responsible for the sin?

The answer to it emerges at once from the principles already laid down as to the nature of God's action. The act of sin is being and is action, and so on both counts proceeds from God. But when we have said this about the act of sin we have said nothing about that which distinguishes it as sinful. What is this? It is evidently some defect in it, some turning aside from good, and so from being, some privation. This, then, which constitutes it as sinful, does not require an efficient, but only a deficient cause, for what is produced by the act as a sinful one is not any being, but a privation and defect in being. Consequently all the sinfulness of the act is attributable to the will which fails and falls away, while all that is positive and of the nature of being, and so good, in the act is attributable to the author of all being, to God.

The explanation which the Thomists give of the reason why the sinfulness of the act of sin is not attributable to God, even though, according to their theory, He predetermines and premoves the will to the physical act which is morally defective or sinful, is based on the same principles as this general one. For they say that the deficiency of this act, morally considered, is to be attributed wholly to the created will which fails of itself in not grasping the good, inasmuch as the man fails in not considering his duty. This failure requires, not a positive and effective motion on the part of God, but only a permissive decree by which such lack of consideration is allowed. Whereas for a good act a positive and effective decree and motion of God is required both for the physical act and for its moral goodness, since here both have the nature of being; for an evil act, a positive decree is required only for the act as physical, while the decree for the act as deficient or sinful is permissive only. God allows the man to fail in his consideration of his duty but in no way moves him to this failure, no such motion being required for what is, in itself, not being or act, but a defect of being. So the predetermination and premotion of God to a good act differs from His motion with regard to an evil act, being in the first case positive and effective with regard both to the physical act and its moral entity, or goodness; while in the second it is positive with regard to the physical act alone and merely permissive with regard to its moral defectiveness, or sinfulness. Thus, as regards the sinful act, God premoves to the act as it proceeds effectively from the will, but not as it proceeds from it defectively, the deficiency arising solely from the cause which is defectible and deficient, namely the man who does not sufficiently consider his moral obligation.

So, without detracting in any way from the universal causality of God, or from His power in working in and with the human will in its self-determination to good, the

Thomists consider that, according to their theory, there is no possibility of attributing the sinfulness to God, or in any way making Him the cause of sin.

What is primary in the Thomist theory of premotion, namely that all the good of human acts is to be attributed to God's motion which works in the very heart of the human will, is well expressed by Von Hugel. He says: 'The scheme of God *plus* man, grace *plus* nature, predestination *plus* free-will—all this putting alongside of each other, as though they were two separate material bodies, what really are two living energies, completely interpenetrating each other' is 'utterly misleading . . . the grace is in the free-will, and the free-will in the grace. Here, again, I think, the clarifying business (of which we are so immensely proud) misleads and impoverishes us; and that so little is it true that, in the spiritual world, two realities cannot (as with two bodies) be in the same place, that, on the contrary, one spirit or spiritual force or idea has not really penetrated the other, unless it *is* in the same point and centre of energising as the other, each as it were passing right through the other, and not adding to the quantity, but profoundly *modifying* the *quality* of the other. Grace so little interferes with, or even simply adds itself on to, or runs parallel with the autonomy of the spiritual personality, that it actually constitutes that personality.'[1]

With this wide view of the interrelations of nature and grace, of God and man, we may conclude our sketch of the philosophy of S. Thomas. Step by step we have climbed the ladder which leads from matter to God, and now, looking back, we can see that each stage of this ascent receives a new meaning from, and is to be interpreted in terms of, this, the last stage. So far reason can guide us, and it remains for faith, prayer, and, at last, vision to unite us with the God of whose existence and attributes we have learned something in the mirror of creatures. All the effort of the reason is valuable only in so far as it leads man along this road The philosophy of S. Thomas shows us where the pathway is;

[1] F. von Hugel, *Selected Letters*, p. 91 (Dent, 1927).

but it is no easy one to follow, for at every step roads which look much more imposing branch off from it.

To understand the philosophy of S. Thomas we must be animated by his spirit: a spirit which is essentially Christian, recognising in reason a true but fallible guide, and one which must therefore always be ready for help and direction from an infallible one. Confidence and humility are thus to go hand in hand in our search for wisdom, the putting of order into things, and directing all to their end, which is God.

BIBLIOGRAPHY

THIS bibliography is not intended to be exhaustive, but to give some indication of books which can be used for purposes of further study.

GENERAL WORKS

A. *Ancient.*

ARISTOTLE, *Opera Omnia.* Bekker. Berlin, 1831–1870.

The Works of Aristotle translated into English. Ed. J. A. Smith and W. D. Ross. Oxford, Clarendon Press. 11 Vols.

Metaphysics. Ed. W. D. Ross. Oxford, Clarendon Press, 1924. 2 vols.

BURNET, J., *Greek Philosophy (Thales to Plato).* Macmillan.

CAPREOLUS, *Defensiones Theologiæ.* Ed. Paban-Pègues. Tours, Cattier, 1900. 7 vols.

GILSON, E., *L'Esprit de la Philosophie Médiévale.* Paris, Vrin, 1932. 2 vols.

The Philosophy of S. Thomas Aquinas. Tr. E. Bullough. Heffer, 1924.

La Philosophie au Moyen Age. Paris, Payot, 1925.

JOHN OF S. THOMAS, *Cursus Philosophicus.* Vives, 1883. 3 vols.

ROSS, W. D., *Aristotle.* Methuen, 1923.

ROUGIER, L., *La Scholastique et le Thomisme.* Paris, Gauthier-Villars.

Collegii Salmanticensis—Cursus Theologicus. Paris, 1870. 20 vols.

SERTILLANGES, A. D., *S. Thomas d'Aquin.* 2 vols. Paris, Alcan, 1922.

Foundations of Thomistic Philosophy. Sands.

STACE, W., *A Critical History of Greek Philosophy.* Macmillan.

TAYLOR, A. E., *Plato : The Man and His Work.* Methuen, 1926.

Aristotle. (The People's Books.) Nelson, 1919.

Platonism and its Influence. Harrap.

THOMAS AQUINAS, S., *Opera Omnia.* (Parma.) Republished in Paris by Vives, 1871–1880.

do. Rome. The Leonine Edition. 15 vols. are at present published, which include the two Summæ, and some of the Commentaries on Aristotle.

Commentaria in Metaphysicam. Ed. M–R. Cathala. Turin, Marietti, 1915.

WULF, M. DE, *Histoire de la Philosophie Médiévale.* Louvain (1924, 5e ed.). 2 vols.

Xenia Thomistica. Rome, Vatican Press, 1925.

ZELLER, E., *Outlines of the History of Greek Philosophy.* Longmans, 1922.

B. *Modern.*

BOX, H. S., *The World and God.* S.P.C.K., 1934.

D'ARCY, M. C., *Thomas Aquinas.* (Leaders of Philosophy Series.) Benn, 1930.

DESCARTES, *Discourse on Method*, etc. (Everyman's Library.)

FARGES, A., *Études Philosophiques.* 9 vols. Paris, Berche et Tralin. 7e ed.

GREDT, J., *Elementa Philosophiæ Aristotelico-Thomisticæ.* Herder. 2 vols.

HUGON, E., *Cursus Philosophiæ Thomisticæ.* 6 vols. Paris, Lethielleux.

LEIBNIZ, *The Monadology, etc.* Ed. R. Latta. Clarendon Press, 1925.

Discourse on Metaphysics, etc. Ed. Montgomery. Chicago, Open Court Publishing Co., 1902.

Philosophical Writings. (Everyman's Library.) 1934.

MANDONNET, P., ET DESTREZ, J., *Bibliographie Thomiste.* Le Saulchoir, 1921.

MANDONNET, P., *Des Écrits Authentiques de S. Thomas d'Aquin.* Fribourg, 1910.

Siger de Brabant. Louvain, 1911.

Manual of Modern Scholastic Philosophy. (Mercier and others.) Kegan Paul, 1932. 2 vols.

Mélanges Thomistes—Bibliothèque Thomiste. Le Saulchoir. Kain, 1927.

MERCIER, D., *Métaphysique Générale.* Paris, Alcan, 1919.

Psychologie. Alcan, 1920. 2 vols.

Critériologie Générale. Paris, Alcan, 1918.

MONACO, N. (S.J.), *Prelectiones Metaphysicæ Generalis.* Rome, 1913.
Theologia Naturalis. Rome, 1918.
Psychologia. Rome, 1917.

PÈGUES, T., *Commentaire Français Littérale de la Somme Théologique.* Toulouse, Privat. 20 vols.

Philosophies Ancient and Modern. Various Authors. A series of small volumes issued by Constable.

REMER, V. (S.J.), *Summa Philosophiæ Scholasticæ.* Editio 5[a]. Rome. Gregorian University.

Stonyhurst Philosophical Series. Longmans.

TAYLOR, A. E., *The Faith of a Moralist.* Macmillan. 1930. 2 vols.
Philosophical Studies. Macmillan, 1934.

WHITEHEAD, A. N., *The Concept of Nature.* C.U.P., 1926.
Religion in the Making. C.U.P., 1927.
Science and the Modern World. C.U.P., 1927.
Process and Reality. C.U.P., 1929.
Adventures of Ideas. C.U.P., 1933.
Nature and Life. C.U.P., 1934.

Works on Special Subjects.

BALFOUR, A. J., *Theism and Humanism.* Hodder & Stoughton, 1915.
Theism and Thought. Hodder & Stoughton, 1923.
A Defence of Philosophic Doubt. Hodder & Stoughton.
Familiar Beliefs and Transcendent Reason. Milford, 1926.

BARRON, J. T., *Elements of Epistemology.* Burns Oates & Washbourne, 1931.

BRAGG, SIR W. H., *The Universe of Light.* Bell, 1933.

BROAD, C. D., *The Mind and its Place in Nature.* Kegan Paul, 1925.
Scientific Thought. Kegan Paul, 1927.

BURTT, E. A., *The Metaphysical Foundations of Modern Physical Science.* Kegan Paul, 1925.

CARR, H. WILDON, *Leibniz.* Benn, 1929.

COFFEY, P., *Epistemology.* 2 vols. Longmans, 1917.
Ontology. Longmans, 1914.

DAMPIER-WHETHAM, W. C. D., *A History of Science.* C.U.P., 1929.

D'ARCY, M. C. (S.J.), *The Nature of Belief.* Sheed and Ward, 1931.

DARIO, J.·M. (S.J.), *Prælectiones Cosmologiæ.* Paris, Beauchesne, 1922.

DE BACKER, S. (S.J.), *Disputationes Metaphysicæ.* Paris, Beauchesne.

DEL PRADO, N. (O.P.), *De Veritate Fundamentali Philosophiæ Christianæ.* Fribourg, 1911.

DESCOQS, P. (S.J.), *Essai Critique sur l'Hylémorphisme.* Paris, Beauchesne, 1924.

Institutiones Metaphysicæ Generalis. Vol. I. Paris, Beauchesne, 1925.

DRIESCH, H., *The Science and Philosophy of the Organism.* A. & C. Black. 2 vols. 1908.

Mind and Body. Methuen, 1927.

EDDINGTON, SIR A. S., *The Nature of the Physical World.* C.U.P., 1928.

New Pathways in Science. C.U.P., 1935.

EINSTEIN, A., *Relativity.* Methuen, 1920.

Evolution in the Light of Modern Knowledge. A Collective Work. Blackie, 1925.

GARRIGOU-LAGRANGE, R. (O.P.), *De Revelatione.* 2 vols. Rome, Ferrari, 1918.

Dieu : Son Existence et Sa Nature. Paris, Beauchesne, 1928. 5e edition. English Translation of the same, by Dom. B. Rose, O.S.B., Herder, 1935.

Le Réalisme du Principe de Finalité. Desclée, Paris, 1932.

Le Sens Commun, la Philosophie de l'Être, et les Formules Dogmatiques. Paris, Beauchesne.

GEDDES AND THOMSON, *Biology.* (Home University Library.) 1925.

GEMELLI, A., (O.F.M.), *Religione e Scienza.* Milan, 'Vita e Pensiero,' 1920.

GENY, P. (S.J.), *Critica.* Rome, Gregorian University, 1927.

GUIBERT, J., *In the Beginning.* (Les Origines.) Tr. G. S. Whitmarsh. Kegan Paul, 1900.

HAAS, A., *The New Physics.* Methuen, 1923.

HALDANE, J. S., *The Sciences and Philosophy.* Hodder & Stoughton, 1929.

HAYNES, E. S. P., *The Belief in Personal Immortality.* Grant Richards, 1925.

HOBSON, E. W., *The Domain of Natural Science.* C.U.P., 1923.
The Ideal Aim of Physical Science. C.U.P., 1925.

HOENEN, P. (S.J.), *Cosmologia.* Rome, Gregorian University, 1931.

HONTHEIM, J. (S.J.), *Theodicea.* Herder, 1926.

INGE, W. R., *The Philosophy of Plotinus.* 2 vols. Longmans, 1923.
God and the Astronomers. Longmans, 1933.

JEANNIÈRE, R. (S.J.), *Criteriologia.* Paris, Beauchesne, 1912.

JEANS, SIR J., *The Universe Around Us.* C.U.P.
The New Background of Science. C.U.P., 1933.
The Mysterious Universe. C.U.P.

JOHNSTONE, J., *The Philosophy of Biology.* C.U.P., 1914.

JOLIVET, R., *La Notion de Substance.* Paris, Beauchesne, 1929.
Le Thomisme et la Critique de la Connaissance. Paris, Desclée, 1933.
Essai sur les Rapports entre la Pensée Grecque et la Pensée Chrétienne. Paris, Vrin, 1931.

JOYCE, G. H. (S.J.), *Principles of Natural Theology.* Longmans, 1924.

KREMER, R. (C.SS.R.), *Le Néo-Réalisme Américain.* Louvain, 1920.
La Théorie de la Connaissance chez les Néo-Réalistes Anglais. Paris, Vrin, 1928.

LODGE, SIR O., *Ether and Reality.* Hodder & Stoughton, 1925.

LOTTIN, O. (O.S.B.), *La Théorie du Libre Arbitre depuis S. Anselme jusqu'à S. Thomas d'Aquin.* (Publications de la Revue Thomiste.)

McDOUGALL, W., *Outline of Psychology.* Methuen, 1924.
Outline of Abnormal Psychology. Methuen, 1926.
Modern Materialism and Emergent Evolution. Methuen, 1929.
Body and Mind. Methuen, 1911.

McWILLIAMS, J. A. (S.J.), *Cosmology.* Macmillan Company, New York, 1928.

MAHIEU, L., *François Suarez.* Paris, Desclée, 1921.

MARÉCHAL, J. (S.J.), *Le Point de Départ de la Metaphysique.* Paris, Alcan.

MARITAIN, J., *Introduction to Philosophy*. Sheed and Ward.
Réflexions sur l'Intelligence et sur sa Vie Propre. Paris, Nouvelle Librairie Nationale, 1924.
Les Dégrés du Savoir. Paris, Desclée, 1932.
Three Reformers. Sheed and Ward.
Sept Leçons sur l'Etre. Paris, Téqui.

MESSENGER, E. C., *Evolution and Theology*. Burns Oates & Washbourne.

MEYERSON, E., *Identité et Réalité*. Paris, Alcan. 3e edition, 1926. English Tr. published by Allen & Unwin.
De l'Explication dans les Sciences. Paris, Payot, 1927.

MOORE, G. E., *Philosophical Studies*. Kegan Paul, 1922.

MORRIS, C. R., *Locke, Berkeley, Hume*. Clarendon Press, 1931.

NEWMAN, CARD. J., *A Grammar of Assent*. Longmans, 1913.

NYS, D., *Cosmologie*. 2 vols. Louvain, 1928.
La Notion d'Espace. Brussels, 1922.
La Notion de Temps. Louvain, 1925.

O'MAHONEY, J. E., *The Desire of God in the Philosophy of S. Thomas Aquinas*. Cork University Press, 1929.

O'NEILL, J., *Cosmology*. Vol. I. Longmans, 1923.

PATTERSON, R. L., *The Conception of God in the Philosophy of Aquinas*. Allen & Unwin, 1933.

PICARD, G., *Le Problème Critique Fondamentale*. (Archives de Philosophie.) Paris, Beauchesne, 1923.

POINCARÉ, H., *Science and Hypothesis*. (English Tr. Walter Scott Publishing Co.)

PRATT, J. B., *Matter and Spirit*. Allen & Unwin, 1923.

PRICHARD, H. A., *Kant's Theory of Knowledge*. Clarendon Press, 1909.

RABEAU, G., *Réalité et Relativité*. Paris, Rivière, 1927.

REID, L. A., *Knowledge and Truth*. Macmillan, 1923.

ROLAND-GOSSELIN, M.D. (O.P.), *Le 'De Ente et Essentiâ' de S. Thomas d'Aquin*. Kain, 1926.
Essai d'une Étude Critique de la Connaissance. Paris, Vrin, 1932.
Aristote. Flammarion, 1928.

ROUSSELOT, P. (S.J.), *L'Intellectualisme de S. Thomas*. Paris, Beauchesne, 1924.

RUSSELL, BERTRAND, *The Problems of Philosophy.* (Home University Library.) 1920.

The Analysis of Matter. Kegan Paul, 1927.

The Analysis of Mind. Allen & Unwin, 1921.

Our Knowledge of the External World. Open Court Publishing Co., 1914.

SCHILLER, F. C. S., *Riddles of the Sphinx.* Macmillan, 1912.

Studies in Humanism. Macmillan, 1912.

SHIPLEY, SIR A. E., *Life.* C.U.P., 1925.

SORLEY, W. R., *Moral Values and the Idea of God.* C.U.P., 1925.

STACE, W., *The Philosophy of Hegel.* Macmillan, 1924.

STOUT, G. F., *The Groundwork of Psychology.* London, 1905.

A Manual of Psychology. London, 1904.

TENNANT, F. R., *Miracle and its Philosophical Presuppositions.* C.U.P., 1925.

THOMSON, SIR J. A., *Biology for Everyman.* 2 vols. Dent, 1934.

DE TONQUÉDEC, J., *La Critique de la Connaissance.* Paris, Beauchesne, 1929.

VANCE, J. G., *Reality and Truth.* Longmans, 1917.

VAN HOVE, A., *La Doctrine du Miracle chez S. Thomas.* Paris, Gabalda, 1927.

VON HUGEL, F., *Selected Letters.* Dent, 1927.

Essays and Addresses on the Philosophy of Religion. Dent, 1924.

Essays and Addresses on the Philosophy of Religion. Second Series. Dent, 1926.

The Reality of God. Dent, 1931.

WARD, J., *Psychological Principles.* C.U.P., 1920.

The Realm of Ends. C.U.P., 1912.

Naturalism and Agnosticism. 2 vols. A. & C. Black, 1899.

WICKSTEED, P. H., *The Reactions between Dogma and Philosophy.* Constable, 1926.

INDEX